Europe and the Financial Crisis

Also by Pompeo Della Posta and published by Palgrave Macmillan

GLOBALIZATION, DEVELOPMENT AND INTEGRATION: A European Perspective (*co-editor*)

Also by Leila Simona Talani and published by Palgrave Macmillan

THE FUTURE OF THE CITY OF LONDON

THE GLOBAL CRASH (*editor*)

THE FUTURE OF THE EMU (*editor*)

THE ARAB SPRING IN THE GLOBAL POLITICAL ECONOMY

Europe and the Financial Crisis

Edited by

Leila Simona Talani
Chair in International Political Economy, Jean Monnet Chair in European Political Economy, King's College London

and

Pompeo Della Posta
Associate Professor in Economic Policy, University of Pisa, Italy

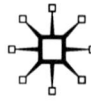

Selection and editorial matter © Pompeo Della Posta and Leila Simona Talani 2011, 2014

Individual chapters © contributors 2011, 2014

All rights reserved. No reproduction, copy or transmission of this publication may be made without written permission.

No portion of this publication may be reproduced, copied or transmitted save with written permission or in accordance with the provisions of the Copyright, Designs and Patents Act 1988, or under the terms of any licence permitting limited copying issued by the Copyright Licensing Agency, Saffron House, 6–10 Kirby Street, London EC1N 8TS.

Any person who does any unauthorized act in relation to this publication may be liable to criminal prosecution and civil claims for damages.

The authors have asserted their rights to be identified as the authors of this work in accordance with the Copyright, Designs and Patents Act 1988.

First published 2011
Published in paperback 2014 by
PALGRAVE MACMILLAN

Palgrave Macmillan in the UK is an imprint of Macmillan Publishers Limited, registered in England, company number 785998, of Houndmills, Basingstoke, Hampshire RG21 6XS.

Palgrave Macmillan in the US is a division of St Martin's Press LLC, 175 Fifth Avenue, New York, NY 10010.

Palgrave Macmillan is the global academic imprint of the above companies and has companies and representatives throughout the world.

Palgrave® and Macmillan® are registered trademarks in the United States, the United Kingdom, Europe and other countries.

ISBN 978–0–230–28554–5   hardback
ISBN 978–1–137–48200–6   paperback

This book is printed on paper suitable for recycling and made from fully managed and sustained forest sources. Logging, pulping and manufacturing processes are expected to conform to the environmental regulations of the country of origin.

A catalogue record for this book is available from the British Library.

A catalog record for this book is available from the Library of Congress.

Typeset by MPS Limited, Chennai, India.

Transferred to Digital Printing in 2014

Contents

List of Figures and Tables	x
Foreword and Acknowledgements	xiii
Preface to the Paperback	xiv
Notes on the Contributors	xxiii

Introduction   1
Pompeo Della Posta

PART I   EUROPE AND THE FINANCIAL CRISIS: GENERAL ISSUES

1 The Regulation of the European Financial Market after the Crisis   9
Pedro Gustavo Teixeira

Introduction	9
The financial crisis: disintegrating markets?	9
The new European Supervisory Authorities	13
The establishment of a European Systemic Risk Board	17
Conclusion: the further development of European integration	20

2 The Monetary Policy Response to the Financial Crisis in the Euro Area and in the United States: A Comparison   28
Domenica Tropeano

Introduction	28
The Federal Reserve's policy response to the crisis	30
The ECB's response	34
The current state of the financial markets in the US	37
The current situation of the financial markets in the euro area	39
Concluding remarks	42

3 Real Divergence Across Europe and the Limits of EMU Macroeconomic Governance   46
Elisabetta Croci Angelini and Francesco Farina

Introduction	46
The evolution of real divergence across EMU economies (1979–2009)	48

	Within-EMU macroeconomic imbalances: an econometric assessment	54
	Macroeconomic imbalances within and between currency areas	62
	Alternative views on EMU macroeconomic governance	64
	Conclusions	69
4	**The Euro in the International Monetary System after the Global Financial and Economic Crisis and after the European Public Debt Crisis**	**74**
	Pompeo Della Posta	
	Introduction	74
	Reasons for the creation of the euro	74
	The performance of the euro during its first decade of existence and the international role of the dollar	77
	The consequences of the global financial and economic crisis in Europe	79
	What future for the international monetary system?	81
	Concluding remarks	86
5	**Europe in Crisis: More Political Integration in the Eurozone is the Solution**	**91**
	Teodoro Dario Togati	
	Introduction	91
	Why is standard macroeconomic theory an obstacle to political integration?	94
	Political union calls for an alternative theoretical perspective	99
	Conclusion	103
6	**Economic Crisis and Industrial Policy in the Union: The Need for a Long-term Vision of Industrial Development**	**107**
	Patrizio Bianchi and Sandrine Labory	
	Introduction	107
	Structure of European industry	108
	The EU as a world economic power	111
	The Lisbon Strategy: an industrial policy for the coherence of the Union at a time of deep transformations	115
	Industrial policy as a long-term vision of development	117
	Concluding remarks	121

Contents vii

PART II THE IMPACT OF THE FINANCIAL CRISIS ON SINGLE EUROPEAN COUNTRIES

7 The UK and the Euro in the Aftermath of the Global Financial Crisis   127
Leila Simona Talani

Introduction	127
The case for the UK to join the EMU after the global financial crisis	127
Why did the UK not join EMU in the first place?	133
Conclusion	138

8 The Greek Debt Crisis: Causes, Policy Responses and Consequences   143
Antimo Verde

Introduction	143
The Greek crisis: the immediate causes and catalyst factors	144
Structural causes	149
Policy responses	150
The EU–IMF Greek rescue plan	151
German measures on short selling and credit default swaps	152
The consequences for EMU	152
The Greek crisis and the Stability and Growth Pact	152
ECB independence and the no-bailout clause	155
The Greek crisis and the 'two-speed EMU': the *restricted solidarity* hypothesis	157
Some concluding remarks	161

9 From Miracle to Crash? The Impact of the Global Financial Crisis on Spain   165
Ramon Pacheco Pardo

Introduction	165
Economic growth and modernization in the 1970s and 1980s	166
The Socialists in power and the boon of EEC membership	168
Economic recession and boom in the 1990s and into the twenty-first century	169
The conservatives in power	171
The global financial crisis and Spain	173
The socialist government and the crisis, step one: denial	174

	The socialist government and the crisis, step two: stern action	177
	Conclusion	179
10	**France: Steering Out of Crisis?**	183
	Susan Milner	
	Introduction	183
	French banking system	184
	Economic outlook in 2010: a fragile recovery	186
	Social and employment policy	190
	Conclusion	194
11	**The Effects of the Financial Crisis on the Italian and US Labour Markets**	198
	Tindara Addabbo, Fahima Aziz and Jack Reardon	
	Introduction	198
	Similarities and differences between the US and Italian labour markets	198
	The effect of the crisis on the Italian and US labour markets	200
	The experience of unemployment in Italy and in the US	207
	The costs of being unemployed in the US in terms of income poverty	209
	Concluding remarks	214
12	**Reaching Out in a Time of Crisis: How External Anchors Assist Southeastern Europe**	218
	Jens Bastian	
	Introduction	218
	The macroeconomic situation	219
	External anchors to the rescue	220
	The Romanian case	221
	The Serbian case	222
	Can Albania and Bulgaria be considered outliers?	223
	Is the crisis assistance discretionary, tilted towards EU members?	225
	Initiatives to support financial sector stability in Southeastern Europe	228
	Cooperation between multilateral lenders and commercial banks	231
	Exit strategies and shaping the reform agenda? The role of external anchors	233
	Conclusion	237

13	**Russia in Crisis: Implications for Europe** *Serena Giusti*	**242**
	Introduction	242
	Russia and the crisis	242
	The effects on Russia's external dimension	245
	The crisis and the post-Soviet space	249
	Conclusion	253
Conclusion *Leila Simona Talani*		**258**
Index		261

List of Figures and Tables

Figures

1.1	The framework for the ESRB risk warnings and recommendations	19
1.2	The 'onion layers' of the integration of the single EU financial market	22
2.1	Securitization in Europe and the US	35
2.2	Commercial and industrial loans	36
2.3	PPI monthly rates of change 2009–10	38
2.4	Change in price of existing family homes	38
2.5	Distress dependence: global	42
3.1	Results of regression 1	50
3.2	Growth rates of ULC in the EMU economies	54
3.3	Results of regression 3	58
6.1	GDP based on PPP	112
6.2	Real GDP growth China, the US and the EU	112
6.3	Gross domestic expenditure on R&D as % of GDP	114
8.1	Five-year credit default swaps	148
8.2	Costs and benefits of monetary union and the restricted solidarity hypothesis	160
11.1	Discouraged workers in the US	203
12.1	Real GDP (%) performance in Southeast Europe	220
12.2	Banking assets in foreign ownership in Southeast Europe	229
12.3	Foreign bank lending in Central and Eastern Europe	229

Tables

1.1	The legal and regulatory system of the single financial market	12
1.2	The European supervisory authorities	13

List of Figures and Tables xi

1.3	The regulatory instruments of the European supervisory authorities	16
1.4	The regulatory instruments of the European Systemic Risk Board	20
3.1	Results of regression 1	52
3.2	Results of regression 2	52
3.3	Results of regression 3	55
4.1	Private and official functions of an international currency	78
4.2	Synthetic index of the degree of reserve currency status of the US dollar, euro and yen, and specific measures of the degree of reserve currency status	79
6.1	Main business indicators of EU industry	109
6.2	Percentage of the value added generated by non-financial business activity in the EU-27	111
6.3	World merchandise exports, by regions and countries	113
6.4	Innovation in main OECD countries	114
7.1	Relative shares of total turnover in London by currencies traded	135
7.2	Overall EMU impact activity on turnover in financial futures and options: principal exchanges	137
8.1	Macroeconomic indicators, PIIGS	145
8.2	The main proposals in tackling the Greek debt crisis: a summary	153
8.3	Foreign-dominated holdings of Greek government securities	156
10.1	Economic growth as % of GDP	187
11.1	Labour force participation rates	199
11.2	Employment rates	200
11.3	OECD harmonized unemployment rates	204
11.4	Long-term unemployment rates, 12 months and over	204
11.5	Multivariate analyses on poverty probability and costs of being unemployed	208
11.6	Multivariate analyses on poverty probability, US	211

12.1	Crisis lending to countries in Central, Eastern, Southeast Europe	221
12.2	EU support for non-EU members in the western Balkans and Turkey	226
12.3	EBRD capital support to UniCredit in Central, Eastern and Southeastern Europe	231

Foreword and Acknowledgements

This volume includes some of the papers that were presented at the international multidisciplinary conference 'Europe in Crisis' that took place on 15 January 2010 at the Villa Schifanoia, one of the locations of the European University Institute (EUI), in San Domenico di Fiesole (Florence, Italy), organized by the EUI Alumni Association.

Although the papers presented ranged from History to Law, in this volume – following the indications of the referees and of the publisher – it has only been possible to include the papers that approached the theme of the conference from the point of view of Economics and Political Sciences. We have also been encouraged to integrate the volume with some other chapters, covering aspects that were not touched upon in the conference but that we consider necessary to make our edited book more complete and appealing.

This is why we invited Francesco Farina and Elisabetta Croci Angelini, Susan Milner, Ramon Pacheco Pardo and Antimo Verde to contribute to our volume with four additional chapters. We thank them for kindly accepting our invitation. Needless to say, we thank all conference participants, both those whose (revised) presentations appear as chapters in this volume, and those whose contributions we have not been able to include here.

The conference and this book would not have been possible without the help and logistical support of the European University Institute. In particular, we would like to thank Yves Mény, former EUI President, Andreas Frijdal, Head of the Academic Service of the EUI, and Judith Przyrowski, who has efficiently helped in the organization of all the activities of the EUI Alumni Association.

Finally, we thank Taiba Batool, Palgrave Macmillan Editor for Economics, for her continuous encouragement and support in getting this volume published.

Pompeo Della Posta
Leila Simona Talani

Preface to the Paperback

Assessing the reaction of the EU to the financial and Euro-zone crises

Overall, the European Union (EU) does not seem to have been particularly well equipped to cope with the financial crisis, nor does it seem to have as yet the political will and capacity to establish an effective regulatory regime for financial services at the regional level (Soedeberg, 2010).

The sovereign debt crisis at the periphery of the Euro-area seems to have been the consequence of the combined effect of the global financial crisis and the structural asymmetries affecting European Monetary Union (EMU) from its establishment.

The European Commission (EC) was taken completely by surprise by the global financial crisis and the subsequent recession. Moreover, European responses to the financial crisis have been fairly scattered and erratic, and EU authorities have not been capable of initiating coordinated responses to the crisis until the very last minute. Equally, macroeconomic responses to the crisis have not been coordinated at EU level. Stimulus programmes were decided at the level of the nation state, had a national scope and produced a number of controversies regarding 'financial protectionism' as relating to the support of national industry or national economic players vis-à-vis their European competitors. This might even have a disruptive impact on the EU as a whole, especially in the wake of the sovereign debt crisis affecting the weakest countries in the Euro-zone. Finally, external support for Europe's periphery has been largely delegated to the International Monetary Fund (IMF) (Cafruny, 2010).

All this must be inserted in the context of the limited potential of the Euro as an international reserve currency.

The current global financial and economic crisis could indeed have stimulated further reflection on the role of the EU and the Euro in the international monetary system and in global economic governance. However, although at the onset of the global crash the weaknesses of the U.S. economy were fairly evident, this did not lead to a run on the U.S. dollar or to a strengthening of the international role of the Euro. On the contrary, the crisis, rather than exposing the limits of global dollar dominance, highlighted the lack of credible alternatives to U.S. power (monetary and otherwise) and the incapacity of the EU to take the lead in the global economy (Plashcke, 2010). To be sure, it was the U.S. Federal Reserve and Treasury, not the EC or the European Central Bank (ECB), that came forward to act as the leading institution in crisis management, in the much-needed role of 'lender of last resort' at the onset of the crisis (Cafruny and Talani, 2012).

There is, finally, little evidence of growing European solidarity in the face of recession. For example, Central and Eastern European countries (CEECs) were in a dire situation as they were experiencing a serious decline in industrial production as well as the bursting of the housing bubble, with all that this entails in terms of capital shortage. This position was further aggravated by the almost complete dominance of the CEEC's banking system by Western, especially Austrian, German, Italian, and Swedish, banks (Cafruny, 2010). The risk was that the CEECs would collapse both economically and socially as a consequence of the outflows of foreign capital. Eventually, the situation was kept under control not so much by the intervention of the EU Commission as by the loans provided by the International Monetary Fund (IMF).

Something more was done to react to the sovereign debt crises affecting Greece and Ireland within the Euro-zone, and spreading quickly to the other at-risk members of the Portugal, Italy, Ireland, Greece and Spain (PIIGS) group. This, however, took the form of mainly ad-hoc decisions providing for impromptu solutions that lacked institutional depth and democratic legitimacy, like the European Financial Stability Facility (EFSF).[1] A more institutionalized rescue mechanism for member states of the Euro-zone under attack for the lack of sustainability of their fiscal position was approved in December 2010, in the form a European Stability Mechanism (ESM).[2] However, it is debatable whether these plans will be likely to solve the problem of credibility and lack of coordination of the European economic governance system.

Overall, despite the establishment of the ESM, it seems inevitable that the only real rescue mechanism for any big Euro-area member state in serious financial strain would be the ECB acting as a hidden lender of last resort.

In reality, the ECB is still far from adopting this role in the Euro-zone area, something that would be more than natural in a currency union. However, in the wake of the collapse of Lehman Brothers in October 2008, the ECB started a novel monetary policy, relying not only on conventional measures, such as interest rate cuts, but also on 'non standard measures', which included 'enhanced credit support' and 'securities markets programmes'. This configures a new role for the ECB as 'hidden/modern lender of last resort' or, as referred to in some scholarly interventions, 'intermediation of last resort' (Giannone et al., 2011). The enhanced credit support relied on (a) increasing the share of liquidity supplied at its Long Term Refinancing Operations (LTROs) relative to its regular main refinancing operations (MROs); and (b) increasing the maturity structure of its LTROs. Most importantly, all the ECB's refinancings would be conducted on a 'fixed-rate full allotment' basis, rather than a variable rate tender format, as used before. In other words, contrary to normal practice, financial institutions were allotted the full amount of liquidity that they wanted at the prevailing interest rate, which was and still is very low.

Moreover, the programme allowed the Eurosystem to accept as collateral in its refinancing operations assets that had become illiquid in financial markets (notably mortgage-backed securities). In its operations, the Eurosystem provided cash loans against the security of these assets. Finally, the Eurosystem increased the number of counterparties eligible for Eurosystem operations from 140 to around 2,000 and started protecting the counterparties' anonymity to avoid domino effects (Giannone et al 2011).

Since 2008, the ECB has successively introduced six-month, 12-month and 36-month terms for LTRO finance. Each of these new issues has been heavily subscribed, with Euro-zone periphery banks in Ireland, Italy, Spain and Greece taking the majority of the first 36-month issue in late 2011. The second 36-month issue was in February 2012, and was also successful with weaker Euro-zone banks.[3]

In addition, in May 2009 the ECB announced a first €60 billion Covered Bond Purchase Programme (CBPP) to purchase Euro-denominated covered bonds issued in the Euro-area over the period until June 2010. A CBPP2 started in November 2011.[4]

The second non-standard component of the ECB's response to the crisis, together with enhanced credit support measures, was the launch in May 2010 of the Securities Markets Programme (SMP). This allowed the Eurosystem to buy both private and public Euro-area debt. Given the constraints of the provisions of the Treaty on the Functioning of the European Union, Eurosystem purchases of government bonds were strictly limited to secondary markets and fully sterilized by conducting liquidity-absorbing operations. On 6 September 2012 SMP was superseded by Outright Monetary Transactions (OMT), which allowed for unlimited purchase of bonds of struggling countries in secondary markets subject to conditionality. Conditionality implies that member states willing to benefit from OMT have to agree to the implementation of a full or precautionary ESM macroeconomic adjustment programme. Also the IMF should be involved in the elaboration and monitoring of the country-specific conditionality. The Governing Council of the ECB maintains the right to initiate, continue and terminate OMT in its full discretion.[5]

In addition to these measures, the Eurosystem continued to provide liquidity in foreign currencies, most notably in US dollars.[6]

Summing up, with its so-called Long Term Refinancing Operations the ECB inaugurated three-year lending programmes that provided virtually cost-free liquidity to banks. Thus, especially in the weakest parts of the Euro-area, banks were incentivized to acquire the sovereign debt of countries under attack, gaining from interest rate differentials. Moreover, the SMP first, and then the OMT, rendered the role of the ECB as a 'hidden lender of last resort' more evident and effective, de facto providing for a sterilized monetization of debt.[7] Despite this, the German government has continued to prevent the ECB from transferring risk to its own balance sheet, as the Federal Reserve Bank has done, thus refusing to give the ECB an official role as 'lender of last resort'.[8]

Furthermore, at the European level, to date, there is nothing like a pan-European regulatory regime for the EU and Euro-area banking and financial systems.

At the end of 2012, four years after the global financial crisis, in the EU and Euro-area, banking and financial supervision remained in the hands of the national central banks (Sapir et al., 2012: 1). Of course some steps have been taken to restructure what had proved to be a highly inadequate European regulatory regime for the financial and banking sector (Teixeira, 2011).

However, the transformation of the existing Committee of European Banking (CEB) supervisors on 1 January 2011 into the European Banking Authority (EBA) based in London, and the establishment of the European Securities and Markets Authority (ESMA) in Paris and of the European Insurance and Occupational Pensions Authority (EIOPA) in Frankfurt to create the new European Supervisory Authorities (ESAs), which were to be inserted in the European System of Financial Supervisors (ESFS), does not seem to have resolved the issue of pan-European banking and financial supervision substantially (Teixeira, 2011). National authorities remain responsible for the day-to-day supervision of individual firms, with the new European architecture only providing an overarching European framework for financial supervision.[9] Moreover, the ESAs themselves comprise high-level representatives of all of the member states' supervisory authorities under permanent chairmanships.[10] They have the power to temporarily ban certain high-risk financial products and activities, such as naked short selling, as well as instructing banks and other financial actors in crisis situations, drawing up standards for national regulators and settling disagreements between them.[11] However, this will be possible only in situations of emergency to be defined by the council, and it is limited by a safeguard clause attributing to the member states the power not to abide by the decisions of the ESAs.[12]

The new ESAs are complemented by a group connected to the Frankfurt-based European Central Bank called the European Systemic Risk Board (ESRB), which monitors the risk of major threats to the economy, such as problems at major banks or asset bubbles (Teixeira, 2011).[13] Although connected to the ECB, the ESRB seems to be mainly a consultative body and its creation did not activate the idle clause in the Maastricht Treaty that gives the ECB a formal role in banking supervisory policy (Art. 105(6)).[14]

Given the shortcomings of these reforms of the EU banking supervision regime, made evident by the evolution of the Euro-zone sovereign debt crisis, at the end of June 2012 the EU leaders agreed to set up a single supervisory authority to oversee 6,000 banks in Europe, with the aim of having the authority in place by the end of the year.

However, many doubts were raised in the course of 2012 on the feasibility and characteristics of even this first step, most loudly from Germany. Eventually, the European Council conclusions on completing EMU, adopted on 18 October 2012, reiterated the need to move towards an integrated financial framework and invited legislators to proceed with work on the legislative proposals on the Single Supervisory Mechanism (SSM), indicating 1 January 2013 as the deadline to agree on the legislative framework. The definition of the legislation needed for its operational implementation would take place in the course of 2013. Most importantly, the European Council noted that only when an effective single supervisory mechanism was established, involving the ECB, could the newly established European Stability Mechanism recapitalize banks directly. This sparked a great deal of discontent, especially within the PIIGS group as some of the weakest countries, most notably Spain, had hoped for a quicker decision regarding direct bank recapitalization from the ESM.

In terms of fiscal policy, the last step in the EU's response to the Euro-zone crisis is the approval by the European Council, on 2 March 2012, of the so-called 'Fiscal Compact' (officially the Treaty on Stability,

Coordination and Governance, TSCG[15]). The Contracting Parties agreed to keep the budgetary position of their general government balanced or in surplus. The fiscal pact falls short of being a real fiscal constitution for the EU, partly because the decision by the UK not to sign it made it impossible to incorporate it into the EU treaties, although the Treaty requires the Contracting Parties to incorporate it into their legal systems, possibly at the constitutional level. In essence, the Fiscal Compact is just an intergovernmental agreement (De Grauwe, 2012). Moreover, notwithstanding the rhetoric, the Fiscal Compact represents little more than a replay of the Stability and Growth Pact, apart from the reference to structural budgets, which, however, is considered by the experts more a complication than anything else (De Grauwe, 2012). Indeed, two things clearly limit the capacity of the Fiscal Compact to be effective: first, there are no provisions for automatic sanctions; and second, the pact allows countries to temporarily deviate from the requirements of having their budgets in balance or in surplus in case of an unusual event outside the control of the government concerned or in periods of severe economic downturn.[16]

In conclusion, far from having been socialized among the members of the Euro-zone and of the EU through the adoption of an actual common fiscal policy and the attribution to the European Central Bank of its natural role as lender of last resort, the burden of the costs of the crisis was inflicted on the weakest countries of the system. This happened through the imposition of savage austerity plans. Indeed, the main characteristic of the EU approach to crisis management, quite apart from the rhetoric about the establishment of a new economic governance system, was 'internal devaluation' with all that this means in terms of pro-cyclical effects, popular resistance, political instability and eventually the threat of disruption of the EU integration process as a whole. It remains to be seen if this is a price worth paying in exchange for fiscal consolidation.

Leila Simona Talani
Chair in International Political Economy
Jean Monnet Chair in European Political Economy
Department of European and International Studies
King's College London

xx *Preface to the Paperback*

Notes

1. See http://www.efsf.Europa.eu/about/index.htm [accessed on 15 December 2010].
2. For more details, see: http://www.consilium.Europa.eu/uedocs/cms_data/docs/pressdata/en/ec/118578.pdf [accessed on 21 December 2010].
3. See Financial Times website: http://lexicon.ft.com/Term?term=long_term-refinancing-operation-_-LTRO [accessed on 18 October 2012].
4. See ECB monetary policy website: http://www.ecb.int/mopo/html/index.en.htm [accessed on 18 October 2012].
5. See ECB website: http://www.ecb.int/press/pr/date/2012/html/pr120906_1.en.html [accessed on 24 October 2012].
6. For a chronological listing of the measures, see the Annex 'Chronology of monetary policy measures of the Eurosystem' in the November 2011 *Monthly Bulletin* [3.15 MB], and for details on the ECB's non-standard measures, including a comparison with the Fed and the Bank of Japan, see 'IV. The ECB's response to the financial crisis' of the former President Trichet's speech 'The ECB's enhanced credit support' (13 July 2009). For details on the ECB's response to the financial crisis, see the article 'The ECB's response to the financial crisis' in the October 2010 *Monthly Bulletin*. For details on the ECB's response to the sovereign debt crisis, see September 2011 *Monthly Bulletin*, Box 5.
7. See http://placeduluxembourg.wordpress.com/2012/03/02/ecb-market-intervention-the-securities-market-programme-smp/ [accessed on 18 October 2012].
8. See Financial Times website: http://lexicon.ft.com/Term?term=long_term-refinancing-operation-_-LTRO [accessed on 18 October 2012].
9. For more details, see: http://www.consilium.Europa.eu/uedocs/cms_data/docs/pressdata/en/ecofin/117747.pdf [accessed on 21 December 2010].
10. http://ec.Europa.eu/internal_market/consultations/docs/2009/fin_supervision_may/replies_su mmary_en.pdf. For more details, see: http://ec.Europa.eu/internal_market/finances/docs/committees/supervsion/20090923/com2009_501_en.pdf [accessed on 21 December 2010].
11. For more details, see: Time http://www.time.com/time/world/article/0,8599,2016359,00.html [accessed on 21 December 2010].
12. For more details, see: http://ec.Europa.eu/internal_market/finances/docs/committees/supervision/20090923/com2009_501_en.pdf [accessed on 21 December 2010].
13. For more details, see: http://www.consilium.Europa.eu/uedocs/cms_data/docs/pressdata/en/ecofin/117747.pdf [accessed on 21 December 2010].
14. For the role of the ECB in banking supervision, see ECB website: http://www.ecb.int/ecb/orga/tasks/html/financial-stability.en.html [accessed on 15 December 2010].
15. For the full text, see: http://www.european-council.europa.eu/media/639235/st00tscg26_en12.pdf.
16. For the full text, see: http://www.european-council.europa.eu/media/639235/st00tscg26_en12.pdf.

References

Cafruny, A. (2010) 'The Global Financial Crisis and the Crisis of European Neo-liberalism', in L. S. Talani (ed.), *The Global Crash*, London: Palgrave, pp. 121–40.

Cafruny, A. and Talani, L.S. (2012) The Consequences of the Global Financial Crisis on Europe, *International Political Economy Yearbook*, Vol. 18, Boulder, CO: Lynne Rienner.

De Grauwe, P. (2012) Interview on http://aregan.wordpress.com/2012/03/20/interview-with-paul-de-grauw/ [accessed on 18 October 2012].

Giannone, D., Lenza, M., Pill, H. and Reichlin, L. (2011) *Non-Standard Monetary Policy Measures and Monetary Developments*, ECB Working Paper Series, No. 1290/January 2011.

Plashcke, H. (2010) 'Challenging the Dollar in International Monetary Relations? The Lost Opportunities of the Euro', in L. S. Talani (ed.), *The Global Crash*, London: Palgrave, pp. 73–100.

Sapir, A., Hellwig, M. and Pagano, M. (2012) 'A Contribution from the Chair and Vice-Chairs of the Advisory Scientific Committee to the Discussion on the European Commission's Banking Union Proposals', Reports of the Advisory Scientific Committee, No. 2/October 2012, on http://www.esrb.europa.eu/pub/pdf/asc/Reports_ASC_1210.pdf?490dce9cc2a2bf39b76ae4b06604b0ca [accessed on 11 October 2012].

Soedeberg, S. (2010) *Corporate Power and Ownership in Contemporary Capitalism: The Politics of Resistance and Domination*, London: Routledge.

Teixeira, P. G. (2011) 'The Regulation of the European Financial Market after the Crisis', in P. Della Posta and L. S. Talani (eds), *Europe and the Financial Crisis*, London: Palgrave.

Notes on the Contributors

Tindara Addabbo is Associate Professor of Economic Policy at the University of Modena and Reggio Emilia, Italy. She has published on the gender impact of public policies, well-being in the capability approach, income distribution and wage discrimination.

Fahima Aziz is Professor of Economics and holder of the Endowed Chair in International Business and Economics at Hamline University, Minnesota, USA. She is a labour economist; her research work includes microcredit financing, gender and race issues in the labour market, and poverty and income inequality.

Jens Bastian is SEESOX/Alpha Bank Visiting Fellow on the Political Economy of South East Europe at St Antony's College, Oxford, UK. Since January 2009 he has also been working as Senior Economic Research Fellow for Southeast Europe at ELIAMEP (Hellenic Foundation for Foreign and European Policy) in Athens, Greece.

Patrizio Bianchi is President of the University of Ferrara, Professor of Applied Economics, President of the Foundation of the Conference of the Italian University Rectors, and Honorary Professor at the South China University of Technology.

Elisabetta Croci Angelini is Professor of Economic Policy in the Faculty of Political Science and Head of the Department of Economic Development, University of Macerata, Italy.

Pompeo Della Posta is Associate Professor in Political Economy at the University of Pisa, Italy, and External Professor at the Stanford Bing Overseas Studies Program in Florence.

Francesco Farina is the Head of the Department of Economic Policy, Finance and Development in the Faculty of Economics of the University of Siena, Italy, where he teaches international economic policy and macroeconomics in the PhD programme. He is the author of books and articles published in international journals on rationality behavior, economic inequality, macroeconomic policies and experimental economics.

Notes on the Contributors xxiii

Serena Giusti is Lecturer in European Politics and Russian Foreign Policy at the Catholic University of Milan, Italy, and Senior Associate Researcher at the Institute for International Political Studies (ISPI–Milan) Programme on Russia and Wider Europe.

Sandrine Labory is Lecturer in the Department of Economics at the University of Ferrara, Italy.

Susan Milner is Reader in French and European Studies at the University of Bath, UK. Her doctoral research was published as *The Dilemmas of Internationalism: French Syndicalism and the International Trade Union Movement* (1990). Her research interests include working patterns and employment practices in the European Union, the social aspects of European integration, including public attitudes, and social capital and associationism in France.

Ramon Pacheco Pardo is Lecturer in European Studies at King's College London, UK. He obtained a PhD in international relations from the London School of Economics and Political Science, where he was also editor of *Millennium: Journal of International Studies*.

Jack Reardon teaches economics in the School of Business at Hamline University in St Paul, Minnesota, USA. He is founding editor of the *International Journal of Pluralism* and *Economics Education*. He is the author of *The Handbook of Pluralist Economics Education* (2009).

Leila Simona Talani is Associate Professor (Reader) in International Political Economy at King's College London. She is also Director of Studies for the Master's in International Political Economy and the Master's in European Public Policy. Previously she was at the University of Bath and the London School of Economics and Political Science.

Pedro Gustavo Teixeira is counsellor to the Vice-President of the European Central Bank (ECB) and Lecturer on the Regulation of the Single European Financial Market at the Institute for Law and Finance of the Goethe-Universität, Frankfurt am Main, Germany. He was formerly Adviser at the Directorate-General Financial Stability of the ECB, which he joined in 1999 after his PhD studies at the Law Department of the European University Institute, Florence, Italy.

Teodoro Dario Togati is Lecturer in Economics at the University of Torino, Italy.

Domenica Tropeano is Associate Professor in the Department of Economic and Financial Institutions, University of Macerata, Italy.

Antimo Verde is Associate Professor in Economics at Tuscia University in Viterbo, Italy. Since 1987 he has taught International Economics at the LUISS University in Rome. Previously he taught econometrics at the same university. He spent study periods at the London School of Economics and Political Science, the International Monetary Fund, Harvard University, Kiel University and Malta University.

Introduction

Pompeo Della Posta

The recent global financial and economic crisis, that after more than two years is still producing its negative consequences on the world economy, has brought about a number of additional effects that it is still difficult to identify and interpret univocally.

It was initially claimed, for example, that the crisis had proved the many fallacies of the neo-liberal paradigm that had been permeating the recent third phase of globalization, started in the second half of the 1970s and characterized by the deepening of the process of trade liberalization, the privatization of the economy and the deregulation of financial markets. In particular, the latter led to the large diffusion of credit derivatives, usually regarded as one of the main causes of the crisis. Given the severity of the economic downturn that has followed the financial turmoil, even the most orthodox followers of the neo-liberal paradigm agreed about the necessity of a temporary public intervention. Needless to say, this was immediately interpreted by neo-Keynesian, post-Keynesian and radical economists as clear evidence that they were correct in arguing that free markets may not always reach a satisfactory equilibrium. The crisis would have proved, then, that despite the many drawbacks it may have, in many circumstances public intervention is in the end unavoidable. For this reason some analysts still believe that the crisis might also mark the beginning of a neo-Keynesian, and maybe neo-protectionist, fourth phase of globalization, following the first one (that coincided with the Victorian age), the second one (that began after World War II and ended with the inflation and exchange rate crises of the 1970s) and the third one described above.

While these interpretations prevailed at the beginning of the crisis, it has only taken a few months for the neo-liberal view to make a comeback, accompanied by the public debt crisis that has been affecting

Greece directly and touching upon some other European countries (Spain, Ireland, Portugal).

It is now difficult, then, to predict what direction economic theories and policies will be taking. Still, it cannot be denied that the crisis made clear that no economic theory can claim any more a moral superiority over the others and that some alternative views, in particular the 'old' Keynesian theory, may still have something to say in Economics. This volume contains a number of chapters in which the Keynesian view appears rather clearly.

Among the culprits of the crisis, many observers include the hegemonic role played worldwide by the US economy and, as a consequence, by the US dollar. As a result, many analysts and commentators argued promptly that the crisis would mark the end of the monetary hegemony of the American currency. Some of them, for example, suggested that the euro might have played a much larger international role, together with the currencies of the emerging economic powers – some of whom, like China and India, were big economic powers already several centuries ago. For the time being, though, the dependency of the European economy on the events occurring in the US, and more generally, the weak European political credibility, undermine any possible larger international role for the euro. The lack of democracy in China, together with the financial restrictions that are still in place in that country, undermine also a potential international role for the yuan renmimbi. In more general terms, it is therefore possible to say that the multilateral international monetary regime that many analysts had envisaged immediately after the burst of the financial crisis may still have a long way to go before materializing and before replacing the current unilateral international monetary regime.

On the contrary, a Bretton Woods III regime may well be on the horizon, still characterized by the hegemony of the US dollar, as has been the case for the previous two phases (the first one started in 1944 and ended with the fall of the fixed exchange rate system in 1972 – Bretton Woods I – and the second one started with the fall of the Berlin Wall and of the Iron Curtain and ended with the recent global crisis – Bretton Woods II).

As the title clearly suggests, the contributors to this volume focus their attention on the consequences of the financial and economic crisis on Europe. Also in this case, however, it is difficult to draw a clear conclusion. Will the crisis increase the centripetal forces that may induce a deepening of the process of integration, so as to lead to a higher degree of political unity? Or will it be the catalyst of all contradictions affecting Europe, so as to threaten the process of European integration and increase the strength of the centrifugal forces? No clear answer can be given, since both elements are present. On the one hand, the impact of the global crisis has certainly been such that the members of the European Union realized that they needed to give a sign of unity in the face of the turbulence and the threats to European economic stability coming from other economic areas. This may plausibly explain the approval, in December 2009, of the Lisbon Treaty and the adoption of the 2020 Strategy, devised in order to orientate and favour the process of economic innovation and growth in Europe. On the other hand, however, we have to consider both the failure of the Lisbon strategy – aimed at making Europe the most competitive economic area in the world – and the risk, envisaged in May 2010, that at least one of the country members of the euro area, Greece, could abandon EMU, maybe followed by some other weak, peripheral European countries and eventually threatening the overall EMU institutional setup.

The perspective to analyze the effects of the financial and economic crisis on Europe, then, has to be twofold: the first one looking at the general effects of the crisis on the European institutional setup, governance and architecture; the second one looking more in detail at the different member countries. This is the approach we take respectively in Part I and Part II of this volume. We describe briefly below the content of the 13 chapters composing it.

Part I includes six chapters.

In Chapter 1, 'The Regulation of the European Financial Market after the Crisis', Pedro Gustavo Teixeira argues that the interlinkages resulting from the process of European financial markets' integration increased the potential for the transmission of economic and financial risks across the single market. He draws a clear picture of the new regulatory framework that has emerged in Europe in order to face systemic risk and avoid new financial crises. The new system is based on two pillars, respectively the European Supervisory Authorities (ESAs) and the European Systemic Risk Board (ESRB), and replaces the framework for financial integration based exclusively on home-country control, mutual recognition and minimum harmonization.

In Chapter 2, 'The Monetary Policy Response to the Financial Crisis in the Euro Area and in the United States: A Comparison', Domenica Tropeano compares the actions undertaken by the Fed and the ECB in response to the crisis. Both central banks have been injecting liquidity into the markets, but while the Fed is committed to keeping both short-term and long-term interest rates at a low level, no such commitment exists in the euro area, probably reflecting the perception of a higher risk of European average debts. Moreover, the ECB seems to be ready to reconsider its relaxed monetary policy should inflation show the least sign of existence.

In Chapter 3, 'Real Divergence Across Europe and the Limits of EMU Macroeconomic Governance', Elisabetta Croci Angelini and Francesco Farina discuss and analyze the current macroeconomic situation in the Eurozone. In their view, the real divergence of Peripheral economies *vis-à-vis* the EMU average and the worsening of macroeconomic imbalances cannot be avoided without a coordinated intergovernmental intervention.

In Chapter 4, 'The Euro in the International Monetary System after the Global Financial and Economic Crisis and after the European Public Debt Crisis', Pompeo Della Posta considers the future perspective for the euro to play an international role together with, or in substitution of the dollar. He concludes that the political fragmentation of Europe is such as to undermine the credibility of the European currency. Although desirable, then, a multilateral international monetary regime may still have a long way to go before materializing.

In Chapter 5, 'Europe in Crisis: More Political Integration in the Eurozone is the Solution', Teodoro Dario Togati also concludes that, in order to favour welfare, competitiveness and growth, the European countries have to realize that it is necessary to increase the degree of integration, thereby moving towards political unification.

In Chapter 6, 'Economic Crisis and Industrial Policy in the Union: The Need for a Long-term Vision of Industrial Development' Patrizio Bianchi and Sandrine Labory discuss the failure of the Lisbon strategy and analyze the perspective of the 2020 Strategy, that has been devised in order to favour European competitiveness and economic growth. Unfortunately, despite the need to have a European industrial policy, the political determination of European countries seems to be lacking in this case too.

The second part of the volume deals with the effects of the crisis on several European countries, namely the UK, France, Spain, Greece, Italy, Southern European countries and a rather important European neighbour, namely Russia. Part II includes seven chapters.

The euro is over a decade old and the UK has not yet decided to adopt it. Despite some timid attempts to revamp the debate about British entry into EMU made by the early Labour administration, the issue has been left aside for a long time, to surge again to the attention of the public only with the explosion of the global financial crisis. Chapter 7, 'The UK and the Euro in the Aftermath of the Global Financial Crisis', by Leila Simona Talani analyzes the above issue, starting from the role played by the City of London in the whole debate about the process of European monetary integration.

In Chapter 8, 'The Greek Debt Crisis: Causes, Policy Responses and Consequences', Antimo Verde addresses the fiscal crisis in Greece in 2010. The chapter is divided into two parts. In the first part the author draws a tentative reconstruction of the *facts*. The second part of the chapter aims at identifying the most important consequences and implications of the Greek crisis from a very delicate point of view: the effectiveness of European fiscal rules (i.e., the Stability and Growth Pact), the independence of the ECB and the meaning and limits of the *no-bailout clause* and, eventually, the future of EMU.

In Chapter 9, 'From Miracle to Crash? The Impact of the Global Financial Crisis on Spain', Ramon Pacheco Pardo underlines how the financial crisis did not create new problems for the Spanish economy. Rather, it exposed previous weaknesses that made Spain ill-prepared to withstand the crisis. After refusing to acknowledge the effects of the crisis on the Spanish economy, the government embarked in a reform programme intended to deal with some of these long-standing weaknesses.

In Chapter 10, 'France: Steering Out of Crisis?', Susan Milner notes how, in many ways, the banking crisis and economic recession provided less of a shock to the French economy than in many other countries. In this chapter, the current state of the French economy and short-term forecasts for growth are reviewed. Debates around policy choices are then presented, focusing in particular on the need to tackle unemployment while also reducing public debt.

In Chapter 11, 'The Effects of the Financial Crisis on the Italian and US Labour Markets', Tindara Addabbo, Fahima Aziz and Jack Reardon evaluate the effects of the crisis on the Italian and US labour markets. In both cases, the socio-economic cost of unemployment – reflected, for example, in the lack of access to health services – can be limited by introducing measures like exemptions for temporary prescription charges for medical specialist visits and exams for the unemployed or redundancy fund recipients and their families.

As Jens Bastian finds out in Chapter 12, 'Reaching out in a Time of Crisis: How External Anchors Assist Southeastern Europe', with the economic crisis starting to assert itself in the second half of 2008 in Southeast Europe, the manner in which governments and central banks initially reacted highlighted a mixture of political unpreparedness – at times outright denial – and exposed manifest institutional limitations to acting quickly and decisively. Crisis management and crisis resistance capacity were both in short supply when a twin external shock started to manifest itself in mid-2008 in the region.

Finally, the aim of Chapter 13, 'Russia in Crisis: Implications for Europe' by Serena Giusti, is to point out the consequences of the global financial and economic crisis for the Russian Federation and its implications for the Russia–EU relationship, the pan-European space and the global balance. Russia has been dramatically hit by the crisis, proving its high integration in the global market.

Part I
Europe and the Financial Crisis: General Issues

1
The Regulation of the European Financial Market after the Crisis

Pedro Gustavo Teixeira[1]

Introduction

The financial crisis challenged the legal and regulatory approach to the integration of the single market for financial services.[2] In this approach, the economic benefits of integration are shared while the related economic and financial risks are not mutualized among Member States. This implies that Member States are compelled to protect their own domestic interests in the case of a crisis. As a result, the financial crisis led to an institutional crossroads: the development of the single financial market should be either constrained to allow Member States to protect their respective financial systems or safeguarded by setting up European structures for regulation and supervision of the single market as a whole.

Against this background, this contribution provides an overview of the main features of the regulatory reform that is taking place in Europe to address the limitations which emerged from the experience with the financial crisis.

The financial crisis: disintegrating markets?

The financial crisis unfolded in Europe in July 2007 with the first reports of subprime-related losses suffered by the European banks and in August 2007 with the freezing of interbank markets.[3] The crisis involved a number of significant events of financial instability, which included a loss of confidence in the soundness of European banks, bank-runs, the prospect of failure of cross-border and domestic financial institutions which required recapitalization measures, and even the financial collapse of an entire country – Iceland – which was part of the EU single financial market as a member of the European Economic Area (EEA). It was later followed by a sovereign debt crisis starting in Greece in May 2010 and later affecting other euro area Member States.

The financial crisis challenged fundamental assumptions regarding the functioning of the single financial market. In particular, Member States took unilateral actions to protect their respective financial system once the crisis occurred, effectively segregating and insulating their domestic markets from the single financial market. For example, certain national measures were only aimed at domestic financial institutions, thus contravening the basic principles of non-discrimination, as well as home-country control and mutual recognition.[4]

Coordination among Member States only emerged at the Paris summit on 12 October 2008, which was the first event ever of its kind bringing together the euro area heads of state and government. It was triggered by the rapidly increasing concern for the integrity of the financial system and the need to restore public and market confidence on financial institutions and markets, particularly within the closely integrated euro area. Accordingly, the euro area Member States agreed at the summit to take a number of national measures within a broadly coordinated framework in order to 'avoid that national measures adversely affect the functioning of the single market and the other Member States'.[5]

In legal terms, the crisis demonstrated that the increased integration of the single financial market gives rise to an unsustainable incompatibility of objectives within the EU's institutional and regulatory framework. In particular, the crisis put into evidence that there is a mutual incompatibility over time between:

1. pursuing financial market integration through free movement of capital and establishment based on the principles of home-country control and mutual recognition, *and*
2. safeguarding the stability of an increasingly integrated market, which progressively increases the level of common economic risks among Member States, *while*
3. retaining nationally based regulatory competences for safeguarding the single market from such common economic risks, and avoiding the mutualization of risks among Member States.[6]

The incompatibility derives basically from the fact that the tools of market integration – 1. home-country control, 2. mutual recognition and 3. minimum harmonization of national laws[7] – provide a framework of incentives to the unlimited expansion of the cross-border provision of services, independently of their country of origin. However, such expansion is not accompanied by the obligation for the home-country to take responsibility for the economic risks stemming from the provision of services in other (host) Member States. Therefore, the framework of the single financial market implies that, as market integration increases, the common economic risks expand. At the same time, nationally based regulatory competences become more and more unable to address such risks, particularly when the degree of integration leads to significant cross-border spillovers.[8]

In this context, the operation of the principles of home-country control and mutual recognition may lead to outcomes which are opposite to those of integration: it will be rational for the home-country to safeguard the assets in its Member State and limit any liabilities *vis-à-vis* host-countries, while the host-country will tend to ring-fence the assets and thus avoid their being repatriated to the home-country.[9] Rather than a mutual sharing of economic risks, the tools of market integration in a crisis may lead to the perverse effects of misallocation of risks and the increase of the related costs among Member States.

The incompatibility of objectives within the framework of the single financial market is similar in terms and in implications to the contradiction that preceded the federalization of monetary policy in the euro area.[10] In particular, the intensification of the common economic risks in the single financial market as a result of integration leads to an institutional crossroads, where either:

1. the competences for the single financial market are transferred from the national to the European level to the extent required to internalize in the regulatory decision-making process both the benefits and risks (potential cross-border spillover effects) of market integration; or
2. there is a renationalization of the single financial market by the Member States to the extent required to safeguard national interests from the economic risks of market integration.

The crisis has also challenged the principle of minimum harmonization of national laws. Such harmonization cannot be limited to the setting of basic and minimum regulatory standards so as to lift the major barriers to the cross-border provision of financial services. The degree of harmonization required for the operation of the single passport would need to be more extensive and deeper than previously so as to safeguard the stability of the single market as a whole.[11]

Finally, the crisis demonstrated the need for a new model for the regulation and supervision of the single European financial market. At the time of the crisis, the guiding principle was that a decentralized system based on the exercise of national responsibilities would be able to regulate the single financial market as a whole. This was reflected in the so-called 'Lamfalussy framework', which represented a multilevel regulatory process combining the traditional EU legislative procedures with the involvement of committees of national regulators in the preparation and implementation of EU law.[12] The premise was that the cooperation among national authorities would replace the need to transfer regulatory competences to the EU level.[13]

At the peak of the crisis, in October 2008, the Commission mandated a High-Level Group chaired by Jacques de Larosière to put forward proposals on improving financial supervision in the EU in light of the financial crisis experience.[14] This led to the development of a new regulatory architecture for the single financial market – a European System of Financial Supervision (ESFS) – which comprises two pillars: the conduct of micro-prudential supervision by a network of three sectoral European Supervisory Authorities (ESAs) and the national regulators; and the

Table 1.1 The legal and regulatory system of the single financial market (2003–10)

Level 1: legislation on principles	Council of Ministers (ECOFIN)			
	European Parliament			
Sectors	Banking	Insurance and occupational pensions	Securities	Financial conglomerates
Level 2: legislation on details through regulatory committees	European Banking Committee	European Insurance and Operational Pensions Committee	European Securities Committee	Financial Conglomerates Committee
Level 3: regulatory convergence through committees of supervisors	Committee of European Banking Supervisors (CEBS) (London)	Committee of European Insurance and Occupational Pension Supervisors (CEIOPS) (Frankfurt)	Committee of European Securities Regulators (CESR) (Paris)	Joint Committee on Financial Conglomerates (comprising CEBS, CEIOPS and CESR)
Level 4: Compliance with EC law	Commission Cooperation among Member States, national regulators, financial industry			

conduct of macro-prudential supervision by a European Systemic Risk Board (ESRB). This new architecture will be in place in 2011 and is analyzed in the following sections.[15]

The new European Supervisory Authorities

The 2009 de Larosière Report identified a number of weaknesses relating to the conduct of financial supervision at the EU level.[16] Such weaknesses included: (1) regulatory failures with regard to financial institutions; (2) the impossibility to challenge regulatory practices on a cross-border basis; (3) the lack of frankness and cooperation between regulators; (4) the lack of consistent powers across regulators; and (5) the lack of means for regulators to take common decisions.[17]

In this context, in its Communication on European Financial Supervision, the Commission considered that the EU had reached the limits of what could be achieved with the Level 3 supervisory committees (see Table 1.1 above). These committees did not provide a mechanism to ensure cooperation and information exchange between national supervisors. In addition, the patchwork of national regulatory requirements may prevent joint action by national supervisors, which may lead to the prevalence of national solutions in responding to EU problems.[18]

The Commission put forward on 23 September 2009 legislative proposals for Regulations of the European Parliament and the Council leading to the setting up of three ESAs,[19] which were then adopted on 24 November 2010.[20]

Table 1.2 The European supervisory authorities

Current institutional setting		The new structures for micro-prudential supervision
Coordination of the three committees on the basis of a Joint Protocol (3L3)	Cross-sectoral	Joint Committee of European Supervisory Authorities
CEBS	Banking	European Banking Authority (EBA)
CEIOPS	Insurance	European Insurance and Occupational Pensions Authority (EIOPA)
CESR	Securities	European Securities and Markets Authority (ESMA)
Colleges of supervisors for banking and insurance groups National supervisors		

The ESAs will take over all the tasks of the supervisory committees and in addition have significantly increased responsibilities, defined legal powers and greater authority than the committees, as follows.

First, the ESAs will issue draft regulatory technical standards in the areas within the scope of the powers delegated to the Commission under EU financial services law and in accordance with Article 290 of the Treaty. The ESAs will submit the draft standards to the Commission, which may then adopt them as delegated acts, thus providing for binding legal effect at the EU level. The Commission may not change the content of the drafts submitted by the ESAs without prior coordination with them.[21] Although the regulatory technical standards will not imply strategic decisions or policy choices, they should allow developing a harmonized core set of standards across the EU, which will provide as much as possible a single rulebook for participants in the single financial market. Furthermore, the ESAs may also issue draft implementing technical standards in the areas where financial services law provides the Commission with powers for issuing uniform conditions for the implementation of EU law in accordance with Article 291 of the Treaty. The procedure for the adoption of these standards by the Commission is broadly similar to the above regarding regulatory standards.

Second, the ESAs may issue guidelines and recommendations to national authorities and financial institutions with a view to ensuring consistent and effective supervisory practices and application of EU law. These guidelines and recommendations will not have a legally binding nature. Instead, a 'comply or explain' procedure will apply, according to which national authorities should provide reasons for non-compliance. Financial institutions may be required to report whether they comply with the guidelines or recommendations addressed to them. The ESAs may also issue recommendations to specific national supervisors, particularly when a supervisor is considered to be diverging EU law, including the technical standards.

Third, the ESAs will be expected to play a coordination role in financial crisis situations – which are defined as adverse developments which may seriously jeopardize the orderly functioning and integrity of financial markets or the stability of the whole or part of the financial system in the EU. In this context, the ESAs may adopt decisions requiring national supervisors to take an appropriate action to address the risks in the crisis situation. The types of action that may be taken will be defined in EU legislation. Furthermore, if a national supervisor does not comply with the decision, the ESAs may adopt a decision directed at a specific financial institution requiring it to comply with the relevant EU legislation.

Fourth, the ESAs will have a range of tools in the area of consumer protection. They will monitor new and existing financial activities and may issue warnings in case a financial activity poses a serious threat to the stability and effectiveness of the financial system. In addition, they may temporarily prohibit or restrict certain financial activities on the same basis.

Fifth, the ESAs will contribute to the efficient and consistent functioning of colleges of supervisors. They may participate as observers in colleges and receive all relevant information shared between the members of the college. In addition, they will have the obligation to establish and manage a central database to make information available to the national supervisors involved in colleges.

Sixth, the ESAs may, in case of disagreements among national supervisors on cooperation, coordination or joint decision-making, take a decision, after an attempt for conciliation, requiring the supervisors to take or refrain from taking action. Moreover, the ESAs can also facilitate the delegation of tasks among supervisors and generally support a common supervisory culture through opinions, reviews and training programmes.

Lastly, the ESAs also have instruments for dealing with systemic risk. In particular, in collaboration with the ESRB, the ESAs will develop a 'risk dashboard', comprising a set of indicators to identify and measure systemic risk. Moreover, the ESAs will also develop criteria for measuring the systemic risk of financial institutions. The institutions posing such risk will be subject to strengthened supervision. The ESAs will also be able to collect information and conduct stress-testing exercises, in cooperation with the ESRB.

Although representing a significant attribution of responsibilities at EU level, the tasks and powers of the new ESAs are largely of a coordinating nature, which falls short of a federal architecture such as the one of the ECB and the Eurosystem.[22] In the words of the de Larosière Report, the new system is:

> a largely decentralised structure, fully respecting the proportionality and subsidiarity principles of the Treaty. So existing national supervisors, who are closest to the markets and institutions they supervise, would continue to carry-out day-to-day supervision and preserve the majority of their present competences.[23]

In this context, an important element of the ESAs legislation is the introduction of a safeguard clause relating to the fiscal responsibilities

Table 1.3 The regulatory instruments of the European supervisory authorities

Tools	
1	Draft regulatory technical standards and draft implementing standards
2	Guidelines and recommendations for the consistent supervisory practices and application of EU law
3	Specific recommendations to national supervisors failing to ensure compliance of financial institutions with EU law
4	Last resort decisions addressed to financial institutions not in compliance with EU law
5	General coordination role of national authorities in crisis situations
6	Decisions addressed to national supervisors in crisis situations
7	Last resort decisions addressed to individual financial institutions in crisis situations
8	Issuance of warnings and temporary prohibition or restriction of financial activities posing a serious threat to financial stability
9	Issuance of opinions to the Parliament, the Council or the Commission
10	Collection of information and setting up of central database
11	Mediation of disagreements between national supervisors, including the possibility to address decisions to national supervisors to take or refrain from taking action
12	Indicators and criteria for assessing systemic risk and stress-testing exercises
13	Instruments and convergence tools to promote a common supervisory culture
14	Conduct of peer review analyses among national authorities

of Member States. In particular, no decision by the ESAs – namely those adopted in emergency situations and for settling disagreements among national supervisors – may impinge in any way on the fiscal responsibilities of Member States.[24] In order to ensure that this is respected, it is provided that, where a Member State considers that a decision by an ESA impinges on its fiscal responsibility, it may notify that the national supervisor does not intend to implement the decision, together with a justification. The ESA shall then inform the Member State as to whether it maintains its decision or whether it amends or revokes it. When the decision is maintained, the Member State may refer the matter to the Council and the decision of the ESA is suspended. The Council shall, within two months, decide whether the decision should be maintained or revoked, acting by qualified majority.

The establishment of the ESAs should enhance significantly the conduct of financial regulation at the EU level. This will be achieved by attributing to the ESAs a set of tasks and powers, which will be conducive essentially to (1) a single EU rulebook for market participants, (2) better coordination at the EU level between national supervisors, and

(3) an enhanced ability of the EU as a whole to respond to a financial crisis.

The establishment of a European Systemic Risk Board

The crisis emerged and developed as a result of the increasing relevance of innovation, as well as the increasingly close links between systemic risk (stemming from structural developments such as financial integration) and financial (between the financial system and the real economy in Europe). Therefore, the crisis reinforced the view that a well-regulated financial market requires a broad monitoring and assessment of the potential risks covering all components of the financial system: so-called macro-prudential supervision.[25] This is in contrast with the scope of micro-prudential supervision, which focuses on the stability of individual financial institutions and aims at ensuring that financial institutions have a strong shock-absorbing capacity and effective risk management.[26]

The de Larosière Report recommended the establishment of a European Systemic Risk Council (ESRC) for macro-prudential supervision, whose tasks would include to 'form judgements and make recommendations on macro-prudential policy, issue risk warnings, compare observations on macroeconomic and prudential developments and give direction on these issues'. The Report also acknowledged that central banks have a key role to play in a macro-prudential framework in view of their role and interest in safeguarding the stability of the financial system.[27] Accordingly, the ESRC would be primarily composed of the members of the General Council of the ECB and it would also be set up under the auspices of the ECB.

The ECOFIN Council of 9 June 2009 renamed the proposed macro-prudential body as European Systemic Risk Board (ESRB), possibly in order to follow the terminology used for the Financial Stability Board by the G-20 in April 2009.[28] On this basis, the Commission presented on 23 September 2009 two legislative proposals which were adopted on 24 November 2010.[29]

First, the ESRB will be entrusted with a set of tasks, which will include (1) the collection and analysis of information, (2) the identification and prioritization of systemic risks, (3) the issuance of warnings where risks are deemed to be significant, (4) the issuance of recommendations for remedial action, (5) the monitoring of the follow-up to warnings and recommendations, (6) cooperation with the ESAs, including on the development of indicators of systemic risk and (7) coordination with the IMF and the FSB, as well as other relevant macro-prudential bodies.

Second, the ESRB's governance structure includes the Chair (the ECB President) and two Vice-Chairs, a General Board, a Steering Committee, a Secretariat, an Advisory Technical Committee and an Advisory Scientific Committee. The Board has a very wide composition. It comprises the ECB President and Vice-President, the EU central bank governors, the three Chairs of the ESAs, the Commission, as well as the Chair and the two Vice-Chairs of the Scientific Committee as members with voting rights. National supervisors and the Chairman of the Economic and Financial Committee are members without voting rights. The Steering Committee sets the agenda and prepares the decisions, while the Advisory Technical and Scientific Committees provide the ESRB with specific expertise and knowledge in all financial sectors. The ECB provides analytical, statistical, administrative and logistical support to the ESRB, which entails also the Secretariat.

Third, the ESRB may request information from the ESAs in summary or collective form, such that financial institutions cannot be identified. If the requested data are not available to those ESAs or are not made available in a timely manner, the ESRB may request the data from national supervisors, national central banks, statistics authorities or, ultimately, Member States. The ESRB may also address a reasoned request to the ESAs to provide data on individual financial institutions.

Fourth, and most importantly, the ESRB has the power and obligation to issue risk warnings and recommendations. They may be addressed to the EU as a whole or to one or more Member States, or to one or more of the ESAs, or to one or more national supervisors. Recommendations may also be addressed to the Commission in respect of the relevant EU legislation. In the case of recommendations, they should specify a timeline for the policy response. The ESRB is also requested to elaborate a colour-coded system distinguishing between different risk levels, which are then applied to warnings and recommendations in order to support their effectiveness.

The addressees of recommendations will have the obligation to communicate to the ESRB their policy response or to explain why they have not acted – an 'act or explain' mechanism. If the ESRB decides that its recommendation has not been followed and that the addressees have failed to explain their inaction appropriately, it shall inform the Council and, where relevant, the ESA concerned.

The degree of effectiveness of the risk warnings and recommendations will be a crucial aspect of the functioning of macro-prudential supervision, since the ESRB will have no legally binding powers to ensure compliance by the addressees of risk warnings and recommendations.

```
┌─────────────────────────┐  ┌──────────────────────┐   Potential addressees of
│ The ESRB may decide to  │  │       COUNCIL        │   ESRB warnings and
│   make warnings and     │  │     COMMISSION       │   recommendations
│ recommendations public  │  │ (copy of all warnings│  ┌──────────────────┐
└───────────▲─────────────┘  │ and recommendations) │  │        EU        │
            │                └──────────────────────┘  └──────────────────┘
┌─────────────────────────┐                            ┌──────────────────┐
│   EUROPEAN SYSTEMIC     │                            │     MEMBER       │
│      RISK BOARD         │◄───────────────────────────►│     STATES       │
└─────────────────────────┘   The addressees of        └──────────────────┘
                              recommendations should   ┌──────────────────┐
┌─────────────────────────┐   communicate the actions  │    EUROPEAN      │
│   The ESRB decides      │   taken or justify why     │   SUPERVISORY    │
│ whether recommendation  │───action was not taken────►│   AUTHORITIES    │
│    has been followed    │   ('act or explain'        └──────────────────┘
└─────────────────────────┘    mechanism')             ┌──────────────────┐
                                                       │    NATIONAL      │
                                                       │   SUPERVISORS    │
                                                       └──────────────────┘
                                                       ┌──────────────────┐
                                                       │   COMMISSION     │
                                                       │ (recommendations │
                                                       │ on EU legislation)│
                                                       └──────────────────┘
```

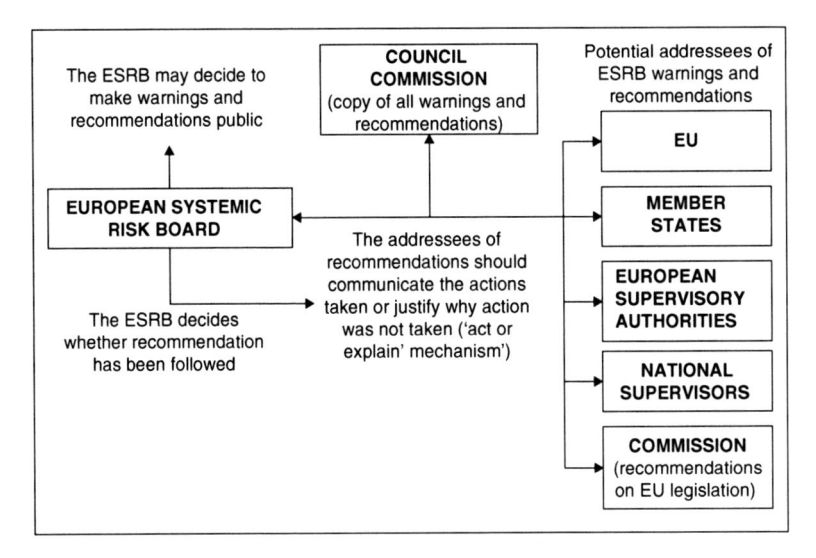

Figure 1.1 The framework for the ESRB risk warnings and recommendations

In this context, the ESRB could rely on the combination of five main tools and mechanisms.

First, the active monitoring by the ESRB on the extent to which its risk warnings and policy recommendations are implemented and the mitigating effects of such implementation on the identified risks.

Second, the regular reporting to the Council and the Commission of the outcome of such monitoring, in order to raise attention and foster action by policy-makers.

Third, the 'act or explain' mechanism mentioned above. The addressees of ESRB recommendations should communicate their actions and provide justification for inaction, not only to the ESRB but also to the Council.

Fourth, the close cooperation with the ESAs, particularly to support the implementation of recommendations addressed to national supervisors. In particular, the ESAs will be required to use their powers to ensure a timely follow-up. Furthermore, when a national supervisor does not follow-up, it has to inform the respective ESA. In its reply to the ESRB, the national supervisor has to take into account the input of the ESA.

Lastly, the right of the ESRB to decide to publish its risk warnings and recommendations on a case by case basis, which may increase the pressure for the prompt corrective actions. Given the sensitiveness of such a publication, it will be expected the decision of the ESRB would be taken

Table 1.4 The regulatory instruments of the European Systemic Risk Board

Tools
1 Issuance of warnings on significant risks to financial stability
2 Issuance of recommendations with a specified timeline for policy response
3 Publication of risk warnings and recommendations
4 Monitoring of the follow-up to the ESRB recommendations on the basis of a comply or explain mechanism
5 If the ESRB decides that its recommendation has not been followed and that the addressees have failed to explain their inaction appropriately, it shall inform the Council and, where relevant, the ESAs concerned
6 The ESRB may request information from the ESAs, and also under certain conditions from the ESCB, national supervisors, or national statistics authorities, or ultimately the Member States. The ESRB may also address a reasoned request to the ESAs to provide data on individual financial institutions.

on an exceptional basis, when serious threats to financial stability are not being addressed to the extent necessary. The Council should be consulted by the ESRB on the publication of warnings or recommendations.

Conclusion: the further development of European integration

The evolution of the law and regulation of the single financial market after the crisis represents a paradigm of the process of European integration as a whole.[30] The progress made in financial market integration gave rise to systemic interlinkages between Member States, which increased the potential for the transmission of economic and financial risks across the single market as a whole. This made the financial crisis a matter of common concern for all Member States.

In this context, the crisis revealed the limitations of a legal and regulatory strategy towards market integration, which is not accompanied by the development of political integration and mutualization of economic and financial risks – ultimately a federal solution for the internal market. The crisis put into evidence, in particular, the mutual incompatibility between 1. pursuing market integration through free movement of capital and establishment, 2. safeguarding the stability of an integrated market as a public good, while 3. retaining national fiscal responsibilities and regulatory competences.[31]

Therefore, the progress in market integration created economic and political dynamics which in turn require further integration to safeguard the progress achieved. This corresponds to the ideal of functional integration, according to which there are functional spillovers when 'incomplete integration undermines the effectiveness of existing policies, thereby creating pressures for new European policies'.[32]

Accordingly, it can be argued that the financial crisis gave rise to a constitutional moment in the EU.[33] This is particularly the case with regard to the economic governance in the euro area, which was called into question by the sovereign debt crisis which followed the financial crisis.

In May 2010, following a significant deterioration in the ability of the Greek state to fund itself in the markets, which threatened to spread to other Member States, the heads of state or government of the euro area provided Greece with 80 billion euros in a joint package with the IMF, which provided 110 billion euros. This was followed by the creation of financial facilities in the form of a European Financial Stability Facility and a European Financial Stabilization Mechanism with a total of up to 500 billion euros (with the IMF providing an additional amount of 250 billion euros), which are able to provide financial assistance in the form of loans or credits to Member States in difficulties.[34] The facilities were activated for the first time at the request of Ireland on 28 November 2010 to cover financing needs of up to 85 billion euros.[35]

These unprecedented measures gave a sense of urgency to the need to strengthen significantly the EU's system of economic governance so as to prevent and mitigate the effects of future crises. On 29 September 2010, the Commission put forward a package of legislative proposals on (i) strengthening the Stability and Growth Pact, (ii) preventing and correcting macroeconomic imbalances, (iii) strengthening national fiscal frameworks, and (iv) a stronger enforcement of fiscal discipline by imposing sanctions on non-compliant Member States.[36] On 21 October, a Task Force chaired by President Van Rompuy set out recommendations for strengthening economic governance, including also on crisis management.[37] Against this background, and also the worsening of the sovereign debt crisis in the euro area, the European Council agreed on 17 December to introduce a Treaty amendment to Article 136 of the Treaty so as to allow the euro area Member States to establish a permanent mechanism to safeguard financial stability from 1 January 2013.[38]

Figure 1.2, below, summarizes the layers peeled away by the process of integration of the single financial market, or, in other words, the fundamental obstacles that were overcome by legal and regulatory integration to fulfil the conditions of a single financial market. Following the experience with the financial crisis and the sovereign debt crisis, the latest obstacle to further market integration is the fiscal sovereignty of

22 The Regulation of the European Financial Market after the Crisis

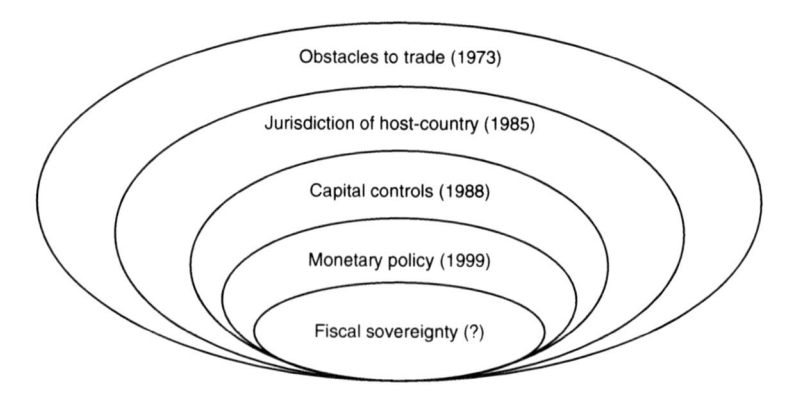

Figure 1.2 The 'onion layers' of the integration of the single EU financial market

(Layers from outer to inner: Obstacles to trade (1973); Jurisdiction of host-country (1985); Capital controls (1988); Monetary policy (1999); Fiscal sovereignty (?))

Member States, which represented a significant constraint in safeguarding the progress made in European integration in the face of the crisis and also in amplifying the competences and powers of the new ESAs as noted above.[39]

Regarding the narrower scope of the single financial market, the setting-up of the ESAs and of the ESRB corresponds to a new model of European financial regulation, which replaces the framework for financial integration based exclusively on home-country control, mutual recognition and minimum harmonization.

In what concerns the ESAs, the new institutional model draws to a large extent from the good experience with the ECB and the European System of Central Banks, which are responsible for the federal competences linked to the Economic and Monetary Union. Their manner of operating – based on the principle of unitary decision-making and executive decentralization of tasks[40] – is rather similar to the framework being proposed for the ESAs: the ESAs agree on regulatory standards which are implemented by national supervisors. Furthermore, the possibility that these standards are adopted by the Commission as European law provides the potential for a high degree of regulatory harmonization, therefore replacing to a certain extent the minimum harmonization concept. Lastly, the ability of the ESAs to mediate between home and host-country regulators, and to support as well the delegation of tasks between them, provides for a managed application of the principles of home-country control and mutual recognition, therefore changing the way they have applied thus far.

On the other hand, the establishment of the ESRB will introduce for the first time the notion of a regulatory public good for the single financial market: the stability of the European financial system. This may be qualified as a condition *sine qua non* for having European-based financial regulation. Previously, the design and implementation of financial regulation was made on the basis of pure national interests, namely the safeguard of the domestic financial systems. European committees and other arrangements then tried to bridge national interests through cooperation mechanisms. With the ESRB, its risk warnings and recommendations have the potential to influence and guide the design and implementation of regulation with a truly European scope. It may therefore be a first step towards a federal solution, in the same way that the emergence of the public good of European monetary stability was a precursor to EMU.

Notes

1. This article takes into account institutional and regulatory developments until 31 December 2010. The views expressed in this article are those of the author and do not necessarily reflect those of the ECB. Comments are welcome to pedro_gustavo.teixeira@ecb.europa.eu.
2. See Teixeira (2010), for the evolution of the law and regulation of the single European financial market. For the regulation of EU securities markets, see Ferran (2004).
3. For a full chronology and description of the global financial crisis, see the 79th Annual Report of the Bank for International Settlements (1 April 2008–31 March 2009), Basel, 29 June 2009, available at http://www.bis.org.
4. For an overview of the lessons from the crisis for the relations between home- and host-country regulators, see Pistor (2010). On the principle of mutual recognition in EU financial services law, see Ortino (2007), as well as Tison (1997).
5. See 'Summit of the Euro Area Countries: Declaration on a Concerted European Action Plan of the Euro Area Countries', 12 October 2008, available at www.ue2008.fr. The spectrum of measures aimed at ensuring appropriate liquidity conditions for financial institutions, facilitating the funding of banks, providing capital to financial institutions so that they continue to finance the economy, recapitalizing distressed banks, ensuring flexibility in the application of accounting rules and enhancing cooperation procedures among EU Member States. The Commission was also requested to act quickly and apply flexibility in state aid decisions. The European Council of 15 and 16 October 2008 endorsed the euro area agreement for the EU as a whole.
6. This was foreseen in Schoenmaker (2009), and characterized as the 'trilemma' of financial stability in the EU: the fact that financial integration, stability and national regulation cannot be pursued at the same time.
7. See Usher (2000), for the concrete application of these principles in EU legislation, as well as Hertig (2001) and Van Gerven and Wouters (1993).
8. In order to address the limitations of the national mandates, the concept of a common European mandate for national regulators was vented in several instances. Such mandate would include an obligation for each national regulator to minimize the collective costs facing Member States. See Hardy (2009).

9. The application of national commercial and insolvency laws implies that the location of assets in the case of the failure of a cross-border financial institution is relevant for the compensation of the domestic creditors. The national regulators cannot rely on assets in one Member State to compensate losses in another. See Herring and Litan (2005).
10. This move towards federalization of monetary policy was based on the realization – diagnosed in the 1989 Delors Report – that the development of the single market necessitated more effective coordination of economic policy between national authorities, as there was a fundamental incompatibility between (i) full freedom of capital, (ii) freedom to provide cross-border financial services, (iii) fixed exchange rate under ERM and (iv) autonomous monetary policy. See Padoa-Schioppa (1997).
11. Harmonization should also include include the legal framework for the safeguarding of financial stability and the management of crises. See the Commission's Communication, *An EU Framework for Cross-Border Crisis Management in the Banking Sector*, COM(2009) 561 final.
12. The framework was first proposed in a report by a High-Level Group chaired by Alexandre Lamfalussy in 2001. For an overview, see Teixeira (2010).
13. See Schinasi and Teixeira (2006).
14. The High-Level Group on Financial Supervision in the EU, February 2009, available at http://ec.europa.eu
15. There have been several European initiatives since 2009 putting forward proposals for regulatory reform. The Economic and Financial Committee mandated, in December 2008, a High-Level Working Group, chaired by Lars Nyberg, to draw on lessons for financial crisis management arrangements (ECOFIN Council Conclusions of 20 October 2009, available at www.consilium.europa.eu). The Commission adopted in May 2009 a Communication on European Financial Supervision, COM/2009/0252 final). The ECOFIN Council in Luxembourg on 20 October 2009 consolidated all these initiatives in a single European roadmap, including actions on (1) the supervisory framework, (2) the framework for crisis prevention, management and resolution, (3) the regulatory framework and (4) promoting the integrity of financial markets (ECOFIN Council Conclusions of 20 October 2009). For an overview of national initiatives, see Recine and Teixeira (2009).
16. See Ferrarini and Chiodini (2009).
17. See paragraphs 152 to 166 of the de Larosière Report. See Begg (2010).
18. See Commission Communication, *European Financial Supervision*, COM (2009) 252 final, 27 May 2009: 8ff.
19. See Recine and Teixeira, 2009, for an analysis of the Commission's proposals.
20. Regulation (EU) No 1093/2010 of the European Parliament and of the Council of 24 November 2010 establishing a European Supervisory Authority (European Banking Authority), OJ L 331, 15.12.2010, p.12; Regulation (EU) No 1094/2010 of the European Parliament and of the Council of 24 November 2010 establishing a European Supervisory Authority (European Insurance and Occupational Pensions Authority), OJ L 331, 15.12.2010, p.48; Regulation (EU) No 1095/2010 of the European Parliament and of the Council of 24 November 2010 establishing a European Supervisory Authority (European Securities and Markets Authority), OJ L 331, 15.12.2010, p.84; Directive 2010/78/EU of the European Parliament and of the Council of

24 November 2010 amending Directives 98/26/EC, 2002/87/EC, 2003/6/EC, 2003/41/EC, 2003/71/EC, 2004/39/EC, 2004/109/EC, 2005/60/EC, 2006/48/EC, 2006/49/EC and 2009/65/EC in respect of the powers of the European Supervisory Authority (European Banking Authority), the European Supervisory Authority (European Insurance and Occupational Pensions Authority) and the European Supervisory Authority (European Securities and Markets Authority) , OJ L 331, 15.12.2010, p.120.
21. In the context of the adoption of the Treaty of Lisbon, the Commission committed explicitly to continue to consult experts appointed by Member States in the preparation of draft delegated acts in the area of financial services. This allows the ESAs to be involved in the preparation of such acts through the issuance of standards. See Declaration 39 on Article 290 of the Treaty on the Functioning of the European Union, annexed to the Final Act of the Intergovernmental Conference, which adopted the Treaty of Lisbon.
22. The ESAs may be characterized as EU agencies with significant independence and autonomy, particularly *vis-à-vis* the Commission. For the characterization of the new European Supervisory Authorities as a new type of European agency, see Chiti (2009).
23. See paragraphs 184 of the de Larosière Report.
24. The recitals of the ESAs regulations clarify that the safeguard clause should only be invoked when a decision taken by an ESA leads to a significant material fiscal impact, and not in cases such as a reduction of income linked to the temporary prohibition of specific activities or products in order to protect consumers.
25. See *The Fundamental Principles of Financial Regulation*, Geneva Reports on the World Economy 11, Centre for Economic Policy Research (CEPR), 2009.
26. See Aglietta and Scialom (2009).
27. On the role of central banks in financial stability, see Padoa-Schioppa (2004).
28. See the Charter of the Financial Stability Board, endorsed at the G-20 Pittsburgh Summit of 25 September 2009, available at www.financialstabilityboard.org
29. Regulation (EU) No 1092/2010 of the European Parliament and of the Council of 24 November 2010 on European Union macro-prudential oversight of the financial system and establishing a European Systemic Risk Board, OJ L 331, 15.12.2010, p.1; Council Regulation (EU) No 1096/2010 of 17 November 2010 conferring specific tasks upon the European Central Bank concerning the functioning of the European Systemic Risk Board, OJ L 331, 15.12.2010, p.162.
30. On the evolution of the legal strategy towards European integration, see Weiler (1999).
31. See Fonteyn *et al.* (2010).
32. See Majone (2005): 43.
33. For an analysis of the constitutional dimension of the financial crisis in the UK see Black (2010): 36ff.
34. Statement of Heads of State or Government of the Euro Area, Brussels 7 May 2010; and Council Regulation (EU) No 407/2010 of 11 May 2010 establishing a European financial stabilization mechanism, OJ L 118/1, 12.5.2010. For an analysis, see Louis (2010).

35. See Statement by the Eurogroup and ECOFIN Ministers, 28 November 2010, available at www.consilium.europa.eu.
36. The Commission put forward on 12 May a Communication which called for reinforcing compliance with the Stability and Growth Pact and extending surveillance to macroeconomic imbalances, as well as setting up a crisis management framework for the euro area. Communication from the Commission on Reinforcing economic policy coordination, COM(2010) 250 final, 12 May 2010. The proposals in this Communication were further developed in the Communication from the Commission on Enhancing economic policy coordination for stability, growth and jobs – Tools for stronger EU economic governance, COM(2010) 367/2. The Communication was then translated on 29 September 2010 into six legislative proposals: three regulations and one directive on the reform of the Stability and Growth Pact and budgetary surveillance, and two regulations for detecting and correcting, also through sanctions, emerging macroeconomic imbalances within the EU and the euro area. The Commission proposals are available at ec.europa.eu.
37. 'Strengthening Economic Governance in the EU', Report of the Task Force to the European Council, 21 October 2010, available at www.consilium.europa.eu.
38. See Conclusions of the European Council of 16-17 December 2010, available at www.consilium.europa.eu. The amendment to Article 136 of the Treaty reads as follows: 'The Member States whose currency is the euro may establish a stability mechanism to be activated if indispensable to safeguard the stability of the euro area as a whole. The granting of any required financial assistance under the mechanism will be made subject to strict conditionality.'
39. See the Decision of the German Constitutional Court regarding the ratification of the Treaty of Lisbon, where the Court argues that 'the fundamental fiscal decisions on public revenue and public expenditure' are 'especially sensitive for the ability of a constitutional state to democratically shape itself' (preliminary version of the English translation made available by the German Court). See paragraph 252 of the Court's Decision: BVerfG, 2 BvE 2/08 vom 30.6.2009, Absatz-Nr. (1 - 421), http://www.bverfg.de/entscheidungen/es20090630_2bve000208en.html
40. See Zilioli and Selmayr (2001).

References

Aglietta, M. and Scialom, L. (2009) 'A Systemic Approach to Financial Regulation: A European Perspective', Working Paper 2009-29, Economix, Université Paris X Nanterre.

Begg, I. (2010) 'Regulation and Supervision of Financial Intermediaries in the EU: The Aftermath of the Financial Crisis', *Journal of Common Market Studies*, vol. 47, no. 5, pp. 1107–28.

Black, J. (2010) 'Managing the Financial Crisis: The Constitutional Dimension', LSE Law, Society and Economy Working Papers 12/2010.

Chiti, E. (2009) 'An Important Part of the EU's Institutional Machinery: Features, Problems and Perspectives of European Agencies', *Common Market Law Review*, vol. 46, pp. 1395–1442.

Ferran, E. (2004) *Building an EU Securities Market*, Cambridge/New York: Cambridge University Press.
Ferrarini, G. and Chiodini, F. (2009) 'Regulating Cross-border Banks in Europe: A Comment on the de Larosière Report and a Modest Proposal', *Capital Markets Law Journal*, vol. 4 (Supplement 1): S123-S140.
Fonteyn W. *et al.* (2010) 'Crisis Management and Resolution for a European Banking System', IMF Working Paper, WP/10/70.
Gleeson, S. (2009) 'Macroeconomic Regulation: New Regulators, New Powers', *Capital Markets Law Journal*, vol. 4 (Supplement 1): S99-S111.
Hardy, D. (2009) 'A European Mandate for Financial Sector Supervisors in the EU', IMF Working Paper WP/09/05.
Herring, R. J. and Litan. R. E. (1995) *Financial Regulation in the Global Economy*, Washington, DC: Brookings Institution.
Hertig, G. (2001) 'Regulatory Competition for EU Financial Services', in Esty and Geradin (eds), *Regulatory Competition and Economic Integration: Comparative Perspectives*, Oxford: Oxford University Press, pp. 218-40.
Louis, J.-V. (2010) 'Guest Editorial: The No-bailout Clause and Rescue Packages', *Common Market Law Review*, vol. 47, pp. 971-86.
Majone, G. (2005) *Dilemmas of European Integration*, Oxford: Oxford University Press.
Ortino, M. (2007) 'The Role and Functioning of Mutual Recognition in the European Market of Financial Services', in *International Comparative Law Quarterly*, vol. 56, pp. 309-38.
Padoa-Schioppa, T. (1997) *L'Europa verso l'unione monetaria*, Roma: Einaudi.
Padoa-Schioppa, T. (2004) *Regulating Finance*, Oxford: Oxford University Press.
Pistor, K. (2010) 'Host's Dilemma: Rethinking EU Banking Regulation in Light of the Global Crisis', Finance Working Paper No. 286/2010, June 2010.
Recine, F. and Teixeira, P. G. (2009) 'Towards a New Regulatory Model for the Single European Financial Market', *Revue Trimestrielle de Droit Financier*, no. 4, pp. 8-18.
Schinasi, G. J. and Teixeira, P. G. (2006) 'The Lender of Last Resort in the European Single Financial Market', IMF Working Paper 06/127.
Schoenmaker, D. (2009) 'The Trilemma of Financial Stability', http://papers.ssrn.com/sol3/papers.cfm?abstract_id=1340395
Teixeira, P. G. (2010) 'The Evolution of the Law and Regulation of the Single European Financial Market until the Crisis', *Revista de Concorrência e Regulação*, vol. 1, no. 2, pp. 209-52.
Tison, M. (1997) 'What is "General Good" in EU Financial Services Law?', *Legal Issues of European Integration*, vol. 24, pp. 1-46.
Usher, J. (2000) *The Law of Money and Financial Services in the EC*, 2nd edn, Oxford: Oxford University Press.
Van Gerven, W. and Wouters, J. (1993) 'Free Movement of Financial Services and the European Contracts Convention', in Andenas and Kenyon Slade (eds), *EC Financial Market Regulation and Company Law*, London: Sweet & Maxwell, pp. 43-79.
Weiler, J. H. H. (1999) *The Constitution of Europe*, Cambridge/New York: Cambridge University Press.
Zilioli, C. and Selmayr, M. (2001) *The Law of the European Central Bank*, Oxford: Hart.

2
The Monetary Policy Response to the Financial Crisis in the Euro Area and in the United States: A Comparison

Domenica Tropeano

Introduction

The financial crisis of 2007–8 has caused the melting down of the financial markets over the world. Globalization, jointly with increased interconnectedness among financial institutions in different countries, has caused a real freezing of many transactions on financial markets. The global aspect of the last crisis is what distinguishes it from previous episodes of financial crises and also from other recent world financial crises such as the Asian crisis. The policy response to the crisis has also been quite similar in the euro area and in the United States, with differences arising from the respective legislative backgrounds. The striking point is that all the most important central banks seemed to be unaware of the dangers of the increasing volume of transactions in financial markets and of the complicated web of mutual relations among financial institutions all over the world for a long time after the crisis started in the United States in August 2007. The Federal Reserve started with a modest lowering of the interest rate, which was followed by many rounds of further falls, but it did not realize the gravity of the problem until halfway through 2008, when it started using less conventional tools and acting, rather than as a lender of last resort, as a market-maker of last resort. The ECB exhibited even less awareness of the global dimensions and gravity of the crisis; in the middle of the financial turmoil, it decided to raise the interest rate, which was already higher than the Federal Reserve's rate, by 0.25 base points. In the following months, however, the ECB aligned its policy to that of the other central banks by lowering policy rates and starting a programme of acquisitions of troubled financial assets from the markets. This programme has been intensified because of the difficulties that European banks had in the light of the crisis of some European countries' government debts. Thus the ECB's role of market-maker of last resort has been strengthened through the covered bond programme and asset purchase programme.The main beneficiaries of this intervention have been commercial banks, which had bad-quality assets on their balance sheets. For example, Irish and Spanish banks, suffering from the consequences of real estate bubbles in their countries, largely used this facility.

At the moment of writing, both the Federal Reserve and the ECB are unwinding the extraordinary emergency measures taken during the crisis by closing the special facilities that have been created to address the problems of liquidity and lack of confidence in counterparties in the markets. The unwinding of these measures will have consequences on market volumes and rates, which are different according to the situations faced in each country by financial intermediaries.

The late recognition of the gravity of the crisis by central banks allowed the repercussions on the real sector to be enormous. However, the introduction of facilities, tailored to the market, has helped markets to work again. This apparent success notwithstanding, monetary policy is now at something of a standstill. It can do nothing more than it has already achieved and, according to the evolution of the macroeconomic variables, it might even make things worse. In all countries we are in what is labelled as a liquidity trap situation. The monetary policy objective of normalizing markets and making them return to doing their jobs has partially been reached, albeit at the cost of severe fiscal expenses, but there are very weak signs of economic recovery and the world risks falling into a situation of abundant money, high unemployment and falling incomes. In the United States the main fiscal expenses have been directed towards the rescue of big financial institutions and thus the stimulus to the real economy has been weak, producing weak recovery signs. In Europe, after a wave of countercyclical fiscal expansions in some countries, heavy fiscal contractions in many countries jeopardize any hope of recovery in incomes and production.

This chapter is organized as follows. In the first section there is a review of the evolution of the crisis in the United States and of the Federal Reserve's measures as a contrast, up to the present situation. The second section deals with the ECB's response to the crisis, distinguishing, among three main phases, non-recognition of the problem, alignment to interest cuts and, finally, direct interventions into the markets. The third and fourth sections will evaluate the achievements of these policies up to now in the US and in Europe respectively. Conclusions will follow.

The Federal Reserve's policy response to the crisis

The crisis started in the August 2007 in the United States and the first sign was a slight increase in the rate of delinquent mortgages. In a disproportionate way this very small disturbance created a disruption in a market whose value was infinitely greater (Dodd, 2007). The way the crisis spread itself to all markets was through the linkages among financial intermediaries' balance sheets. In particular, even markets for assets that were considered as totally safe, such as commercial paper issued by firms for their short-term financing needs, were affected. The reason behind this rapid spread was that intermediaries in the commercial paper market had on their balance sheets other assets linked to the mortgage market. The failure of mortgage purchasers to honour their debt affected the value of the assets resulting from the securitization of mortgages. Intermediaries that were poorly capitalized and under-regulated were the dealers in this very important segment of the market. The sudden awareness of counterparty risk that arose in the market meant that their assets found no purchasers. Because they had no other means of financing, they were compelled to give up their function of market-makers. They had no right to central bank refinancing. After this first episode the Federal Reserve continued to lower interest rates but it seemed unaware of the fact that lowering the rates did not solve the liquidity problems of the financial institutions that used to finance themselves on the market. The liquidity offered flowed to banks that, however, would not lend it to other financial institutions but rather kept it on their balance sheets as idle or excess reserves. At some point the monetary authorities realized that they had to allow many financial institutions which were not eligible to refinancing to access credit facilities and that they could mobilize excess reserves by ordinary banks offering interest on reserves held at the central banks.

Since the money injected into the market through the normal channel, banks refinancing, did not reach the parts of the financial system where it was badly needed, the authorities changed the rules by allowing non-financial institutions to be refinanced by the central bank. At the same time they introduced a form of remuneration previously absent for deposits held by banks at the central bank. So they were collecting the excess reserves idle in banks' balance sheets and through various facilities they were lending to non-bank financial institutions. The turmoil in the commercial paper market subsided for almost a year and a new episode of severe strain in that market was registered only after the Failure of Lehman Brothers in September 2008. Despite the freezing in the interbank market, nothing more happened in the year before the Lehman Brothers bankruptcy, which triggered a new wave of disruption, falling asset prices and the like. The reason for that slow pace of the spreading of the financial crisis is not evident by merely looking at statistics. It has been reconstructed in a very stimulating way in a narrative paper by Ferguson and Johnson (2009). In the whole of the year between September 2007 and September 2008 the Federal Reserve, jointly with other private financial institutions, participated in the so-called shadow bailout. Paulson, the Treasury Secretary in the Bush government, fearing the presidential elections scheduled to happen in November 2008, tried desperately to avoid the spreading of the crisis, attempting to postpone it to after the election.

Particularly important is the role played by government-sponsored institutions, namely the giant Fannie and Freddie – previously public financial institutions operating in the private mortgage markets. They bought an enormous amount of mortgages that nobody wanted to buy (Ferguson and Johnson, 2009). In particular they were authorized to buy riskier mortgages. In March 2008 there was the rescue of Bear Sterns organized by Paulson and Bernanke (respectively Treasury Secretary and Chairman of the Federal Reserve). J. P. Morgan bought Bear Sterns. Before this happened, the New York Fed took over $30 billion of bad assets in Bear's portfolio for its own account. The transaction was intermediated by a corporation to which the Fed loaned $30 billion. Paulson had a role in the transaction in so far as he wrote a letter allowing the NY Fed's losses to be deducted from what the Fed remits to the Treasury annually. The losses would thus become a burden of the US taxpayer. Then J. P. Morgan Chase bought Bear and saved a lot of money which would have been lost if Bear had declared bankruptcy (Ferguson and Johnson, 2009: 19–20). Later, the government took over the two giant intermediaries in the mortgage market, whose assets were 40 per cent of the US GDP. It also promised to purchase mortgage securities from them, which was forbidden by law. As a consequence of this, the government opened short-term credit lines for both of them at the New York Fed. In September 2008 Lehman Brothers declared bankruptcy and was not rescued, while AIG, the giant insurance company, was.

The rescue of AIG meant that the government actually paid all the money that AIG should have paid to other big counterparties – like Goldman Sachs, for betting by means of CDS. After the shadow bailout failed and the interbank market was still frozen, the Fed started its special facilities programme, which meant that, as Johnson and Ferguson write, it was no longer supporting private markets but actually replacing them (Johnson and Ferguson, 2009: 41). It took all this time for the Fed to understand that the interbank market or, better, the market for fund exchanges among financial institutions was no more governed by the federal funds rate. Many studies have reported what happened: there were extensive runs on commercial paper, on the repo and on the money market mutual funds markets (Gorton, 2008; Kacperczyk and Schnabl, 2010). The 'haircut', the borrowing rate on repurchase agreements, skyrocketed in the period 2007–9. The markets for some credit derivatives, which were used as collateral in the repo market, practically ceased to exist (see Gorton and Metrik, 2010).

The Fed seemed not to have realized that a liquidity problem in these markets might have destroyed the whole payments system. Though its interventions into the markets were successful in so far as they replaced markets that had suddenly disappeared, little effort was made to avoid the same disgraceful situation repeating itself in the future. The measures taken by both the Fed and the Treasury were shaped as emergency measures, which had to be temporary. Most of the special facilities have already expired and the unwinding of these emergency measures is depicted as successful. The possibility that, if all these emergency measures were necessary, the financial system architecture in itself may have been flawed, has not yet arisen in official institutions' declarations; neither has the question been tackled in the recently approved new law on the financial system.

Minsky repeatedly wrote that in a system with a large non-bank financial institutions sector the central bank is no longer able to control the money market. Securitization in turn adds further difficulties to the central bank's action (Minsky, 1982; 2008; Tropeano, 2010).

The market for securitization has almost ceased to exist since 2007. Most of the new securitizations are in reality resecuritizations of products that were previously rated AAA; half of the new issue of securitized products has been made through TALF, the term auction liquidity facility (IMF, 2010). The danger arises that when banks and other institutions try to roll over existing securitized products, either they will not succeed or they will succeed but only at increasing costs. In turn this will raise the cost of financing for small and medium enterprises (*ibid.*). In the opinion of the writer, the only possible solution is that the Federal Reserve intervenes again in the market and purchases massive amounts of these securities. The Fed has already bought a large quantity of asset-backed securities. The possibility of further interventions in this direction, with the Fed continuing to use non-conventional tools, has not been excluded by Bernanke (2010).

Also Krugman, in a recent contribution to *The New York Times*, has stressed that, in order to avoid the current situation triggering a double-dip recession, the Fed should purchase other risky assets even if this means increasing the risks it bears on its balance sheets. He advocates also a role for a more expansionary fiscal policy and strongly opposes the so-called deficit hawks. In his previous work on the liquidity trap and the financial crisis in Japan (Tropeano, 2010b) he seems to share the same ideas that Bernanke has expressed on how to get out of a liquidity trap. Essentially, in order to avoid deflation, the central bank has to make people believe that it is targeting a reasonably high level of inflation. Bernanke (2010) agrees that one of the tools still at disposal of the central bank is precisely to create inflation expectation.

The market for derivatives, in contrast, has never ceased to work and some of the most dangerous products from the viewpoint of systemic instability, such as credit default swaps, have even experienced an increase in the volume of issues and in the liquidity of the market. Some scholars even recommend their use in their proposal for reform of financial regulation. They argue that, since the reform of regulation must be market-based, credit defaults are the ideal tool by which to evaluate how risky financial institutions are (Hart and Zingales, 2010).

The shadow banking system has not shrunk after the crisis. The non-banks, such as money market mutual funds, still receive a lot of money as various sorts of deposits. The awareness that, as Gorton and Metrick (2010) argue, shadow banking is effectively banking, has not inspired any revision of their role by the authors of the recently passed law on financial reform. Even now, Paul Volcker, when asked in an interview why the money market mutual funds are not eligible to central bank refinancing in the financial reform law that has been approved by the US Parliament, seemed not to grasp the problem at all (see Levy Economics Institute, 2010).

To summarize, the Fed did not understand the structural problems that had accumulated in the US financial system before the crisis erupted and those structural problems are still present. Chairman Bernanke has theorized and implemented a quantitative easing policy mainly consisting of massive injections of liquidity into the system through both usual and unusual tools. Being now aware that the macroeconomic problems linked to the financial crisis have not been solved, he is planning to use more doses of the same remedies. Thus, presumably, the short-run interest rate will be kept near zero for a longer time than previously thought and eventually the large-scale asset purchase programme will be continued to lower further the long-term interest rates.

The ECB's response

The ECB's response to the crisis, apart from the initial mistake of raising interest rates, was similar to that of the Fed. The ECB, however, did not intervene in the rescue of failing big financial institutions, contrary to what the Federal Reserve has been doing during the 'shadow bailout' period. The recapitalizations of banks have been performed instead by the governments of the countries where the banks were located. The ECB has injected in the system a lot of liquidity and issued guarantees for private bonds. Some of these measures are being withdrawn. The liquidity previously given to banks, for example, has been returned at maturity without big problems.

The European Central Bank has not used facilities aimed at particular markets because of the different structure of European markets compared to those in the US. For example, given that money market mutual funds are not as important in the European financial structure, there has been no run on them. The crisis has not caused a contraction in the volume of transactions in the commercial paper market either because it is not a significant factor for the financing of enterprises in Europe. The run on repo, instead, may have crossed the ocean because it has been one of underlying causes of the freezing of the interbank market. The rise in the haircuts and the margins for derivatives transactions has surely hit European financial institutions. The problem was aggravated by the foreign exchange denominations of all these securities. It is noteworthy that, though the crisis developed in the US, the dollar appreciated throughout 2008. All the payments linked to the repurchase agreements and derivatives, whose underlying assets were denominated in dollars, had to be made in dollars. Though the European banks could access liquidity by the ECB, the euro funds had to be swapped into dollars, which needed willing counterparties and a liquid foreign exchange swap market (Pozsar *et al.*, 2010: 33). The problem was eased by the swapping of some operations between the Fed and the ECB. Though the European banks had in their portfolio many toxic assets, those assets were issued and sold by foreign counterparties. The complex piling of markets and intermediaries' interconnections that triggered the diffusion of the crisis in the United States was not present in Europe. In particular, securitization has been more limited in amount in Europe with respect to the United States (see Figures 2.1 and 2.2 below).

The transmission of the crisis in Europe was rather linked to cross-border transactions and financial globalization. Though the toxic assets were not generated in Europe and in Europe as a whole there has not

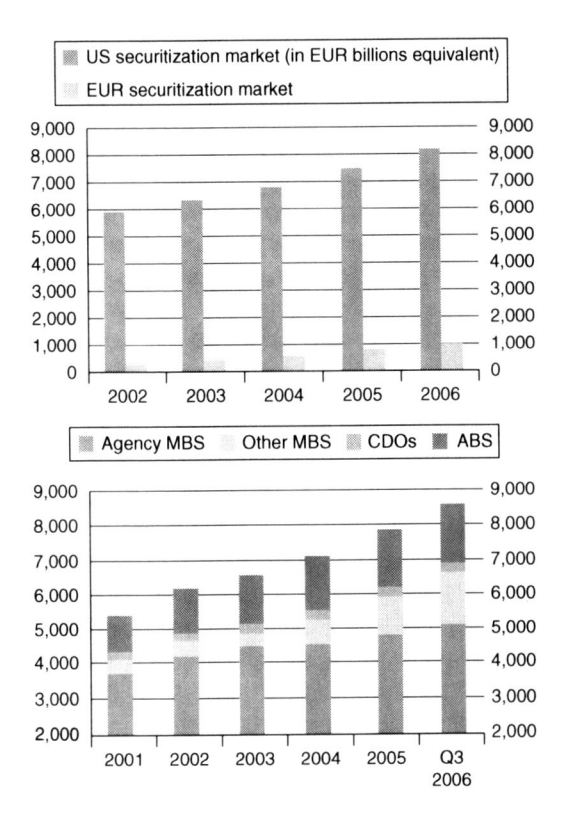

Figure 2.1 Securitization in Europe and the US
Source: ECB (2007, p.26).

been a real estate boom leading to a bubble, all of these products, which were the by-product of excessive lending in the housing market in the US, passed to the other side of the ocean. In this environment, the task of the central bank *was simply to restore the working of the interbank market rather than to replace the private financial markets.*

The only relevant intervention in the private markets made by the ECB has been in the market for covered bonds. Covered bonds are bonds secured by a pool of cover assets on the issuer's balance sheet. Cover assets consist mainly of mortgage loans and public bonds, assets which are considered as safe. Covered bonds, in contrast to asset-backed securities, are claims of the bond-holders against the monetary and financial institutions that have issued them. About 30 per cent of all debt securities issued by monetary and financial institutions in the euro area are covered bonds (see ECB, 2007). Since July 2009, the ECB has been purchasing covered bonds for a total amount of 60 trillion euro. Recently, the ECB has launched another facility, the Securities Markets Programme, which allows the bank to buy not only private securities but also public bonds. The total amount of securities purchased, up to the time of writing, under the two programmes is 100 billion euro.

Given the different weight that banks have in Europe with respect to non-bank financial institutions, the main problem that Europe is facing now is linked to the conditions in the markets when, and this will happen very soon, these banks will have to refinance huge amounts of maturing bonds. Since most banks still have government guarantees on their bonds and the situations of governments is not terribly healthy, the risk premia for holding both banks' and governments' debts of certain countries may well increase.

Purchases of public bonds by the ECB have been implemented because of the difficulties of some weak members of the European Union. *They were not part of a deliberate strategy to lower long-term interest rates as they have been in the US.* This would not work in the same way as in the US in any case. In the European Union there are many public debts belonging to different states but denominated in the same currency. The action by the central bank is aimed at lowering the interest rates on the debts of the states that have been attacked by speculation. Those countries were compelled to pay very high interest rates on new debt issued because of the increase in risk premia. *Ultimately, the aim of the central bank may be to reduce the interest differential between different European countries' public bonds*

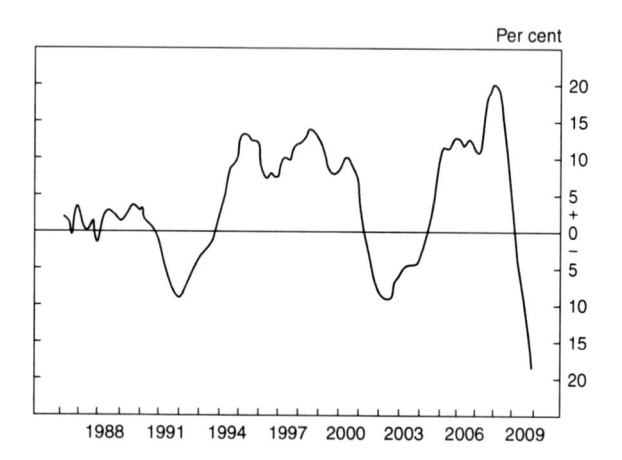

Figure 2.2 Commercial and industrial loans
Source: Federal Reserve (2010).

rather than to lower long-term interest rates. According to official accounts, the ECB many times has expressed worries about inflation and made plans to raise interest rates but, fortunately, it did not do this (see Figure 2.2).

The current state of the financial markets in the US

In the US, the measures taken by the central bank to inject liquidity have produced an increase in the monetary base M1. This increase, however, has not affected the supply of credit. Strangely enough M1 is bigger than broad money aggregates (Keen, 2009). The data on commercial and industrial loans, which are strongly decreasing, confirm this point.

The reason is that the demand for credit supply is missing. In the US, the lack of demand may be explained by the fact that the households are saving more to pay past debts, and investment has not started to grow again after the crisis. Thus, all the liquidity goes to the giant financial institutions generated by the disorderly rescues made up during the crisis, which may speculate again on anything from the weak European states' debts to commodity and raw materials prices. The choice of derivatives products that was available before the financial crisis is still there. Even if markets have been revitalized, liquidity for those markets is still not warranted.

Interest rates are at historical lows, both short term and long term. Stock prices have risen again near to their pre-crisis levels. But if this brings relief to some financial institutions' balance sheets, it does not resolve the problems of all the people who now have to repay loans which are higher than the value of their houses. The prospects for recovery are thus dim.

The price levels of different assets are showing different tendencies. The producer price levels fell during the first year of the crisis, thus making deflation possible. These rose, though slowly, until March 2010, but, after that point, started falling again because of failing consumer confidence and persistent high unemployment (see Figure 2.3 below).

The stock price index, instead, shows a very pronounced recovery with respect to the post-crisis period. The home price index fell heavily during 2008, while the fall was mitigated in 2009–10 by the intervention of the Fed to sustain the mortgages market and by fiscal discounts to home purchasers, which now have expired. In Figure 2.4, we see the fall in home price index because of the crisis.

Another effort of the administration is to keep very low interest rates for all maturities to help people who took a variable-rate mortgage to service it. Most mortgages have a fixed interest rate for the first years

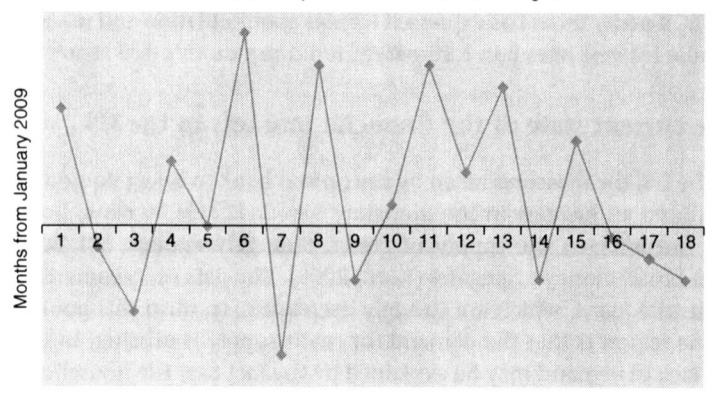

38 *Monetary Policy Response to the Financial Crisis*

Figure 2.3 PPI monthly rates of change 2009–10
PPI = Producer Price Index
Source: Federal Reserve Board of Governors Statistics.

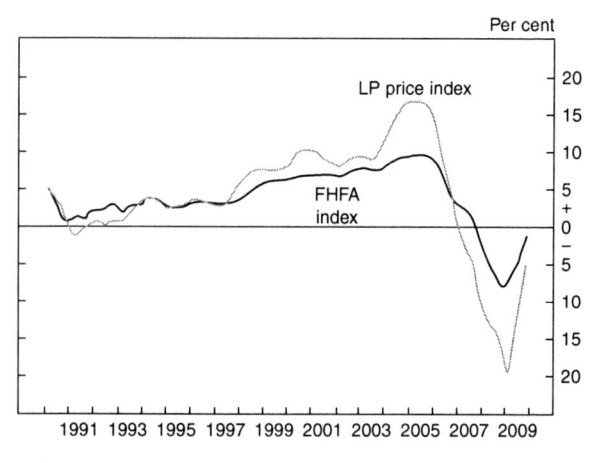

Figure 2.4 Change in price of existing family homes (1990–2009)
Source: Federal Reserve (2010).

and then become variable-rate mortgages. For those who have not yet reset to variable, the lower interest rates may help. The problem is that if the value of the house falls too much with respect to the mortgage value foreclosures and/or strategic defaults are likely to occur. IMF (2010) forecasts an increase in the rate of strategic defaults in the coming years. The evolution of home prices as time goes on is thus decisive. Until now, the government has done a lot to sustain the prices of financial assets, but it has not introduced any measure to relieve the conditions of distressed home owners. It is reasonable to expect that they will have to restrain consumption to pay off their debt. Thus, after years of falling saving ratios, the saving rate is and will be increasing.

The effects of rising stock prices with very low interest rates on the balance sheets of financial institutions are very different according to the specialization of the same institutions. The big financial institutions that have survived the crisis through public money infusions and mergers now may continue to do their business under improved conditions. They have posted gains in recent balances and these gains come from trading activity. Even without considering arbitrage and speculation, if they just charge a fee for trading in assets, which is calculated as a percentage of the value of assets, the recovery of asset prices obviously causes an increase in their trading revenues. Moreover, their interest margin has increased rather than decreased. This may be due to the fact that now, thanks to their bigger size and to the moral hazard speculations induced by the rescues, they are getting funds at a rate which is still lower than that paid before the crisis. Due to their size and to the implicit government guarantee, they are now perceived as safer than they were before the crisis. On the contrary, a large number of smaller commercial banks dispersed through the country has a reduced interest margin due to the very thin difference between lending and borrowing rates; these banks have to cope with increasing non-performing loans and perspective recapitalizations (Federal Reserve, 2010).

As a conclusion, it can be stated that the main beneficiaries of this policy of quantitative easing have been the big banks, which have increased their trading revenues, and the rentiers, the owners of wealth in the form of financial assets. If the trend in the relative prices of assets continues in the future, it will increase inequality as measured by the ratio of stock prices to house prices. The richer households, whose net wealth is positive and whose wealth has a higher share of financial assets, will be favoured in comparison to the poorer households, who have a negative net wealth due to the mortgage debt (Tropeano, forthcoming).

The current situation of the financial markets in the euro area

In Europe also the main stock market indexes have returned again to their pre-crisis levels. The main difference with respect the US is that financial markets are less layered and non-bank financial institutions are less important with regard to shares of assets, though there are big differences among countries within Europe. Moreover, in Europe there has not been a bubble in housing prices in general; Ireland, Spain and some Eastern European countries that do not have the euro as their currency yet are the exceptions to this. Private debt as a ratio to GDP is important only in countries like Ireland, Spain and Portugal, but for the remaining ones this is not an emergency situation. This means that the painful process of saving more, so as to be able to generate revenues to pay past debts, should weigh less on the aggregate demand of the Eurozone. In theory, households on low incomes should not worry about the high debt contracted in the past. In theory this should help the recovery of the Eurozone, thereby leaving more space for aggregate demand increases. However, this is not the case. The monetary policy of the ECB, like that pursued by the Federal Reserve, by pursuing a policy to ensure that stock prices reach a high level again may have favoured richer families, which have positive net wealth and own the biggest share of financial assets. The same cannot be said of the rest of population. The most striking thing is that, in Europe, many countries have engaged in strong fiscal contractionary policies, which aim at reassuring international capital markets regarding the ability of governments to honour their debts. These policies have been implemented in different measure by many countries, which find themselves in different conditions. The result is just to aggravate the consequences of the crisis and to postpone the recovery. In those countries where the fiscal contraction policy has been in place for the longest time, the fall in aggregate demand and the rise in unemployment is stunning (see the case of Ireland). The worsening of public finances in many countries, though not all of them (a notable exception is Greece), is due to the expenses accrued in rescuing failing financial institutions, which, in the European accounts, weigh directly on the balance sheets of the governments that have intervened. In the US, with the Federal Reserve acting as a quasi-fiscal agent of the state, often in a non-transparent way (Ferguson and Johnson, 2009), some of these costs are still on the balance sheet of the central bank, though improperly. In some of the fiscal contractions in Europe, the packages include explicit reductions in nominal salaries of employees, something which reminds us of the reduction in nominal wages, implemented during the 1929 crisis by the fascist government in Italy and of its disastrous consequences.

The recovery of financial asset prices is less important in Europe than it is in the United States. The reasons are the following:

1. The savings propensity out of wealth is higher in Europe than in the United States, so no significant effect on consumption can reasonably

be expected. In Germany the propensity to save out of wealth increased in the period before the crisis rather than falling.
2. The weight of pension funds and other institutional investors, which have in their portfolios stocks and other financial assets, is quite limited with respect to the US.
3. Though, in some countries, there has been a real-estate bubble, there has been no extraction of rents from the value of the houses on the part of European families, as it has happened in the US. Thus a fall in the value of houses though impairing the ability of families to repay debt has no direct consequence on consumption through the wealth effect.

The crisis in Europe has simply been a consequence of the globalization of finance and, in particular, of the global dimension of the interbank market. The interconnections between European and US banks have survived the financial crisis. The European banks, to invest the abundant savings and the many borrowed funds, have purchased huge quantities of financial assets born and packaged in the wild and unregulated US markets. The losses they have suffered because of this very unwise policy, aimed at increasing the return to shareholders through leverage, have been borne by the state and now, through taxation and spending cuts, they will be transferred to the citizens.

Since consumption was not dependent on debt, there has not been a reduction in demand due to the burst of a bubble. The strong fall in output growth is mostly due to the contraction in trade flows. In most European countries, given the stagnation of domestic aggregate demand, the most important source of income growth has been exports. European countries could not avoid the painful output contractions following the burst of the bubble in the US. Still worse, given that the weakness of domestic demand was due to low wages, not supplemented by wealth or debt injections, and high inequality, the measures taken to overcome the financial crisis risk perpetuating the existing situation. People with low wages, unemployed or precariously employed will see their situation worsened, while the people who already enjoyed capital gains and high salaries will not notice big changes with respect to the past.

Moreover, given that the interconnections between European and US giant financial institutions are still important and that the markets for derivatives are still unregulated in the US, it is quite probable that any further disturbance or crisis in the US market will spread itself to Europe in exactly the same way as it has done before. Securitization markets are relatively frozen in the US, but derivatives markets are flourishing again and are gaining liquidity and depth. The recent Dodd–Franck Financial

Stability Act does not address the problem of systemic instability within the financial system. The more conservative attitude towards financial regulation in Europe cannot avoid the spreading of disturbances through interconnected markets.

After the financial crisis, the banking systems in the US and in Europe appear to have increased their interconnectedness. A recent study by the IMF (IMF, 2010) has calculated that the probability that a distress in one of the two banking systems spreads itself to the other one has increased after the crisis with respect to the pre-crisis level (see Figure 2.5 below).

Concluding remarks

The monetary policy responses by the Federal Reserve and the ECB to the devastating financial crisis of 2007–8 are based on some common elements, but they diverge in their general philosophy. The Federal Reserve, throughout the first year of the crisis, attempted to use traditional liquidity injections, while at the same time strongly participating in Paulson's shadow bailout with interventions. From March 2008 onwards the Fed started the special facilities programmes that have replaced private markets rather than simply supported them. The balance sheet of the Fed has swollen and, in particular, it contains more

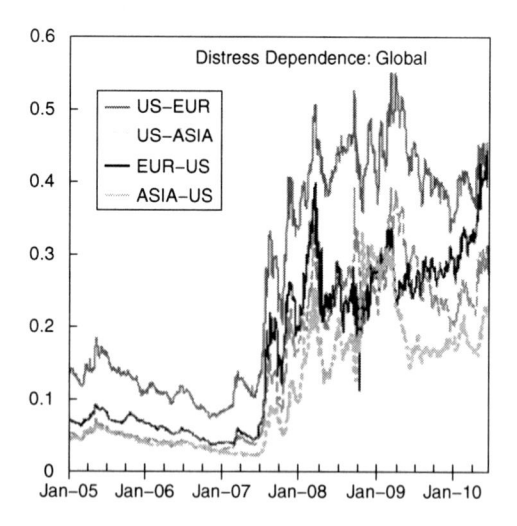

Figure 2.5 Distress dependence: global
Source: IMF (2010).

than $1 trillion of mortgage-backed securities. These interventions have been justified by the emergency situation created by the crisis and were underpinned by Bernanke's monetarist faith that, in the end, by pumping into the system infinite quantities of money, inflation will rise and deflation will be avoided. The central bank did not seem to be aware of the structural flaws in the architecture of the US financial system. Neither did the legislators that drafted the recent Dodd–Franck Act, which has been approved by the US Congress. The strategy of the Fed, according to Bernanke's speeches, is to continue to keep the short-term interest rate close to zero in the future and to go on with asset purchases that will lower the long-term interest rates.

The ECB, after the initial unhappy move of raising the interest rate in the midst of a crisis, has done more or less the same. It has injected liquidity into the system through usual and unusual tools. It has also in part purchased middle- or long-term assets in the markets, but its interventions in this respect have been both quantitatively and qualitatively less important than those made by the Fed. The ECB has intervened particularly in the market for covered bonds, an asset used by financial institutions to finance themselves, and recently in the market for public bonds. The difference with respect to the US is that the European financial system is less layered than that of the former. The weight of the non-bank financial institutions on total assets is less pronounced and the problem of managing a complex and highly interconnected financial system less urgent. Only some countries have experienced a real estate bubble, but the diffusion of derivatives products in Europe is much lower than in the US. The problems linked to derivatives and securitization do not directly concern the ECB. This notwithstanding, however, given that the interconnectedness between US and European banking institutions has increased after the crisis, the danger that any distress in the US market will be transmitted to the European financial system is higher now than in the past. Moreover, while the philosophy of the Fed is to lower and lower interest rates because this will avoid deflation and will help the indebted families to repay their debt, no such philosophy – based on a sort of liquidity trap monetarism – lies behind the ECB's action. In Europe short-term interest rates are very low but the ECB has repeatedly warned that they will be raised to avoid an unlikely inflation. Long-term interest rates are not so low as in the United States, probably because the riskiness of European average debts is perceived as higher than that of the US. No deliberate strategy of lowering long-term interest rates by resorting to unusual tools has been announced by the ECB. It is indeed likely that, because of the increased costs of funding for banks, of the recapitalizations they need and of the non-performing loans that will emerge in the future, those rates will be higher than now. A higher interest margin, however, should favour traditional banking activity. While in the US there is a commitment by the Central Bank to maintain both short-term and long-term interest rates at a low level, no such commitment exists in the euro area. If the countries that mostly influence the decisions of the ECB, like Germany, experience a rapid recovery, increased pressure to raise interest rates is likely.

Unfortunately, the idea that a restrictive fiscal policy will induce markets to trust governments and thus lower the cost of debts and help the recovery is gaining consensus on both sides of the Atlantic. No attention is being paid to mounting unemployment. Thus, the combination of a very lax monetary policy and a restrictive fiscal policy will lead us to a situation where wages and aggregate demand will be depressed while eventually gains arising from arbitrage and speculation will flourish. Many references to the Japanese crisis in the 1990s have been made in the current debate on economic policy. Perhaps it should not be forgotten that one of the by-products of the quantitative easing policy of the Bank of Japan was the growth of a very profitable and long-lasting carry trade.

References

Bernanke B. (2010) 'Semiannual Monetary Policy Report to the Congress Before the Committee on Banking, Housing, and Urban Affairs', US Senate, Washington, DC, 21 July 2010, http://www.federalreserve.gov/newsevents/testimony/bernanke20100721a.htm. For the complete video of the testimony, see http://banking.senate.gov/.

Dodd R. (2007) 'Subprime: Tentacles of a Crisis', *Finance and Development* (December): 15–19.

European Central Bank (2007) *The Euro Bond and Derivatives Markets*, June 2007.

European Central Bank (2010) 'Extraordinary Measures in Extraordinary Times', Occasional Paper n.117 by S. M. Stolz and M. Wedow.

Federal Reserve (2010) 'Profits and Balance Sheet Developments at US Commercial Banks in 2009', *Federal Reserve Bulletin*, May 2010.

Ferguson, T. and Johnson, R. (2009) 'Too Big to Bail: The "Paulson Put," Presidential Politics, and the Global Financial Meltdown', *International Journal of Political Economy*, vol. 38, no. 2, pp. 5–45.

Gorton, G. B. (2008) 'The Subprime Panic', Yale ICF Working Paper No. 08-25. Available at SSRN: http://ssrn.com/abstract=1276047.

Gorton, G. B. and Metrick, A. (2010) 'Securitized Banking and the Run on Repo (July 14, 2010)', Yale ICF Working Paper No. 09-14. Available at SSRN: http://ssrn.com/abstract=1440752.

Hart, O. and Zingales, L. (2010) 'Curbing Risk on Wall Street', *National Affairs*, no. 3, pp. 20–34, www.nationalaffairs.com.

International Monetary Fund (2010) 'United States: Publication of Financial Sector Assessment Program Documentation – Financial System Stability Assessment', IMF Country Report No. 10/247 Washington, DC.

Kacperczyk, M. and Schnabl P. (2010) 'When Safe Proved Risky: Commercial Paper during the Financial Crisis of 2007–2009', *Journal of Economic Perspectives*, vol. 24, no. 1, pp. 29–50.

Keen S. (2009) 'Bailing Out the Titanic with a Thimble', *Economic Analysis and Policy*, vol. 39, no. 1, pp. 1–24.

Levy Economics Institute of Bard College (2010) 'Proceedings Annual Hyman Minsky Conference 2010', Paul Volcker Q&A, http://www.levyinstitute.org/conferences/minsky2010/.

Minsky, H. (1982) *Can 'It' Happen Again? Essays on Instability and Finance*, New York: M. E. Sharpe.

Minsky, H. (2008) 'Securitization', Jerome Levy Economics Institute Policy Note No. 2.

Pozsar, Z., Adrian, T., Ashcraft, A. and Boesky, H. (2010) 'Shadow Banking', Staff Report no. 458, Federal Reserve Bank of New York.

Tropeano D. (2010) 'The Current Financial Crisis, Monetary Policy and Minsky's Structural Instability Hypothesis', *International Journal of Political Economy*, vol. 39, no. 2 (Summer 2010), pp. 41–57.

Tropeano, D. (forthcoming) 'Quantitative Easing in the United States after the Crisis: Conflicting Views', in Rochon L.-P. (ed.), *Central Bank Policies and Financial Crises*, Cheltenham: Edward Elgar.

3
Real Divergence Across Europe and the Limits of EMU Macroeconomic Governance

Elisabetta Croci Angelini and Francesco Farina

Introduction

As an effect of financial globalization,[1] the traditional transmission mechanism of macroeconomic disturbances based on trade flows has been substituted by the much faster international financial transmission. The financial crisis, stemmed in 2007 from 'moral hazard' in the creation of derivatives by banking institutions in the United States, rapidly crossed the Atlantic. European banks loaded with the overpriced derivatives created through the securization of the US subprime mortgages started deleveraging in 2008–9, so that credit conditions tightened and the mutual creditworthiness among banks progressively faded out. The credit crunch and gloomy profit expectations led to a huge drop in output in the economies of the European Economic Monetary Union (hereafter: EMU) The unprecedented amount of liquidity granted to financial institutions by the European Central Bank (hereafter: ECB) avoided the drying-up of the interbank financing, and the consequent implosion of the market functioning. To revive aggregate demand after substantially negative growth rates, some EMU governments also made recourse to expansionary fiscal interventions.

The recession is doomed to aggravate the macroeconomic divide which has widened within Europe since its inception. The EMU is undergoing two major sources of macroeconomic imbalances. First, a divide has opened within the EMU since its inception between Peripheral countries,[2] where a declining competitiveness caused a soaring current account deficit, and some Core countries,[3] where a real appreciation caused the accumulation of current account surpluses. Second, the ratio of the public deficit and debts over the GDP have enormously deteriorated, because both the accumulation of negative output gaps and

European governments imitating the United States government and transferring the banking sector's debt to the public sector.[4]

Underneath the successful start of the monetary union, these two questions unveil the fragility of the overall European institutional setting. The rigid statute of the ECB, which limits monetary interventions in favour of the private and the public sector of Member States, and the severe constraints imposed on national fiscal authorities by the Stability and Growth Pact (hereafter: SGP), make the EMU macroeconomic governance manifestly inadequate to face the challenges posed by the interconnectedness of globalized financial markets. On the one hand, the ability of Ireland, Greece and Spain to withstand the challenges of the participation in the EMU is under scrutiny, due to the financial markets expecting their banks to undergo bankruptcies and/or public debt default. On the other hand, the commercial and investment banks of the large Core countries are burdened by the high-risk private and public assets of the Peripheral countries. Macroeconomic governance in the EMU lacks institutions devoted to organize a system of mutual risk insurance to prevent the formation of Member States' current account deficit and/or public deficit and debt. The absence of a common fiscal policy magnifies uncertainty after macroeconomic imbalances within the EMU continuously exposes the euro to a loss of credibility.

This chapter argues that the deterioration of trade balance and/or of fiscal sustainability in some EMU countries is not only the outcome of a domestic failure in preserving competitiveness and/or in pursuing fiscal discipline. Indeed, the origin of the EMU macroeconomic imbalances is rooted in the national economic systems, as the different risk premia borne by the public debt of EMU governments demonstrate. Yet, the economic integration process has brought about increasing interconnections among the productive and the financial sectors, which ask for the strengthening of common policies among the EMU countries.

The opposite trends of real depreciation in many Core EMU economies and real appreciation in Peripheral EMU economies witness a self-aggravating path of real divergence across Europe depending on the inconsistency between growing *spillovers* and the inadequate governance of macroeconomic imbalances among EMU countries. The message of the chapter is that the major inadequacy subsiding the EMU construction lays in the absence of a fiscal union to cope with systemic crises.

The chapter is organized as follows. In section 2, econometric estimates explore the reaction of real effective exchange rates (hereafter: REER) to output gaps, and the contribution of price flexibility to the recovery in competitiveness after a shock. Section 3 presents the evolution of domestic demand, primary balance, and current account during the various stages of the monetary integration process, and, through a regression model, investigates whether the output gap or a deterioration in the REER originate the current account deficits. Section 4 differentiates between macroeconomic imbalances across countries occurring within or between currency areas. In section 5, real divergence across Europe is evaluated in the light of monetary and fiscal policies within a monetary union characterized by numerous spillovers. Section 6 concludes.

The evolution of real divergence across EMU economies (1979–2009)

The analysis of the main determinants of the evolution of real exchange rates and competitiveness within the Eurozone distinguish three phases. The first one is the 'hard EMS' period,[5] when the fixed (but adjustable) exchange rate mechanism (hereafter: ERM) had tight (± 2.25 per cent) upper and lower bands.[6] In the aftermath of the structural change consisting of capital markets' complete liberalization, the British pound and the Italian lira were kicked out of the EMS. The 'soft EMS', laid out with the passage to ± 15 per cent ERM bilateral bands in 1993, appeared inadequate to rigidly restrain national monetary policies and sustain the credibility of a fixed exchange rate regime. Hence, the second phase coincides with the 'Maastricht' period, when the four criteria[7] endorsed by the Maastricht Treaty in 1991 represented the enforcement mechanism, the compliance to which would have warranted the admission to the monetary union. The third phase is the 'EMU' period, the present full-fledged monetary union.

The European governments that progressively got involved in the monetary integration process failed to adequately foresee the complex trade-offs brought about by this valuable programme. It is still widely debated whether tight monetary and fiscal policies should be held responsible for the increase in unemployment suffered by many Peripheral countries and for two decades of high real interest rates yielding poor growth rates and the accumulation of public debt. On the positive side, the macroeconomic performance after a shock certainly improved, as the loss of autonomy suffered by the monetary and fiscal authorities reinforced market adjustment. On the negative side, the macroeconomic governance of the integration process failed to cope with the consequent soaring macroeconomic volatility. In particular, the European governments failed to agree on a coordinated solution of the spillovers across the EMS economies, to which the Peripheral countries were remarkably exposed. It was hardly admitted that the goal of fostering nominal convergence by enforcing restrictive macroeconomic policies, through monetary and fiscal authorities 'tying their hands', was bound to rule out much of the stabilization capacity of macroeconomic policies (Farina and Tamborini, 2004).

Therefore, the first question is whether the monetary integration process, by fostering the demise of competitive devaluations, succeeded in strengthening the competitiveness of the European economies.

By pegging their monetary policies to the deutschmark (DM), the Bundesbank being the best performer for low inflation, the EMS countries switched from the *beggar-thy-neighbour* policy of competitive devaluations to limited realignments within the fixed bilateral parities. Yet, the huge increase in unemployment rates, brought about by restrictive monetary and fiscal policies, progressively weakened the credibility of the commitment of the *n-1* central banks to effectively curb inflation. Just at the outset of capital movements' liberalization, financial operators had many opportunities to put under pressure the national central banks and exploited them by gaining speculative arbitrage profits across the EMS currencies, finally provoking the 1992–3 collapse of the 'hard' EMS. Establishing the ECB solved the 'common pool' problem (each EMS central banks' governor could be tempted to engineer a competitive devaluation by provoking a 'surprise inflation').

Figure 3.1 presents the evolutionary path followed by the REER measured by unit labour costs (hereafter: ULC) of the European economies in the three periods. Provided that perfect price flexibility applies, nominal variations are expected to directly shape real exchange rate variations. A theoretical prediction is that an exchange rate regime switch emphasizes the role of imperfect markets. With the passage to a fixed exchange rates regime, under nominal rigidities the adjustment in relative prices after a shock is prevented, and a sharp drop in the REER volatility ensues (Monacelli, 2005). During the two decades when the EMS functioned as the engine for nominal convergence, nominal rigidities have been extremely important in decoupling the real from the nominal exchange rates after a shock.

The empirical evidence in Figure 3.1 confirms the prediction that under flexible exchange rates the REER volatility is higher than in a fixed exchange rates regime. Along with the evolution towards more stable bilateral parities (no realignments took place during the 'hard' EMS period (1987–92), nor in the 1993–9 period of wide bilateral bands), in all countries the REER volatility declines as shocks are no longer offset

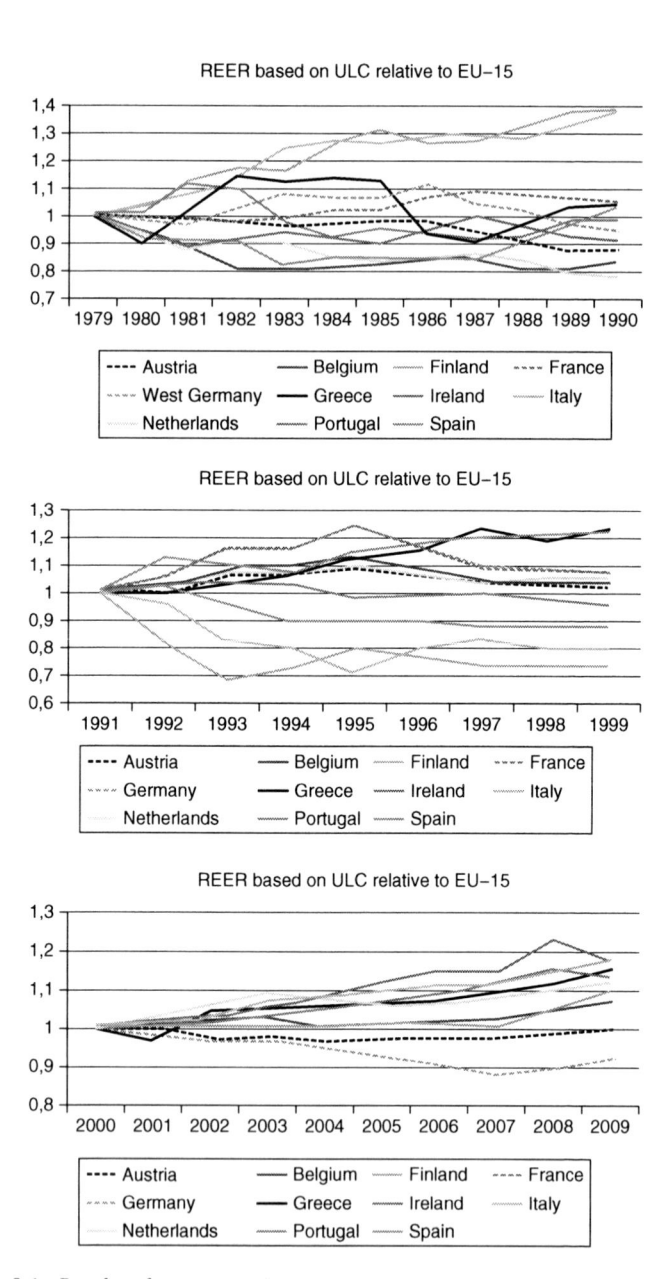

Figure 3.1 Results of regression 1
Source: Own calculations on Ameco dataset.

by nominal exchange rate adjustment. As mentioned above, however, a divide has opened among the ULCs of the EMU economies. We first investigate to what extent the single market and macroeconomic policies accompanying monetary integration favoured a more competitive environment. The aim is to achieve a deeper understanding of the evolution of real divergence across the European economies resulting in the present widening pattern:

Regression 1: $\Delta \log REER_t = \alpha_t + \beta_1 \Delta \log REER_{t-1} + \beta_2 outputgap_{t-1} + u_t$

Table 3.1 displays the results of a regression where changes in the REER (based on ULCs relative to the European average) is a function of both changes in the lagged REER measuring the inertia in the market adjustment, and the lagged output gap measured as the deviation of actual from potential output (computed by the Commission services).[8]

The positive sign of the output gap coefficient means that the reduction in ULC secures some relief in competitiveness after a negative shock. The reaction of REER to output gap absorbs around one third of a shock. However, the closer the period to the inception of the monetary union, the more the coefficient expressing inertia (the lagged relative REER) shrinks, indicating that market adjustment via diminishing wages and prices becomes more sluggish and, by consequence, divergences among national inflation rates and distances from potential output become more persistent. This is expected, given that in approaching the monetary union the fading support provided by nominal exchange rate realignments was transferring the whole weight of market adjustment on the ULC.

The question can be posed about whether on the road to the single currency the industrial systems were forced to moderate their price setting, independently from the relief in the trade balance obtained by means of nominal devaluations. To investigate to what extent the moderate recovery of competitiveness after a shock was driven by price adjustments,[9] regression 2 insulates changes in the price levels within the European economies. The price reaction to the output gap, measured independently from the export and imports elasticities, allows verification as to what extent the integration process strengthened the market adjustment, depending on the wage and productivity dynamics, the recourse by firms to Calvo pricing, and the pattern of the transmission of wage increases from the manufacturing to the service sectors (i.e., the Balassa–Samuelson effect):

Table 3.1 Results of regression 1

	1979/2009	1979/90	1979/99	1991/9	1991/2009	2000/9
Δ log REER$_{t-1}$	0.21449	0.22502	0.21633	0.19116	0.19334	0.13495
t	(4.3822)***	(2.9751)***	(3.6300)***	(1.9111)*	(2.8963)***	(1.4443)
output gap$_{t-1}$	0.31846	0.27141	0.31587	0.39111	0.36286	0.30298
t	(-4.7441)***	(2.3548)***	(3.5030)***	(2.6042)***	(4.4434)***	(4.6457)***
R^2	0.1319	0.1120	0.1237	0.1419	0.1549	0.1836
nobs	341	132	231	99	209	110

Note: Significance levels: *** significant at 1 per cent; ** significant at 5 per cent; * significant at 10 per cent.

Table 3.2 Results of regression 2

t	1979/2009	1979/90	1979/99	1991/9	1991/2009	2000/9
Δ log P$_{t-1}$	0.65547	0.73492	0.70749	0.58714	0.49346	-0.07931
t	(16.5009)***	(15.5036)***	(19.3070)***	(9.47927)***	(6.9128)***	(-0.4325)
output gap$_{t-1}$	0.25005	0.23797	0.22059	0.19092	0.22444	0.35223
t	(5.8192)***	(3.9902)***	(5.0556)***	(3.0421)***	(3.7792)***	(3.4642)***
Δ log NEER$_{t-1}$	-0.21632	-0.19770	-0.17838	-0.10209	–	–
t	(-6.3291)***	(-4.7218)***	(-5.7039)***	(-2.1232)***		
R^2	0.6290	0.8058	0.7574	0.6811	0.2523	0.1013
nobs	341	132	231	99	209	110

Note: Significance levels: *** significant at 1 per cent; ** significant at 5 per cent; * significant at 10 per cent.

Regression 2:
$$\Delta \log P_t = \alpha_t + \beta_1 \Delta \log P_{t-1} + \beta_2 outputgap_{t-1} + \beta_3 \Delta \log NEER_{t-1} + u_t$$

The regression results show that the price reaction to an output gap diminishes from the 'hard EMS' period to the 'Maastricht' period. The coefficients reduce up to 1999, revealing that the contribution of price flexibility to competitiveness has been much lower than that stemming from nominal devaluations. The values of these coefficients, as well as those of regression 1, show a declining capacity of market adjustment to absorb output gaps. In particular, the higher coefficients in the 2000/9 column cannot be taken as a proof of an increased price reaction to output gaps after the structural change of monetary union. Just as in regression 1, in the last period statistical significance fades out.

The expectation that the single market and the single currency, by favouring a reduction in nominal rigidities, would have strengthened the market reaction to negative shocks is not verified. The absence of a substantial improvement in price flexibility asks for further investigation.

It is well known that economic and monetary integration reshaped not only the corporate governance of industrial and banking firms, through mergers and acquisitions, but also the market structure.[10] On the one hand, the increase in intra-EMU trade (more than half of EMU members' foreign trade) was favoured in the largest economies by the diffusion of monopolistic competition markets (many durable consumption goods appear among both imports and exports in the largest EMU economies). More similar intersectoral matrices of domestic output are likely to reduce the frequency of asymmetric shocks hitting specific countries. On the other hand, the removal of barriers to trade, by enabling the small European economies to specialize in productions attuned to their comparative advantages, may have spurred the search for specialization, thus increasing the probability of asymmetric shocks.[11] However, empirical evidence shows that the formation of a Europe-wide business cycle is still to come, as the synchronization across EMU economies' business cycles has come about only in terms of a drastic reduction of co-movements with the world cycle (European Commission, 2010).

This lack of business cycle synchronization helps interpret the failure of both regression 1 and 2 in detecting substantial competitiveness recovery and price flexibility after a shock during the EMU period. As documented by Figure 3.2, in the first ten years of monetary union a gap widened between Core countries, with labour productivity dynamics faster than wage dynamics, and Peripheral countries, exhibiting

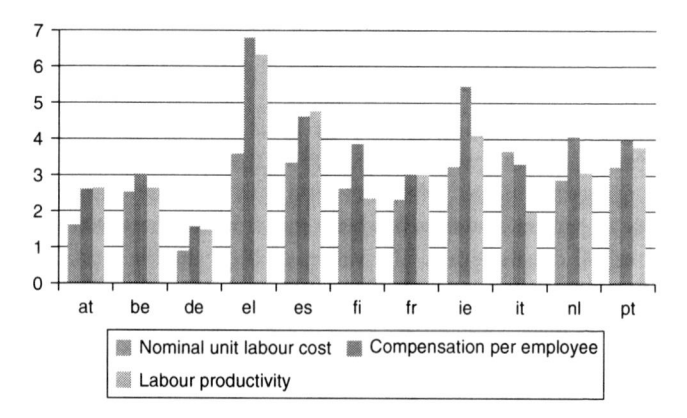

Figure 3.2 Growth rates of ULC in the EMU economies (1999–2009)
Source: Own calculations on Ameco dataset.

the opposite trend. Some Core economies, particularly Germany, have augmented their total factor productivity (hereafter: TFP), while in Peripheral economies different degrees of regulation in goods and labour markets have propagated symmetric shocks at different speeds.

Within-EMU macroeconomic imbalances: an econometric assessment

The econometric estimates conducted so far suggest that economic and monetary integration did not secure the strengthening of a common pattern of market adjustment, which has remained heterogeneous across the EMU economies. To investigate the evolution of real divergence across Europe in more depth, we estimate a regression model meant to explore the causality chain linking the two lagged independent variables of regression 1 (the REER and the output gap), together with the primary balance, to the evolution of the current account:

Regression 3:
$$currentaccount_t = \alpha_t + \beta_1 \log REER_{t-1} + \beta_2 outputgap_{t-1} + \beta_3 primarybalance_{t-1} + u_t$$

The main results of regression 3 are:

1. A robust negative relationship between the current account and both lagged dependent variables of regression 1 (output gap and REER) during both the EMS (1979/90) and the Maastricht (1991/9) period.

Table 3.3 Results of regression 3

	1979/2009	1979/90	1979/90	1979/99	1991/9	1991/2009	2000/9
constant	0.76396	0.34260	0.38401	0.61926	0.82150	0.83929	0.54993
t	(8.072)***	(2.828)***	(3.005)***	(5.996)***	(3.623)***	(4.352)***	(1.058)
log REER$_{t-1}$	−0.37596	−0.17062	−0.19136	−0.30596	−0.40526	−0.41332	−0.26594
t	(−8.028)***	(−2.863)***	(−3.043)***	(−6.019)***	(−3.613)***	(−4.307)***	(−1.020)
outgap$_{t-1}$	−0.56273	−0.47739	−0.51930	−0.48915	−0.73119	−0.69890	−0.08709
t	(−3.542)***	(−2.789)***	(−2.874)***	(−3.917)***	(−4.716)***	(−3.453)***	(−0.252)
primary balance $_{t-1}$	0.54487	0.09739	0.18941	0.41145	0.73472	0.78602	0.61440
t	(7.527)***	(1.166)	(1.737)*	(6.312)***	(7.291)***	(9.182)***	(4.916)***
dummy periphery	−0.95716	−0.66442	−0.67207	−0.98402	−1.0775	−0.78414	−0.80361
t	(−7.635)***	(−4.698)***	(−4.837)***	(−7.869)***	(−4.265)***	(−3.057)***	(−1.031)
drift REER	0.45382	0.32282	0.32532	0.48151	0.52210	0.36294	0.36030
t	(7.277)***	(4.617)***	(4.752)***	(7.797)***	(4.164)***	(2.842)***	(0.929)
drift prim.balance	–	–	−0.00332	–	–	–	–
t	–	–	(−2.540)**	–	–	–	–
R^2	0.4190	0.2221	0.2368	0.3260	0.4698	0.5374	0.6511
nobs	341	132	132	231	99	209	110

Note: Significance levels: *** significant at 1 per cent; ** significant at 5 per cent; * significant at 10 per cent.

The rationale is that, when investment lags behind savings, declining economic activity contributes to improving the trade balance. Yet, it remains to be explained why during the EMU period (2000/9) the coefficient significance is lost just as in the two previous regressions.

2. A positive relationship between the dependent variable (current account) and the public primary balance becomes significant, as time goes by. As shown in Table 3.3, for the first period its significance is obtained by adding a primary balance drift that allows slightly different coefficients for Core and Periphery countries. The strengthening of the link between the primary balance and the current account since 1990 is coherent with the Maastricht Treaty implementation in 1992. In fact, the fiscal retrenchment imposed by the Maastricht criteria for fiscal policy could have determined an improvement in the current account. Though, despite primary balance being significant, the econometric relationship fails to be significant in the last period.

3. The heterogeneity between Core and Periphery countries, which comes to light by including in all regressions a dummy (identifying Peripheral countries with regression 1) as well as a drift on lagged REER. With the exception of the EMU period, both coefficients are always statistically significant and their values almost always result in a sign changed. This is especially telling for the REER drift, pointing at a positive association between the REER and the current account for the Periphery countries.

In our regression model the two lagged variables cease to determine the trade balance in the EMU period. Thus, the positive and significant correlation between the coefficient linking the current account to the public deficit might indicate a role for the primary balance in explaining the current account, according to the 'twin deficit' hypothesis stemming from the Mundell–Fleming model (Mundell, 1960).[12] The 'twin deficit' has manifested in the United States in the second half of the 2000s, when the creation of a public deficit following the 9/11 demand shock causally determined the opening of a current account deficit. Instead, the 'twin deficit' hypothesis does not seem to apply to the EMU, where the reaction to the shock was characterized by a lack of 'fiscal activism', so that the negative output gap ended up in the worsening in the EMU countries' public deficit over GDP. Overall in the EMU period, the impact of the SGP limits on the public deficit has rendered fiscal policies of stabilization pro-cyclical especially in those Peripheral countries burdened by high public debt (Farina and Ricciuti, 2006). Since in the EMU period the compliance with the SGP constraints curbed automatic stabilizers and made discretionary fiscal policy of stabilization not viable, the significant positive correlation with the current account might then signal a downward variation of the primary balance triggering a downward variation of the trade balance in the same year.

We are still short of an explanation for the loss of significance for the coefficient linking the current account and both lagged dependent variables of regression 1 (output gap and REER) during the EMU period (2000/9). Figure 3.3 shows the evolution of overall macroeconomic equilibrium through the paths of the private, public and foreign sectors for 11 EMU economies during the 30 years from 1979 to 2009. During the pre-EMU period, in many EMS economies wage dynamics have been overtaking labour productivity dynamics in the short run, so that a real appreciation (i.e., increasing ULC), and the consequent negative output gap, induced a trade deficit. As indicated by regression 3, up to the inception of the monetary union the path of the saving–investment balance in many European economies seems to be correlated to the path of the net exports more than to the public primary balance.

The evaluation of the EMU period is more difficult. We exploit the hint of an heterogeneity between Core and Periphery countries suggested by the dummy and the drift on lagged REER (see point 3 above). The hypothesis is that a different determination of the overall macroeconomic equilibrium may pertain to Core and Peripheral countries, depending on the REER or the output gap being decisive in the evolution of the current account. Let us then evaluate this rationale.

During the world demand expansion (2004–7), the enlargement of current account surpluses enjoyed by Germany was due to both wage moderation and a constant productivity growth fostering real depreciation.[13] Thus, in this large export-led economy a depreciating REER facilitated the transfer of excess savings into the financing of the exports boom of 2004–7, with the overall macroeconomic equilibrium resulting from a substantial fiscal consolidation. In the other very open small Core economies, large trade deficits have added up to excess savings, due to the REER following a continuously rising path after monetary unification.[14] An excess demand has given rise to a huge current account deficit in two Peripheral countries: in Ireland, where the long period of high growth rates had provoked rising imports, and in Spain, where the output boom in 2004–7 boosted imports. Finally, a falling output, coupled with a soaring REER, has resulted in massive deterioration in both public finances and the trade balance in Greece.[15]

This mixed evidence invites the question whether the output gap or competitiveness (the proxy of which being the REER) is the major determinant of the current account. The European Commission's answer

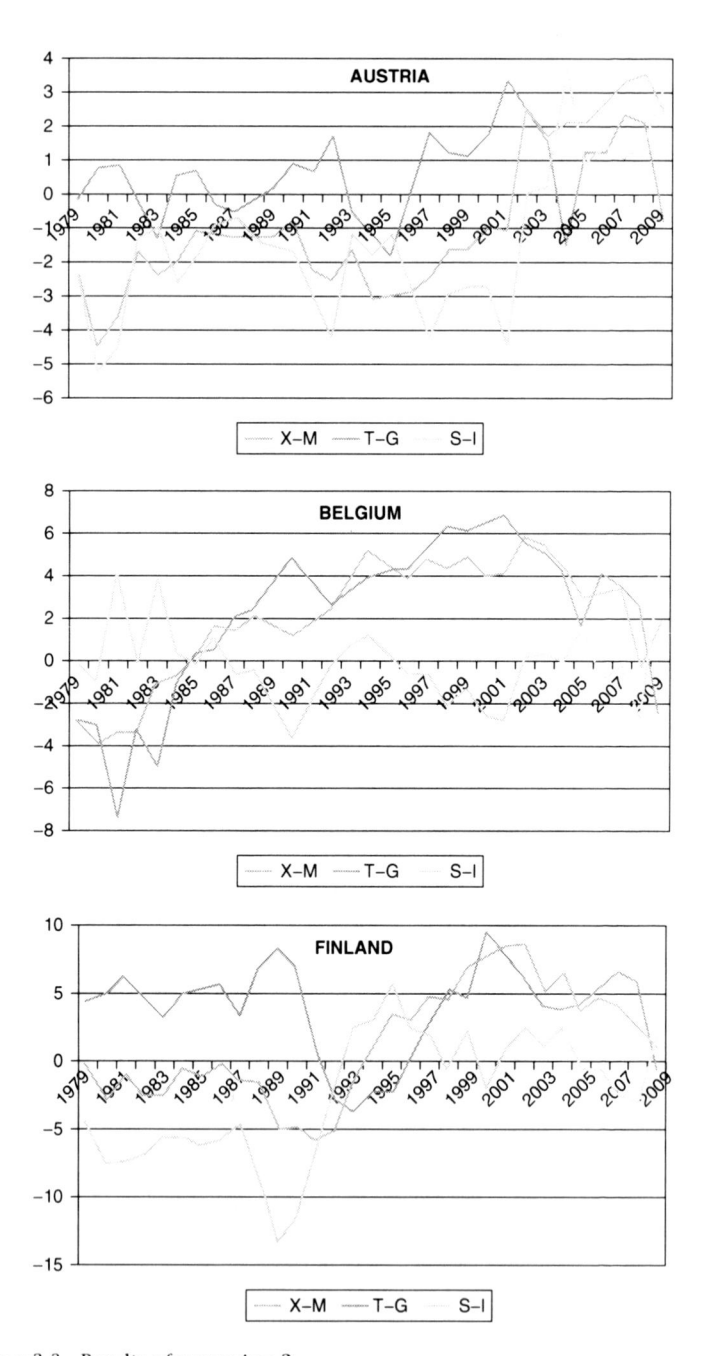

Figure 3.3 Results of regression 3
Note: Own calculations on Ameco dataset.

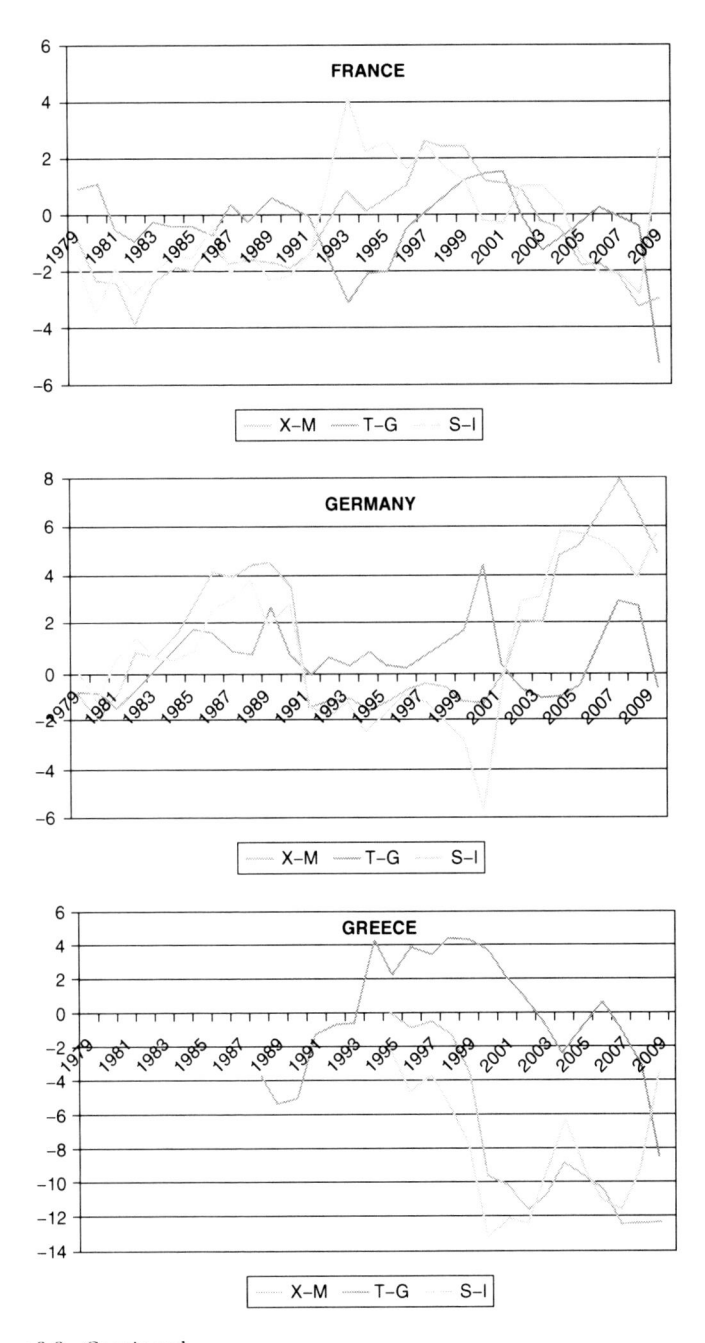

Figure 3.3 Continued

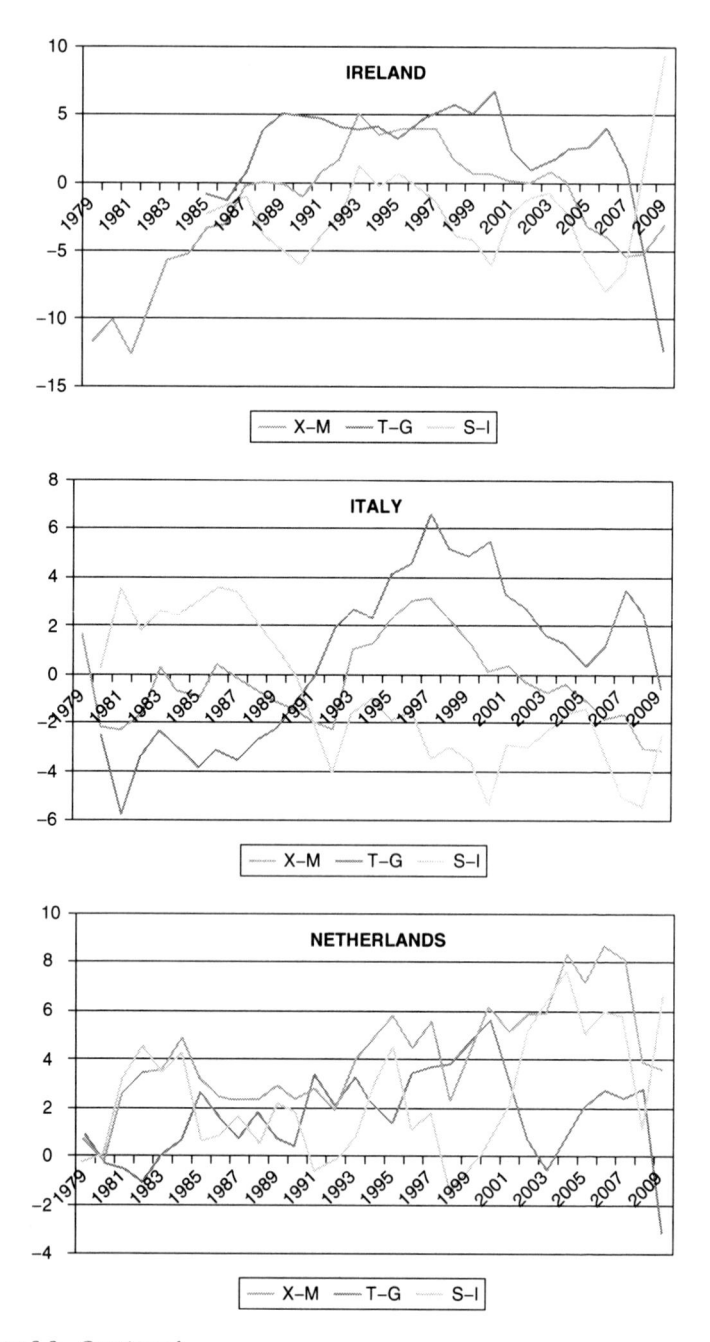

Figure 3.3 Continued

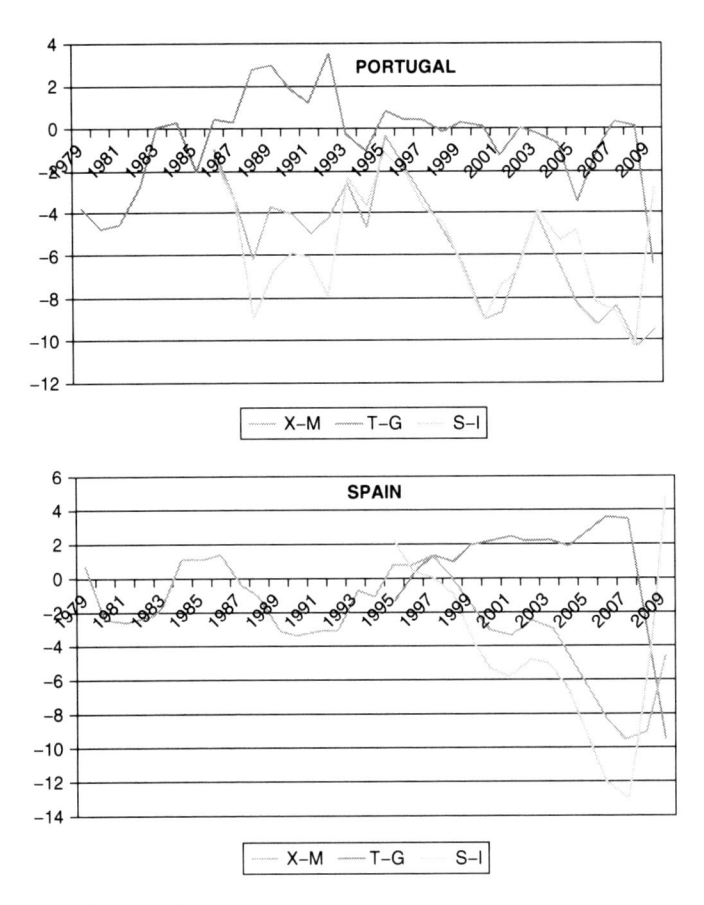

Figure 3.3 Continued

is that the domestic demand impulse prevails.[16] We propose a more nuanced evaluation. In fact, Regression 3 introduces a drift separating the Core from the Periphery. The results are significant, but are in the last period. The introduction of the REER drift reveals a different pattern of economic performance for Core and Peripheral countries up to the inception of the monetary union. Since, in the last decade, which precisely corresponds to the end of nominal exchange rate adjustment, the econometric model is no longer significant, we conclude that a structural break has occurred. Therefore, it would not be insightful to assess dominance either of the output gap or of the ULC in the current account evolution. This evaluation can be complemented by descriptive evidence.

In 1999–2003, Peripheral countries experienced a depressed domestic demand, which brought about a positive correlation between the REER (appreciating, due to the downward wage rigidity) and the current account (improving, due to imports falling faster than exports). On the contrary, during the world demand boom of 2004–7, the common monetary policy led to very low real interest rates in high-inflation countries (e.g., Spain), so that a rapid domestic demand expansion, also fuelled by financial and housing bubbles, pushed up wages and prices and thus the REER, but as soaring imports were overtaken by gains in market shares, the current account improved.

Our investigation has stressed the central role played by the REER and the output gaps respectively in widening macroeconomic imbalances within the Eurozone during the ten years after monetary union. Given that the weight of aggregate demand is greater than the REER in determining current account balance, the Peripheral countries' macroeconomic equilibrium heavily relies on the level of economic activity. Yet, the slow growth rate of the European economies since the 1990s has rendered aggregate demand structurally weak, with a dangerous decline in potential output. This is a clue that full employment does not depend only on ULC but also on the appropriate balance between domestic and foreign demand across the EMU economies. The next section highlights that the refusal of the leader country to take responsibility for the EMU growth performance causes the Peripheral countries to be short of policy instruments to cope with their macroeconomic imbalances.

Macroeconomic imbalances within and between currency areas

During the recession following the 9/11 worldwide shock, Germany – seeking to comply with the 3 per cent SGP limit for the public deficit/GDP ratio – refrained from opening a deficit in the primary balance. The excess formation of savings mainly reached foreign operators and Germany enjoyed a surplus in the trade balance.

Since more than half of the trade of Germany occurs within the EMU, a German economic policy traditionally oriented to take control of domestic demand amounts to a '*beggar-thy-neighbour*' strategy inflicted by the dominant country on the other countries of the Eurozone, which will unavoidably suffer from a deficit in their trade balance. A similar trade-off takes place between the US and China, whereby the ruling global power brings about too high a domestic demand while the main emerging economy struggles to boost its exports to the US by manoeuvring an undervalued exchange rate, and devotes the international reserves stemming from trade surpluses to absorb the US public debt (two-thirds of which is owned by China and Japan). The renmimbi and the yen do not directly suffer if the fiscal sustainability of the US worsens.[17] On the contrary, the euro volatility in financial markets is not simply the result of financial markets negative expectations about the 'deviating' countries current account and fiscal sustainability, but also stems from increasing integration across European financial markets. The mergers and acquisitions accompanying monetary unification have magnified the interconnectedness across the EMU banks, so that the overall EMU banking sector today holds liabilities many times larger than the overall EMU countries' public debt. Since commercial and investment banks in Germany and in France have accumulated large amounts of high-risk financial assets issued by Peripheral EMU governments with shaky public finances (e.g., Greece), the trade imbalances between the surplus and the deficit of these countries belonging to the same currency area do not cancel out but sum up.

The trade imbalances between Germany and the remaining EMU economies differ with respect to the China–United States connection also from the real economy vantage point. In both situations, the first country refuses to correct macroeconomic imbalances by letting its counterpart increase exports. The US economy keeps enjoying an excess investment over its savings, due the worldwide excess demand of $US- denominated financial assets induced by the 'search for quality' in portfolio investments. Moreover, the United States can hope to promote more exports towards China after the Chinese government promises to revalue the renmimbi *vis-à-vis* the $US. On the contrary, the German government abstains from an expansionary fiscal stance aimed at rising domestic demand, which leaves the Peripheral EMU countries with no economic policy alternative to a deep deflation to re-equilibrate their relative current accounts. This is the clue bringing to light that the Core–Periphery real divergence is rooted in the mismatch between the economic boundaries connecting the Eurozone and the political boundaries separating the EMU Member States.

The German government explains its reluctance to foster a higher domestic demand to substitute for excess exports with the diverging efficiency of the Core and the Periphery productive systems. The strength of German exports is ascribed to the domestic ULC decreasing trend determined by wage moderation and productivity growth. Yet, interconnectedness matters not only for public debt flows within European financial markets, but also from the point of view of trade surpluses and deficits. Germany has benefited from real depreciation *vis-à-vis* the other European economies suffering a real appreciation. During the two decades of the 'hard EMS' and 'Maastricht' periods, German exports were boosted by the real depreciation warranted by the diminishing compensation of inflation differentials through the Peripheral countries' periodic nominal devaluations. Besides, German firms were the main beneficiaries of the positive externality resulting from a lowering exchange rate uncertainty on EMS bilateral parities, due to DM pegging by the *n-1* central banks. Germany's real depreciation has continued during the Maastricht period and, to a larger extent, also after monetary unification, when the expansion of German exports to EMU markets reached its peak. Hence, the leading European country could be held responsible for having conceived the monetary integration process not as a cooperative effort for the 'common good' of improving the macroeconomic performance of the European economy as a whole, but for securing the macroeconomic stability needed to pursue a 'beggar-thy-neighbour' strategy in Europe.

Are German authorities right? The rationale underpinning the German economic policy needs be evaluated by a theoretical assessment of the manipulation of the macroeconomic equilibrium by monetary and fiscal authorities.

Alternative views on EMU macroeconomic governance

In the theoretical literature, it is highly debated whether macroeconomic instability stems from market distortion and public finances mismanagement in single countries, or from inadequate EMU macroeconomic governance.

The view of the European Commission is inspired by the New Classical Economics, which considers European integration as limited to a market liberalization process. A diminishing competitiveness or a soaring public deficit has to be counteracted by Peripheral countries through their independent implementation of reforms, so to avoid undermining monetary stability and fiscal sustainability, respectively secured by the ECB and the SGP. The argument against policy coordination within EMU is that possible mismatches between national macroeconomic performances and the common institutional framework by no means are to be ascribed to the latter. Since macroeconomic imbalances are rooted in *country-specific* structural deficiencies, no further centralization of powers should be devised (Tabellini and Wyplosz, 2006). To shrink their real divergence *vis-à-vis* the EMU average, Peripheral economies should engage in the strengthening of market adjustment through a 'complementary' strategy, that is the combination of wage and fiscal retrenchment aimed at prompting the needed real depreciation.

This rationale is questionable. The tenet that economic and monetary integration process had to do with the worsening of *country-specific* inefficiencies, and each country's independent capacity to re-equilibrate macroeconomic imbalances, is challenged by widespread spillovers across Europe. The path to the establishment of a supranational monetary policy like the ECB, and the adoption of the SGP supranational fiscal constraints, are doomed to magnify spillovers by impinging differently on the different economies.

As for monetary policy, the 'one size fits all' ECB's monetary stance faces different national output-inflation *trade-offs*. A downward variation of the interest rate, the only ECB policy instrument, affects EMU countries to a different extent, depending on how much the real interest rate is affected by the domestic inflation rate. Given the limited room for nominal interest rates cuts under the low ECB inflation target, after a shock with different propagation effects across the EMU (e.g., the 9/11 shock or the recent financial crisis) the economies exhibiting a higher-than-EMU-average output loss suffer from a monetary policy under-stabilization bias (Farina and Tamborini, 2004). By the same token, in economies exhibiting a higher-than-EMU-average inflation rate following an expansionary business cycle (e.g., the 2004–7 world demand boom), a lowering trend of nominal interest rate renders the real interest rate almost nil or even negative.

Our econometric estimates show a positive correlation between a higher REER (as an effect of labour productivity dynamics falling behind wage dynamics) and an improving current account (due to sustained exports led by the world demand boom despite rising wages and prices). This result suggests that a widening real divergence across Europe was also due to the inflationary domestic demand expansion triggered by negative real interest rates in some Peripheral countries, such as Ireland and Spain. The common monetary policy has prompted the easy financing of speculative financial positions and/or investment projects in low-productivity sectors, and these allocative distortions ended up in financial or housing bubbles.

As for fiscal policy, the evergreen debate on the size of the fiscal multiplier has not yet come to a clear assessment of the question (Perotti, 2005). Therefore, the evaluation of national fiscal stances is still strongly influenced by the theoretical pre-analytical assumptions.

The New Keynesian Economics maintains that the positive impact of a fiscal impulse through the domestic channel (the fiscal multiplier) is larger than the negative impact through the financial channel (that is, how the public budget, the EMU interest rate, and the euro exchange rate feeds back on each country's aggregate demand). In addition, the positive effect through the trade channel (the relationship between domestic economic activity and intra-EMU trade) prevails over the negative effect due to the financial channel (that is, a fiscal impulse in one country increases aggregate demand abroad). Hence, a Keynesian expansionary effect ensues both domestically and in the other EMU countries.

The New Classical Economics, instead, anticipates a negative impact of the fiscal impulse on aggregate demand (due to the so-called non-Keynesian effects based on the Ricardian equivalence). Moreover, the financial channel is stronger than the trade channel, thus preventing a fiscal expansion in one country from raising the output level in the other countries.

The European Commission stays in between these two views. According to the theoretical underpinnings of the SGP, the overall effect of a fiscal impulse in one country of the Eurozone is mixed, as the Keynesian expansionary effect applies domestically, while abroad the negative impact of the financial channel overwhelms the positive impact of the trade channel, mainly because a rising interest rate negatively impacts on aggregate demand (Tamborini, 2004). Hence, the European Commission dictates to national fiscal authorities to keep the public budget balanced in the medium run, and let the automatic stabilizers work during downswings, thus taking advantage of the positive fiscal multiplier. The problem of the financial channel being stronger than the trade channel will be dealt with by the SGP rules. By abstaining from discretionary fiscal policies EMU governments avoid disturbing the ECB's control over the interest rate, as the EMU financial markets will be relieved from excess public bonds issuing. Once this sole possible source of spillovers across Member States was stopped, there would be no fear of a deflationary spiral spreading over the Eurozone after simultaneous restrictive fiscal policies, and so no need for intergovernmental coordination.

It is very difficult to assess how heterogeneity in market adjustment across EMU countries affects this theoretical reasoning. It has been argued that the stabilization efficacy of fiscal policy has improved passing from the Maastricht Treaty to the EMU period, as the decreased elasticity of fiscal impulses to output gap demonstrates that under the SGP rules the pro-cyclicity of fiscal stances was converted into 'neutrality' (Galì and Perotti, 2003. Yet, by computing discretionary fiscal policy as a deviation from the fiscal impulses required by the SGP, the lower coefficient linking the cyclically adjusted public balance to the output gap seems to be the outcome of a larger amount of fiscal revenues devoted to debt decumulation. During downswings, the fiscal impulses have been waived, and in some high-debt countries the compliance with the 3 per cent deficit/ GDP limit even requires the 'sterilization' of automatic stabilizers (Farina and Ricciuti, 2006). This judgement of a 'deflationary bias' embedded in the SGP is confirmed by a simulation demonstrating that in a monetary union nominal rigidities magnify the countercyclical efficacy of fiscal impulses.[18] Moreover, empirical work has been conducted, showing that the size of automatic stabilizers, which already amounted to no more than a quarter of the original shock till the 1990s (Fatas and Mihov, 2001), further shrank after a variety of fiscal reforms in Europe aimed at reducing the generosity of social expenditures (Creel and Saraceno, 2008). It is apparent that the more competitive market environment promoted by economic and monetary integration encourages workers and firms to take more risks. Yet, coping with increased uncertainty requires the strengthening, not the rolling-back, of social protection. Less regulated labour markets will hardly be socially consented under a macroeconomic governance unable to preserve the efficacy of the social protection system to counteract an increasing macroeconomic volatility (Fitoussi and Le Cacheux, 2009).

Overall, it is apparent that spillovers across the EMU countries – possibly resulting in macroeconomic imbalances – are also stimulated by the heterogeneous impact of the common monetary policy on the various EMU economies and by the common SGP rules constraining national fiscal policies. Hence, the German reluctance to take responsibility for the EMU growth performance is not fully justified. Within a monetary union, the macroeconomic imbalances of a single country cannot be overcome exclusively by the implementation of its own macroeconomic governance.

The divide, shown by our econometric estimates for the EMU decade, between Core and Peripheral countries for REER and current account is a clear signal that the present design of macroeconomic governance is inadequate. On the one hand, the 'one size fits all' ECB monetary policy cannot cope with spillovers put in motion by financial integration, heterogeneous labour market institutions (employment protection legislation, minimum wage, temporary or long-term wage contracts, degree of centralization of labour negotiations, etc.) and systems of social expenditures differently impinging on fiscal stances in different EMU countries. In the EMU *second best* world of markets with nominal rigidities, monetary authorities should refrain from pursuing the inflation-targeting strategy advocated by New Classical Economics, and put into practice a tighter coordination with national wage contracts and fiscal stances.[19] On the other hand, disentangling the impact of the fiscal policy of stabilization from the transmission of the shock, as well as the other countries' fiscal impulses of different size, is a difficult matter. Under a monetary union, the propagation of a symmetric (or asymmetric) shock greatly differentiates within each economy, depending on its own specific degree of sectoral specialization and on the varying characteristics of markets and institutions. Granted that in a monetary union with nominal rigidities the countercyclical efficacy of fiscal impulses is magnified (Galì and Monacelli, 2008), the stringency of the SGP rules is unsound. Hence, the complementarity between enhanced labour market flexibility and fiscal consolidation – the cuts in wages and in public expenditures invoked by the European Commission (Buti *et al.*, 2009) – could provoke a huge fall in output ending in a long-lasting deflation. Instead, the substitutability between the labour market and the public deficit adjustment should be preferred, as the peril of a depressed aggregate demand after spillovers fuelled by the complementarity strategy would be avoided.

To counteract asymmetric shocks or the asymmetric propagation of symmetric shocks, the appropriate policy mix between the market adjustment and the fiscal stance has to be chosen. Under low inflation, the best mix is a fiscal contraction with nominal wage increases, while under low real interest rates a fiscal expansion with wage moderation has to be preferred.[20]

For this strategy to be welfare enhancing for the whole Eurozone, negative spillovers across countries are to be minimized. The policy mix has to be implemented through an intergovernmental coordination, rather than through the independent re-equilibrating strategy by each EMU country tackling its own macroeconomic imbalances. Were all countries implementing a contraction in aggregate demand independently, without internalizing negative output spillovers abroad, 'beggar-thy-neighbour' strategies could further spread negative spillovers across the monetary union (De Grauwe, 2009b).

This approach to the EMU macroeconomic governance, as an alternative to the European Commission one, ascribes macroeconomic imbalances to the growing interconnectedness across globalized financial markets. The central role played by interconnectedness in the current crisis[21] recollects the interpretation of self-accelerating recessions proposed by Fisher, Keynes and Minsky, in terms of debt deflation, the savings paradox and financial fragility, respectively, and suggests the appropriateness of a cooperative management of macroeconomic instability (De Grauwe, 2009b). The chaotic management of the recent crisis developed within the Eurozone is a case in point. Regulatory interventions aimed at curbing the 'moral hazard' exhibited by deviating governments are obviously needed, but the *no-bailout* clause is flawed. This ban on mutual insurance ignores the existence of spillovers across Member States, and puts the euro in danger by bringing to light that the main weakness of the EMU construction is the absence of a political union. The recent ECB interventions in the secondary public bonds market have benefited both EMU government affected by fiscal sustainability problems (e.g., Greece) and the owners of its public debt, who are spread within the monetary union. The 'last resort' provision of funds internalizing a deficit of a Member State substitutes for the missing mutual risk insurance across EMU economies.

Conclusions

Since the inception of the Eurozone, it was clear that the monetary union was not going to render European macroeconomic governance more cooperative in favouring real convergence after having accomplished nominal convergence.[22] In the pre-EMU years, the institutional weakness of the economic integration consisted of the absence of a common central bank conducting an anti-inflationary monetary policy. In the EMU years, the institutional weakness of the economic integration consists of the absence of institutions devoted to cope with the problem of domestic failures transformed in systemic risks due to the complex spillovers developing across EMU economies. The shortcomings embedded in the macroeconomic governance at the time of writing are not addressed because these interdependences are not recognized. Under this macroeconomic governance, where the inflation targeting monetary policy and the SGP constraints are not concerned about spillovers within the EMU, the sole remaining instruments for conducting economic policy in Europe consists of supply-side and fiscal reforms to be implemented on an individual basis. The European Commission refrains from promoting policy coordination, following the view that market competition, through the retrenchment of labour market and fiscal interventions, will prompt wage and price flexibility, and deliver much faster shock adjustments (Issing, 2008).

Yet, it is unclear how the real divergence of Peripheral economies *vis-à-vis* the EMU average can be confronted while ignoring that macroeconomic imbalances are self-aggravating without a coordinated intergovernmental intervention. In a monetary union with complex interconnections and spillovers across markets and governments, the 'complementarity' strategy of wage cuts and fiscal retrenchment conveys the risks of a profound deflation in the Eurozone, as the EMU countries would be pushed to activate simultaneous real depreciations. If all EMU governments were to keep relying on 'beggar-thy-neighbour' policies, and challenge trade shares to other EMU economies in a sort of 'race to the bottom' in real depreciation, there would be no point in continuing the EMU construction.

The macroeconomic governance in the Eurozone would benefit from a mutual risk insurance provided by the pooling of resources in the public budget of a central government, to be redistributed to individuals and/or regions hit by a temporary or a permanent shock (Farina and Tamborini, 2004; De Grauwe, 2009a). A first step in this direction could consist of funding a larger European public budget, to pursue fiscal policy of stabilization by choosing the policy mix optimizing output-inflation trade-off at the Eurozone level, just as the ECB monetary policy is geared on the EMU-average inflation and output gaps. The intergovernmental coordination of a centralized fiscal policy 'activism' with national wage dynamics and fiscal stances could control the tendency towards macroeconomic imbalances and shield macroeconomic stability in the Eurozone as a whole.

Notes

1. During the last three decades, the level of foreign assets in the balance sheets of financial institutions has been multiplied by five relative to world GDP.
2. Greece, Ireland, Italy, Portugal and Spain.
3. Austria, Belgium, Finland, France, Germany and the Netherlands. Obviously, up to 1990 econometric estimates refer to data for West Germany.
4. The total amount of financial assets issued by the EMU governments in 2010 has soared, on average, above 70 per cent of the Eurozone GDP, while the SGP imposes a limit of 60 per cent, which should be observed at each country's level.
5. The European Monetary System (EMS) was launched in 1979 with the explicit objective to establish in Europe the 'public good' of monetary stability.

6. Italy in 1979–89, and the United Kingdom in 1990–2, were allowed much larger (± 6 per cent) bilateral bands.
7. The Maastricht Treaty envisaged three stages towards full monetary integration, linking the participation to the monetary union to the EMS countries' compliance with the almost full convergence to the three best performers for inflation and nominal interest rates, together with the thresholds of 3 per cent for the public deficit/GDP and 60 per cent for the public debt/GDP ratios.
8. The long-term stability shown by the EMU REER *vis-à-vis* the US$ and the yen ensures that the divergent national trends with respect to the average EMU REER are not biased by fluctuations of the overall Eurozone REER.
9. Drawing on Honohan and Lane (2003), the P variable, representing the GDP deflator, is calculated as REER/NEER.
10. An indirect clue of augmented similarities across EMU productive systems is that the percentage of foreign direct investment within the Eurozone soared from a fifth to a third of total GDP.
11. The hypothesis whereby the process of economic integration is bound to accelerate industrial specialization within the European Union is raised by Krugman (1991).
12. In the Mundell–Fleming model a causality nexus goes from the opening of a deficit in the primary balance to the opening of a deficit in the current account. Under flexible exchange rates, a deficit-financed fiscal expansion provokes – through capital inflows determined by a higher interest rate – a real appreciation, so that the decline in net exports eventually leads to a current account deficit. Under fixed exchange rates, a deficit-financed fiscal impulse stimulates the GDP growth, so that the subsequent rise in imports prompts a current account deficit.
13. Besides, the exploitation of economies of scale in large corporations and non-price factors (namely, a raise in the quality of products) also contributed to increase exports.
14. The exception is the Netherlands, where soaring exports counterbalanced the negative impact of the real appreciation on the current account.
15. The huge output slump of 2007–9 has led to the fast reversal of current account surpluses, mainly in Germany, Austria and Finland. Current account deficits shrank in Ireland (where huge wage cuts triggered a large real depreciation) and, to a lesser extent, in Italy and France (European Commission, 2010).
16. 'Stronger relative demand pressures in a given Member State tend to fuel import demand and depress the current account. Differences in export performance – and therefore price competitiveness – have also contributed to the divergence of current accounts but, in most Member States, this has been of secondary importance compared with domestic demand factors' (European Commission, 2010: 8).
17. However, the value of the $US reserves of the Central Bank of China would be eventually affected by a long-term declining trend of the $US.
18. 'Our simulations under the optimal policy mix of a representative economy's response to an idiosyncratic productivity shock show that the strength of the countercyclical fiscal response increases with the importance of nomi-

nal rigidities. Such a finding may call into question the desirability of imposing external constraint on a currency union's members ability to conduct countercyclical fiscal policies, when the latter seek to limit the size of the domestic output gap and inflation differential resulting from idiosyncratic shocks' (Galì and Monacelli, 2008: 117).
19. It has been demonstrated that under nominal rigidities optimal monetary policy can neither be employment-targeted nor inflation-targeted, as social welfare is maximized when monetary creation averts these two extreme regimes (Blanchard and Galì, 2010).
20. 'For a better coordination of wage and fiscal adjustments ... it would have been better for Portugal to combine *fiscal contraction and wage increases* in the 1990s, in exchange for *fiscal expansion and wage decreases* in the 2000s' (Blanchard, 2007: 32; italics in original).
21. The excess savings in emerging countries in search of financial investment have been matched by the issuing of $US-denominated financial assets. This financing of the huge US trade and public deficits, by virtue of the role of international means of payment of the $US, was an incentive for the United States' commercial and investment banks to increase the supply of high-risk financial assets (Caballero *et al.*, 2008).
22. 'Germany's strategy to tie Peripheral Europe to the conservative monetary policy of the Bundesbank through the EMS agreement then was conducive to the creation of a competitive advantage in favour of Core Europe. Under this interpretation, the 'asymmetric' functioning of the EMS ... was not 'neutral' to the trade competition between Germany and Peripheral Europe... If the ECB were urged to follow a tight monetary policy, Peripheral Europe could be exposed to deflationary pressures greater than those that were determined by the asymmetric functioning of the EMS, so as to widen the real divergence between the two areas' (Farina, 2001 (1999): 307-8).

References

Blanchard, O. (2007) 'Current Account Deficits in Rich Countries', MIT, Department of Economics, Working Paper Series, no. 6.

Blanchard, O. and Galì, J. (2010) 'Labor Markets and Monetary Policy: A New-Keynesian Model with Unemployment', *American Economic Journal: Macroeconomics*, no. 2: 1–30.

Buti M., Rüger, W. and Turrini, A. (2009) 'Is Lisbon Far from Maastricht? Trade-offs and Complementarities between Fiscal Discipline and Structural Reforms', *Cesifo Economic Studies*, no. 55: 165–96.

Caballero, R. J., Farhi, E. and Gourinchas, P. O. (2008) 'An Equilibrium Model of "Global Imbalances" and Low Interest Rates', *American Economic Review*, no. 98: 358–93.

Creel, J. and Saraceno, F. (2008) 'Automatic Stabilisation, Discretionary Policy and the Stability Pact', in J. Creel and M. Sawyer (eds), *Current Thinking on Fiscal Policy*, Basingstoke: Palgrave Macmillan.

De Grauwe, P. (2009a) 'The Fragility of the Eurozone's Institutions', *Open Economies Review*, no. 21: 167–74.

De Grauwe, P. (2009b), 'Keynes' Savings Paradox, Fisher's Debt Deflation, and Banking Crisis', mimeo.
European Commission (2010) 'The Impact of the Global Crisis on Competitiveness and Current Account Divergences in the Euro Area', Special Issue. http://www.europe.xorte.com/0,3,The-Impact-of-the-Global-Crisis-on-Competitiveness-and-Current-Account-Divergence-in-the-Euro-Area,11592.html as accessed on 4 January 2011.
Farina, F. (2001) 'Monetary Policy and Competitiveness in the Euro Area', in M. Franzini and F. R. Pizzuti (eds), *Globalization, Institutions and Social Cohesion*, Berlin: Springer-Verlag (Italian edn, *Globalizzazione, istituzioni e coesione sociale*, Rome: Donzelli, 1999).
Farina, F. and Ricciuti, R. (2006) 'L'évaluation des politiques budgétaires en Europe. Règles budgétaires et marges de manouvre', Revue de l'OFCE, 99: 275–301.
Farina, F. and Tamborini, R. (2004) 'Set a Sufficiently Ambitious Budget Target and Let the Automatic Stabilizers Work." Can it Really Work in the European Monetary Union?', *Open Economies Review*, 15: 143–68.
Fatas, A. and Mihov, I. (2001) 'Fiscal Policy and Business Cycles: An Empirical Investigation', *Moneda and Credito*, no. 212: 167–205.
Fitoussi, J. P. and Le Cacheux, J. (eds) (2009) *Report on the State of the European Union, vol. III, Crisis in the EU Economic Governance*, Basingstoke: Palgrave.
Galí, J. and Perotti, R., (2003) *Fiscal Policy and Monetary Integration in Europe CEPR Discussion Papers* 3933, CEPR Discussion Papers.
Galì, J. and Monacelli, T. (2008) 'Optimal Monetary and Fiscal Policy in a Currency Union', *Journal of International Economics*, no. 76: 116–32.
Honohan, P. R. and Lane, P. (2003) 'Divergent Inflation Rates in EMU', IIIS Discussion Paper no.5, July.
Issing, O. (2008) *The Birth of the Euro*, Cambridge: Cambridge University Press.
Krugman, P. (1991) 'Increasing Returns and Economic Geography', *Journal of Political Economy*, no. 99: 483–99.
Monacelli, T. (2005) 'Into the Mussa Puzzle: Monetary Policy Regimes and the Real Exchange Rate in a Small Open Economy', *Journal of International Economics*, no. 62: 191–217.
Mundell, R. (1960) 'The Monetary Dynamics of International Adjustment Under Fixed and Flexible Exchange Rates', *Quarterly Journal of Economics*, no. 74: 227–57.
Perotti, R. (2005) 'Estimating the Effects of Fiscal Policy in OECD Countries', Proceedings, Federal Reserve Bank of San Francisco.
Tabellini, G. and Wyplosz, C. (2006) 'Supply-side Reforms in Europe: Can the Lisbon Strategy be Repaired?', *Swedish Economic Policy Review*, no. 13: 101–56.
Tamborini, R. (2004) 'One "Monetary Giant" with Many "Fiscal Dwarfs": The Efficiency of Macroeconomic Stabilization Policies in the European Monetary Union', in A. V. Deardorff (ed.), *The Past, Present and Future of the European Union*, Palgrave: London.

4
The Euro in the International Monetary System after the Global Financial and Economic Crisis and after the European Public Debt Crisis

Pompeo Della Posta

Introduction

The creation of the euro, more than ten years ago, was accompanied by the expectation that it would play a significant role in the international arena. Some observers even argued that it might have challenged the international role of the $US (hereafter: dollar). Data suggest, however, that while the use of the euro as a reserve currency, as a vehicle currency, or as a unit of account has been higher than that of legacy currencies, it did not really acquire an international rank.

Moreover, while the recent financial and economic crisis might have undermined the international credibility and reputation of the US economy, and as a result of the dollar, paradoxically the negative economic consequences that it has been playing on the euro area and the lack of a satisfactory European political response might have made even more apparent its weaknesses. The yuan renmimbi (hereafter: yuan) is likely to play a growing role in a future, possibly multipolar, world but the Chinese political, financial and economic structure has still to undertake many changes before its currency may acquire an international status.

Reasons for the creation of the euro

The creation of the European Economic and Monetary Union (EMU) and the euro has many different explanations, relating to history, politics and economics.

The most important historical event to mention is the fall of the iron curtain and of communism.[1] In November 1989, the Berlin Wall was symbolically and physically abated and in 1991 West and East Germany were allowed to reunite. This reunification, however, could not occur without the approval of the countries that emerged as the winners of World War II, including France. As a matter of fact, a reunited Germany, with its about 80 million people, not only changed the economic geography of Europe, but it also implied a significant modification of the European political weights, previously characterized by the presence of four countries (France, Germany, Italy and the UK) of comparable size. Moreover, the memory of the tragedy of both World War I and World War II was still there, together with the historical responsibilities of Germany.[2] As a result of all this, France, represented by its President François Mitterrand, in order to approve the reunification, requested a sign of the German commitment to give up its past ambitions of economic hegemony over Europe. Renouncing the use of the prestigious DM was seen precisely as a credible sign that Germany would be willing to find in the success of the overall European continent the motivations for its own economic success.[3]

Fixed exchange rates, moreover, were necessary not to hinder the intense intra-European trade favoured by the success of the creation of the EEC. The adoption of a single currency, as opposed to a system of irrevocably fixed exchange rates, however, was privileged because, among other reasons – including the benefits resulting from price transparency and from the reduction of transaction costs, it would have removed the possibility of speculative attacks against the adhering currencies.[4]

The creation of the euro has also to do with the ambition (particularly characterized by France, but also, to a lesser extent, Germany) to challenge the international role of the dollar. The ambiguity of this objective is such that, while the 1970 Werner Plan for monetary unification[5] referred explicitly to it, the process of monetary unification – starting with the creation of the European Monetary System (EMS) first and continuing with EMU later on – never did so, most likely also for reasons of diplomacy *vis-à-vis* the US.

If the euro were to replace or just to flank the dollar as a currency of international rank, it would act at the world level as an international reserve, as a unit of account and as a means of exchange, both at the private and at the official level (Krugman, 1984). This means, for example, that the euro area countries could do what the US has been doing so far, namely selling financial activities in exchange for imports (reserve value function); pricing raw materials, and in particular oil, in euros rather than dollars, so as to avoid the negative effects of exchange rate fluctuations (unit of account function); enjoying seigniorage as a result of the use of the euro in international transactions (means of exchange function).

These benefits have been enjoyed by the US, not only under the Bretton Woods regime, that explicitly assigned to the leader country an 'exorbitant privilege',[6] but even under the flexible exchange rate system that followed, due to the lack of alternatives and to the fact that the dollar kept being perceived as a 'safe haven' (the so-called Bretton Woods II).[7]

Being a reserve currency, however, does not imply only privileges, as is well explained by the Triffin's dilemma: if a currency is demanded at the international level, the consequence is its appreciation *vis-à-vis* foreign currencies, thereby implying a current account deficit of the leader country (see Carbaugh and Hedrick, 2009). It is easy to understand that this is not precisely in the interest of Germany, the third-largest exporting country in the world.[8] It is in the interest of Germany, instead, to protect its competitiveness by setting up around itself something like an absorbing cushion, obtained by fixing the exchange rate with the European trading partner countries.

The appropriateness of monetary unification in Europe had to be evaluated by considering the conclusions of the theory of Optimum Currency Areas (OCAs), which identifies the requirements that should be satisfied to guarantee the optimality of giving up both monetary and exchange rate autonomy. The traditional criteria are well known (see, for example, Della Posta, 2003) and refer mainly to the probability and relevance of asymmetric shocks; the homogeneity of the productive structure of the participating countries; the presence of automatic absorbing mechanisms, represented mainly by the flexibility and mobility of the factors of production; and the degree of openness of the economy. Credibility theory, that was booming in the 1980s, even suggested that retaining monetary independence would have been detrimental rather than beneficial, since it would have simply increased inflationary expectations and it soon became the 'new' OCA theory (Tavlas, 1993), replacing it and providing the theoretical justification for the appropriateness of the European monetary unification, even in the case in which the traditional OCA criteria were not satisfied.

Some contributions even argued, later on, that OCA criteria would have been satisfied endogenously, as the synchronization of the European business cycle following the European monetary unification seemed to show (Frankel and Rose, 1998). The euro could be launched then, in confidence that it would produce net benefits to the countries adopting it.

The performance of the euro during its first decade of existence and the international role of the dollar

The first decade of life of the euro has been characterized by several phases that can be synthesized by referring to the behaviour of the dollar–euro exchange rate. While just before the beginning of EMU the ECU (the accounting currency that preceded the introduction of the euro) appreciated slightly *vis-à-vis* the dollar in the anticipation of the creation of the single currency, the euro depreciated largely up to the introduction, on 1 January 2002, of the actual euro banknotes and coins (over the years 1999–2001, the euro only existed as an accounting device). During this initial period it reached its minimum, falling down to 0.8252 on 26 October 2000. The following years, however, have been characterized by an appreciation of the European currency (although it did depreciate during 2005), reaching the maximum of 1.5990 on 15 July 2008. A period of depreciation of the euro followed, connected with the financial crisis. The crisis should have reflected in a weaker dollar, given the fundamental weaknesses of the US economy that, according to many observers, were at the origin of the financial crisis. This has been, indeed, the case for most of 2009, with the dollar–euro exchange rate reaching the level of 1.5090 at the beginning of December. After this date, however, a period of sustained depreciation of the euro followed, leading the exchange rate to the level of 1.2010 on 9 June 2010. The reasons for such depreciation of the euro have to do with the European public debt crisis that will be discussed below.

The uncertain performance of the euro over the first decade or so of its existence, then, does not suggest that it managed to replace – in fact, not even to flank – the dollar as an international currency, as data also show clearly.[9]

Krugman (1984) spelled out in detail the implications of the functions to be fulfilled by an international currency, both at the private and at the official level, as synthesized in Table 4.1 below, so as to allow its international rank to be measured.

Needless to say, the three functions exhibit a strong complementarity, implying that an international currency enjoys economies of scale (not surprisingly, Bobba *et al.*, 2007, show a high correlation between the use of a reserve currency made by a country and the currency of denomination of the foreign debt of the country itself).

By looking at only some of these features (o2 and o3, p1 and p3), McKinsey (2009) constructs an index of the international rank of a

Table 4.1 Private and official functions of an international currency

Use of the currency	Private	Official
Means of payment	(p1) Vehicle	(o1) Foreign exchange intervention
Unit of account	(p2) Invoicing	(o2) Currency peg
Reserve of value	(p3) Holdings of financial assets	(o3) Central banks' holdings of foreign reserves

Source: Krugman (1984).

currency (see Table 4.2 below), from which the dominance of the dollar clearly emerges.[10]

Although the quota of foreign reserves held in dollars at the world level has been decreasing steadily, it remains significantly high compared to the next currency, namely the euro (as to the first quarter of 2010, the dollar quota of the allocated foreign reserves decreased to 61.5 per cent, down from 63 per cent in 2009).[11] It is also interesting to observe how the level of euro-denominated foreign reserves held by both developed and less developed countries (LDCs) increased steadily during the first years of EMU and substantially stabilized from the end of 2003 onwards.[12]

The Chinese central bank reflects such a tendency, since about 62 per cent of its current foreign reserves are dollar denominated, while less than half of that percentage is kept in euros. The Chinese accumulation of dollar-denominated foreign reserves is also a consequence of the fixed exchange rate policy that it has been following to preserve its competitiveness against the US, and that is often blamed by analysts and commentators in the economic press.

If, on the one hand, the creation of the euro, in 1999, was expected to determine a reduction of the quota of dollars on the world foreign reserves, the 1997–8 South-East Asian crisis, instead, obliged developing and LDCs to increase the level of dollar-denominated foreign reserves, in order to enhance their protection, especially in the presence of a dollar-denominated foreign debt. As a matter of fact, the level of foreign reserves after 1999 increased steadily, with the share of developing countries doubling, from 33 per cent to 66 per cent of the total (IMF, 2010).[13]

By doing so, however, the US has been encouraged to absorb resources well beyond its own possibilities. This is why it is usually argued that the recent global financial crisis has been determined by the global savings glut that allowed the US to run trade deficits, willingly financed by China and other surplus countries. The excessive accumulation of dollars as foreign reserves by the central banks of all countries in

Table 4.2 Synthetic index of the degree of reserve currency status of the US dollar, euro and yen, and specific measures of the degree of reserve currency status (% of total)

	Synthetic index of the degree of reserve currency status (% of total)	Specific measures of the degree of reserve currency status (% of total)				
		Foreign reserves	Bonds rated AAA	Share of global bond issuance	Forex transactions	Countries that peg
US dollar	51	63	30	35	86	72
Euro	24	27	20	28	37	26
Yen	6	3	6	3	17	1

Source: McKinsey (2009).

the world – and especially those of the developing and LDCs – is synthesized by the figures relative to China, whose dollar-denominated foreign reserves almost reach 12 per cent of the US GDP and exceed 50 per cent of its own GDP.[14]

It is inevitable to conclude that if the leading role of the dollar at the world level has a responsibility in the building up of the recent global financial crisis, the international monetary and economic architecture needs to be deeply modified.

The consequences of the global financial and economic crisis in Europe

The 1980s and 1990s, characterized by capital movement and financial liberalization, had been hit by recurring exchange rate and financial crises, affecting mainly the 'periphery' of the world economic system. The explanations for such crises were usually found in the macroeconomic imbalances of the countries affected by the crises (as, indeed, had been the case in the 1970s). As a result, the IMF provided loans to LDCs that were applying for financial support only after the latter had accepted the conditionality programmes imposed on them.

With the benefit of hindsight it is possible to argue that the stability objective pursued by the IMF was myopic, ill focused and biased, stressing and penalizing in a probably excessive way the (public sector) imbalances characterizing the world periphery, while substantially ignoring those (mainly relative to the private sector financial markets), that were piling up at the centre of the economic system. This is not surprising, if we consider that the IMF has a Euro-Atlantic nature: the voting weight of the US and the European countries in it is much higher than that of the remaining countries.

The global *financial* crisis quickly became a global *economic* crisis, which made necessary the resurrection of the Keynesian toolkit centred on government intervention. The US engaged in a $800 billion fiscal stimulus, while European countries provided further evidence of the lack of fiscal policy coordination among themselves. In order to absorb the negative effects of the crisis, many European governments pushed up excessively their fiscal expansion and, in the end, under the pressure of speculation, euro countries undertook a 120 billion euro intervention to support Greece. When, a few days later, the public debt crisis looked menacing for countries like Spain, Portugal and Ireland, the EU agreed, in a joint effort with the ECB and the IMF, to provide resources up to the amount of 750 billion euros.[15] Observers and analysts who were claiming that the crisis had clearly proven the limitations of neo-liberal policies and the unavoidability of government intervention had to accept, therefore, the rebuttal coming from free-market supporters, who were warning against the dangers of government intervention. Some of the peripheral European countries, whose national accounts were not sound, have been on the verge of a confidence crisis. The most significant case has been the one of Greece, whose public debt was the object of a devastating speculative attack. It can hardly be claimed, however, that the Greek public debt crisis is further proof of the bad consequences of government intervention into the economy. What happened in Greece was a case of fraudulent behaviour, where the government that ruled the country from 2004–9 manipulated the national accounts to hide the growing fiscal deficit and public debt. As it would be inappropriate to take the Madoff case as a decisive argument to conclude that the hedge funds industry is to be forbidden, it would also be inappropriate to take the Greek experience to conclude that all government interventions are characterized by an expansionary bias and the hands of governments should therefore be tied. Moreover, it should be considered that two other European high-debt countries, Italy and Belgium, realized that their initial conditions were such as not to allow them any fiscal expansion, even in the presence of the severe negative, symmetric shock represented by the global financial crisis.

The European public debt crisis has made clear the moral hazard problem emerging in the presence of a lender of last resort. Still, the dangers associated with bank runs are too large to privilege the game theoretic aspects that suggest providing the 'right' incentives to market participants. This is the dilemma that has emerged with the Lehman Brothers case, in which the US government preferred to play the 'free market game', rather than the 'regulated market game'. The outcome of the crisis has dramatically proved the importance of preserving market confidence, even if that may appear as costly and 'unfair'. It might certainly be true that by granting full insurance, the markets might not behave in the appropriate way, but the answer to this problem has to come from a different set of regulations. A similar dilemma affected Europe in the recent case of Greece, where an undisciplined and fraudulent government cheated on its national accounts. Despite the no-bailout clause, however, the European governments decided to intervene to save the whole of the euro construction, given that the benefits that it produces for European countries (especially Germany!), are much higher than the costs of such an intervention.

What future for the international monetary system?

A unipolar world?

The crises that occurred during the 1980s and 1990s, hitting mainly the periphery of the world economy, did not induce any serious reconsideration of the structure of international arrangements, nor of the economic model to be followed. The impact of the recent crisis, however, may have been such as to mark the end of the neo-liberal, III phase of globalization, and the beginning of a more balanced IV phase, in which a neo-Keynesian view of the economy may prevail.[16] It is also often argued that the dollar, after the global financial and economic crisis, cannot maintain its international leadership. The huge US current account deficit, together with the large 'fiscal stimulus' undertaken by the Obama administration, might contribute at some point to undermine both the credibility of the US institutions and the supremacy of the dollar in capital markets. A further problem for the US might be the unemployment rate, which is close to 10 per cent, and that in the longer run might weaken the credibility of the currency. There may be no major problems if the US runs a current account deficit, if we believe in the global savings glut, dark matter, or Bretton Woods II hypothesis. If a current account deficit implies unemployment, however, the situation may be radically different. The point would be, then, to identify the currency that might aspire to challenge the international role of the dollar.

Kenen (1983) spelled out the preconditions for a currency to acquire international status: 1. a large-sized economy, with substantial global trade; 2. a relatively closed geographical area; 3. lack of exchange controls; 4. broad, deep and liquid capital markets; and 5. sound macroeconomic policies.

Salvatore (2002) concentrates instead on just two main aggregates: relative economic size (whose components have been taken to be the share of world GDP and the share of world merchandise exports) and the financial structure (bank deposits and bank loans, outstanding debt securities – issued by corporations, financial institutions and the public sector – and stock market capitalization).

With the benefit of hindsight, and especially by considering the effects produced by the recent financial and economic global crisis, together with those resulting from the European public debt crisis, it is possible to argue that a more comprehensive classification should be followed, that hinges upon and extends the previous ones. According to it, a currency may aspire to acquire an international role, depending on how it ranks in terms of the four different criteria discussed below.

1. Relevance of international trade and economic dimension of the country more generally (which can be seen as associated with the private part of the transactions and unit of account functions).
2. Relevance of financial markets (to be interpreted as directly associated with the private sector's reserve of value function). This is certainly a more important point, since, as it is well known, financial transactions are much more relevant today than commercial ones, not only in determining the exchange rates, but, for example, in providing a more rapid and complete transmission mechanism from one economy to the others.
3. Inertia and network externalities. This is an element which is also connected to the fact that once a currency is used, for example, as a unit of account, it is also used as a store of value, and international transactions are also likely to take place in that currency (Fratianni et al., 1998).
4. Economic and political relevance of a country: as it has been stressed in the points 1 and 2 above, the larger the economy (both real and financial), the more likely it is that its currency will acquire international status. The stability, credibility and reputation of a given *currency*, upon which international confidence is based, however,

are also crucially dependent on the political stability, credibility and reputation of the *country* (or countries) issuing that currency. This aspect can be seen as closely associated with the reserve and the unit of account function, both at the private and official level, but it certainly affects also the means of payment function.

By referring to the criteria outlined above, it is possible to say that for the time being neither the euro nor the yuan qualify to replace the dollar. Of course, there are differences between China and Europe (especially after the Greek crisis), but the dollar qualifies dramatically better in those aspects. This is due to two basic weaknesses affecting both the euro and the yuan, relating to the role played, on the one hand, by financial markets and, on the other hand – and more importantly – by the lack of political credibility.

Will the euro be the next leading international currency?

It can be argued, rather paradoxically, that the financial crisis has weakened the perspectives for a future international role of the euro,[17] for at least two main reasons.

First of all, the financial crisis has proved the strict dependence of Europe on the US. The financial crisis originated in the US and spread to the whole world, but it affected mainly Europe, due to the fact that European companies own a significant share of US financial activities.[18]

The reasons for the capital inflow into the US have a lot to do with the sophistication of the US financial markets and with the credibility of such a country. A peculiarity of the US is also that it is able to borrow in the short term and lend in the long term, which has to do with the fact that multinationals make a lot of foreign direct investments into less developed and developing countries. This aspect, however, does not seem the dominant one, since financial innovations and structural market changes may well revert the current situation, so as to induce a quick adaptation of network externalities to a new currency.[19]

The second and more important element to explain the continuing supremacy of the dollar *vis-à-vis* the euro is, then, the political weakness of the EU, resulting not only from the political division among the European countries, but also from the lack of economic coordination among them, implying a lack of political credibility. As a matter of fact, while the US on average has experienced an increase in the budget deficit, which is higher than in Europe, only the financial markets of the latter have been subject to speculative attacks.

It is often claimed that the continuing relevance of the dollar *vis-à-vis* the euro is mainly due to inertia. To justify this position, the historical experience of Great Britain *vis-à-vis* the US is often reported. The euro area, however, is not to the US what the US was to Great Britain. The size of the European economy is not of a different scale than that of the US, and it is not possible to identify any European economic supremacy over the US. In fact, over the last three decades the rate of growth of Europe has been systematically lower than that of the US. The theme of the catching up of Europe *vis-à-vis* the US has been on the table since the creation of the EEC in 1957. The Lisbon strategy, a *fiasco* of the recent European policy, was devised precisely not to loose track, in fact to overtake, the US in terms of technological development. For the euro to play the role of means of payment, unit of account and store of value at the world level, however, the euro area would really need to make progress on all of the preconditions that need to be satisfied.[20]

Posen (2008) argues that the presumed recent shift of Chinese foreign reserves from dollars to euros may just reflect the appreciation of the euro, so that a change in the *value* of the dollar reserves would have taken place rather than a deliberate change in the *composition* of the overall foreign reserves. Such a change has occurred indeed, but it has affected less than 10 per cent of the foreign reserves that have been accumulated over the period 1997–2007.[21]

Will the yuan be the next leading international currency?

Political credibility is the key element in explaining the continuing supremacy of the dollar, not only *vis-à-vis* the euro, but also over the Chinese yuan. Both the political weakness of Europe, and the lack of democracy of the Chinese political system explain the permanence of the dollar leadership in international financial markets.

A further problem with the yuan is that the Chinese financial markets allow for neither capital mobility, nor currency convertibility: unless both capital mobility and currency convertibility are guaranteed, it will be impossible to consider the yuan as an international currency, no matter the relevance and the size of the Chinese economy.

According to Ferguson and Schularick (2009), however, the yuan has already been playing an international role – for example, in the pegging that the Central Bank of the People's Republic of China has been exercising over time *vis-à-vis* the dollar. Such a policy of pegging and systematic undervaluation of the yuan (which has not followed the 'rules of the game' of international trade and finance) implies an undervaluation with respect to the euro too. Moreover, the current international role of the Chinese currency is proved by the fact that the size of the Chinese foreign exchange reserves is such as to condition the valuation of the dollar and, as a result, of the euro.

Still, the deliberate choice of the yuan as in international currency will not occur before the financial and political problems identified above are solved.

A multipolar international monetary regime?

The global financial crisis has also made more likely a radical reform of the international monetary system. China is among the countries invoking it, given the weakness and the loss of credibility of the US that many observers consider, rightly or wrongly, as the main culprit of the crisis itself, particularly because of the lack of caution in the way financial markets and instruments have been liberalized and left free to operate.

China has recently proposed (followed by other emerging countries, including Russia), to replace the dollar with SDRs as international currency, in order to avoid the asymmetry of the future current international monetary system.

The Chinese proposal may be interpreted as a way to take advantage of the weakness of the US in order to prepare the ground for the substitution of the dollar with the Chinese yuan as an international currency, thereby bypassing the euro.

Of course, the reasons for which China may want her currency to acquire an international status are the same as Europe. The gradual reduction of the role of exports as opposed to internal demand that may characterize China's future, may only increase the convenience for China to have an internationally ranked currency.

The picture is complicated by the fact that Russia would also want to have a role in the international monetary system. The game played by China, however, paradoxically is that of keeping at bay the Russian (and European) ambitions, by keeping the dollar relatively strong: until China can be sure that it has the chance to replace the dollar, the best way to keep away other potential entrants is to maintain the dollar at the centre of the system.

It is unavoidable not to think that in the future the potential international role to be played by the euro may be substantially obscured by the BRIC countries (Brazil, Russia, India and China): today they account for about 15 per cent of world GDP, but in 20 years' time the sum of their GDP will be higher than the one of G-7 countries and Chinese GDP will be higher than that of the US. The recent approval of the Lisbon Treaty is the least Europe could do to try to resist as much as possible this trend.

It is possible to argue, then, that the current financial and economic crisis may also mark the passage from a *unipolar* world, which gained strength by the fall of the Berlin Wall in 1989, to a *multipolar* one, in which China, Brazil, India and Russia – just to name the most important countries – will have a voice in taking decisions in a common, coordinated way together with the US and Europe.[22]

Such a situation would present at least two advantages. First of all, it would allow diversification of the risk of those who held a single reserve currency (Eichengreen, 2005). Second, and more importantly, it would avoid the piling up of global imbalances resulting from the Triffin's dilemma,[23] which may have been at the roots of the financial crisis.

The passage from a unipolar to a multipolar arrangement, however, is far from immediate, since the former allows benefiting of network externalities and increasing economies of scale. The trade-off, then, is between the *efficiency* granted by network externalities and economies of scale in a *unipolar* system, as opposed to the *stability* favoured by the presence of more than one international currency in a *multipolar* system. Of course, favouring efficiency or stability may imply taking one direction or the opposite one. It could be argued that the efficiency-orientated, neo-liberal policies, followed over approximately the last three decades, led to the unipolar regime that has characterized the III phase of globalization.

Concluding remarks

Many authors argue that the world leadership of the dollar has some responsibility in the building up of the recent global financial crisis, and as a result they conclude that the international monetary and economic architecture needs to be deeply modified. One possibility would be for the euro or the yuan to replace the dollar as international reserve currency, but both potential entrants present major weaknesses *vis-à-vis* the incumbent. Moreover, replacing one currency with another would leave the international system exposed to the same problems.

A different possibility would be, then, to move from a unipolar to a multipolar arrangement. Such a change, however, is far from immediate, since it would imply losing the *efficiency* granted by network externalities and economies of scale in a *unipolar* system. It is too early to conclude that the objective of *stability* and the associated neo-Keynesian policies (as opposed to the *efficiency* that was the objective of the neo-liberal policies that have been followed over the past three decades), may play such a strong role as to induce the passage towards a multilateral regime that may characterize a new IV phase of globalization. This would be the necessary way to follow, though, to avoid any devastating financial and economic crisis occurring again in the future.

Notes

1. The Cold War and the opposition between communist and democratic countries was also one of the main reasons that led, with the signing of the Treaties of Rome in 1957, to the beginning of the process of European integration, with the creation of the European Economic Community (EEC).
2. It should not be forgotten, however, that the dramatic consequences of the unreasonably punitive sanctions imposed on Germany by the Versailles Treaty in the aftermath of World War I had been lucidly anticipated by John Maynard Keynes in a famous booklet on the economic consequences of peace.
3. It is not by chance, then, that EMU dates back to the Maastricht Treaty, signed in December 1991 and approved by the adhering European countries over the course of 1992.
4. As the recent events have made clear, however, while a monetary union removes by definition the possibility of balance of payments crises, it cannot rule out the occurrence of a public debt crisis on the participating countries, if the latter retain fiscal independence.
5. The Werner Plan, however, envisaged a monetary unification to be realized through the irrevocable fixing of the existing currencies, rather than through the abandonment of the respective national currencies.
6. This is the expression used by Charles De Gaulle, the President of the French Republic, 1958–67.
7. Dooley *et al.* (2003).
8. As it will be discussed more in detail below, for the time being this is not in the interest of China either.
9. The survey of the literature that follows in the current paragraph draws partly on Benetton (2010).
10. Data on p3 are implicitly assumed to be summarized by the data relative to 'Bonds rated AAA' and 'Share of global bond issuance', but stock market capitalization and the weight of the banking sector might have also been included. Similarly, p1 is implicitly assumed to be summarized by data on 'Foreign exchange transactions', although such a voice includes both the transactions due to international trade and those relative to the exchange of financial assets.

11. The dollar is the global reserve currency despite the fact that the US economy represents only a fifth of the world economy.
12. It should be kept in mind, however, that the composition of about 45 per cent of world reserves is not identified, a share that has increased in the last few years, and that was about 25 per cent up to the year 2002.
13. Two additional reasons for the accumulation of foreign reserves (and on the leading role of the dollar in the international arena) have been identified in the steady increase in oil price (that took the form of a commodity bubble) that preceded the breaking up of the financial crisis and in the sophistication of the US financial markets.
14. During the Bretton Woods I agreement, instead, Germany and Japan accumulated foreign reserves that were well below 2 per cent of the US GDP and well below 10 per cent of their respective national GDP (Dooley et al., 2003).
15. Tropeano, in this volume, compares and discusses the monetary policy responses of the Fed and the ECB.
16. It is possible to argue that the I phase of globalization was the one characterizing the Victorian age, up until the outbreak of World War I, and the II phase ranged from the end of World War II to the end of the 1970s, when globalization took a new impetus due to the abandonment of Keynesian policies and the adoption of neo-liberal ones, characterizing the III phase of globalization, ranging from the end of the 1970s to the time of writing.
17. The ECB monitors at regular intervals the international status of the euro. See, for example, ECB (2009).
18. According to the CESifo (2010), financial integration, rather than international trade is the more relevant channel of European dependence. The world recovery, and in particular the European one, however, relies upon the US recovery, so that the US will be encouraged to go back to the pattern of current account deficit that they followed in the past: in my view, the dependency channel represented by international trade is therefore still rather strong.
19. EMU would receive a decisive push forward, then, if it could include the British capital and financial markets (Carbaugh and Hedrick, 2009).
20. Problems of institutional credibility of the euro area may also be due to the lack of coincidence between the former and the EU.
21. See Benetton (2010). A different point is the one raised by Lee (2006), who refers to what is called a 'rebalancing behaviour', according to which once a given *quota* has been optimally determined central banks operate in such a way as to keep its *value* constant. When a currency depreciates, therefore, they increase its quantity, so as to keep constant the value of the quota in the portfolio.
22. A multipolar world was envisaged already by Krugman in 1984, when the possible candidates to flank (not to replace) the dollar were identified with the DM and the Japanese yen.
23. Some authors analyze the role of Special Drawing Rights as a possible future international reserve currency (see, among others, Carbaugh and Hedrick, 2009; McCallum, 2009; Williamson, 2009a; 2009b; Swaminathan and Aiyar, 2009).

References

Benetton, M. (2010) 'L'Evoluzione delle Valute Internazionali dall'Introduzione dell'Euro alla Crisi: Verso un Sistema Multi-Valutario?', Tesi di laurea, Corso di laurea in Scienze Economiche, Università di Pisa.
Bobba, M., Della Corte, G. and Powell, A. (2007) 'On the Determinants of International Currency Choice: Will the Euro Dominate the World?', Working Paper, Inter-American Development Bank.
Carbaugh R. and D. Hedrick (2009), 'Will the Dollar be Dethroned as the Main Reserve Currency?', Global Economy Journal, vol. 9, no. 3.
CESifo (2010) The EEAG Report on the the European Economy 2010, Munich: IFO Istitute for Economic Research.
Della Posta, P. (2003) 'Vecchie e nuove teorie delle aree monetarie ottimali', E-Papers Series of the Department of Economic Sciences, Discussion Paper no. 5, Pisa University, January.
Dooley, M., Folkerts-Landau, D. and Garber, P. (2003) 'An Essay on the Revived Bretton Woods System', NBER Working Papers 9971.
ECB (2009) The International Role of the Euro, July.
Eichengreen, B. (2005) 'Sterling's Past, Dollar's Future: Historical Perspectives On Reserve Currency Competition', NBER Working Paper no. 11336
Ferguson, N. and Schularick, M. (2009) 'The End of Chimerica', Harvard Business School Working Paper, October.
Frankel, J. and Rose, A. (1998) 'The Endogenity of the Optimum Currency Area Criteria', Economic Journal, vol. 108, no. 449 (July), pp. 1009–25.
Fratianni, M., Hauskrecht, A. and Maccario, A. (1998) 'Dominant Currencies and the Future of the Euro', Open Economies Review, vol. 9, no. 1, pp. 467–91.
IMF (2010) Composition of Foreign Exchange Reserves (COFER), IMF, April.
Kenen, P. (1983) 'The Role of the Dollar as an International Currency', Group of Thirty Occasional Paper No. 13, New York: Group of Thirty Frenkel and Sondengard, 1998.
Krugman, P. (1984) 'The International Role of the Dollar: Theory and Prospect', pp. 261–78, in J. F. O. Bilson and C. Marston (eds), Exchange Rate Theory and Practice, Chicago: NBER and University of Chicago Press.
Lee, E. (2006) 'The Euro's Challenge to the Dollar: Different Views from Economists and Evidence from COFER and Other Data', Working Paper, IMF, June.
McCallum, T. (2009) 'China, the US Dollar and SDRs', prepared for Shadow Open Market Committee meeting of 21 April.
McKinsey (2009) 'An Exorbitant Privilege? Implications of Reserve Currency for Competitiveness', Discussion paper, McKinsey Global Institute, December.
Papaioannou, E. and Portes, R. (2008) 'The Euro as an International Currency vis-à-vis the Dollar', Working Paper, London Business School and CEPR.
Posen, A. (2008) 'Why the Euro will not Rival the Dollar', Commentary, International Finance 11:1, 2008: pp. 75–100.
Salvatore, D. (2002) 'The Euro: Expectations and Performance', Eastern Economic Journal, vol. 28, no. 1, pp. 121–36.
Swaminathan, S. and Aiyar, A. (2009) 'An International Monetary Fund Currency to Rival the Dollar? Why Special Drawing Right Can't Play That Role', Papers, Cato Institute for Global Liberty and Prosperity, July.

Tavlas, G. S. (1993) 'The "New" Theory of Optimum Currency Areas', *The World Economy*, vol. 16, pp. 663–85.

Williamson, J. (2009a) 'Understanding Special Drawing Rights', Policy Brief, Peterson Institute for International Economics, June.

Williamson, J. (2009b) 'Why SDRs Could Rival the Dollar', Policy Brief, Peterson Institute for International Economics, September.

5
Europe in Crisis: More Political Integration in the Eurozone is the Solution

Teodoro Dario Togati

Introduction

There is no doubt that the world economy has recently faced one of the worst global crises since the Great Depression. It is also quite indisputable that Europe is one of the worst affected areas. Not only do European growth rates tend to be lower than those of the US or emerging economies, but also even the existence of the Eurozone is at risk. The sovereign debt of various European countries, such as Greece and Spain, has come under massive speculative attack on financial markets, despite the fact that other countries are even more indebted. For this reason, several euro members have approved various austerity plans that threaten a double-dip scenario.

The big questions that naturally arise are the following: what accounts for this crisis of the European model, and in particular of the Eurozone, and how to face it? In a recent issue, *The Economist* mentions three alternative stances. The first is the French view, which considers the crisis as due to a lack of political integration which governments should now seek to remedy:

> the chaos, that has spread from Greece to Southern Europe shows the eurozone needs a core of dirigiste powers to run Europe in a more political and less technocratic way. To limit 'unfair' competition, they want things like Europe-wide labour standards and some harmonisation of taxes. They want to oversee transfers of communal cash to the euro's weakest members. (*The Economist*, 2010a: 11)

The second is the German view that regards fiscal indiscipline by a number of southern countries as the key problem for the Eurozone to tackle. In order to save the euro, 'Germany wants a harsh system of rules, enshrined by treaty if need be, that would ban countries from spending too much' (*ibid.*). The third is that suggested by most academics and endorsed by *The Economist* itself, according to which Europe's relative lack of flexibility and competition on labour and product markets with respect to other areas turns out to be its main drawback. In this view, a vast menu of liberal reforms is the proper solution: 'The crisis offers the best chance at revival since the 1980s. To rediscover its vigour and boost its economic growth, Europe should free its economy and set up the single market' (*ibid*). However, *The Economist* also realistically recognizes that, in view of the political obstacles to the implementation of such reforms, a suboptimal solution for the Eurozone is likely to emerge after all; namely, it will 'muddle through':[1]

> Tidy minds contemplating the contradictions between the euro's two most important members foresee either integration or collapse. They argue that without a clear political mechanism to cope with wayward countries, the euro is doomed to repeat the sort of crisis it has suffered this year. One day this view may be proved right. But tidy minds underestimate the European art of compromise ... and they overlook the determination in Europe to make the euro stick ... For the moment, therefore, the most likely outcome is neither collapse nor a dash towards integration, but for the eurozone to muddle through. (*Ibid.*)

According to *The Economist*, to 'muddle through' is certainly suboptimal, since it 'avoids problems, it does not solve them' (*ibid.*). In particular, it condemns Europe to experience a relatively slow growth rate for many years to come. I agree. Unlike *The Economist*, however, we suggest that more political integration is the proper, rational way forward, at least for the Eurozone members (for a similar view, see, e.g., Eichengreen, 2010; Krugman, 2010; Soros, 2010; Stiglitz, 2010).[2] But the key issue is: why is this preferred outcome very unlikely to happen and 'muddle through' bound to prevail instead? To answer this question is the aim of this chapter. It attempts to underline the obstacles to political integration, following a research strategy which parallels that pursued by *The Economist*, seeking to explain why its preferred solution (i.e., structural reforms) is not easy to implement in practice.

The main view put forward in the chapter is that mere national interest or 'selfishness', though obviously important, is not the sole obstacle to greater political integration. It interacts with another, more intellectual, obstacle: namely, the conscious or unconscious reliance of most governments, officials, academics and policy-makers alike on the prescriptions of orthodox macroeconomic theory concerning stability and growth issues, a theory which today is labelled as 'New Neo-classical Synthesis' and characterizes most modern textbooks. Indeed, a number of arguments discouraging political integration quite simply follow from the application of this theory to the European case. One can note, for example, that it inspires the pillars of what can be termed as the current 'economic constitution of Europe' linked to the introduction of the euro, namely the Maastricht Treaty and the SGP (Stability and Growth Pact) on the one hand and the one-sided emphasis on structural reforms on the other.[3] These two pillars, which are widely regarded as necessary preconditions for growth, imply that monetary policy and acceptance of strict budget rules are all Eurozone countries need to share; apart from market unification, individual countries' growth is regarded as the product of national factors and policies (such as structural reforms). This framework thus simply dismisses the very possibility of active or discretionary fiscal policy for Europe as a whole, certainly requiring a higher degree of coordination among states, despite the fact that most countries in the world, including the US (which is otherwise taken as the benchmark in many cases), do not hesitate to implement major strategic anti-cyclical plans, such as the Obama plan, when facing serious recession or deflation scenarios as we currently are.

But this is not all. It can be shown that standard theory is ultimately responsible even for the 'muddle through' outcome itself. The point is that its precepts are quite difficult to implement in practice. Thus governments experience a growing sense of frustration and are bound in the end to get stuck out on a limb; as a result, not only do they fail to cooperate more strictly but they also tend to become more suspicious of each other.

The two factors just mentioned are mutually reinforcing: it is because it apparently best suits national interests to leave individual countries alone to pursue growth that the current economic constitution is adopted. The central thesis defended in this chapter is that this circle should be broken. In my view, as Europe's stagnation shows, it is quite wrong to believe that individual countries benefit from this constitution. In principle, they could be much better off under an alternative constitution, one requiring a higher degree of political integration.

The main implication of my view is that any progress towards political integration depends upon individual states understanding the strategic reasons why they could gain from it. This understanding should not be seen as the inevitable outcome of a long historical process of evolution, of the slow maturation of some kind of European identity that will make it almost natural for national governments to accept deferring their prerogatives to some communal entity. Although the *natura non facit saltum* argument is certainly plausible and to a large extent correct, in my view history must be somehow 'guided'. Just as the introduction of the euro was not 'necessary', not somehow written in the genes of Europeans and thus bound to happen anyway, so making the Eurozone work properly calls for lucid determination and strategy. In particular, I suggest that people's eventual understanding that integration is better than the status quo crucially depends upon the existence and popularity of a quite different theoretical framework for stability and growth than the current one, a framework capable of inspiring a different 'economic constitution' for Europe. In other words, greater political integration to this end will occur only if policy-makers in individual countries reject the current macro theories and embrace an alternative one stressing the advantages of political integration.

To discuss such issues this chapter is organized as follows. In the first section, I focus on the arguments against political integration that are somehow justified by standard theory. The second focuses instead on arguments in favour of integration, which derive from an alternative framework broadly inspired by Keynesian theory.

Why is standard macroeconomic theory an obstacle to political integration?

Standard macro theory is a key obstacle to political integration for a number of reasons. Some of these directly follow from its principles (e.g., they influence the key features of the 'economic constitution' of Europe, such as the Maastricht Treaty and the SGP, which implies only a low degree of integration). There are also indirect reasons, however. The point is that such orthodox principles are difficult to implement in practice, so governments are structurally bound to be 'pragmatic' and search for suboptimal compromise solutions within the existing economic constitution: that is, the 'muddle through' outcome described by *The Economist*. The best way to discuss both types of reasons is to analyze the alternative stances expressed in the current political debate about the European crisis, which are all influenced heavily by standard theory.

One major reason why standard theory directly discourages political integration is that it leads governments – like Germany's – to place a major emphasis on fiscal discipline, and more in general tight demand policies, as a precondition for growth. The general idea behind this principle is known as Say's Law, according to which the market system based on rational agents and flexible prices works efficiently so that supply creates its own demand, full employment is the rule and there is no need in principle for any public support to private demand. If governments spend too much, they will simply end up by crowding out private investment and/or generating inflation.

Clearly, this idea inspires the current 'economic constitution' of the Eurozone, which was devised to support the introduction of the euro. Now there is no doubt that this constitution calls for only a relatively modest degree of political integration between the euro members: all they need to share is a unified monetary policy aimed at the strict control of inflation. According to standard theorists, however, this is the maximum achievable degree of unification. Strictly speaking, even a unified monetary policy is too much. As argued, for example, by Tabellini (2010), it is too stringent for some countries (for example, Spain is different from Germany) and certainly there is no need to have also a unified fiscal policy. The only form of 'fiscal' coordination between countries at the European level which is implied by the current constitution is in 'negative' terms, according to which individual countries are obliged to comply with fixed criteria (and even tend to balanced budgets) and, if they fail to do so, they are forced to implement restrictive policies, even in critical periods such as these, in order to avoid sanctions or market punishment.

But fiscal discipline is difficult to implement in practice. The point is that this framework takes stability of the private sector for granted (that is, consumption or investment are seen as responding smoothly to price incentives). It thus leaves governments unarmed when facing serious crises, such as the current one, where demand instability leading to lower income and higher budget deficits (due to lower taxes and higher expenditures) clearly emerges. However, it would be wrong to believe that even in this case the standard framework and the current constitution simply break down and the need for a greater degree of cooperation as well as political integration between Member States becomes self-evident. This is so for at least two reasons. First, recessions are normally seen as temporary and policy-makers concur that they can be dealt with by some flexibility in the timing of fiscal adjustment required by the current constitution, especially if inflation fails to emerge as in the current period. This is one of the main features of the 'muddle through' scenario.

Second, the standard model is the benchmark which people use to assess states of the economy which greatly diverge from the norm even for long periods of time, as in the case of Europe. This means that if the world does not conform to the model, it is not necessarily because demand is low as Keynesians would suggest. It may well be for opposite reasons: namely, because of supply-side problems due to the existence of a number of structural obstacles to the efficient working of markets.

Indeed, this is one the most popular explanations of the European crisis to be found in articles in the academic literature and authoritative publications, such as *The Economist*. They suggest that although Europe does well in certain areas, the success of its economic model is impaired by old structural problems, such as the relative lack of flexibility and competition on labour and product markets with respect to other areas (see, e.g., Steltzer, 2010; *The Economist*, 2010a; 2010b). This basic thesis goes back at least to the 1990s, when Europe started to lag behind the US, and comes in various, not mutually exclusive, versions, ranging from the emphasis on demographic factors (e.g., Europe is 'old', a relatively static society where mobility is scarce and immigration is not sufficient to reinvigorate it: see, e.g., Alesina, 2010; Steltzer, 2010) to that on 'institutional' ones (e.g., Europe is more corporatist than the US and is lagging behind in promoting the institutions of capitalism, e.g., Phelps, 2006). However, the emphasis on the supply-side factors in the crisis of Europe also underlies the views of more heterodox economists when recently claiming that the key problem of the Eurozone is that it fails to be an optimal currency area (e.g., Stiglitz, 2010; Krugman, 2010).

On these grounds, we can now understand the second reason why standard theory directly discourages political integration: it leads governments to place emphasis on structural reforms. Indeed politicians are convinced that this should be the way forward to solve problems.[4] But what is the link between structural reforms and low political integration? To answer this question, we only need to recall that, according to standard theory, the reason why tight demand policies need to be pursued at all costs is that they create the conditions for growth; that is, once price and fiscal stability are achieved, growth can take place almost automatically as it is driven by supply factors. For our purposes, the key point to note is that, when applied to Europe, this framework implies that competitiveness and growth do not need any degree of coordination between countries. Indeed, according to the current economic constitution inspired by the orthodox principles, all the central European authorities should do to favour competitiveness for all Eurozone members, apart from approving regulations to unify markets, is to keep inflation low. For the rest, competitiveness and growth must be pursued by national governments alone in the form of supply-side policies (e.g., labour market policies). Given institutional differences across countries, in these areas competition between countries is better than harmonization (see, e.g., Tabellini, 2010). The following quote from *The Economist* gives a clear idea of the current menu of structural reforms, with an indication of the normative 'division of labour' between central authorities and national governments:

> The single market remains half-built ... the EU is 30% less productive than America in services ... Whole areas, such as health care, are exempted from EU-wide competition. Likewise, some high-tech industries, such as telecoms, have been protected ... the EU has a costly, fragmented patent system ... energy supply has not been properly liberalised; debts are hard to collect across borders ... In Spain and Italy privileged workers are protected ... Europeans retire too early everywhere. (*The Economist*, 2010a: 11)

Again, structural reforms are difficult to implement in practice for a number of reasons. Defenders of this perspective, like *The Economist*, suggest that obstacles are purely political in essence: 'The barrier to reform has always been political, not economic' (*ibid.*). Subscribing to this view, Tabellini suggests, for example, that the actual implementation of the structural reforms project is undermined by the institutional architecture of the Eurozone, which makes the normative division of labour just mentioned quite problematic. In particular, he notes that the 'soft coordination' method, which prevails today among European nations, is responsible for the substantial failure of the Lisbon strategy (see Tabellini, 2010). By placing everything at the same level, this method turns out to be ineffective where strong European intervention is needed and redundant where national government responsibility is needed.[5]

In my view, however, another obstacle is standard theory itself. The point is that this theory regards even recessions as caused essentially by supply-side problems. Although demand shocks may hit a stable economy, it is only when price rigidities or market imperfections impair swift market adjustment that prolonged deviations from the norm occur. This approach leaves governments to seek to follow its precepts relatively unarmed when facing serious crises, such as the current one, due to the prolonged instability of the demand side, induced by factors such as confidence crises, inequitable income distribution, credit crunch and stock market volatility. It is not surprising therefore that, when dealing with such crises, governments become pragmatic: that is, they do the right things without understanding why; they instinctively seek to remedy such effective demand failures rather than insisting on reforms. For this purpose, they discover the virtues of more explicit political coordination. For example, in the recent crisis many countries have been working together to engineer financial intermediaries' bailouts rather than leaving them to go bust (as focusing on 'structural reforms' should have implied). In my view, this gap between actual policy 'forced by events' and wrong economic theory is one of the key explanations for the 'muddle through' scenario. However, once again it should be noted that pragmatism alone does not lead to a change in the current constitution. The latter is meant to apply at least to 'normal times', exceptions being allowed in emergency times only. This is the reason why the structural reform rhetoric accompanied by the fiscal discipline requirement has recently assumed new vigour in the policy agenda of many governments soon after the first signs of recovery in European economies.

It would be wrong to believe, however, that the negative influence of standard theory on political integration follows simply from the two principles just mentioned: that is, the insistence on fiscal discipline and structural reforms combined with the difficulty of implementing them in practice. Another influence results from the fact that standard theory also leads commentators to represent political integration in negative terms: that is, as a 'violation' of the right economic model. It essentially regards it as reflecting dirigisme (that is, an attempt to impose the will of the state over market forces) or protectionism to defend the costly 'European social model'. Indeed, according to *The Economist*, a 'European economic government' within an inner core of Eurozone members:

> means politicians meddling in monetary policy and a system of redistribution from richer to poorer members, via cheaper borrowing for governments through common Eurobonds or outright fiscal transfers ... fiscal and social harmonisation: e.g. curbing competition in corporate tax-rates or labour costs. (*The Economist*, 2010b: 23)

Other elements of this project include: bailout mechanisms as a way to impose the will of the state over 'speculators', protectionism (e.g., French car industry) to keep globalization (especially within Europe's own borders) at bay and, above all, defence of the 'European social model' (old-age pensions and unemployment benefits):

> single nations are too small to maintain high-cost social-welfare models in the face of global competition. But the EU, with its 500m people, is big enough to assert the supremacy of political will over

market forces. For such politicians, European diversity is a problem because it undermines the most advanced (meaning expensive) social models. Such competition must be curbed with restrictions on labour migration from eastern Europe, subsidies for rich-country production and lots of harmonisation – including ... a European minimum wage. (*Ibid.*: 26)

Clearly, in the light of negative assessments such as these it becomes quite difficult for policy-makers and governments to advocate political union. Once again, it is not surprising that the 'muddle through' scenario emerges as the most likely outcome of the current situation in Europe.

Political union calls for an alternative theoretical perspective

In the previous section, I have suggested that at the roots of the current 'muddle through' scenario, which condemns Europe to relative stagnation, lies the combination between a wrong macroeconomic model inspiring the current economic constitution in the Eurozone and governments' failure to implement the actual policy measures that follow from this model. In this section, I argue instead that to overcome this suboptimal scenario and grow at a more reasonable pace the Eurozone calls for higher political integration. However, for this purpose this area needs to rely on a new economic constitution, based on an alternative theoretical framework, capable of integrating stability and growth issues in a better way than orthodox theory does. The basic idea underlying this framework is to reject the two basic premises of the orthodox policy framework, namely monetary and financial stability, as preconditions for growth and reliance on structural reforms to stimulate growth directly by influencing the supply-side factors. I argue instead that aggregate demand factors represent the 'true' drivers of growth and this idea leads me to draw very different conclusions with respect to standard analysis. A good way to present this alternative framework and its policy implications very briefly is to consider the reasons why the current economic constitution, while apparently favouring the national interest of individual countries, is bound in the end to discourage their growth.

Let me start by noting that, by focusing on inflation control as a precondition for macro stability and growth, this constitution tends to favour export-led growth in countries such as Germany and Italy. A few drawbacks in this model of growth can easily be singled out.

First, such countries tend to experience low internal demand, which many Keynesian economists regard as one major cause of Europe's relative decline (see, e.g., Fitoussi, 2010). In principle, a stronger Union, in which more resources are allocated to central government than is the case today, could more easily address this issue (for example, by using appropriate fiscal tools).

Second, by calling for external engines of growth, such as the US, this model condemns Europe to a certain degree of political minority (as second violin to use Bauman's metaphor: see, e.g., Bauman, 2008, ch. 6). There is little doubt that higher political integration could be a remedy to this state of affairs.

Third, this model rests on the idea that the only weapon to gain competitiveness which is available for individual members of the Eurozone, given the impossibility of devaluating, is to reduce costs. However, this neglects other dimensions of competitiveness, such as quality or identity, which are especially important for Europe in the face of strong globalization trends. German goods are competitive because the 'made in Germany' label guarantees their excellent quality, not because they are cheap. For this reason, aware of their difficulty in competing in terms of costs alone on global markets, the priority of European governments should be to develop more effectively a different model of competitiveness based on innovation and research. Rather than leaving individual countries alone to gain this kind of competitive edge as happens today, a more politically integrated Eurozone would pursue this goal by seeking to promote as added value something like a European identity, 'made in Europe' as a distinct brand, synonymous with high-quality standards, partially overlapping, but not necessarily in conflict with, other existing strong national brands, such as 'made in Germany' or 'made in Italy'.

In the end, the model of growth implied by the current constitution is not internally consistent. The insistence on monetary and fiscal stability as preconditions for growth is certainly aimed at increasing the euro's reputation on financial markets. However, one by-product of this policy is to undermine the very export-led growth in the Eurozone pursued by this constitution: indeed, due to its strong reputation, the euro has been constantly overvalued in recent years with respect to key currencies, such as the dollar or the yuan, thus crowding out those goods which are more exposed to price competition by emerging countries. A higher degree of political integration would perhaps break this vicious circle by changing the source of the euro's reputation. The strength of the euro as a global reserve currency in the international monetary system should derive primarily from political union itself and Europe's ability to grow rather than from the anti-inflationary obsession of the European Central Bank. In my view it is quite wrong to leave the latter alone to fill a political void for one simple reason: low inflation per se is simply not a sufficient condition for growth.

Let us now turn to the second pillar of the current economic constitution, namely the one-sided emphasis on structural reforms as a direct way to stimulate growth. It is sufficient to note here a basic drawback in this approach. In my view, it fails to work not just because of political opposition, but also because it ignores the 'true' drivers of growth. Strictly speaking, I am not claiming that structural reforms and the supply factors are irrelevant for growth, but that they influence outcomes only indirectly through aggregate demand factors. For example, it is misleading to suggest that relative low productivity growth in Europe is simply due to structural factors, such as inefficient labour market, high taxes, bad infrastructure and the inefficiency of the state or technological gap especially in services. It is necessary to recognize that this phenomenon is primarily due to low aggregate demand and that the structural factors just mentioned play a role by undermining the propensity to invest or consume. The key problem of macroeconomics is that the latter are malleable factors; they fail to respond in a mechanical way either to changes in market prices, such as interest rates, or to changing structural factors, such as those mentioned above. In contrast with standard theory, in which such factors exercise a separate, direct influence on productivity growth (as the very notion of the production function implies), in my Keynesian vision they exercise an indirect and 'chemical' influence (that is they do not act separately), especially on investment. But this is not all. If we focus on this variable we can list a vast array of other determinants. Apart from the well-known, key factors, such as psychology, convention and cultural matrix, which are grouped under the 'expectations' label, investment also depends upon a complex and 'chemical' combination of institutional factors including those such as education and public expenditure underlying R&D, which are often labelled as 'the national system of innovation'. It is possible perhaps to summarize all these influences on investment by using the term 'trust'. In this way, we suggest that all the factors mentioned above combine in an unpredictable manner to determine outcomes and a key role in this combination is played by policy. Indeed, 'trust' can be seen as the product of a state's ability to coordinate factors such as education, welfare, cultural resources; these factors do not influence separately income growth as in orthodox stories based on the production function, but in combined form through institutional mediation.

It is important to note a few significant implications of this alternative stance. First, although structural reforms may be important (there is no doubt, for example, that low taxation and good infrastructure may attract investment from abroad), they may fail to stimulate investment in a context in which expectations are depressed and austerity plans are devised, such as the current one. This is the reason why the twin pillars of the current constitution fail to work. Structural reforms and monetary and financial stability are both seen as separate, though complementary, preconditions of growth when in fact they may be in contrast with each other and are, at least partly, the product of growth. For example, higher growth rates make it easier to repay or sustain debt and achieve financial stability (for a similar view, see, e.g., Krugman, 2010).

Second, this approach attributes a positive role to welfare. While the standard model regards welfare as a burden in view of its full employment assumption (as already noted, those like *The Economist* who follow its precepts regard the 'European social model' as too expensive), in my view, instead, welfare is a positive factor for stability and growth because it increases 'trust'. It can be argued, for example, that the problem is not simply to consume more; there is a lack (rather than too much) of public demand especially for relational goods, concerning services, such as assistance, health, culture and education, which may be able to stimulate investment. In this way, my approach seeks to overcome the gap between the economic visions that emphasize the positive role of factors such as culture, welfare and income redistribution (e.g., Sen's capabilities approach) on the one hand and the current macroeconomic paradigms on the other.[6]

In the end, this approach reveals a major weakness in the Eurozone, namely that it lacks trust and trust-generating policies. A stronger form of political union would also remedy this weakness. What I mean by this is that European countries still behave too much as national economies and still fail to coordinate effectively factors such as education, welfare and cultural resources. This is perhaps the main reason behind the failure of the Lisbon strategy, which is a set of goals without the ability to act to pursue them.

In conclusion, it should be noted that by representing economic principles buttressed by law, apparently endowed with higher degree of objectivity, the current constitution itself inevitably favours the status quo and encourages people to regard any deviation from its norm in negative terms. It thus somehow justifies commentators, such as *The Economist*, in describing political integration in the Eurozone as a necessary move towards protectionism or dirigisme, when it actually means instead greater chances to favour growth by allowing active fiscal policy in difficult times such as these, an option which is not available today for individual countries except in negative terms as violation of the SGP.[7] In other words, I suggest that what is missing in Europe today, due to a lack of political integration, is the fiscal counterpart of what already exists at the monetary level – that is, the common currency and monetary policy between a number of countries (for a similar view, see, e.g., Benigno, 2010; Reichlin and Borri, 2010; Soros, 2010; Stiglitz, 2010). It must be noted that what is at stake is not just the possibility to carry out countercyclical plans, such as the Obama plan. Clearly, such plans are costly and Europeans may not be prepared to pay more taxes to allow central government to implement them. However, a stronger form of political union in the Eurozone is desirable even if it does not increase the tax burden for its citizens. For example, debt financing would certainly be much easier and markets could tolerate more European debt than the current sum of individual national debts. It is sufficient to think, for example, that while today the sovereign debt of each Eurozone country is left alone to face markets, common eurobonds representing a cohesive political will should have a much stronger appeal; even if bigger deficits for the Eurozone as a whole are difficult to manage, there is little doubt that eurobonds could be more easily digested by markets than the sum of, say, Greek, Italian and Spanish bonds.

A final remark on the dividends of political integration should be added. The arguments presented so far are clearly quite general. Needless to say, many new problems are raised by a higher degree of integration: for example, how to determine the share of eurobonds that each single country could issue. In principle, only a centralized fiscal authority working under a new constitution appears able to solve this problem. However, it is not a sharp dichotomy between old and new constitution that I ultimately wish to underline. Some positive steps towards a better European cooperation can and have already been taken in the present institutional context, especially when facing exceptional events, such as the Greek crisis. It is important that Member States do not miss further opportunities to move in this direction.

Conclusion

The main conclusion that follows from this chapter is that the key problem of the Eurozone is represented by the insufficient degree of political integration between its members. The chapter also identifies two mutually reinforcing factors that account for this outcome. The first is the traditional concern for narrow national interest, which underlies, for example, the constant political in-fighting between key countries such as France and Germany. The other one is governments' actual reliance upon standard macro theory as a source of inspiration of the current 'economic constitution' and policies such as the recent austerity plans implemented in various European countries when still facing a very uncertain economic scenario. These factors account for the current 'muddle through' scenario which is a suboptimal state halfway between complete deflagration of the Eurozone on the one hand and the economic success which its members hoped for when adhering to the single currency project but has never been achieved on the other.

As a way out of this state of affairs, this chapter concludes that it is important to make people realize: 1. that the current constitution does not serve national interests well since it condemns Eurozone members to slow growth rates; 2. that such interests are best pursued by accepting a higher degree of political integration as the necessary premise for devising a new economic constitution, allowing Eurozone members in particular to carry out a full-blown discretionary fiscal policy like other federal states, such as the US. This chapter has tried to show that this constitution cannot be *ad hoc*, a mere expression of pragmatism, but must rely on an alternative theoretical framework capable of integrating stability and growth issues in a better way than orthodox theory does.

Notes

1. According to the Free Dictionary, which is available on the web, 'muddle through' means 'to manage to get through something awkwardly'.
2. As Krugman puts it, 'So the only way out is forward: to make the euro work, Europe needs to move much further toward political union, so that European nations start to function more like American states' (Krugman, 2010).
3. Indeed 'the single currency was always supposed to drive structural reforms, as once profligate countries were forced by the rules, and their peers, to live within their means' (*The Economist*, 2010b: 24).
4. For example, *The Economist* quotes Juncker, prime minister of Luxembourg, as claiming that 'We all know what to do, but we don't know how to get re-elected once we have done it' (*The Economist*, 2010a: 11).
5. According to Tabellini, stronger European intervention is needed for policies to unify markets, especially in environment, telecoms and information and those providing public goods, such as research and infrastructures, where it is not necessary to deal with other supply-side reforms.
6. This critique applies not just to standard neo-classical theory, unable to accommodate a positive role for welfare in view of its full employment assumption, but also to current versions of the Keynesian paradigm which are

often criticized for neglecting these factors in view of its aggregative nature (see Sen, 2009).
7. This negative bias against European political integration emerges clearly when commentators carry out international comparisons. For example, while the US is widely regarded as the best incarnation of capitalism in line with the neo-classical model, commentators comparing it favourably with the Eurozone tend to forget that it does implement a full-blown discretionary fiscal policy.

References

Alesina, A. (2010) 'Terapie alla greca per un'Italia più sana', *Il Sole 24 Ore*, 4 May.
Bauman, Z. (2008) *Does Ethics Have a Chance in a World of Consumers?*, Cambridge: Harvard University Press.
Benigno, P. (2010) 'Se tocca all'euro salvare l'Europa', *Il Messaggero*, 10 May.
Eichengreen, B. (2010) 'Drawing a Line under Europe's Crisis', *The Vox*, 17 June.
Fitoussi, J. P. (2010) 'Contro chi giocano i mercati', *La Repubblica*, 3 May.
Krugman, P. (2010) 'The Making of a Euromess', *The New York Times*, 14 February.
Phelps, E. (2006) 'Macroeconomics for a Modern Economy', Nobel Prize Lecture, 8 December.
Reichlin, P. and Borri, N. (2010) 'Un modello Usa per la UE', *Il Sole 24 Ore*, 13 May.
Sen, A. (2009) 'Capitalism Beyond the Crisis', *The New York Review of Books*, vol. 56, no. 5, 26 March.
Soros, G. (2010) 'Soros: L'euro? E' a rischio. Una moneta incompiuta', *Corriere della Sera*, 15 April.
Steltzer, I. (2010) 'The EU needs Long-term Solutions to Come of the Eurozone Crisis', *The Wall Street Journal Europe*, 29 March.
Stiglitz, J. E. (2010) 'Can the Euro be Saved?', *The Project Syndicate*, 5 May.
Tabellini, G. (2010) 'Il fantasma di un piano URSS e l'Europa 2010', *Il Sole 24 Ore*, 10 January.
The Economist (2010a) 'Can Anything Perk Up Europe?', 10 July.
The Economist (2010b) 'Staring into the Abyss', 10 July.

6
Economic Crisis and Industrial Policy in the Union: The Need for a Long-term Vision of Industrial Development

Patrizio Bianchi and Sandrine Labory

Introduction

In this short chapter, we discuss the need for industrial policy in the Union beyond the crisis. We define industrial policy in a wide sense. The term is often taken in a restrictive sense, as selective intervention to support specific firms or specific industries. This selective intervention was the so-called 'constructivist' approach prevailing in the EU (EEC at the time) up to the mid-1980s. The approach to industrial policy changed thereafter, focusing on providing the conditions for business to develop rather than directly intervening in markets. In the EU, this is the approach defined by Martin Bangemann in his famous 1990 report, which constituted the basis for the industrial policy adopted in the EU in the 1990s and enshrined in the Maastricht Treaty. This approach is horizontal, in that measures apply to all firms and industries without discriminating or favouring specific 'champions'. In the 1990s, the very term 'industrial policy' was abandoned because taken to mean the old approach of the past that was not pro-competitive. Rather, other terms were used such as 'competitiveness policy'. The broad objective of industrial policy is then to favour the competitiveness of firms, by ensuring appropriate conditions (macroeconomic stability, respect of competition rules, efficient regulation, R&D programmes and so on).

The chapter argues that, at the end of the 1990s, this approach showed limits since the competitiveness of European business relative to the rest of the world, and especially relative to traditional rivals like the US and Japan, was not substantially improved. In addition, EU business competitiveness was increasingly challenged by firms from emerging countries, especially the BRIC (Brazil, Russia, India and China) countries, but also the Asian Tigers.

On the other hand, the EU constitutes an important economic power in the world, especially after the 2004 and 2007 enlargements. This note illustrates the main features of the structure of European business more recently, concluding that the EU as a whole is one of the first traders in the world, one of the first production poles and one of the first R&D and innovation producers.

The EU is therefore an economic giant. However, it is a political miniature. The reason is that European Member States have difficulties in speaking with one voice, as shown by recent events such as the recovery plans after the financial crisis and the reaction to the Greek crisis.

The chapter suggests that adopting an industrial policy in the classical meaning of the term could resolve this paradox. We do not mean a return to constructivist or interventionist industrial policies of the post-war period, which tend to be protectionist. Rather, we mean an industrial policy defined in a wide sense, as a long-term vision of industrial development in an open economy or, specifically in the EU, an open, integrated and knowledge-based economy. Only such a vision can mobilize Member States towards a common goal and bind them to the European integration process.

The Lisbon Strategy has been a success in defining such a long-term vision. Ambitious goals are needed to induce appropriate improvements. However, ambitious goals also require political commitment, which has been lacking after the adoption of the Lisbon Strategy (Prodi, 2008).

We argue in this chapter that the failure of the Lisbon Strategy does not mainly result from the incoherence of its objectives but from the lack of political commitment to the strategy. To show this, the argument runs as follows. Section 2 examines the structure of European industry, simply taking Eurostat data, showing obviously that the EU as a whole is one of the first economic powers in the world. Section 3 analyzes the German syndrome, while section 4 shows to what extent the Lisbon Strategy and now the 2020 Strategy could resolve this paradox. Section 5 concludes on the necessity for long-term visions of development, especially after the financial crisis, a political leadership such as that which guided and regularly relaunched the European economic integration process throughout its history.

Structure of European industry

Table 6.1 below shows that five EU countries account for about three-quarters of both the total value added produced in the EU and total

Table 6.1 Main business indicators of EU industry (2006)

	Enterprises		Turnover		Value added		Persons employed	
	1,000s	% of EU-27	€ million	%	€ million	%	1,000s	%
EU-27	20,156	100	22,311,165	100	5,650,016	100	129,773	100
BE	402	2.0	796,132	3.6	153,621	2.7	2,446	1.9
BG (1)	240	1.2	61,857	0.3	9,845	1.4	1,816	1.4
CZ	857	4.2	324,538	1.5	67,605	1.2	3,539	2.7
DK	207	1.0	435,662	2.0	117,563	2.1	1,783	1.4
DE	1,774	8.8	4,322,906	19.4	1,152,541	20.4	21,501	16.6
EE	43	0.2	36,191	0.2	7,453	0.1	423	0.3
IE	93	0.5	330,514	1.5	90,911	1.6	1,089	0.8
EL	829	4.1	289,033	1.3	69,552	1.2	2,589	2.0
ES	2,632	13.1	2,053,175	9.2	536,808	9.5	13,908	10.7
FR	2,332	11.6	3,197,686	14.3	795,262	14.1	14,663	11.3
IT	3,847	19.1	2,773,486	12.4	631,343	11.2	15,177	11.7
CY (1)	43	0.2	20,770	0.1	6,960	0.2	211	0.2
LV	67	0.3	38,855	0.2	8,734	0.2	643	0.5
LT	126	0.6	48,179	0.2	10,016	0.2	932	0.7
LU	23	0.1	76,252	0.3	14,419	0.3	210	0.2
HU	543	2.7	239,036	1.1	42,005	0.7	2,536	2.0
NL (2)	494	2.5	986,469	5.1	234,001	3.7	4,679	3.7
AT	283	1.4	506,149	2.3	137,648	2.4	2,434	1.9
PL (1)	1,407	7.2	514,471	2.5	121,985	6.0	7,576	6.0
PT	861	4.3	318,413	1.4	71,397	1.3	3,301	2.5
RO (1)	412	2.1	139,957	0.7	28,188	3.2	4,038	3.2
SI	96	0.5	67,831	0.3	15,758	0.3	597	0.5
SK	53	0.3	89,333	0.4	18,050	0.3	961	0.7
FI	204	1.0	340,696	1.5	82,469	1.5	1,268	1.0
SE	542	2.7	605,539	2.7	161,613	2.9	2,720	2.1
UK	1,621	8.0	3,547,762	15.9	1,072,552	19.0	17,737	13.7
5 Bigs (D, F, I, UK, S)		60.6		71.9		74.2		64

Notes:
1. Data for 2005.
2. Number of enterprises and numbers of persons employed, 2005; value added and turnover, 2004.
3. Data for Malta are not available.
Source: Eurostat (2009).

EU sales. Indeed, Germany, the UK, France, Italy and Spain produce about 74.1 per cent of the total value added in the EU-27 non-financial business activities, while they employ about two-thirds of the total workforce. Italy and Spain have a larger number of enterprises than

Germany, France and the UK, providing evidence of higher firm dimension in the latter three countries.

Poland is the sixth ountry in terms of value added (percentage of total EU-27 value added), followed by the Netherlands, Romania and Sweden.

Regarding the sectors in which European non-financial business firms operate, the most important sector appears to be non-financial services: more than half (55.5 per cent) of the value added generated by non-financial business enterprises originates from services (Eurostat, 2009), while industry accounts for about a third (35.5 per cent) of the value added of all non-financial business activities. The rise in services is due to the phenomenon of outsourcing whereby firms increasingly rely on services realized outside the frontiers of the firms, besides services for families. Business services represent 15.8 per cent of the total value added of the non-financial business sector. Among the more traditional manufacturing sector, the most important in terms of value added are metals and metal products (4.3 per cent), fuel processing and chemicals (4 per cent) and electrical machinery and optical equipment (3.6 per cent). In contrast, wholesale trade and retail trade and repair represent respectively 9.2 per cent and 7.4 per cent of the total value added produced by the non-financial business sector in the EU. The three largest sectors in the EU-27 economy are business services (15.8 per cent of total value added), wholesale trade (9.2 per cent) and construction (9.0 per cent).

In terms of location of industrial activities, the evidence (Eurostat, 2009) is that industrial activities have moved east in the EU, since these activities are concentrated in Germany, and Eastern and Central Europe. Non-financial services are concentrated in the north – the central part of the EU, namely the UK, Benelux and northern Germany, and in the west and south of France, together with the Parisian region (Île de France). In contrast, financial services are concentrated in Belgium, the Netherlands, Luxembourg, France, North Germany, the UK, Ireland, Denmark, south Sweden and south Finland.

European industrial activity is thus diversified across countries and regions, although the five largest countries account for a disproportionate share of the total value added created in non-financial business activities (more than a half). Purely manufacturing activities have moved to the new members, where labour costs are lower. Older members tend to specialize in services, denoting a strong move to the tertiary sector.

The financial crisis caused a steep fall in industrial production in the Union in 2009, especially in the euro area: for an index amounting to 100 in July 2005, industrial production reached 110 in April 2008 and

Table 6.2 Percentage of the value added generated by non-financial business activity in the EU-27

Non-financial business economy	100
Industry	35.5
Mining and quarrying	1.6
Food, beverage and tobacco	3.5
Textiles, clothing, leather and footwear	1.1
Wood and paper	1.4
Fuel processing and chemicals	4.0
Rubber and plastics	1.4
Other non-metallic products	1.4
Metals and metal products	4.3
Machinery and equipment	3.4
Electrical machinery and optical equipment	3.6
Transport equipment	3.5
Furniture and other manufacturing	0.9
Network supply of electricity, gas and stream	3.2
Recycling and water supply	0.6
Construction	9.0
Non-financial services	55.5
Motor trades	2.9
Wholesale trade	9.2
Retail trade and repair	7.4
Accommodation and food services	3.2
Transport and storage	7.1
Media and communications	6.2
Real estate, renting and leasing	6.0
Research and development	0.4
Business services	15.8
Business activity as % of total EU-27 value added	75.8
Non-financial business activity as % of total business activity	73.9

Source: Eurostat (2009): 19.

fell to 89 in April 2009, to slowly recover up to more than 96 in April 2010.[1] The crisis hit European industry sharply, but it is recovering. As we argue elsewhere (Bianchi and Labory, 2010), what the crisis reveals is that there are long-term structural trends that have to be addressed by industrial policy, namely the increasing worldwide competition due to the growth of new competitors, mainly from BRIC countries.

The EU as a world economic power

In order to complete the overview of EU business activity, a comparison with the rest of the world is useful. Figure 6.1 below shows the level of GDP of the US, China and the EU: it clearly shows that the EU, taken as a whole, is an economic giant in the world, since its GDP is higher than that of the US and of China. It also shows that, while the US and European GDP slightly reduced during the financial crisis, Chinese GDP continued to rise.

In terms of variations and GDP growth, the effects of the 2008 financial crisis appear more clearly (see Figure 6.2 below), as does the rapid growth of the Chinese GDP.

As for trade, the EU also represents an important block worldwide, as shown by Table 6.3 below.

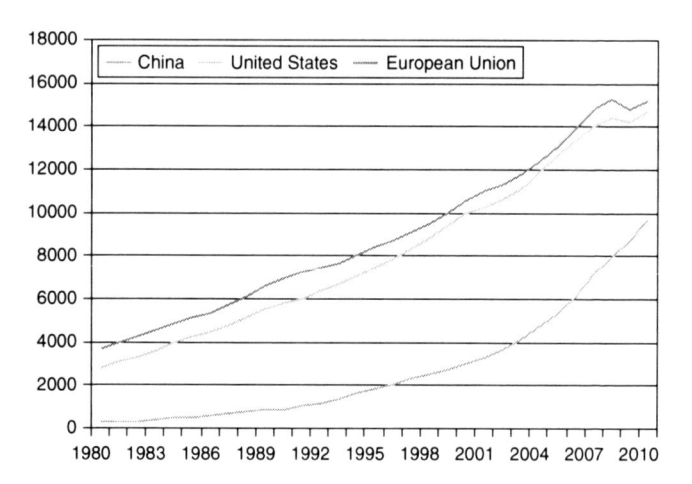

Figure 6.1 GDP based on PPP (current international $ billion)
Source: IMF data mapper (2010).

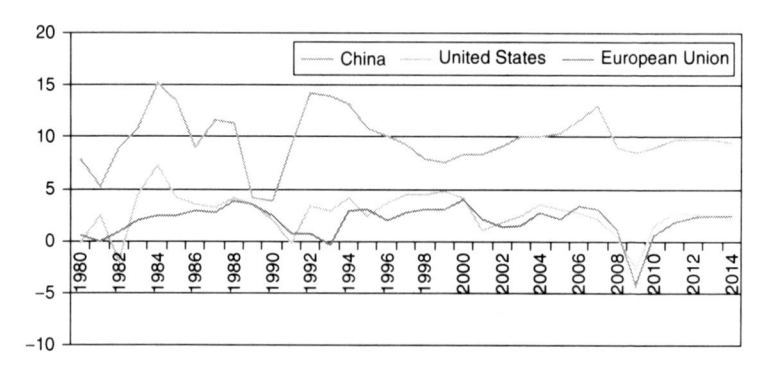

Figure 6.2 Real GDP growth China, the US and the EU (1980–2014)
Source: IMF data mapper (2010).

Table 6.3 World merchandise exports, by regions and countries

	1983	1993	2003	2008
World	100	100	100	100
North America	16.8	18.0	15.8	13.0
USA	11.2	12.6	9.8	8.2
Canada	4.2	4.0	3.7	2.9
Latin America	4.4	3.0	3.0	3.8
Brazil	1.2	1.0	1.0	1.3
Argentina	0.4	0.4	0.4	0.4
Europe	43.5	45.4	45.9	41.0
Germany	9.2	10.3	10.2	9.3
France	5.2	6.0	5.3	3.9
Italy	4.0	4.6	4.1	3.4
UK	5.0	4.9	4.1	2.9
EU	31.3	37.4	42.4	37.5
Africa	4.5	2.5	2.4	3.5
Middle East	6.8	3.5	4.1	6.5
Asia	19.1	26.1	26.2	27.7
Japan	8.0	9.9	6.4	5.0
China	1.2	2.5	5.9	9.1
India	0.5	0.6	0.8	1.1

Source: *International Trade Statistics*, WTO (2009).

The EU has represented, since the 1980s, more than a third of all world exports. The Asian share of world exports has risen in the period from about a fifth to more than a quarter. The US share of world exports reduced by 3 per cent points, from 11.2 per cent in 1983 to 8.2 per cent in 2008.

In terms of R&D and innovation, European countries are among the countries which invest more in new sectors, as shown by data on R&D expenditure as a percentage of GDP (Figure 6.3). The EU as a whole invests about 2 per cent of GDP in R&D, with high variation across Member States: Italy invests only 1.1 per cent of GDP, while Scandinavian countries such as Sweden and Finland respectively invest about 3.6 per cent and 3.5 per cent of GDP in R&D. Among new Member States, the Czech Republic is the country which invests most in R&D expenditure as a percentage of GDP (1.5 per cent). Asian countries such as Japan, including emerging ones such as Korea, heavily invest in R&D. China has been investing in R&D more than Japan since 2006.[2]

In terms of innovation output, Table 6.4 shows, besides R&D intensity which is derived from R&D expenditure as a percentage of GDP, the number of patents per capita, showing that Japan and Germany are the

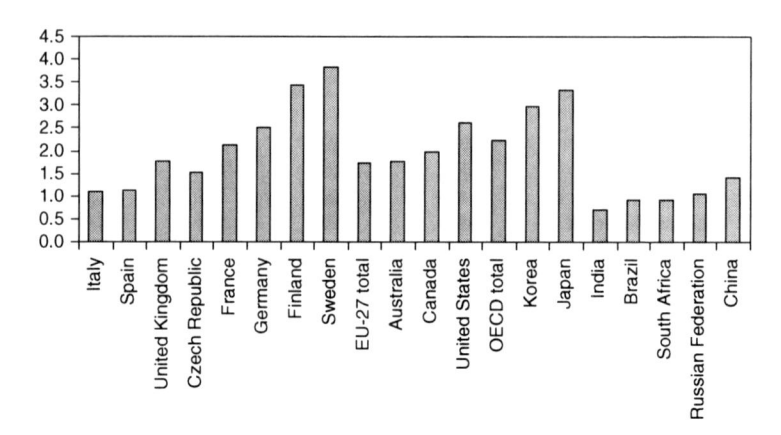

Figure 6.3 Gross domestic expenditure on R&D as % of GDP (2008)
Source: OECD (2008).

Table 6.4 Innovation in main OECD countries

	R&D intensity (2007)	Patents per capita (2005–7)
Canada	101.1	63.4
France	115.3	117.8
Germany	148.1	222.1
Italy	47.7	38.4
Japan	212.1	335.3
UK	94.7	80.6
USA	158.0	157.4

Source: OECD (2008).

most innovative from this point of view, followed by the US, France and the UK over the period 2005–7.

European countries therefore have relatively little weight on their own in the world, but, taken as a whole, they represent an important world economic power. However, since the beginning of the new century they have had increasing difficulty in speaking with one voice and in coordinating their policies. The failure to achieve the Lisbon Strategy objectives, the problems with the Stability and Growth Pact, the divergences emerging in external policy concerning the Iraq and Afghanistan wars and the failure in the ratification of the European Constitution in 2005 are numerous signs of this difficulty. The European Constitution has been saved by the simplified Treaty signed in Berlin in 2007, adopted in Lisbon in December of that year and, finally, ratified and coming into force in December 2009. A common strategy to face the financial crisis was discussed in Brussels in December 2008, but coordination of national efforts has been weak, so that the crisis plan has been just a sum of the national parts without exploiting much synergy. Even in the face of a major crisis of the European Monetary Union, European countries have not been able to agree and commit on a strategy on their own and they had to recourse to the IMF to face the Greek emergency.

The Lisbon Strategy: an industrial policy for the coherence of the Union at a time of deep transformations

In 2000, when Romano Prodi was still President of the European Commission, a long-term strategy for economic growth and employment was agreed and signed by all EU members in Lisbon. This strategy had a major objective, that of transforming the EU into the most competitive, knowledge-based economy by the year 2010. This broad objective was very ambitious – so ambitious that it did not aim to be realistic; rather, it aimed at mobilizing all EU members towards a common high goal that would renew commitment to the economic integration process. Its broad character was also probably chosen in order to leave room for different policy approaches to be adopted at Member States' level, be they more or less liberal, more or less focused on social or environmental issues.

In the following years, though, the Lisbon Strategy turned out to be a failure, for four main reasons. First, it was so broad that it appeared difficult to divide into coherent sub-objectives and action programmes. Second, each country adopted particular national reform programmes without much interaction at European level. The European Commission started monitoring national progress towards the achievement of the Lisbon objectives, but the exercise tended to be perceived by Member States as a sort of classification of the countries into good and bad pupils. Perhaps the excessive width of the strategy prevented the open coordination method[3] from functioning, since confronting and sharing experiences is more difficult when the objectives are many. For instance, coordinating on a specific policy question, such as developing a new technology or implementing some tax or voluntary agreement to reduce certain pollutants' emissions, may be easier, since the choice of instruments is clear and specific, while the potential gains from coordination are more easy to identify (for instance, pooling resources for the development of the new technology in a common European R&D programme). Third, some EU countries have been particularly limited in their ability to implement national reform programmes: countries in the Eurozone have had strong budget constraints in order to fulfil the Growth and Stability Pact and could not widely use fiscal policy to the aim of the Lisbon Strategy. Fourth, the objectives of the strategy may have appeared extremely far away for the new EU Member States, which had just transformed into market economies and found themselves at earlier stages of economic development than older members.

However, the Lisbon Strategy could have represented an important occasion for the European Union. In the end of the 1990s, the enlargement of the EU and the start of EMU created enormous challenges to the Union, enlarging membership hence political voices and economic disparities on the one hand, while deepening the economic integration process, with the monetary union, on the other hand. Enlarging meant increasing membership, political and economic disparities, while economic union meant deepening of the economic integration process but only between a restricted number of members. The risk of divide within the EU was therefore significant, new members embarking, unlike previous entry into the European Community, at very low levels of economic development, despite the strong support from the Union since the fall of the Berlin Wall and despite the significant transition period (about ten years). The Lisbon Strategy aimed at unifying all members towards common goals that had to be defined broadly because the only common denominator was very broad, given the very high divergence. In the past, the European Community tried first to reduce divergence and then define common goals and policies: for instance, the long transition period allowed before creating EMU was aimed at allowing the main economic indicators of future members to converge. Similarly, a common technology and science policy was started only in the 1980s, when Member States had reached an advanced level of economic development and a complete reconstruction after World War II.

The possibilities of coordination of national reforms reaching the Lisbon Strategy objectives may have been too weak, given these strong divergences – mainly between new members concerned by their economic and political transition, while EMU members were primarily concerned about the credibility of the common currency and the problems of the limited possibility for fiscal policies.

In the meantime, the worldwide competitive context was changing and putting increasing pressure on European business, which called for new supporting policies. The European Commission therefore came to a realization on industrial policy in an enlarged Union facing globalization. This realization highlighted that European industry could only gain in competitiveness by coordinating effort and exploiting synergies between instruments and between countries wherever possible. Therefore, the European Commission underlined that the new industrial policy had to be *integrated*.

Industrial policy as a long-term vision of development

Industrial policies can be defined as instruments aimed at guiding a structural adjustment process that impacts not only on the economic growth of countries but also on their social and civil development, hence also their political equilibrium, both within countries and between countries. These wider objectives of industrial development were stressed by classical economists such as Adam Smith (1776) and underlined by contemporary economists such as Sylos Labini (2006).

One key result of classical economists is precisely that economic growth is an instrument for the wider social and cultural development of societies. In Smith, the 'wealth of nations' is not just the total product of the country, but also equity and justice. The division of labour, hence industrial development, is a key determinant of the wealth of nations.

In the EU, industrial policies are necessary not only for the development of national industry, but also, more importantly, to favour the structural adjustment necessary in the economic integration process (Bianchi and Labory, 2009). The economic integration process is not just a process whereby national markets are put together so that firms can operate in the integrated market just as it is, efficient firms adjusting and remaining while non-efficient firms just leave the market. Economic integration indeed requires substantial institutional changes that have deep consequences for the division of labour (in Smithian terms). Economic integration requires the elimination of tariff and non-tariff barriers. The latter cannot be eliminated suddenly with a law but require a structural adjustment than can take much time. In fact, institutional barriers represent specific institutional conditions of a country that create obstacles to the import of goods or services from other countries. They can depend on consumer preferences, in turn depending upon cultural, social or religious traditions. Other institutional barriers include product regulations that impose specific standards on products sold on the national market. Another non-tariff barrier is the difference in growth models across countries – for instance, in the relation between family ownership and financial capital, or between state ownership and capital markets. The national specification of institutions that regulate economic development and the related political balances can constitute a non-tariff barrier, not only to the entry of external operators but also of the mobility of national operators abroad. In the same manner, the set of informal rules defined within social groups constitutes a non-tariff barrier. For instance, in the US bankruptcy is socially accepted while in Europe it tends to reduce social prestige, implying that European entrepreneurs may be more risk-averse and less prone to set up business in other Member States in the wider market.

Hence the economic integration process has deep implications on the institutional organization of a country and market integration requires a redefinition of the formal and informal rules that govern individuals' interactions. This process is very long, as has been shown by the long time period necessary to reach an advanced, but not complete, integration of the European single market.

As stressed by classical economists, the market is a social construct that requires rules in order to properly function. These rules concern property rights, modes of exchange (contract law) and the opportunities of distribution of the generated wealth. When individuals have the rights and capability to exchange on markets, markets must be constructed through the definition of collective rules that could allow the realization of positive dynamics between these individuals.

Industrial policy is made of actions aimed at both defining individual rights to exchange and at developing individual and collective capacity and competencies to exchange. In other words, industrial policy is made of instruments aimed at favouring institutional stabilization, at guiding structural adjustment and at consolidating the grouping of complementary specializations.

The economic integration process can thus be seen as a process whereby the extent of the market is increased, thereby allowing a wider labour division beyond national frontiers and therefore firm networks; unifying elements not only include geographical proximity and dependence on a government, they can also include the possibility of delineating new mechanisms for the definition of common institutions. The economic integration process is not only economic but, inevitably, also political.

It is therefore necessary to specify the effective historical conditions in which social aggregation processes are realized, and define industrial policy on this basis. The common market must be progressively built, on the basis of the ethical value of individual rights. The role of the state regarding the market is not to determine collective dynamics in an authoritarian manner, but to guarantee the functioning of the decentralized decision-making system.

Such a system only functions if public goods exist that keep individuals together. The most important such public good is the set of rules that guarantees the growth of the group through time. In this sense, the definition of public goods is crucial because it provides the group with a collective identity.

It is precisely in this sense that the Lisbon Strategy represented an industrial policy in a classical sense. It provided a vision of long-term development for the Union, with an ambitious objective regarding the development of the Union. In a sense, the Lisbon Strategy was aimed at being a public good for the Union, just as the single market and common policies are.

It is probably for this reason that it has been redefined and relaunched for the next period, in the 2020 Strategy. The 2020 Strategy is not fundamentally different from the Lisbon Strategy. It defines a development path for the Union through three particular (and broad) objectives: a focus on innovation and the knowledge-based economy ('smart growth'), an attention to the environment ('sustainable growth') and to social cohesion (employment, standards of living, in the term 'inclusive growth'). The European Commission has proposed to realize these objectives through seven initiatives, in the fields of innovation, education and training, the digital economy, environmental efficiency, industrial policy (in the sense of enterprise policy), labour market policies and policies against poverty. These objectives and broad initiatives can only be shared by all Member States, which have to define national reform plans to meet these objectives. Once again, the European Commission will monitor progress towards the 2020 objectives.

The Lisbon and now the 2020 strategies constitute therefore industrial policies as long-term visions of industrial (and wider) development, but only to a certain extent. These strategies indeed represent long-term visions only in so much as they formulate long-term objectives and very broad categories of actions. However, they are not complete 'visions' because they do not identify the structural elements and structural changes required to reach the identified development path. The identification of these structural elements is left to Member States, which individually implement the instruments most fitted to national conditions.

The importance of these structural elements is highlighted in Adam Smith's view of structural dynamics. The 'wealth of nations' is determined by the capacity to organize production and to learn. It is the capacity to organize production in forms that are appropriate to the extent of the market that determines the strategic position of firms and economic growth. The regulated opening of markets in a tariff union and subsequently an economic union thus constitutes an industrial policy because it induces firms to reorganize relative to the new market and to the new rivals.

Economic integration is thus the first industrial policy of the EU, because it leads to a direct confrontation of productive organizations that were previously protected by national institutions. The opening to Central and Eastern European countries has constituted, in the last decade, an important engine of economic development both for new and old members of the EU.

However, the market opening and integration process can be hurdled by some actions of the state, such as state aid. The first Treaty of the European Union, the Treaty of Rome, which created the European Economic Community, therefore prohibited state aid that would favour domestic firms at the expense of firms coming from other Member States, and allowed state ownership but on condition that it was not used to protect national champions.

The protection of the competitive process, in the sense of avoidance of abuse of dominant positions and of cartels, therefore constitutes the second industrial policy in an economic integration process.

To this second pillar was added across the years, and specifically from the 1980s onward, attention to territories and to innovation, since they can make competition more dynamic by allowing new entrants to markets. Territories matter because industrial development generally starts at that level, when there are 'good' institutions, especially for education and research, social guarantee and security, that determine conditions for agglomeration and for firm creation. Innovation as a factor for economic change cannot be reduced solely to technology; it also applies to organizational and social innovations, when knowledge and learning are considered as the main factors for growth (Bianchi and Labory, 2004).

All those elements were put together at European level in both the Lisbon Strategy and the 2020 Strategy, which called for more research and innovation, a more dynamic business environment, higher investment in training and education and a general industrial restructuring towards production systems and products that could preserve the environment. This requires coherent macroeconomic policies and a clear regulation framework for capital markets, an increasing political cohesion, in order for disequilibrium effects not to be created. In addition, it requires a common opening towards developing countries in order to ensure a balanced globalization.

The Lisbon Strategy has progressively evolved towards a more articulated set of instruments, but its main obstacle has been a lack of exploitation of synergies at European level, Member States deciding and implementing strategies at national level without much coordination given the above-mentioned limits of the open method of coordination. This method implemented by the European Commission indeed aims at favouring a process of convergence of national industrial policies, in the sense of promoting a set of actions geared towards industrial development, towards the wider objectives of the EU, but it has remained an exercise of exchange of information between Member States without a strong commitment towards collectively resolving European competitiveness problems.

President Barroso himself seems to recognize the main difficulty of the Lisbon Strategy, namely the lack of political commitment to its implementation. He argues in the preface to the 2020 Strategy (European Commission, 2010): 'We need to accept that the increased economic interdependence demands also a more determined and coherent response at the *political* level' (emphasis added). Member States should indeed gear instruments to national conditions, but they also should try to benefit from transnational synergies by coordinating their actions.

Concluding remarks

The history of the last 20 years has shown how the progressive and pragmatic approach is the most appropriate for the EU. The last enlargement raised numerous questions, of both an economic and a political nature. From an economic point of view the entry of Central and Eastern European countries has substantially increased the disparities in living conditions within the EU. From a political point of view, the last enlargement has raised questions about the capacity of the Union to accommodate the entry of such a large number of countries, hence of interests and voices in the negotiations at European level. The difficulties arising in the adoption of solutions to these uncertainties show the width of the problem.

These difficulties arise in a worldwide context characterized by what we call 'globalization', characterized by the evolution towards a multipolar world, with new world powers or, more precisely, returning powers, since China and India have returned to the role of world powers they used to have a few centuries ago. This multipolar world established in a context of high instability, with wars, terrorism and economic and financial crises.

The only approach that can be adopted to exit from the crisis is based on market opening, together with clear and stringent rules and measures to promote the transformation of the economy into a knowledge-based economy respecting the environment and ensuring social cohesion. This 'integrated' approach, however, only functions if numerous instruments are implemented in a coordinated manner at European, national and regional levels, thereby offering a governance of the system, complex and articulated, necessary to escape from authoritarian temptations prevailing in crises.

The European Commission's proposal for a new Strategy for the Union for the period 2010–20 states that 'the exit from the crisis should be the point of entry into a new sustainable social market economy, a smarter, greener economy, where our prosperity will come from innovation and from using resources better, and where the key input will be knowledge' (2009: 2). 'By acting together on a common vision, we can make the whole more than the sum of its parts' (2009: 4).

The 2020 Strategy was adopted in June 2010, but without a strong political commitment towards it. 'Intergovernmentalism' still prevails, without clear actions to coordinate national efforts. The strategy stresses the importance of both fiscal consolidation and measures to promote growth, but does not explain how these two objectives can be combined. The strategy also highlights relevant objectives, identifying a development path for the Union to which countries have to provide the instruments and structural elements so that the path is effectively taken at European level.

The Union, however, appears today as a Union of small and selfish interests, where each country aims at taking most individual benefits, not showing concern for collective benefits, whereas the worldwide context would require the union of grand designs that it has been in the past. As stressed by President Prodi in a speech in Munster in March 2010, the Union appears as a sum of conveniences that are negotiated through compromise up to the compromise of all compromises, which has been the Lisbon Treaty.

In this context, the new Union must be cured from the 'German syndrome', which has until now determined its growth, namely the paradox of an economic power that remains a political miniature. For this purpose, the Union should relaunch integration and collective action which, in a time of crisis, tends to vanish in favour of a focus on national strategies and performance. The structural adjustment necessary for the deeper integration of countries in the Eurozone and the convergence of new members, beyond the recovery plans after the crisis, must go back to the industrial policies elaborated in the last years in the EU, namely the policies aiming at providing the conditions for industrial development primarily by activating a nexus between innovation and territory, that allowed the Union to integrate progressively and peacefully in the last 60 years.

The core of the European project just lies there. The European project was initiated in the most tragic years of World War II, and aimed at a European community that could be a factor for peace and prosperity for the whole world. Given the difficulties in realizing a political union, the founding fathers of the European community chose to create the need for more political integration from the realizations in the field of economic convergence. After the last enlargement, and in the world political and economic context, the need for political unity is even greater in order to reduce economic disparities within Europe and, most of all, to allow European countries to have a voice and a geopolitical weight in the new multipolar world. In the current context industrial policies with long-term perspectives are more important than ever before, as economic instruments implemented to reach political means – that is, in the role they generally had in a historical perspective.

Without a common grand project the Union is likely to have a marginal role in the new multipolar world. As stressed by Romano Prodi, the absence of the US President Obama at the 20th anniversary of the fall of the Berlin Wall was a sign of this marginality, especially since he preferred to be in China.

Notes

1. http://epp.eurostat.ec.europa.eu/cache/ITY_PUBLIC/4-14092010-AP/EN/4-14092010-AP-EN.PDF.
2. http://www.oecd.org/document/27/0,3343,en_2649_201185_37770522_1_1_1_1,00.html.
3. Method by which Member States are invited to pursue the same objectives and experiences are confronted and shared so that best practices can diffuse in the EU.

References

Bianchi, P. and Labory, S. (eds) (2004) *The Economic Importance of Intangible Assets*, London: Ashgate.
Bianchi, P. and Labory, S. (2009) *Le nuove politiche industriali dell'Unione europea*, Bologna: Il Mulino.
Bianchi, P. and Labory, S. (2010) 'Economic Crisis and Industrial Policy', *Revue d'Economie Industrielle*, vol. 129–30, pp. 301–26.

European Commission (2009) Commission Working Document. Consultation on the Future 'EU 2020' Strategy, COM(2009) 647/3, Brussels.
European Commission (2010) 'Europe 2020. A European Strategy for Smart, Sustainable and Inclusive Growth', COM(2010) 2020, Brussels, 3 March 2010.
Eurostat (2009) *European Business: Facts and Figures*, Luxembourg: Eurostat.
IMF data mapper, http://www.imf.org/external/datamapper/index.php.
OECD (2008) *OECD Factbook*, Paris: OECD.
Prodi, R. (2008) *La mia visione dei fatti. Cinque anni di governo in Europa*, Bologna: Il Mulino.Smith, A. (1776) *The Wealth of Nations*, 2 vols, London: J. M. Dent & Sons, 1960 reprint.
Sylos Labini, P. (2006) *Torniamo ai classici. Produttività del lavoro, progresso tecnico e sviluppo economico*, 2nd edn, Rome: Editori Laterzat.
WTO (2009) International Trade Statistics, web-site: http://www.wto.org/english/res_e/statis_e/its2009_e/its09_toc_e.htm, as accessed on January, 4th, 2011.

Part II
The Impact of the Financial Crisis on Single European Countries

7
The UK and the Euro in the Aftermath of the Global Financial Crisis

Leila Simona Talani

Introduction

The euro is over a decade old and the UK has not yet decided to adopt it. Despite some timid attempts to revamp the debate about British entry into EMU made by the early Labour administration, the issue was left aside for a long time, to surge again to the attention of the public only with the explosion of the global financial crisis.

Why were British academics and politicians tempted to reopen the debate about EMU in the aftermath of the global financial crisis? Has the monetary union helped to limit the damages of the crisis or has it accentuated them, exposing the weaknesses of an economic crisis whose political dimension is still far from being properly addressed (as the Greek fiscal crisis clearly demonstrated)?

This chapter answers the above questions, addressing the issue of the role played by the City of London in the whole debate about the process of European monetary integration.

The case for the UK to join the EMU after the global financial crisis

The case for joining EMU has never been as pressing as at the start of the global financial crisis. Leading scholars and public opinion-makers in the UK joined the debate promoting accession in various occasions (Bishop *et al.*, 2009).

Mike Artis,[1] quoting Keynes, attributes to the changed economic climate the need to rethink British position towards the euro (Artis, 2009). When the euro was launched, the British economy enjoyed a long period of economic growth with almost no inflationary pressures compounded by a strong pound. None of these circumstances applies today. Moreover, contrary to what the City of London believed, the European Central Bank policy has been well considered and well conducted and effectively sheltered euro area countries from the worse consequences of the crisis (*ibid.*: 12). Iceland's fate is an instructive example for the UK not to follow. Although certainly Iceland is smaller than the UK, the British GDP has certainly fallen in recent years. And, even more certainly, financial globalization rendered smaller countries more vulnerable than ever. In conclusion, joining the euro area would allow the British economy to enjoy all the advantages of a big economy in a world economic climate which is more unstable and uncertain than before (*ibid.*: 13).

The need to overcome the rhetoric about the five economic tests is advocated by Iain Begg.[2] The 'current febrile economic environment' (Begg, 2009: 20) should open up the debate on whether they are still appropriate. The five tests were set out in 1997 by the then Chancellor, Gordon Brown, to assess whether or not the economic benefits of euro membership exceeded the costs and therefore justified joining. However, their purpose was also a political one, namely to avoid taking a decision until 'the time is ripe'. In 2003, an in-depth assessment of the five economic tests ruled out the possibility of joining 'for the time being'. However, the tests could not forecast the current financial and economic crisis and crucially overlooked the connection between the currency regime and financial stability. The credit crunch has made clear that this approach is inappropriate and that, in a situation in which financial markets are globally interconnected, membership of the euro area would shelter the British economy (*ibid.*: 22), not to mention the fact that the much-needed regulatory reforms that will have to ensue from the crisis could require a much higher level of governance than the national one, and therefore the UK could be left away from key decision-making tables (*ibid.*: 22).

Also according to Willem Buiter[3] the economic case for the UK to adopt the euro in the present circumstances is overwhelming (Buiter, 2009: 40). Indeed, reviewing the five economic tests in the light of the global financial crisis, there is no doubt in the opinion of Buiter that they are all fulfilled. Leaving aside the third test (investment) and the fifth test (growth, stability employment), which would be satisfied if and only if the other three are satisfied, he assesses the first, second and fourth tests. The main new finding of this analysis is that the global financial crisis is in itself a powerful and sufficient argument for the UK to enter the EMU as soon as possible. This is because it adds a financial stability dimension to the already strong optimal currency ones (*ibid.*). Concluding, the author advocates immediate UK membership to the euro zone. This is supported by, on the one hand, the conventional optimal currency area criteria (convergence, flexibility, labour mobility, fiscal flexibility). Moreover, with the global crisis a new financial stability criterion has emerged. Membership of the euro zone is essential for the UK to avoid a triple financial crisis (a banking, currency and sovereign debt crisis). These crises would be inevitable otherwise because the UK belongs to a group of countries characterized by a new inconsistent quartet: 1. a small country with 2. a large internationally exposed banking sector, 3. a currency that is not a global reserve currency and 4. limited fiscal capacity relative to the possible size of the banking sector solvency gap. Euro zone membership would eliminate the third member of the quartet and by reducing liquidity risk premia, and could even reduce the impact of the fourth element (*ibid.*: 57).

The fall in the value of the pound is what most worries Graham Bishop in his statement in support of British entry.[4]

According to David Lea,[5] saving the pound means making it the 'Euro Pound' (Lea, 2009: 126). The free-fall of the pound should be considered unacceptable even by the most chauvinist of Britons. The reason why it is happening is, according to Lea, first, the role of financial services in the UK's economic structure and, second, after the banking collapse, the inevitable fiscal expansionary policy. To give stability to the British economy it is imperative to stabilize the exchange rate with the main trade partner of the UK, which is the euro area. Consequently the British government has to admit that the five economic tests have been met and allow the country to enter the euro zone (*ibid.*: 135).

The question, therefore, is only whether to join the euro by a rational decision or through a crisis, according to John Palmer (Palmer, 2009: 142).[6]

Stefan Collignon[7] reintroduces in the debate the political dimension, addressing the issue of how sovereignty and democracy can help in promoting the case for British membership of the euro area (Collignon, 2009: 61). His argument is based on the need to guarantee European democracy as the next step of European integration after the adoption of the single currency. Entry of the UK into EMU would contribute to increasing the level of European democracy, legitimizing the process of European integration further (*ibid.*: 68).

Politics is at the heart of Brendan Donnelly's intervention in the debate (Donnelly, 2009: 78).[8] The silence of all British political parties regarding EMU in the face of the global financial crisis is yet more proof of the dysfunctionalism of the British political system where European questions are concerned. The case proposed by the then Chancellor of the Exchequer, Gordon Brown, that British distinctiveness and economic and financial superiority made it unthinkable to join the euro, has been blatantly disproved by the events ensuing from the crisis. British distinctiveness as an economic model has proved to be fraught with dangerous errors, which will bring the UK to a more severe recession than that of any of its neighbours. Also, in the opinion of Nicolas Stevenson,[9] there is no doubt that the myth of the superiority of UK economic performance, on the basis of which the decision not to join EMU in 1998 was taken, should be abandoned (Stevenson, 2009: 169).

In his analysis, Niels Thygesen[10] demonstrates to what extent this idea that the UK could not join the euro area by virtue of a superior framework for macroeconomic policy was wrong, especially in the light of the most recent events. Besides, political considerations in the UK public debate weighing against any such participation cannot be discarded (Thygesen, 2010).

For Richard Basset (Basset, 2009: 13) the issue of British membership of the euro area is indeed mainly a political one. The problem is to obtain consensus in public opinion on a policy which is badly needed in the light of the global financial crisis. The gravity of the crisis, the dramatic devaluation of the pound and, again, the Icelandic experience, suggest that a change of opinion of the British public is desirable (ibid.: 15). Moreover, it is apparent to the author that the Bank of England has misjudged the situation and is endangering British economic future with its too low interest rate policy. And this is apparent even to the 'man in the street' (ibid.: 16). However, there is a major obstacle to British entry: at present a referendum held on euro membership would offer little guarantee of success for the pro-euro cause. The media are not helping the cause, with Murdoch positively boycotting it.

However, not all British media are currently against joining the single currency. David Seymour, a former political editor of the Mirror Group, is an enthusiastic supporter of UK entry to the euro. He also believes that a referendum on the subject could be won. Indeed, although only months before the referendum of 1975 on continued membership of the Common Market polls indicated that British public opinion was opposed, the result was almost two to one in favour (Seymour, 2009: 148).

One of the hottest topics of discussion in the wake of the global financial crisis is that of banking supervision. The need for global economic governance of the banking and financial sector has been underlined in a number of international forums and enjoys the support of leading world politicians, not least the US President Obama.[11] David Green, former Head of International Policy at the Financial Services Authority (FSA), assesses to what extent it matters for the UK to be out of the euro and European supervision (Green, 2009). When the euro was launched, the idea of having pan-European banking and financial supervision seemed pretty theoretical and therefore it really didn't matter if the single market coincided with the single currency area. In fact, even in the euro area banking and financial supervision remained in the hands of the national central banks. Moreover, when, after some discussions, a separate banking supervision committee at EU-wide level was created, the Committee of European Banking Supervisors, this was not only outside the ECB but was also physically located in London, on the model of the UK's FSA. Besides, as London clearly became the dominant financial centre of Europe, the UK was substantially involved in the drafting of the Financial Services Action Plan, and never marginalized for not being part of the EMU (*ibid.*: 99). The current crisis might bring into question the assumption that being outside the EMU does not matter for supervision. Indeed, the role of the Central Bank as the lender of last resort, which has been highlighted by the current situation, has also put in evidence the need for the Central Bank to exert a closer control on the banking and financial institutions. An idle clause in the Maastricht Treaty gives the ECB a formal role in banking supervisory policy. Although this has not yet been activated, it is evident that euro area Central Banks have a forum to coordinate their interventions in the banking systems from which the UK is excluded. Also many euro area banks have been active in London and their supervisory authorities have noticed how much of the business leading to the crisis was conducted in the British capital where, however, they do not have jurisdiction. This might propose again the need for the UK to join the euro area to have a say on the future outlook of banking and financial supervision in Europe (*ibid.*: 101).

A parallel argument is proposed by Dirk Hazell.[12] Financial services regulation failed to move with the times, provoking disaster. However, this gives Europe a historically unprecedented opportunity to build an exceptionally strong and effective capital market by enacting proper common regulation. If the British government wants to keep the centrality of the City of London as the financial market of Europe, it cannot afford to remain outside this process and needs to take the decision to join the EMU (Hazell, 2009: 110).

According to Will Hutton,[13] it is finally 'Time to be brave' (Hutton, 2009: 112). The idea that Britain is doing fine outside the euro and will continue to do so, has been called into question by recent financial events. His argument is that euro membership must be considered as a strategic move allowing Britain to keep its leadership of the international financial markets and, equally, to boost its knowledge-intensive manufacturing and service sectors. Britain would finally be at the heart of a major currency block, which will increasingly shape the world's international financial system. Moreover, it would support its industrial sector by adopting the euro at a favourable exchange rate and stabilizing its interest rate policy (ibid.: 118).

The excessive risk-taking attitude of global financial markets in general and the City of London in particular is also at the heart of Richard Laming's intervention in the debate over UK's entry into EMU.[14]

Let's face it, adds Peter Sutherland,[15] adopting a counterfactual analysis, the UK would have had fewer problems during the financial crisis if it had entered EMU in 1998 (Sutherland, 2009: 184). And even if the UK was better off staying outside during the first ten years of the euro, it is now time to rethink this decision (Münchau, 2009: 136) according to the opinion of Wolfang Münchau.[16] Economic circumstance over the next ten years are doomed to change so profoundly that the balance between the benefits of joining and the costs will be overturned. First of all, finance will not any longer be the main specialization of Britain; the country will have to find a new one. Second, the era of global free-floating exchange rates will come to an end slowly as floating exchange rates have not aided current account adjustment. In Europe, this would mean that accession to the euro zone would continue, and all of Eastern Europe EU, plus Denmark and Iceland, will join. This would leave the UK in the unsustainable position of an independent exchange rate country at the fringes of a stable exchange rate block. The exchange rate of the pound would be more volatile; investors would ask higher interest rates. Membership of the euro would help reducing those risks. Concluding, the external situation will change so dramatically that the past benefits of staying out will be wiped out. This change will ultimately be reflected by change in public opinion (ibid.: 140).

The majority of the analyses reported above insist on the changes that the global financial crisis will have not only on the British economic strategy, but, more importantly, on the structure itself of the British economy. It seems almost inevitable that the role of the financial sector will decline, although it does not emerge clearly what would take its place. Moreover, the centrality of the City of London as the 'European' financial capital or as a global financial power has been allegedly put in danger by the crisis. This has led the economists and commentators above to identify as a solution joining the euro area. Indeed, it is not the first time more integration of the UK into Europe has been advocated as the panacea of sudden and seemingly otherwise irresolvable problems of the British economy. This happened before, notably when the UK decided to enter the Exchange Rate Mechanism (ERM) of the European Monetary System (EMS) in October 1990, to leave it shortly thereafter in September 1992. And there have also already been, according to the scholars, moments in the development of the British capitalist structure in which it seemed as if the power of the City had been finally overcome. But somehow the City has always been able to emerge again as the dominant actor of the British socio-economic scene. Will this happen again? Maybe it is too soon to say, but having a look at the reasons underlying British decision not to enter EMU in the first place might shed some light on the future position of the UK towards the euro.

Why did the UK not join EMU in the first place?

The British stance towards the whole process of European monetary integration has been deeply influenced by the City of London's preferences. It is therefore logical to think that the future British government's position towards entry into EMU is also likely to be deeply affected by the City's preferences and interests. It becomes thus necessary to analyze why the UK decided not to join EMU which, in turn, is related to the impact that EMU was perceived to have on the City of London. Indeed, such an impact is also one of the five economic tests to enter EMU set by the Labour Chancellor of the Exchequer on 27 October 1997. In this section, therefore, the impact of EMU on each individual market of the City of London, and on the institutions acting in them, will be studied and conclusions drawn on the advantages and disadvantages for London as a leading financial centre from the establishment of a European single currency area.

Well-developed money markets, both sterling and foreign currencies' ones, are a key feature of the UK financial system, making a major contribution to, and being partly the result of, London's position as a leading financial centre (Talani, 2000). A market-orientated environment, notably the absence of minimum reserve requirements, is a particular strength of these markets. In the wake of the establishment of EMU, the City's position as a participant could have been very adversely affected, if onerous reserve requirements were imposed by the ECB at zero interest rates or at interest rates lower than market ones. London is a leading international, not only European, financial centre, and thus its competitive position towards New York or Tokyo would be greatly undermined by the imposition of similar restrictions. Moreover, onerous reserve requirements could spur the developments of off-shore euro money markets, as the EU banks minimize the amount of deposits subject to punitive charges, which, if the UK were inside the EMU area, would necessarily be set outside the City of London, possibly in one of its international rival financial centres: this, of course, makes a very strong case against Britain's participation in EMU altogether. Indeed, if the UK did not participate in EMU, sterling and other London-based money markets would clearly continue in existence, while an ECB regime with reserve requirements set higher than those in the UK, which means any requirement since in the UK there is none, could help the competitive position of sterling markets or let London become the centre for Euro-euro deposit trading, as it would become a natural location for excess liquidity seeking to escape the onerous, or even not so onerous, ECB regime. Moreover, the City's position as an international money market centre, namely, its dominant position in the already established euro currency and euro commercial paper markets, would not suffer any threat (*ibid.*).

Moving to the London Foreign Exchange market, when EMU was established it was already the largest in the world, with a daily turnover of $464 billion in 1995, an increase of some 60 per cent compared to three years earlier and more than the turnover of New-York and Tokyo combined (British Invisibles, 1996), and with a market share in steady growth of 30 per cent in 1995. The majority of its activity was linked to the $US and its dominant role in global trade, focusing, in particular to the $/£, $/DM and $/yen trades with the $/DM business predominating in the spot market, while in the forward market trades in the three currency pairs were of the same magnitude (see Table 7.1 below).

The market was a wholesale one dominated by banks, accounting for over 70 per cent of trading, and its truly international nature was made clear by the fact that non-UK-owned banks were responsible for almost 80 per cent of market turnover, while sterling was involved in less than 20 per cent of all transactions (BBA, 1996: 31). Given its evident global character, if the UK remained outside the EMU area, the competitive threats for London as a centre for foreign exchange trading activity were judged to be fairly low while, on the contrary, it was anticipated that the City would still remain a major location for euro trading. The loss of revenues consequent on the disappearance of former currencies would clearly be directly proportionate to the number of currencies participating

Table 7.1 Relative shares of total turnover in London by currencies traded (1995)

	%		
	Spot	Forward	Total
£/US$	3.1	8.3	11.5
US$/DM	11.8	9.7	21.5
US$/yen	5.7	11.3	17.0
US$/Swiss franc	1.7	3.7	5.5
US$/French franc	0.9	4.5	5.5
US$/Canadian$	0.5	1.9	2.4
US$/Australian$	0.4	1.2	1.6
US$/lira	0.4	2.9	3.4
US$/peseta	0.2	1.8	2.1
US$/other EMS	0.8	5.1	5.9
US$/other	1.2	2.9	4.2
£/DM	2.8	0.4	3.2
£/other	0.4	1.0	1.3
DM/yen	1.9	0.3	2.2
DM/other EMS	4.8	0.9	5.7
ECU denominated	1.1	3.0	4.1
Other cross currencies	2.3	0.8	3.1

Source: *Bank of England Quarterly Bulletin*, November 1995.

in EMU, as well as dependent on the turnover of euro trading. However, it would certainly be lower if sterling did not take part in the single currency area, since trading in sterling would not disappear.

On the other hand, if the UK entered the single currency area, the disappearance of trades between former national currencies in the EMU area would account for less than 20 per cent of turnover on the London market, a lower proportion than that estimated for the other European Foreign Exchange, and, again, this loss could be overcome by trading in euros (Levitt, 1996a). Overall, the London Foreign Exchange would remain neutral to EMU whether sterling entered or whether it did not enter, the only likely implications being legal ones, namely the need for agreement on relevant market conventions and of legal preservation of contracts continuity in conversion from previous currencies to euros.

Finally, as far as the infrastructure is concerned, the fact that most of the foreign exchange trades are settled on a bilateral basis means that there will not be the same need for centralized infrastructural preparation that will be required in the money whole markets.

As far as capital markets are concerned, the transition to a single currency would have an immediate impact on the City-based government and corporate debt markets, including the euro markets, even if the UK did not participate. Regarding the corporate bond market, if the UK participated from the outset, UK corporations would have the option, but not the obligation, to issue bonds denominated in euros in the transition phase from 1 January 1999 until 1 January 2002, but after the latter date, all new issues would have to be in euros. This raised two major issues, the first one concerning the resolution of legal problems relating to continuity of contracts (BBA, 1996: 14) and the other one relating to the ability, if not need, for companies to redenominate in euros any existing debt before start of phase 3, with all that it implied in terms of costs and of the decision over the legal framework in which to effect these operations. However, corporations could, of course, continue to issue debt in other non-EMU area currencies, and also via the euro bond market, allowing for the development and establishment of a Euro-euro bond market – that is, an off-shore market in bonds denominated in euros, which, were the UK inside EMU, would obviously be outside London, thus certainly undermining London's share of primary and secondary international bonds trading. If the UK did not participate in EMU, then UK corporations could still issue euro-denominated debt, either as foreign bonds within an EMU-area state, or as euro bonds in the Euro-euro bond market which, with the UK outside EMU, would certainly be located in London.

With respect to the British government's bond market, if the UK participated in EMU from the outset, new gilt issues after 1 January 1999 would be denominated in euros, as would new central government debt issues in all EMU area states. However, as the credit risk posed by each central government issuer would still differ, pricing of all such debt would also show differences. Regardless of EMU, primary market activity would remain nationally orientated, at least as long as restriction on cross-border primary dealing was not withdrawn, while secondary market activity would concentrate in London as it did already. This scenario would be unchanged even if the UK did not enter the EMU, but a potential threat would arise if EMU area states lifted the local presence requirements for the primary market for central government bonds only for each other, and not for non-participants: UK-based firms would then miss an opportunity to compete for this business. Some concerns were also expressed over the ability of the City to maintain its share in non-sterling business, including that of the new euro market. We have seen above how unfounded similar concerns were (Talani, 2000).

At the time, it was felt that the impact of EMU on the London share markets would be gradual. If the British government decided to enter, the London market could benefit from the ending of currency restrictions on the investment of institutional investors in the EMU area, but at the same time the advent of the single currency might reduce the number of individual stock exchanges in which the investors might seek listing, thus intensifying the competition with the City (*ibid.*).

In the event that the UK did not participate in EMU, equity markets would continue in sterling. However, it was possible that issuers from within the EMU area would wish to trade in euros on the SEAQ.

Overall, the City seemed confident that, if preparations were carried out in due time, and British markets had adequate access to euro liquidity and payments mechanisms, and, generally, if the EMU countries did not adopt discriminatory measures, then the UK, even outside EMU, could live with its competitive pressures (*ibid.*).

Regarding the derivative markets, if the UK participated in EMU then all exchange-listed contracts related to sterling interest rates, along with other EMU area interest rate contracts and the ECU contract, would cease to exist and be replaced by a euro rate contract. As well over 90 per cent of trading volume in interest rate and bond products was at that time composed of assets in currencies which could potentially be replaced by the euro, it would be of critical importance for the London International Financial Futures and Options Exchange (LIFFE) to win a high market share of the new markets (see Table 7.2 below).

If the UK did not take part in EMU, then sterling rate and gilt contracts would continue to be traded, so that the proportion of trading volume that would be replaced by euro-denominated contracts would be around 70 per cent. In reality the LIFFE did not have any problems in keeping its dominant position after the establishment of EMU, despite

Table 7.2 Overall EMU impact activity on turnover in financial futures and options: principal exchanges

Rank	Exchange	1994 turnover (million contracts)	% potential EMU impact*
1	Chicago Mercantile Exchange	156.31	10.65%
2	LIFFE	148.73	92.27%
3	Chicago Board of Trade	139.48	0%
4	Marché à Terme International de France	93.1	91.65%
5	Deutsche Terminbörse	49.32	41.84%

Note: * Percentage of volume of trade in any potential EMU currency interest rate or bond instrument in relation to the total volume of financial contracts.
Source: BBA (1996).

the UK remaining outside it. Also in the over the counter markets (OTC) there was no scope for competitive threats in the event of the UK remaining outside EMU (Talani, 2000).

Moving to the impact of EMU on some key City services, as far as fund management was concerned, according to the Institutional Fund Managers' Association, the direct impact of EMU on the industry was likely to be fairly limited (BBA, 1996). Although the extension to the whole EMU area of currency matching rules, requiring up to 80 per cent of assets to be denominated in the currency in which the liabilities arise, would increase the scope of asset diversification in the common currency area, thereby also increasing the opportunities for banks with fund management capabilities (Levitt, 1996a), UK fund managers could benefit from the impact on currency matching rules even in the case of non-participation in EMU.

The City of London was also extremely competitive in corporate banking thanks to its undisputed expertise and professionalism. However, competitive pressures from within the single currency area were expected to increase a lot with the entry of the UK into EMU, since corporations would be likely to rationalize treasury operations and existing banking relationships in the EMU area. Also competitive pressures from outside might have increased as a consequence of the imposition within EMU of a relatively onerous regime – for example, reserve requirements, on the banking industry. The impact on corporate banking would clearly be less if the UK did not participate in EMU (BBA, 1996).

Finally, as UK insurers were much more involved in the US market than their European counterparts and the most of the London market business was conducted in dollars, EMU impact on this business was judged to be fairly limited.[17]

Conclusion

In conclusion, as the Thatcher government's 'wait and see' attitude towards the Exchange Rate Mechanism of the European Monetary System perfectly matched the British financial sector preferences for a set of monetarist practices inconsistent with the pegging of the exchange rates, also the British government's 'wait and see' attitude towards the Maastricht way to EMU concealed a balance between the pros and the cons of EMU for the City of London, which is still erring on the cons side.

That the preferences of the British financial community might change after the global financial crisis is, of course, a possibility that cannot be discarded *a priori*. However, it is possible to claim, on the basis of the analysis of the impact of EMU on the City's markets and institutions, that, *rebus sic stantibus*, the City of London would still prefer the British government to avoid committing the UK to EMU.

Indeed, as the success of the City of London has always been determined by its ability to adapt to the changing environment, its markets and institutions will certainly be able to react to the global financial crisis. However, it is precisely this capacity to adapt quickly to react to the changing global environment that can be raised for discussion by entry of the UK into EMU. In turn, this 'pragmatic adaptation' has been recognized by the scholars interested in the development of the British capitalist elite as an almost 'ontological feature' of the British financial sector.

In 1998, as today, British participation in EMU certainly undermined this capacity of the City of London by first of all imposing restrictions on the working of its markets and institutions. In general, the City loses by being submitted to external controls. Moreover, entry into the EMU will affect the City's international primacy by eliminating the possibility for London to keep its role as the main off-shore market in euro or euro-denominated assets,[18] a role that, were the UK to join EMU, would certainly be developed by one of its major world competitors.

Finally, it is also necessary to take into consideration the domestic economic consequences of joining a monetary union. These are usually included in the all-embracing expression of loss of sovereignty, and in the case of the City of London this would mean losing the possibility to influence domestic monetary and exchange rate policies.

Given all this, it should not be particularly surprising that the debate over the entry of the UK in the euro area has not yet been officially reopened by the British government and, in the opinion of the author, it is unlikely to be reopened despite the global financial crisis.

Notes

1. Michael Artis is currently the Welsh Assembly Government Visiting Research Professor in the University of Swansea. He is a Fellow of the British Academy and Research Fellow of the Centre for Economic Policy Research.
2. Iain Begg is Professor at the European Institute, LSE. See Begg (2009): 20.
3. Willem H. Buiter is Professor of European Political Economy European Institute, London School of Economics and Political Science, CEPR and NBER.

140 *The UK and the Euro in the Aftermath of the Global Financial Crisis*

4. For the past two decades, Graham Bishop has specialized in the deregulation of Europe's financial markets due to the Single Market programme and monetary union. He has been an adviser to both the House of Commons and House of Lords on EU financial issues, a member of several key European Commission committees and represented the European Parliament in monitoring the integration of EU capital markets.
5. David Lea (Lord Lea of Crondall), AGS TUC, 1977–99, Vice-President ETUC, 1994–9; Treasury Advisory Group on the Euro, 1998–9.
6. John Palmer is a leading writer and commentator on European Union affairs. From 1975 to 2006 he was the Brussels-based European Editor of the *Guardian*. From 1996 to 2006 he was the Founding Political Director of the European Policy Centre in Brussels. He is an experienced radio and television broadcaster. Current positions: Member of the Advisory Council of the European Policy Centre, Brussels; Member of the EU Advisory Board of the European Foundation for Management Development, Brussels; Member of the Advisory Council of TASC (Think Tank for Action on Social Change), Dublin; Member of the Advisory Board of the Federal Trust, London; Visiting (Practitioner) Fellow with the European Institute, the University of Sussex, UK; Member of the Advisory Group of the Governance of Globalization Network, Globus et Locus, Milan.
7. Stefan Collignon was a professor at the London School of Economics and Harvard University and now teaches at Sant' Anna School of Advanced Studies, Pisa, www.stefancollignon.eu.
8. Brendan Donnelly was a Member of the European Parliament from 1994–9 and a founder of the Pro-Euro Conservative Party (1999–2004). Previously he worked for the Foreign and Commonwealth Office, the European Parliament and the European Commission.
9. Nicolas Stevenson is Head of European Equity Strategy at Mirabaud Securities in London. He has worked in European economic and financial analysis for over 30 years. He writes in his personal capacity.
10. Emeritus Professor of Economics, University of Copenhagen; Member of the Delors Committee on EMU, 1988–9.
11. See *Financial Times*, various issues.
12. The first European General Counsel and Compliance Director of Daiwa Securities, Dirk Hazell was an arbitrator at the SFA and ran IPMA before becoming the CEO of the Environmental Services Association in 1999. With an MA from the University of Cambridge, where he was an Exhibitioner, he is a barrister.
13. Will Hutton is Executive Vice-Chair of the Work Foundation, Professorial Fellow at the LSE and regular columnist for the *Observer*. He has written a number of books, including *The State We're In*, *The Writing on the Wall* and *The World We're In*. Will Hutton writes in a personal capacity.
14. Richard Laming is Director of Federal Union and Secretary of the European Movement.
15. Peter Sutherland is a former EU Commissioner. He writes in a personal capacity.
16. Wolfgang Münchau is associate editor and columnist of the *Financial Times*, with a special focus on European economics and politics, and global finance. Together with his wife, the economist Susanne Mundschenk, he has founded

eurointelligence.com, an internet service that provides daily comment and analysis of the euro area, targeted at investors, academics and policy-makers. Wolfgang was one of the founding members of *Financial Times Deutschland*, the German-language business daily, where he served as deputy editor from 1999 until 2001, and as editor-in-chief from 2001 until 2003. *FT Deutschland* is now firmly established.
17. In fact, in these cases premiums are usually kept down by reliance on high investment returns.
18. In its December 1997 report on the euro, the Bank of England clearly claims:
'The introduction of the Euro represents an opportunity for London rather than a threat. There will be a vigorous Euro-euro market in London, just as there is a vigorous Euro-DM, Euro-franc, Euro-$ and Euro-yen now.' See Bank of England (1997): 12.

References

Artis, M., (2009), 'British Membership of the Euro: Time to Think Again?', in G. Bishop *et al 10 Years of the Euro: New Perspectives for Britain*, London: John Stevens.
Bank of England (1997) *Practical Issues Arising from the Introduction of the Euro*, no. 6, 10 December.
Basset, R. (2009) 'Winning Hearts and Minds: The Battle for British Public Opinion', in Bishop *et al.*, *10 Years of the Euro: New Perspectives for Britain*, London: John Stevens.
Begg, I. (2009) 'Time to Look Beyond the Five Tests?', in Bishop *et al.*, *10 Years of the Euro: New Perspectives for Britain*, London: John Stevens.
Bishop, G. (2009) 'Britain's Eternal Vulnerability: Sterling', in Bishop *et al.*, *10 Years of the Euro: New Perspectives for Britain*, London: John Stevens.
Bishop, G., Buiter, W., Donnelly, B. and Hutton, W. (2009) *10 Years of the Euro: New Perspectives for Britain*, London: John Stevens.
BBA (British Banking Association), Association for Payment Clearing Services, London Investment Banking Association (1996) *Preparing for EMU: the implication of European Monetary Union for the banking and financial markets in the United Kingdom*, Report of the EMU City Working Group, London: BBA, APACS, LIBA, September, Background Papers, Money Markets.
British Invisibles (1996) *Invisibles Facts and Figures*, London: BI.
Buiter, W. (2009) 'The Overwhelming Economic Case for the United Kingdom Adopting the Euro', in Bishop *et al.*, *10 Years of the Euro: New Perspectives for Britain*, London: John Stevens.
Collignon, S. (2009) 'Sovereignty, Democracy and the Euro' in Bishop *et al.*, *10 Years of the Euro: New Perspectives for Britain*, London: John Stevens.
Crosby, N. (2009) 'The European Consequences of David Cameron', in Bishop *et al.*, *10 Years of the Euro: New Perspectives for Britain*, London: John Stevens.
Donnelly, B. (2009) 'The Silence of the Lambs', in Bishop *et al.*, *10 Years of the Euro: New Perspectives for Britain*, London: John Stevens.
Green, D. (2009) 'The Euro and European Supervision: Does the UK Being 'Out' Matter?', in Bishop *et al.*, *When the Facts Change I Change My Mind*. Hazell, D.

(2009) 'Securing Sustainable Capital Markets', in Bishop *et al.*, *10 Years of the Euro: New Perspectives for Britain*, London: John Stevens.

Hutton, W. (2009) 'Time to be Brave ...', in Bishop *et al.*, *10 Years of the Euro: New Perspectives for Britain*, London: John Stevens.

Laming, R. (2009) 'Should Britain Join the Euro? A Lesson from History', in Bishop *et al.*, *10 Years of the Euro: New Perspectives for Britain*, London: John Stevens.

Lea, D. (2009) 'Let's Save the Pound: Make it the Euro-Pound', in Bishop *et al.*, *10 Years of the Euro: New Perspectives for Britain*, London: John Stevens.

Levitt, M. (1996a) 'European Monetary Union: The Impact on Banking', Royal Institute of International Affairs Conference, 13–14 March, London.

Levitt, M. (1996b) 'EMU: A View from the Banking Sector', *Journal of European Public Policy*, vol. 3, no. 3, September: 499–514.

Münchau, W. (2009) 'The Benefits of Euro Area Membership from a Purely Economic Perspective', in Bishop *et al.*, *10 Years of the Euro: New Perspectives for Britain*, London: John Stevens.

Palmer, J. (2009) 'Joining the Euro: By Rational Decision or Through Crisis?', in Bishop *et al.*, *10 Years of the Euro: New Perspectives for Britain*, London: John Stevens.

Seymour, D. (2009) 'A Fight We Can Win', in Bishop *et al.*, *10 Years of the Euro: New Perspectives for Britain*, London: John Stevens.

Stevenson, N. (2009) 'Sterling and the Myth of UK Economic Performance', in Bishop *et al.*, *10 Years of the Euro: New Perspectives for Britain*, London: John Stevens.

Sutherland, P. (2009) 'Facing Reality', in Bishop *et al.*, *10 Years of the Euro: New Perspectives for Britain*, London: John Stevens.

Thygesen, N., (2010) 'Rebuilding Euro Governance', web-site: hhttp://www.project-syndicate.org/commentary/thygesen5/English as accessed on December 4, 2010.

Talani, L. S. (2000) *Betting For and Against EMU*, London: Ashgate.

8
The Greek Debt Crisis: Causes, Policy Responses and Consequences

Antimo Verde

Introduction

A dramatic debt crisis erupted in Greece at the beginning of 2010 when everyone believed the world economy was recovering well and before expected. After a protracted period of hesitation, due to the the doubts of Angela Merkel, the German Chancellor which worsened the crisis, eventually, the EU decided to bailout Greece. An impressive 750 billion euro Greek rescue plan has been approved.

The European Council has set up a 440 billion euro European Financial Stability Facility and 50 billion euro in loans from the IMF, while the European Central Bank has been called on to buy Greek bonds and to stabilize markets of public and private bonds.

However, despite the EU and the Greek government's policy measures to quell financial unrest, the sovereign debt crisis is not over. At the time of writing, it affected Ireland and is threatening to spread to Spain, Portugal and Italy. It might well be hypothesized that it goes well beyond the problems arising from the fiscal positions of Greece and peripheral European economies: it crucially touches the future of EMU.

To verify this hypothesis, this chapter is divided into two parts. In the first part an attempt will be made to reconstruct the *facts*. This will imply identifying the immediate causes as well as the catalyst factors which sped up the crisis or made it critical (section 2); the structural causes (section 3) and, finally, policy responses to the crisis (section 4).

In the second part, the most important consequences and implications of the Greek crisis will be addressed from the following points of view: the effectiveness of European fiscal rules (i.e., the Stability and a Growth Pact), the independence of the ECB and the meaning and limits of the *no-bailout clause* and, eventually, the future of EMU. With respect to the latter, a model of a *two-speed Europe* will be provided.

Some short concluding remarks close the chapter.

The Greek crisis: the immediate causes and catalyst factors

Starting from the analysis of the immediate causes of the crisis and those factors which accelerated and/or made it critical, it seems to the author that the following aspects should be considered:

1. The dramatic Greek public finance situation, which had allegedly been hidden, for years.
2. the faltering behaviour of the German Chancellor Angela Merkel;
3. the consequences of the international financial crisis, which erupted in 2007;
4. the economic imbalances among EMU Member States.

Below, each of these aspects will be tackled more in detail.

The dramatic public finance situation

The immediate reasons of the speculative attack against Greek sovereign debt are basically two:

1. the disarray of public finance;
2. the alleged creative accounting and manipulations of budgetary figures carried out for years by the Hellenic authorities.

At the time of writing, public debt in Greece is close to 120 per cent of GDP, while the deficit/GDP ratio exceeds 13.5 per cent.[1] Before the launch of the rescue package on 10 May 2010, Greece was believed close to default and risks of contagion to other weak countries highly probable, especially in Portugal, Ireland, Italy, Greece and Spain (PIIGS). Table 8.1 shows that economic growth, the key variable for the evolution of fiscal aggregates, is now dramatically low everywhere. Indeed, one immediate cause or catalyst factor of the crisis is the gloomy Greek economic outlook, after some years of satisfactory growth.

If for Greece and for Italy public debts are worrying, in the case of Portugal vulnerable variable is foreign debt and for Spain, growing external imbalances. However only Greece, had both high fiscal deficit and high debt amongst the weaker Eurozone Member States. This made the Greek problems extreme.

Table 8.1 Macroeconomic indicators, PIIGS (2007–9)

Indicators countries	Deficit/GDP 2007–08–09	Debt/GDP 2007–08–09	Growth 2007–08–09	Interest rate 2007–08–09	Inflation 2007–08–09	Current account/GDP 2007–08–09
Greece	–5.0; –7.6; –14.2	95.7; 99.2; 115.1	4.5; 2.0; –2.0	4.5; 4.8; 5.1	2.8; 4.1; –	–14.2; –14.4; –
Portugal	–2.5; –2.8; –9.4	63.6; 66.3; 76.8	2.4; 0; –2.6	4.4; 4.5; 4.2	2.8; 2.5; –	–9.4; –12; 1; –
Irland	0.1; –7.2; –14.2	25.0; 43.9; 64.0	6.0; –3.0; –7.1	4.3; 4.5; 5.2	4.8; 4.0; –	–5.3; –5.3; –
Italy	–1.4; –2.7; –5.3	103.5; 106.1; 115.8	1.5; –1.3; –5.0	4.4; 4.6; 4.3	1.8; 3.3; –	–2.4; –3.4; –
Spain	1.9; –4.0; –11.1	36.2; 39.7; 53.2	3.6; 0.9; –3.6	4.3; 4.3; 3.9	2.8; 4.0; –	–10.0; –9.6; –

Source: Datastream.

Foreign investors soon reached a consensus on what to do: get rid of Greek public bonds. Thus their interest rates jumped upwards, as the risk premium *vis-à-vis* German Bunds – a measure of Greece default risk – touched unforeseen highs.[2] Greek credit ratings rapidly deteriorated.

The faltering behaviour of Germany

One factor that made the Greek crisis critical has doubtless been Angela Merkel's behaviour. For a long time, at least up to the eve of the EU–IMF decision to approve the 750 billion euro rescue maxi-package, Berlin was stubbornly against the bailout of the leftist Greek government led by Andreas Papandreou. Why? It is possible to identify three reasons behind Angela Merkel's behaviour. First, the Treaty explicitly ruled out any hypothesis of bailout, since it would have been interpreted as general incentive to moral hazard. On top of this, Germany has always conceptualized its role as the guardian of budgetary discipline. Second, it seemed that Greece did not deserve help from the EU due to the alleged falsification of its budgetary figures. Third, Merkel could not afford to ignore, on the eve of a polling test,[3] the opposition of German voters and taxpayers towards any financial help to the Greeks.

The German stance on Greece bailout eventually changed quite rapidly after pressure from the Obama administration and this allowed EU—ECB–IMF to approve the rescue plan which had the merit of lessening the gravity of the crisis.

Had Merkel shown a credible willingness to help Athens at the outset, the crisis would have been less dramatic, as investors would have been less worried. As we will see shortly, Germany also played a role as one of the catalyst factors of the Greek crisis.

The 2007 world financial crisis

The Greek sovereign debt crisis might be seen as the prosecution of the global financial crisis. The main consequences of the latter, indeed, were on the one hand, a huge spreading of unsafe investments and, on the other hand, the prospect of a substantial increase in demands for financial resources due to the fiscal stimuli. These circumstances made investors more cautious in selecting debtors.

In the Greek case, investors feared default because of the large scale of government renewable debt, the prospect of a messy and costly restructuring of it and the lack of credibility. The Argentinian default on $82 billion represents a recent, costly and unpleasant precedent. From a general point of view, it is possible to identify some similarities between the global financial crisis and the sovereign debt crisis in Greece. Both got under way in secondary sectors of the international financial markets and of the European Monetary Union respectively. In the case of subprime debt, this took the form of collateralized debt obligations consisting of government-supported mortgage-backed securities. In the case of Greek bonds, it was the European Monetary Union subprime debt, long magically believed to be as safe as German Treasury bonds. Instead, once the crisis erupted, the reality came to the surface.

In both cases, an important catalyst factor has been external imbalances. In the case of the global financial crisis external imbalances interested the relations between the US and China, plus other surplus countries. In the case of Greece they referred to the relations between Germany and the other EMU Member States.

External imbalances

As far as the consensus goes, the main cause of the Greek crisis was that its public finances were in disarray. However this is not the whole story. A closer look at reality shows that, sometimes, the ultimate cause of fiscal deterioration is not in fiscal policy itself, but elsewhere. For example, Spain, Ireland and the United Kingdom, have recently experienced an impressive worsening of their fiscal stances, although their situation was healthy just a few months ago. By contrast, at the moment they are lagging behind countries which usually have fragile state accounts, like Italy. As regards the overall fiscal situation, states that were better off yesterday are worse off today.

Actually the evolution of fiscal aggregates is affected by many factors arising from the private sector – capital outflows, real estate bubbles etc. – which have nothing to do with fiscal policy, but rather with *macroeconomic imbalances*, domestic and external ones.

Macroeconomic imbalances have been underlined by the financial market reactions penalizing the above-mentioned countries which, despite their better initial public finance conditions (lower deficit or debt level), have been characterized over recent years by large current account deficits, lower productivity, higher unit labour costs and inflation, strong dependency on foreign direct investment (FDI). These are – all factors usually reflecting a permanent loss in competitiveness (see Figure 8.1).

In particular, it is important to underline the role of (*serious*) *external* imbalances. These are a worrying problem for several EMU Member States, including Greece. In these countries, current account deficits (a measure of the external imbalance) turned into external liabilities and high public debt levels (ECB, 2010).

Actually external imbalances have characterized the Eurozone for a long time, with Germany on the other side of the imbalances. Germany has a large and lasting current account surplus, while all the other

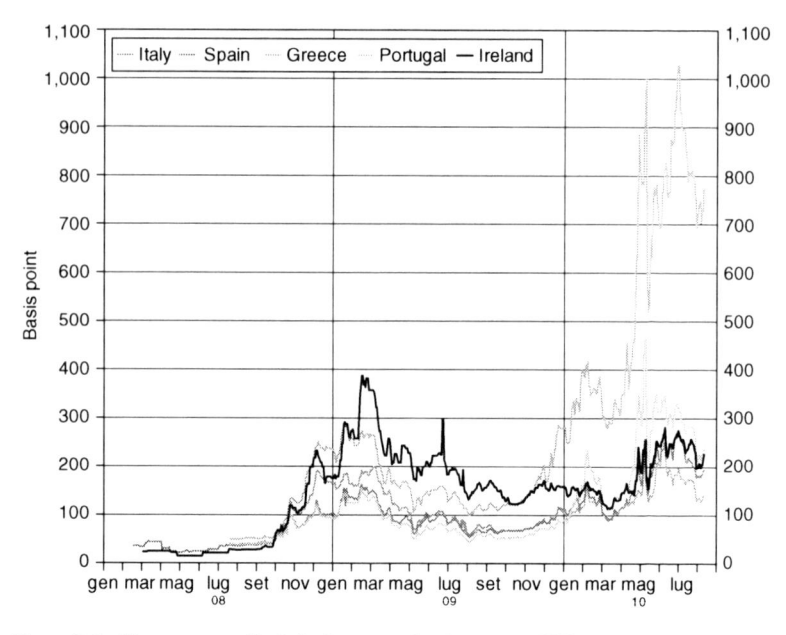

Figure 8.1 Five-year credit default swaps (basis points, US$)
Source: Reuters EcoWin.

countries report large and persistent deficits against it, because factor productivity and competitiveness in Germany largely outweigh other countries'. The latter, therefore, systematically transfer national savings to the former. Moreover, their persistent current account deficits imply losses in output, employment and rising public deficit and debt.In contrast, a more dynamic growth and the improvement of fiscal global stance derive from persistent current account surpluses. From this point of view, then, Germany appears to be the only country gaining from the current macroeconomic situation in EMU: it can exploit its higher competitiveness while its partners are prevented from improving as they can not devalue any more. Thus, according to this, the worsening of the budgetary situation might have its roots in persistent external imbalances, more than (or not only in) the fiscal policy itself, even if it is admittedly difficult to assess its importance.

The appropriate cure for *debt crisis* associated to significant external imbalances is, in turn, represented by reducing them improving competiveness and, with respect to the surplus country, stimulating its internal demand.[4]

Structural causes

Instead, structural causes of the Greek crisis are to be found in the economic characteristics of EMU. In the first years of the 1990s, many empirical studies showed the (then future) EMU would not be an optimal currency area (Blanchard and Katz, 1992; Sachs and Sala-i-Martin, 1992; Krugman, 1993; Bayoumi and Eichengreen, 1993; Bayoumi and Masson, 1995; Fatàs, 1997; Obstfeld and Peri, 1998; Verde, 2003).

Actually, the conditions required by the traditional theory of optimum currency areas (OCA) for two or more countries to create an optimal monetary union (namely, high degree of economic cycle synchronization, high degrees of labour mobility, high degree of fiscal federalism, high degrees of financial integration) were not met by EMU Member States. The main consequences of this conclusion were clear cut: 1. in the future Union, economic tensions among regions would be frequent as asymmetric shocks would prevailed; the Union would be fragile and crisis-prone; 2. for its Member States costs would be higher than benefits. These conclusions and related risks, however, were completely ignored by the states' signatories of the Maastricht Treaty. Why?

Here are some explanations: 1. the experience largely showed that no one monetary union has been built having in mind the traditional OCA theory's criteria; 2. the belief that *symmetric* shocks would prevail after the birth of the Union; 3. the belief that benefits would outweigh costs.

The 2010 Greek experience has clearly shown that while point 1 is undoubtedly true, points 2 and 3 were excessively optimistic. Against the risks of asymmetric shocks, both the European Commission (1990) and Frankel and Rose (1998) had presented largely accepted hypotheses regarding positive evolution and changes for the better of the Union. In particular, Frankel and Rose (1998) suggested that the above-mentioned criteria for an OCA are *endogenous*: it is the very creation of the Union which generates them, thanks to the increase in the trade exchanges within the Union which would make national economic cycles more synchronized. Thus, even if criteria are not met *ex ante*, before the constitution of the Union, they will be fulfilled *ex post*.

On the other hand, in any case, the EMU benefits will exceed costs, irrespective of the actual existence of the preconditions needed to join the Union. This was the main conclusion of the *modern approach to the choice of the exchange rate regimes* prevailing in the 1990s. Unlike the traditional or Mundellian OCA theory (Mundell, 1961; McKinnon, 1963; Kenen, 1969), which focused on costs, the modern approach stresses benefits of monetary unions. Fixed and adjustable exchange rates are, more than policy instruments, a real problem for policy-makers, since they can be tempting targets for speculators, while flexible rates could be sources of widespread instability. Thus, giving the exchange rate up while joining a monetary union is the optimal and most beneficial solution: this is the starting point of the modern approach to a monetary union. In other words, according to this approach, the risks of EMU membership can be overlooked. Moreover, speculative attacks will no longer be possible. These conclusions have not been unanimously accepted, but Europeans are *de facto* used to ignoring both asymmetric shocks and costs of a monetary union.

However, one important lesson from the Greek crisis is that it reminds us of the structural vulnerability of the EMU, because asymmetric shocks, as well as macroeconomic imbalances within the Union, are always possible and thus the costs given by the loss of exchange rates and of national monetary policies remain important.

In particular, it has shown that speculative attacks can occur also in a monetary union, the target being sovereign public bonds instead of national currencies, which can even lead to default of the state. Also in this case, speculative attacks against national bonds can spread by contagion to other Member states.

Policy responses

The Hellenic government, as well as the European Union and the International Monetary Fund adopted a number of policies to face the debt crisis. Below some of the most relevant are detailed.

The Papandreou government's cuts to the deficit

As far as domestic policies are concerned, at the beginning of 2010, the socialist government, led by George Papandreou, passed a very restrictive package aimed at cutting the deficit by 12 per cent of gross domestic product in three years – that is, 30 billion euro in the period 2010–12 (*Financial Times*, 30 April 2010).

The package included: cuts and freezes in public sector pay and hiring – 13th and 14th monthly salary abolished; short-term contracts not renewed; changes to the pension system – average retirement age raised to 67 years from the current 53; an increase of 2–3 points in VAT and other taxes; sale of state corporations; and closure of more than 800 state entities (*Financial Times*, 30 April 2010). In addition, a Anti-corruption legislation was approved by Parliament on 18 May (*Financial Times*, 19 May 2010).

Papandreou's austerity package resulted in strikes and protest demonstrations by the leftwing and unions against the government. These were strongly opposed by the government which has thus shown its determination to deliver the massive fiscal tightening that is needed to make the country governable. The fierce commitment to the fiscal consolidation served also the interests of other Eurozone countries – in the first place Germany – keen to show their taxpayers that the Greeks would be able to return their loans.

The EU–IMF Greek rescue plan

After having wasted valuable time because of Ms Merkel's faltering behaviour, on 10 May 2010 a very important and sizeable rescue plan to bail out Greece was approved. The EU and IMF provided 750 billion euros, dividedas follows:

- IMF loans up to 250 billion euros;
- 60 billion euros from the EU;
- EMU-backed loan guarantee for 440 billion euros (*Financial Times*, 11 May 2010).

This package has far-reaching intentions going well beyond the bailout of Greece. It aims to tackle the Eurozone's debt problem, avoiding the risks of 'another Greece'.

The most important aspects of the rescue plan are basically two: 1. the European Stabilization Fund; and 2. the ECB securities markets programme to intervene in private and public debts markets.

According to the rescue plan, 440 billion euros would be provided by a Stabilization Fund or *European Financial Stability Facility* (EFSF) managed by a *Special Purpose Vehicle* which issues loans backed by guarantees up to 440 billion euros by EMU countries, plus Sweden and Poland (*Financial Times*, 11 May 2010). The Stabilization Fund will last three years and its main purpose is to act as an instrument of crises management – that is, its task will be to handle every financial crisis involving EMU Member States.[5] On the other hand, the ECB will intervene on public and private debt markets, purchasing securities to avoid tensions and to stabilize them; the Central Bank will intervene with extra measures to boost Eurozone liquidity.

This last aspect is clearly the most controversial, since it is in sharp contrast with Article 123 of the Treaty banning the ECB from purchase of Member States' public bonds, to guarantee its independence from national governments.

Both these issues will be tackled more in detail further on in this chapter.

German measures on short selling and credit default swaps

Among the policy responses to the Greek debt crisis, we can include the measures banning short selling[6] and credit default swaps or CDS,[7] adopted by German authorities to hamper speculation against Greek sovereign bonds. Many economists believe these measures are ineffective or even harmful (see *Financial Times*, 20 May 2010: 4).

The consequences for EMU

The Hellenic public finance crisis exploded in the first months of 2010 and immediately proposals were advanced by economists and officials of international institutions to tackle it. Table 8.2 summarizes some of them to clarify their consequences for the future of EMU.

Summing up, the most important implications for the Euro-zone appear to be the following:

1. the limits of the Stability and Growth Pact;
2. the independence of the ECB and the meaning of the *no-bailout clause*;
3. the lesson of the Greek crisis for the future of EMU.

The Greek crisis and the Stability and Growth Pact

With regard to fiscal policy, the EMU institutional framework is based on numerical fiscal rules and procedures. They state that national public accounts must be kept in order: the deficit/GDP ratio cannot exceed 3 per cent in 'normal times'; monetary funding of deficits and bailouts of struggling governments are banned.

However, the Greek crisis has shown that neither fiscal rules (i.e., the Stability and Growth Pact (SGP)), nor the ban of bailouts has been effective. The rationale of the Treaty's numerical fiscal rules is obvious: they are visible and therefore checkable. Moreover the Treaty refers to two fiscal criteria – the deficit *and* the debt ratios – to keep both short- and long-term aspects of state budgets under control. To make the fiscal rules effective, the Treaty provides for a *preventive arm* – or *multilateral surveillance* – to facilitate control by the European Commission of national budgetary projections, and a *repressive mechanism* – the so-called

Table 8.2 The main proposals in tackling the Greek debt crisis: a summary

Even if many of the proposals economists put forward in the aftermath of the 2010 Greek debt crisis are doomed to remain without effects, it can be interesting to sum them up, adding new elements to the crisis, to its causes and possible solutions.

a) **Otmar Issing** (*Financial Times*, 16 February 2010): **A Greece bailout would be a disaster.** According to the former member of the ECB's Executive Council, the question of whether to bail out struggling EMU Member States is absolutely unacceptable. Indeed, once Greece was rescued it would be inevitable that other Member States would want a bailout from the same troubles. Financial markets would soon be able to identify the next countries under attack. Ensuring bailouts would mean the demise of the European fiscal rules.

b) **Tommaso Padoa-Schioppa** (*Financial Times*, 19 February 2010): **The bailout is inevitable.** According to Tommaso Padoa-Schioppa, another former member of the ECB Executive Board, refusal to rescue Greece would imply the end of the monetary union, conceived as the way to force its Member States towards political union. The Greek crisis should be seen as an opportunity to accelerate in this direction.

c) **Pisani-Ferry-Sapir** (*Financial Times*, 2 February 2010): **The best solution is to call in the IMF.** The rescue of Greece could be ensured by the International Monetary Fund, the main international institution engaged in the management and funding of the financial crises.

d) **Pisani-Ferry-Sapir** (*Financial Times*, 29 April 2010): **A new scheme of funding sovereign debt crises.** The EMU needs a mechanism whereby the Member States with unsustainable sovereign debt problems could face them, involving creditors in an orderly way.

e) **Martin Feldstein** (*Financial Times*, 17 February 2010): **The solution is Greece's temporary withdrawal from the Eurozone.** To meet the Union's budgetary constraints, Greece should cut public spending and raise taxes by more than 10 percentage points of Gross Domestic Product.

Were this goal actually reached, Greece would be in a deep recession with millions of unemployed; the unemployment rate already exceeds 10 per cent. Politically unsustainable tensions would arise. All this could be avoided if it were possible to give Greece the chance of a temporary withdrawal from the Union, regaining its currency and devaluing it. Thus devaluation could favour the current account of balance of payments, spur output and employment and mitigate budgetary and financial problems. Greece could temporarily leave the Eurozone, committing itself to enter the Union with a devalued exchange rate.

f) **Daniel Gros and Mayer** (2010): **EMU needs a European Monetary Fund.** The Greek crisis could be addressed by creating a European Monetary Fund devoted to manage sovereign debt crises within the Union. A similar institution was already provided for within the European Monetary System, but it was not implemented.

g) **Dominique Strauss Kahn** (*Financial Times*, 12 May 2010): **A short-term public transfer** from some healthy European Member State to those in financial trouble.

Excessive Deficit Procedure (EDP) – concerning sanctions against deficits/ GDP ratios defined *excessive* – that is, exceeding the reference parameter of 3 per cent (Verde, 2006).

The Greek crisis proved the failure of the SGP; in particular, that of its preventive arm. The Greeks have sensationally confirmed that even well-designed rules can be bypassed. Indeed, the crisis seems to strengthen a widespread opinion suggesting that rules are useless: reliable governments don't need them, while those fiscally undisciplined are prone to successfully bypassing them.

In the aftermath of the Greek crisis, the Stability Pact is at the centre of general criticism. Indeed, first its crisis in 2003 and then its 2005 reform had already significantly reduced its credibility. As it is well known, it was Germany and France who provoked the crisis and then inspired the reform. They had already breached the reference parameter of 3 per cent in 2002 and refused to allow the EDP to be opened against them. Moreover, since 2005, it has been up to Ecofin – that is, to the Member States themselves – to have the last word in deciding if one or more of them have breached the Pact; the EDP might be reopened, making the infliction of sanctions very improbable, if not impossible (*ibid.*).

However, it has been the Greek crisis which has fully unveiled its intrinsic limits. After the Greek events, European officials and (some) national policy-makers have stressed the need to strengthen the implementation of fiscal rules and procedures; in particular, increasing the level of automaticity of EDP procedures and sanctions.

According to the Germans, for instance, EMU countries should gradually adopt a *balanced budget rule*.[8] Clearly this is a doomed proposal, but the suggestion advanced by Schäble, the German finance minister, proves the lasting intent of the leader country of the Union to move resolutely towards a dramatic tightening of the Stability Pact.

However, what is at issue is not the Pact's degree of tightness, but the possibility it could be circumvented. Indeed, essentially two reasons can explain its failure: 1. creative accounting and data manipulation, as well as the lack of an effective and independent watchdog, and 2. the lack of any mechanism to eract to a financial crisis, once it has exploded. At the moment, however, the proposal for changes to the Pact is at the centre of a heated debate involving the Commission, the ECB and Ecofin.

The belief that the Pact's reform should be considered within an overall scheme targeted at reinforcing economic governance in EMU has clearly grown. Thus, the purpose of reinforcing the European fiscal rules is envisaged alongside with other crucial goals: 1. addressing serious macroeconomic imbalances; 2. implementing an adequate framework for crisis management; and 3. favouring structural reforms (ECB, 2010).

On this topic some suggestions could easily be derived from previous analysis. For instance, the creation of an independent fiscal agency aimed at removing any risk of manipulation of budgetary data could be crucial. Moreover, appropriate mechanisms to signal significant macroeconomic imbalances and differences in competitiveness within the Eurozone could be critical. Finally, EMU would need a crisis management instrument, providing financial support for Member States in trouble and able to minimize moral hazard while reinforcing incentives towards sound fiscal policies.

In this vein, the European Financial Stability Facility, approved in May 2010, appears an excellent starting point. As Prodi, the former Italian prime minister, stated: it has been one of 'inevitable steps towards economic governance that were not possible when the euro was created' (*Financial Times*, 21 May 2010: 9).

ECB independence and the no-bailout clause

The enforcement mechanism of the European fiscal rules works in this way: Member States must curb their public deficits; to force them to do so, monetary funding of their deficit as well as their bailouts are formally banned.

The *no-bailout clause* rules out any rescue of Member States in trouble and the independence of the ECB is crucial to make this ban credible. It would oblige Member States to fiscally correct behaviours, preventing unsustainable public debt and moral hazard.

It is worth remembering that ECB independence was required to win over strong German resistance to joining EMU, since it was seen as a necessary condition to ensure price stability. The ban on bailouts and the independence of ECB are the two sides of a coin.

However, according to many economists the no bail-out clause is inevitably meaningless. Indeed, when a Member State is experiencing a speculative attack and impaired access to private credit, it is difficult to conceive how the Union – that is, the ECB or other Member States – could refuse to rescue it. Actually it is very probable that considerable amounts of securities issued by the country under attack appear on the balance sheets of banks and financial institutions of other Member States. The following generalized financial crash could result in the end of Monetary Union as well as possibly the European Union. Thus, the question is: can the ECB refuse to purchase the national bonds under speculative attack[9] putting the future of the Union as a whole at risk? This question was asked before the birth of the euro and it has re-emerged in the aftermath of the Greek crisis.

Table 8.3 Foreign-dominated holdings of Greek government securities (euro billions, end Q3, 2009)

	Banks	Insurance Companies	Mutual funds pension funds	Monetary authorities	Others	Total	% of total
Greek residents	42	—	29	—	6	77	26
All non-residents	83	49	47	33	6	218	74
France	18	20	3	7	2	50	17
Germany	19	6	2	—	—	28	10
Italy	5	8	6	—	1	20	7
Belgium	7	2	5	—	3	17	6
Netherlands	6	2	7	1	—	15	5
Luxembourg	6	—	9	—	—	15	5
Other Eurozone	10	6	—	1	—	19	2
Eurozone (exc Greek)	72	44	33	9	6	164	56
UK	8	—	1	—	—	9	3
other	3	4	13	24	—	44	15
Grand total	125	49	76	33	12	295	100

Source: *Financial Times*, 29 April 2010.

The lesson for EMU which can be drawn from this crisis is clear cut. The no-bailout clause, the ban of purchasing government bonds, is not very meaningful as it could prove fatal for the future of the Union. And indeed it has been *de facto* cancelled, with remarkable implications for ECB independence.

The Central Bank has been pushed, under (political) pressure from the European Council and the Ecofin as well, to purchase Greek bonds and to stabilize public and private bond markets. It has been a baleful shock to ECB credibility and the ECB President of the Executive Board, Jean-Claude Trichet, hastened to state that the liquidity put into the system would be rapidly withdrawn.[10] From now on, the categorical imperative should be to rebuild ECB credibility, avoiding ongoing defence of a clause that is dangerous and inane, like banning bailouts.

Let us come back to Ms Merkel's stance in the debate on the rescue package for Greece, which we have already hinted at. As we saw, she initially exhibited a strong hostility against the bailout of the Greek government. There is nothing surprising in that behaviour: Germany has always been a supporter and defender of the ECB independence and the related *no-bailout clause*. However, this time one important and new aspect came to the surface.

Merkel's behaviour was backed by German public opinion, which was fiercely against the rescue of Greeks who don't meet the European fiscal constraints, work less and retire before German people and so on. The lesson from the Greek events is that Germans are unwilling to pay for people of other Member States and, more important, this attitude is widespread in the Union,[11] with clear-cut implications for the *long-term* prospect of EMU. In other words, the Hellenic events have made evident a clear weakening of *solidarity* among the Member States of the Union.

This is the main lesson from the Greek crisis and this is the starting hypothesis, concerning the future of EMU, of a *two-speed EMU* approach (Verde, 2009).

The Greek crisis and the 'two-speed EMU': the *restricted solidarity* hypothesis

The Greek crisis has shown, at least up to a certain point, a worrying lack of solidarity among EMU Member States. What, in a monetary union, does solidarity mean? Why is it crucial? In general terms, we can define solidarity as the willingness to help all other Member States, in particular providing financial support for governments in trouble, without any 'clear' return.

However, solidarity can mean a range of things, from a minimum level, what is required for the implementation of monetary union, to a maximum beyond which macroeconomic stability is at risk and incentives to moral hazard are real. Greek events, in fact, have shown an unwillingness 'to pay a single euro' in rescuing other countries, expressed by German people[12] and shared by citizens of other Member States.[13] More than a denial of solidarity, these attitudes suggest a surfacing new concept of solidarity which is blended with that of *perceived* proximity or similarity among EMU Member States from the economic, political, cultural and religious points of view.

In other words, if we analyze the Greek crisis as previously described, it seems that a *restricted* definition of solidarity looks likely to prevail in EMU: the willingness to help is restricted to the *club* of countries (e.g., the rich and competitive ones) which *perceive themselves* economically, politically and culturally close to each other. All that leads to a perception by the involved countries that the Union is their *own*. Moreover, this restricted solidarity can be shored up by the need to maintain macroeconomic stability and prevent any opportunistic behaviour.

Thus, if the Member State in trouble is not a member of the 'club' (e.g., a poor or less competitive country like Greece) the rescue problem could be hampered by one or more countries of the 'club', which may (as they actually did in the Greek case) claim they are acting with the sole goal of the Union's stability. Thus the problem could be overcome only by the political will of the Union as a whole, precisely as happened in the case of Greece with the European Council's decision of 10 May 2010. In contrast, no problem would arise when it is a Member State enjoying the restricted solidarity that is under attack.

From a general theoretical point of view, the definition of restricted solidarity works like a criterion or condition required for two or more countries to create or join an *optimal and long-term sustainable* monetary union. But it can be seen as a criterion in a context quite different from that of the 1960s traditional theory on optimum currency area (OCA),[14] already hinted at in section 3. According to this theory, once a monetary union is created it lives forever. This conclusion is strengthened by Frankel and Rose (1998), who suggest that the required conditions to make the union optimal can surface *ex post*, thanks to the creation of the union. At the centre of this traditional approach there is the macroeconomic adjustment problem. In the restricted solidarity approach, – monetary union (the EMU) is not optimal – that is, for some of its member countries costs outweigh benefits; moreover, the Union as a whole is not sustainable in the long term, as political union is ruled out by Member States. At its centre there is the mechanism which leads to the disintegration of the Union or, better, to a two-speed EMU. This mechanism is 'restricted solidarity'. It rests on national public opinions, on political, cultural, religious considerations: all factors crucial for every viable monetary union but excluded in the traditional analysis. 'Restricted solidarity' defines the *optimal dimensions* of (a restricted) monetary union. We can imagine these dimensions as due to trade-offs between the benefits deriving from the size (number of states) of the Union and the costs of heterogeneity of preferences (political, cultural, etc.) existing among member countries. Benefits are those usually tied to the introduction of a single currency. Costs are, in this case, due to the heterogeneity with other member countries, in part potentially translating in the need of financial support (e.g., a rescue package) in their favour.

Other implications of this definition of restricted solidarity are worth emphasizing. Certainly, in a large monetary union there exist many differences – economic, cultural, political, customs and so on – within its population. Among them, while choosing a group or club of countries who share a perceived common sense of homogeneity, it is very probable that they are very close or similar from the *economic* point of view. This would mean that the involved Member States would be characterized by an adequate synchronization of economic cycles[15] and that they could form an optimal monetary area as compared to the larger one, which does not represent an optimal union. If the union comprised only these countries, benefits would exceed costs and the probability of bail-outs would be very low.

The dimension of this restricted optimal monetary union, derived from the definition of restricted solidarity, is not immutable, as it can be changed, enlarged or restricted according to the policies carried out by the Union and to the economic and political context. Thus, heterogeneity or similarities within the Union are influenced by economic, harmonization and institutional policies aimed at reducing economic imbalances, as well as legal, regulatory and wealth disparities across regions, and by the economic context, such as the development of intra-Union trade exchanges or lasting crisis scenarios.

The restricted solidarity is significantly affected by national public opinions, which governments cannot afford to ignore, and even if subject to an evolutionary process (point 2), the restricted solidarity is *given* – that is, it is a *datum* for the Union as a whole. In presence of particular shocks, like financial crises or asymmetric shocks, it could push the Union towards different results. Anyway, considered in a *long-run perspective*, the problems posed by this limited, but supposedly prevailing, form of solidarity could force the EMU towards a multispeed structure, or towards political union, which, however, needs much greater solidarity in the form of unlikely widespread political agreement.

In particular, if the Greek crisis spreads to other countries outside the 'club', EMU could be pushed towards a two-speed union, defined by a restricted solidarity and ending up with new borders of the Union. In this case, however, the risk is that the Union's border-redrawing process could be carried out not only by Member States but *within* them too.

In the aftermath of the Greek crisis, Zingales (2010) has spoken about north and south *euros*: the first regarding the northern, rich and competitive countries, the latter circulating in the south of EMU in poor and not competitive countries, like Italy, Greece, Spain, Portugal and Ireland.

This hypothesis might be considered as a partial outcome of the approach proposed here and, taking into consideration the risk which have just been hinted at, I it is possible to suppose that particularly advanced areas in Italy (so-called Padania) and Spain (Catalonia) could be included in the north Eurozone, with dramatic political consequences.[16]

160 *The Greek Debt Crisis*

Overall, the prospect of European political union is very remote and nebulous: nobody really wants it and it cannot succeed with current macroeconomic imbalances and vast wealth disparities.[17] Thus the *two-speed EMU* remains the most probable medium-term scenario.

In Verde (2009), a simple formalized model of 'two-speed EMU', according to the restricted solidarity hypothesis, is proposed. In the model, EMU disintegration is explained by the refusal by some Member States to rescue others because of the perceived lack of solidarity or ownership from some of them.

Let us consider a *reference Member State* (e.g., Germany) and let us number all the other countries according to the decreasing level of economic, political, social and cultural similarities with it. Thus, the country labelled 1 is the country *closest* to the reference one from those points of view (e.g., Austria) and so on. Now, let us put on the *y axis* of Figure 8.2a below costs and benefits deriving from Union membership (C, B) and on the *x axis* the number of Member States of the Union (N) classified according the mentioned criterion.

According to my approach, there could be, for each reference state, an optimal number of countries (N*) for which the hypothesis of restricted solidarity works. Thus, for our reference country, the union formed by the states going from 1 to N* is optimal: its advantages outweigh costs. A larger union, going from 1 to N, is not optimal because of higher costs and loss of ownership, this one due to the lack of cultural and social closeness. If for each of the first N* reference states the same results

(a) C, B = costs and benefits of the union
N = number of Member States
N* = optimal dimension of monetary union

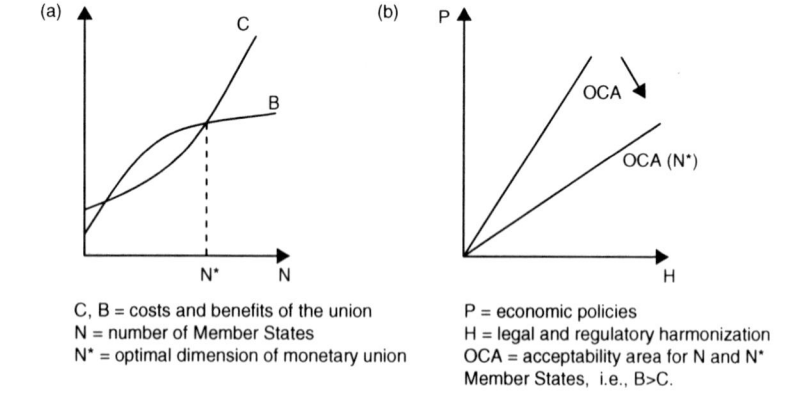

(b) P = economic policies
H = legal and regulatory harmonization
OCA = acceptability area for N and N* Member States, i.e., B>C.

Figure 8.2 Costs and benefits of monetary union and the restricted solidarity hypothesis

occur, N* is the optimal dimension of the monetary union, for the states involved.

In Figure 8.2a above, when the number of states is N*, the optimal dimension is reached. It should be clear that if N>N*, where N is the initial number of Member States of the original OCA, the area of optimality of the union is going to reduce from OCA (N) to OCA (N*) as in Figure 8.2b above, where, on the y and x axes, we have economic (P) and harmonization policies, respectively.

Some concluding remarks

The Greek crisis has gone well beyond its own turmoil as a peripheral country. This chapter has summarized the 'facts' – that is, the causes and policy responses to the crisis. It has been possible to establish a bridge between causes and consequences for EMU arising from the Greek events. Some of the latter concern the EMU policy framework, that is – the European fiscal rules or SGP and the independence of the ECB. But the most important impact of the Greek crisis has involved the very long-term sustainability of EMU as it made evident the lack of solidarity – that is, the vocal hostility of some Member States to help (to support financially) Greece, as well as other countries at risk of contagion. The context evident after the Greek crisis is that of a monetary union which is not optimal and, in absence of a political union, doomed to disintegrate. The author identifies in restricted solidarity – involving a group of countries which perceive themselves to be close to each other from the economic, political, cultural and common sentiment points of view – the mechanism able to lead the EMU towards a two-speed union.

Notes

1. However, it is worth remembering that in its *On Government Deficit and Debt Accounting*, published in 2002, the European Commission gave Member States the freedom to use derivatives to adjust deficit/GDP ratios.
2. In times of crisis it is very difficult to evaluate the risk premium because of its strong volatility: this has actually happened in the current Greek crisis.
3. The state election in North Rhine-Westphalia of 9 May 2010.
4. 'EMU economies display wide and sometimes increasing imbalances. At the heart of the matter is Germany, Europe's strongest economy. Fixed European exchange rates provide disproportionate support for Germany's export-oriented economy by making its industrial sales extremely competitive throughout most of Europe, increasing Germany's export surplus to record levels, and deflecting its attention from the necessary task of stimulating domestic demand – an outcome that would help both itself and its neighbours' (Marsh, 2010: 3). However, the data concerning the balance of trade

162 *The Greek Debt Crisis*

of the first month of 2010 show steady increases of Gerrman imports from other EMU Member States.
5. However, the Fund is temporary: this could be a problem.
6. In truth, short selling investors sell securities they do not own in the expectation of profiting from a fall in the share price before they have to deliver the securities. They don't even see the assets: at maturity they collect the difference or profit. However, an investor will gain in a falling market, but he is exposed to unlimited losses should the securites gain value. In normal short selling an investor borrows the assets he sells.
7. Credit default swaps (CDSs) are essentially similar to short selling. Indeed, the buyer (who buys insurance against a default from either a company or country) can profit if the outlook of the entity deteriorates since the premium for that default risk will rise and he can profit by selling the insurance. In some cases the investor buys credit insurance to protect his portfolio from such a risk, but most buyers simply want to express a negative bet. As such, buying CDS without any of the entity's debt is an exposed short bet.
8. In 2009 the German government committed itself to limit the public deficit/GDP ratio within 0.35 per cent by 2016.
9. For a model of speculative attack on monetary union, see Verde (2010).
10. According to Jean-Claude Trichet, the ECB President, the ECB action to shore up confidence in the Eurozone by buying government bonds is totally different from US or UK quantitative easing. 'We will withdraw all the liquidity injected into the financial system' (*Financial Times*, 17 May 2010: 3).
11. It is confirmed by the *Financial Times*/Harris poll, according to which Germans are strikingly more hostile than other Europeans (*Financial Times*, 22 March 2010: 1).
12. With some important exceptions, like that of the former finance minister Theo Waigel, the 'father' of the Stability and Growth Pact.
13. See note 11.
14. The idea of (usual) solidarity as criterion for an optimal currency area is not new. Eichengreen (2006: 432), talking about Asian monetary integration, writes: 'Asian countries possess neither ... nor the solidarity needed to offer extensive financial support. ... Hence there is little prospect of early monetary union.'
15. As we know (see section 3), synchronization of economic cycles is one criterion required by the traditional theory of OCA for the optimality of currency areas.
16. See La Malfa (2010). According to La Malfa, an Italian MP, there is the risk that EMU disintegration would entail national boundaries being redrawn as well. In this case, the rich regions of the north of Italy could move away from the rest of Italy, leaving a huge public debt problem for the southern regions, with dramatic economic and political consequences.

It is worth obeserving that Alesina and Spolaore (2003) have outlined the relationship between European monetary integration and and the increase in demand from regions of independence or autonomy. According to these two authors, once a region is a member of a common currency area and can enjoy free trade, the incentive for the region to seek independence or autonomy increases, as governments are much less important for the economy of the region. Moreover, Drèze (1995) suggests that Europe should develop towards

a union of regions – that is, a loose federeration of independent regions, because European national governments have become too small for certain prerogotives and too big for others. So their existence is being threatened both from above – the union – and from below – regional governments.
17. This was confirmed by the stiff resistence from Member States against the EU's 'euro taxes' plan (see *Financial Times*, 10 August 2010).

References

Alesina, A. and Spolaore, E. (2003) *The Size of Nations*, London and Cambridge, MA: MIT Press.
Bayoumi, T. and Eichengreen, B. (1993) 'Shocking Aspects of European Monetary Integration', in F. Torres and F. Giavazzi (eds), *Adjustment and Growth in the European Monetary Union*, Cambridge: Cambridge University Press.
Bayoumi, T. and Masson, P. R. (1995) 'Fiscal Flows in the United States and Canada: Lessons for Monetary Union in Europe', *European Economic Review*, vol. 39, no. 2 (February), pp. 253–74.
Blanchard, O. and Katz, F. (1992) 'Regional Evolutions', *Brookings Papers on Economic Activity*, vol. 1, pp. 1–61.
Drèze J. H. (1995) 'Regions of Europe: A Feasible Status to be Discussed', *Economic Policy 17*, pp. 206–307.
Eichengreen, B. (2006) 'The Parallel-currency Approach to Asian Monetary Integration', *The American Economic Review*, Papers and Proceedings, May, pp. 432–6.
European Central Bank (2010) *Reinforcing Economic Governance in the Euro Area*, Frankfurt, June.
European Commission (1990) 'European Economy: One Market, One Money', *European Economy*, no. 44.
European Commission (2002) *On Governement Deficit and Debt Accounting*, Brussels.
Fatàs, A. (1997) 'EMU, Countries or Regions? Lessons from the EMS Experience', *European Economic Review*, vol. 41, pp. 207–47.
Frankel, J. and Rose, A. K. (1998) 'The Endogeneity of the Optimum Currency Area Criterion', *Economic Journal*, July, pp. 1009–25.
Gros, D. and Mayer, T. (2010) 'Financial Stabilty beyond Greece: Making the Most Out of the Euro(pean) Stabilization Mechanism', available at www.vox.eu.org/index php? Q=node 5028.
Kenen, P. (1969) 'The Theory of Currency Areas: An Eclectic View', in R. A. Mundell and A. K. Swoboda (eds), *Monetary Problems in the International Economy*, Chicago: University of Chicago Press.
Krugman, P. (1993) 'Lessons of Massachusetts for EMU', in F. Torres and F. Giavazzi (eds), *Adjustment and Growth in the European Monetary Union*, Cambridge: Cambridge University Press.
La Malfa, G. (2010) 'L'unità nazionale è finite da tempo', *Il Riformista*, 20 May 2010.
Marsh, D. (2010) *The Euro: The Politics of the New Global Currency*, New Haven and London: Yale University Press. McKinnon, R. (1963) 'Optimum Currency Areas', *American Economic Review*, September, pp. 717–25.

Mundell, R. A. (1961) 'A Theory of Optimum Currency Areas', *American Economic Review*, September, pp. 657–65.

Obstfeld, M. and Peri, G. (1998) 'Regional Non-adjustment and Fiscal Policy', *Economic Policy*, vol. 26, pp. 207–47.

Sachs, J. D. and Sala-i-Martin, X. (1992) 'Fiscal Federalism and Optimum Currency Areas: Evidence for Europe from the United States', CEPR Discussion paper no. 632.

Verde, A. (2003) 'E' l'UEM un'area valutaria ottimale?', *Rivista economica del mezzogiorno*, vol. 3, Rome: Svimez.

Verde, A. (2006) 'The Old and the New Stabilty and Growth Pact along with the Main Proposals for its Reform: An Assessment', *Transition Studies Review*, vol. 3, pp. 475–96.

Verde, A. (2009) 'In and Out of Monetary Unions: Lessons from, and Risks for the EMU. An Alterative Approach to Monetary Union', in L. S. Talani (ed.), *The Future of EMU*, New York: Palgrave Macmillan, pp. 110–43.

Verde, A. (2010) 'A Speculative Attack on a Monetary Union: Lessons from the 2010 Greek Crisis', Working Paper no. 10, cattedra di economia internazionale della facoltà di economia della università la Tuscia.

Zingales, L. (2010) '9 maggio San Beato-Due euro sono migliori di uno?', *Il Sole 24 ORE*, 9 May.

9
From Miracle to Crash? The Impact of the Global Financial Crisis on Spain

Ramon Pacheco Pardo

Introduction

The financial crisis that struck in 2007 affected developed countries more than emerging and developing markets, and European economies more than those in other regions. Yet, the effects of the crisis on developed members of the EU were uneven. Some were hit as a result of their over-reliance on banking, finance and trade, suffering a temporary setback but with positive long-term prospects due to their competitiveness. Germany and the United Kingdom are examples of this. Differently, the crisis exposed the deficiencies of a number of EU economies which benefited from the sustained period of economic growth that began in the mid-1990s but which did not result in an improvement of their competitiveness. Hence, countries such as Greece, Ireland and Spain were hit by the crisis much harder than other EU economies. Even as they left the worst of the crisis behind in 2010 their economic prospects remained poor.

In the case of Spain, economic problems date back to the 1970s. Even though the country benefited from a 40-year period of almost uninterrupted economic growth, successive governments failed to introduce the necessary reforms to make the economy more competitive. High unemployment, budgetary deficits and excessive inflation have been the key indicators of this lack of competitiveness. Behind the façade of the two Spanish 'economic miracles' of the 1960s–70s and 1990s–2000s there has been an over-reliance on tourism, construction and cash inflows associated to EU membership. Hence, when the first two were hit by the financial crisis and the latter ceased to act as an economic umbrella, structural deficiencies made the economy suffer a painful blow. Whereas more competitive European economies were able to start recovering in mid- to late 2009, Spain barely scraped out of recession in the first quarter of 2010. By the middle of that year, the Spanish government even had to act to restore market confidence in an economy deemed by some to be as weak as Greece's.

This chapter will first trace the development of the Spanish economy from the mid-1960s to the early 1990s. It will emphasize how Spain modernized thanks to low value added industries and services, but then failed to build on them to become a more competitive economy. Unemployment, budget deficits and high inflation will be used to showcase this problem. The chapter will then explain how the economic boom that began in 1994 and the effects of the crisis that hit the country from 2007 can only be understood with reference to the way in which Spain modernized. Hence, the financial crisis did not create new problems for the Spanish economy. Rather, it exposed previous weaknesses which made Spain ill-prepared to withstand the crisis. After refusing to acknowledge the effects of the crisis on the Spanish economy, the government embarked in a reform programme intended to deal with some of these long-standing weaknesses.

Economic growth and modernization in the 1970s and 1980s

Spain had transitioned from an agrarian society to a modern industrialized economy in the late 1960s and early 1970s. Throughout early Francoism the Spanish economy had relied on state companies and family-owned businesses. State intervention in the market and high tariffs ensured that the Franco regime controlled an uncompetitive economy with great imbalances. Yet, mass emigration to the booming economies of Western Europe and a patriarchal social model constraining the access of women to the workforce kept unemployment low, limiting social unrest. Elites benefited from their close links to the Franco regime, and labour saw its economic well-being improve after decades of instability. Hence, demand for market-orientated reforms was minimal.

The situation changed in 1964, when the first of three consecutive quadrennial development plans was approved. Spain engaged in a process of state-led industrialization. The country transitioned from an economy in which the agricultural sector was the largest and ample capital controls were the norm, to an economic model based on the industrial and services sectors in which foreign aid and investment were actively sought. Heavy industries, tourism and investment in infrastructure became the new pillars of the Spanish economy (Balfour, 2000). There is no agreement on whether these changes took place thanks to the reforms introduced by the Franco regime or in spite of them. However, there is little doubt that by the early 1980s Spain was a modern economy with solid foundations for the first time in decades, in spite of the oil shocks a few years earlier.

Paradoxically, the economic success of the two previous decades had created three important problems for the Spanish economy. First, unemployment grew dramatically. From almost full employment in the mid-1970s, the unemployment rate went up by over 10 percentage points, peaking at 17.8 per cent of the labour force in 1985 (OECD, 2010). This was the result of labour flows from agricultural areas to urban centres in search of better salaries, together with the inability of Western European economies to absorb Spain's surplus labour, which they had been doing until the economic slowdown of the 1970s (Lieberman, 1995: 201–2). As we shall see below, Spain is yet to be able to solve the problem of persistent high unemployment.

Second, budgetary deficits increased rapidly. The public sector had been behind the process of economic growth and modernization. The expansion of energy-intensive industries such as car-making, machinery production and shipping made Spain heavily dependent on energy imports, especially Middle Eastern oil. The combination of a decline in exports from state-run companies due to the economic slowdown in Western Europe, growing energy costs following the oil shocks of 1973 and 1979–80, and large social security costs because of the implementation of redistributive policies prevented the government from being able to control the deficit (*ibid.*: 254–6). Similarly to the case of high unemployment, budget deficits have persistently afflicted Spain until today.

Third, inflation rose sharply. From 1973 to 1984 annual inflation was consistently above 11 per cent. While inflation rates gradually came under control in other advanced economies once the effects of the oil shocks of the 1970s were over, the rate in Spain did not fall below 3.5 per cent until 1997 (OECD, 2010). High inflation in the early 1980s slowed domestic demand and reduced the competitiveness of Spanish labour, since salary increases in many industries closely tracked inflation rates, which they still do today. Therefore, high inflation steadily eroded the competitiveness of a Spanish economy unable to match the productivity of other developed countries (Lopez-Claros, 1988: 30–1). As with high unemployment and budget deficits, high inflation still is a major problem of the Spanish economy.

The Socialists in power and the boon of EEC membership

The Socialist Party (Partido Socialista Obrero Español, or PSOE, in Spanish) swept the 1982 general elections, obtaining a majority in both houses of parliament which allowed it to govern without the constraints of a coalition government. Concurrently, talks to join the European Economic Community (EEC) seriously took off. First discussed in 1962, Spanish membership of the EEC had not been a realistic option during the Francoist dictatorship of 1939–75. Afterwards, the transition period had opened up the prospects of joining the EEC. However, domestic reform and consolidation of a democratic regime had taken priority. The election of the Socialist Party in 1982 symbolized the successful transition to a pluralistic political system. Accession to the EEC was perceived as akin to the 'reintegration' of Spain in Western Europe. In June 1985 Prime Minister Felipe González signed the accession agreement. A few months later, in January 1986, Spain joined the EEC (Crespo MacLennan, 2000).

A solid parliamentary majority and the prospects and later materialization of membership of the EEC allowed the Socialist Party to follow an ambitious reform agenda. One of the first decisions the government took after its election was the devaluation of the currency, the peseta. This was followed by other measures to show international markets that the government was serious about managing the Spanish economy. Some investors and institutions had regarded the Socialist Party suspiciously because of its historical links to international socialism and domestic trade unions. However, their fears were swiftly dispelled. Monetary and fiscal policies were tightened to try to bring the budget deficit under control. In addition, loss-making public companies were closed or sold, uncompetitive industries were reconverted and labour costs were reduced through wage moderation while labour market flexibility was increased (Recio and Roca, 1998: 141–3 and 149–51). Overall, state interventionism in the economy began to be reduced to the levels of other Western European countries.

More importantly, capital inflows grew exponentially thanks to private investment and economic aid from the EEC in the form of structural funds. The reduction in public investment was more than offset by these inflows. Both Spanish companies and the government greatly benefited from them (Sosvilla-Rivero and Herce, 2004). Sectors such as banking, fixed-line telecommunications, oil and insurance tapped on this investment, as well as know-how transfers, without having to face significant foreign competition, since the Spanish government negotiated long transition periods before these sectors were opened to European providers.

Subsequently, Spanish companies expanded into Latin America and other European countries (Salmon, 2001: 95–6). Furthermore, economically less developed regions received an extra boost in the form of EEC cohesion funds (Harrison and Corkill, 2004: 180–1). By the end of 1989, only four years after Spain had joined the EEC, the country's GDP had more than doubled.

Notwithstanding the undeniable benefits from joining the EEC, the government was unable to substantially change the structure of the Spanish economy before the years of boom came to an inevitable end. When the recession of 1992–3 struck, unemployment still hovered over 13 per cent, public debt as a percentage of GDP was lower than in 1986 but still above 4 per cent (OECD, 2010), and inflation was almost 6 per cent (*ibid.*). In addition, Spain's trade deficit had more than trebled because the lowering and eventual phasing out of tariffs to European imports led to a huge inflow of more competitive high value added products from other EEC members, such as cars, household utensils and pharmaceuticals. Furthermore, some regions, especially Andalusia and Extremadura, and some sectors, most notably agriculture, became to a large extent dependent on EEC transfers for their economic functioning (Viñals, 1992). Spain had not built on the boom of the 1980s to solve its major structural problems, improve the competitiveness of its economy or move up the economic value chain.

Economic recession and boom in the 1990s and into the twenty-first century

In the summer of 1992 Barcelona hosted the Olympic Games, watched by hundreds of millions of people around the world. In October of the same year the Universal Exposition of Seville closed after almost six months. Forty million visitors made this exposition the third most attended ever. These two events were perceived by Spaniards as a coming-out party for the country. Not only was Spain a fully consolidated democracy, but also its economic development made it capable of hosting two of the most popular and expensive events in the world simultaneously. Spanish economic power allowed Spain to absorb the costs of these loss-incurring events.

The optimism raised by the Olympic Games and the Universal Exposition came to an abrupt end with the recession that afflicted Spain in the last two quarters of 1992 and the first two quarters of 1993. The crisis was much more severe than in other EEC members. GDP growth came to a standstill (OECD, 2010). Unemployment grew more rapidly than in the rest of Europe with permanent, full-time employment being particularly hit (*ibid.*). In spite of this inflation remained stubbornly high, staying above 4.5 per cent between 1992 and 1995 (*ibid.*). It seemed that Spain had a hangover from the boom that followed accession to the EEC, worsened by the sudden end to the construction spree associated to the Olympic and the Exposition projects.

Spaniards had not experienced a recession since 1981, so the Socialist government had no experience in dealing with a severe economic slowdown and rapidly increasing unemployment. To enhance the competitiveness of the Spanish economy, the government implemented three currency devaluations in 1992–3. This helped to increase exports when other European economies started to recover. The devaluation of the peseta helped to give a boost to incoming tourism. This sector was reinforced from Spain's successful hosting of the 1992 Olympics in Barcelona and Exposition in Seville (González and Moral, 1996: 739–54).

A second policy to improve the economic situation was the progressive reduction in interest rates to stimulate domestic demand. Between 1990 and early 1993 interest rates had hovered around 15 per cent. From then onwards they started to fall to under 10 per cent in 1995 (Ayuso *et al.*, 2006: 31). Business and consumer confidence improved, and investment in machinery and durable goods slowly began to recover. Both trends would continue after the election of the conservative Popular Party (Partido Popular, or PP, in Spanish) to power in March 1996.

However, the main engine behind Spain's economic recovery and eventual boom after the 1992–3 recession was the entry into force of the Maastricht Treaty in November 1993, along with the second phase of the Economic and Monetary Union of the European Union (EMU), initiated in January 1994. This gave credibility to the Spanish economy and currency beyond any policies that the government may have decided to implement. It also helped to stabilize the Spanish economy, which would go on to grow above the EU's average for 14 consecutive years.

Inward investment and financial flows grew as the prospects of Spain joining from the onset the EU single currency envisioned in the Maastricht Treaty increased. Restrictions on capital movements among EEC members had already been abolished in July 1990.[1] However, Spain only began to benefit from the free flow of capitals in earnest once investors were assured that Spain was a candidate to join the EU's single currency. This made the prospects of future currency devaluations like the ones implemented in 1992–3 unlikely. Eventually, Spain would be using a strong currency supported by a credible European Central Bank. It was expected that other macroeconomic indicators such as public deficit, inflation and unemployment would be reduced to the levels of countries such as Germany and France.

The conservatives in power

The period between 1996 and 2007 was marked by what many analysts have called a second 'Spanish economic miracle', after the one in the 1960s and 1970s. In 1995 economic growth in the euro region outpaced Spain's for the last time until 2008 (OECD, 2010). During this period Spain accounted for one third of all jobs created in the EU. Meanwhile, Spanish multinational corporations engaged in a process of overseas expansion which placed some banks, telecommunication businesses, energy companies and fashion groups among the leaders in their respective fields. For most of this period the conservative Popular Party was in power. Yet, the Socialist Party was also behind this sustained period of economic growth.

In March 1996, the Popular Party won the elections. The party had to form a coalition with Basque, Canarian and Catalan regionalists to govern. The Popular Party's three coalition partners shared its economic ideology: further liberalization and deregulation of the capital and labour markets, privatization of public companies and lowering of the tax burden. This was not a radical departure from the policies carried out by the previous government. Rather than sweeping changes to the policies introduced by the socialists, the conservatives tweaked some of them, accelerated others, and left unchanged those that they considered were working well.

The first major task that the new government set to achieve was compliance with the Maastricht convergence criteria to enter EMU. According to the Treaty on European Union (TEU, art. 104 and 109)[2] Member States seeking to join the euro had to achieve and respect five criteria, namely 1. an inflation rate no more than 1.5 per cent higher than the average of the three best-performing Member States, 2. interest rates of long-term government securities no more than 2 per cent above the average of the three best-performing Member States, 3. an annual government budget deficit no higher than 3 per cent of GDP, 4. a national debt lower than 60 per cent of GDP and 5. membership of the exchange-rate mechanism under the European Monetary System for two consecutive years without currency devaluation. When the conservatives had come to power in 1996, Spain did not fulfil criteria 3 and 4, was barely complying with criteria 1 and 2, and there were many doubts about whether it could observe criteria 5.

To ensure that Spain would meet the convergence criteria in time, the conservative government tightened the fiscal policy and reduced market rigidities further. GDP grew by 4 per cent (OECD, 2010) and unemployment decreased over 1 percentage point in 1997 (*ibid.*), helping to increase tax receipts and reduce social welfare costs. By May 1998, when the countries set to adopt the euro from the onset were to be decided, Spain was in compliance with the convergence criteria. Hence, on 1 January 1999, it was one of 11 founding members of the euro.

Membership of the euro provided an extra boost to the Spanish economy. Between 1999 and 2001 growth averaged 4.4 per cent (*ibid.*). In 2001 the unemployment rate was reduced to 10.4 per cent, the lowest figure since 1980 (*ibid.*). Inflation stabilized around the 3–3.5 per cent mark, the lowest rate in decades (*ibid.*). The budget deficit comfortably remained below the 3 per cent threshold (*ibid.*). In short, Spain reached sustained macroeconomic stability for the first time in decades. It could be argued that the country finally had an economy that resembled that of other Western European countries.

Since monetary policy had been transferred to the European Central Bank created in June 1998, fiscal and labour policies and liberalization became the major tools to drive economic growth. The conservative government followed the path of its socialist predecessor and cut public spending. After the binge prior to the 1992 Olympics and Exposition, investment in infrastructure and other public works had significantly slowed down. These austerity measures continued under the government led by the Popular Party. In addition, a public administration wage freeze was introduced and only a quarter of retiring civil servants were replaced. With regards to the labour market a new contract was introduced. Redundancy costs were lowered and the grounds for justified dismissals were broadened (Murphy, 1999: 65–74).

Perhaps the biggest change between the socialist and conservative governments took place in the area of privatization, liberalization and deregulation. The new government significantly accelerated privatization of public sector companies. The goal was not to improve the overall efficiency of the economy but rather to raise capital and reduce the state deficit. Only railways and subways, television and radio services, post and coal-mining escaped privatization. Nevertheless, privatization preceded liberalization and deregulation (Comín, 2008: 713–16). The result was that state monopolies in sectors such as telecommunications, electricity, oil or natural gas were transformed into private monopolies. When these markets were completely opened up to competition in the early 2000s, former state monopolies enjoyed a competitive advantage which they still maintain ten years later.

In spite of the success of the Spanish economy after the recession of the early 1990s, several problems still afflicted the country. To begin with, high unemployment, trade deficits and budgetary deficits did not disappear. In addition, inflation, while lower, persistently remained around 1 percentage point above the EU average. Second, labour productivity did not close the gap with other EU economies. In fact, taking into account population growth Spanish economic growth lagged behind most other developed countries, a result of stagnant productivity gains. In short, the structural weaknesses present at the end of the first Spanish miracle had not been dealt with.

Furthermore, and related to the previous point, Spain's economic growth was heavily dependent on a housing bubble and increasing inward tourism. The Spanish economy failed to capitalize on years of economic growth to diversify and move up the value chain. In addition, the labour market remained ill prepared to face globalization-induced competition. Successive waves of labour market liberalization had not offset costs derived from remaining rigidities and higher costs due to the strength of the euro. Despite sustained economic growth since the 1960s, the Spanish economy still relied on low value added industries and services. As we shall see in the next section, these are key factors to explain why Spain was hit by the 2007–10 financial crisis harder than most other advanced economies.

The global financial crisis and Spain

The worst financial crisis since the Great Depression began in 2007 in the United States and rapidly spread around the world. In general, developed economies in the West suffered more than their Asian counterparts or emerging markets. Of all developed economies, no other had a recession for as long as Spain did. The Spanish economy contracted for six consecutive quarters, throughout the second half of 2008 and the whole of 2009. When the country hobbled out of recession, in the first quarter of 2010, its GDP grew by a meagre 0.1 per cent. In short, the crisis affected Spain as much as any other economy in spite of the country not being a big financial centre and having a relatively healthy banking system. What explains the Spanish economy being hit harder by the financial crisis than most others?

By the time the Socialist Party regained power in March 2004, rebalancing the economy would have meant a painful restructuring. Economic growth following the 1992–3 crisis had been led by a housing and tourism boom. Even in 2007, when the crisis had already arrived, the building sector still accounted for around 18 per cent of

Spanish GDP (INE, 2010). Tourism accounted for a further 11 per cent of GDP.[3] Together, these two sectors employed 21 per cent of all working Spaniards (*ibid.*). In short, the Spanish economic miracle was to a large extent based on two sectors of little productivity.

Moving the economic model away from these two labour-intensive sectors would have taken time. Hence, the José Luis Rodríguez Zapatero administration implemented an economic policy modelled on that of the previous government. Labour-intensive industries such as agriculture, textiles and car manufacturing were offered public help to make up for their loss of competitiveness against foreign rivals and avoid lay-offs. Regions such as Andalusia, Extremadura and Galicia remained to a large extent dependent on EU transfers. One of the few notable deviations from the conservative government's economic policy was an expansion of social benefits for groups such as new parents and first-time home buyers. However, these policies made the budget deficit grow bigger. Above all, construction and tourism remained as the two main growth engines (Royo, 2009).

When the first signs of the global financial crisis arrived in 2007, Spain was unprepared to withstand prolonged economic upheaval. Unemployment, at 8.3 per cent, was still above the EU average and high for a country that had been growing for 14 consecutive years (OECD, 2010). Inflation stubbornly remained above the EU average (*ibid.*). The current account deficit stood at about 10 per cent of GDP, one of the largest among developed economies (Blanchard, 2007: 3). Having transferred control over monetary policy to the European Central Bank and with new EU Member States attracting capital in search for greater returns and a greater share of structural funds from Brussels, the socialist government did not have the tools used to escape the previous crisis: currency devaluations and relying on inward investment and aid.

The socialist government and the crisis, step one: denial

Similarly to other European countries, the global financial crisis began to affect Spain in late 2007, a few months after the problems that began with defaults in the American subprime mortgage market spread to other developed countries. However, the government and some economic agents at first thought that the Spanish economy would be relatively shielded from the problems in the United States. Thanks to stringent regulation imposed in the years after the death of Francisco Franco, the Spanish banking system was deemed to be better positioned to withstand the crisis than most Western counterparts. Banks had been forbidden from investing in the subprime market and had high capital provisions, making them less exposed to defaults by mortgage holders or to capital liquidity shortages (Royo, 2009: 24–5, 28). Hence, the banking system was strong and it seemed that this would sustain the Spanish economy throughout the crisis.

As a result, the government thought that Spain would not need to implement the measures that other countries were introducing to sustain their economies. This was partly driven by economics, since it was genuinely believed that Spanish banks were solvent enough to propel up the economy. But it was also motivated by political calculations. Spain was due for a general election in March 2008. The socialist government did not want to run a campaign focused on the need for painful yet necessary austerity measures. However, even after Prime Minister Rodríguez Zapatero was re-elected the government still communicated a positive message. Truly tough measures would not be announced until May 2010, when the severe Greek debt crisis threatened to spread to Spain as well.

Between the onset of the crisis and the moment when the government announced a sweeping reform package, the Spanish economy suffered greatly. Arguably, it was the job market sector of the economy that was hit hardest. In 2007, unemployment was at 8.7 per cent, still high but at its lowest since 1979 (OECD, 2010). Furthermore, the economically active population stood at 65.6 per cent, an all-time record. This rate was similar to France's and less than four points below Germany's, which would have been considered unthinkable, even at the turn of the twentieth century (Eurostat, 2010).[4] The female employment rate of 54.9 per cent was particularly remarkable in a country in which Francoist morals had relegated women to the traditional role of housewives (*ibid.*). Even though wage restraint in the previous years had meant that the salary differential with euro area members had stagnated at around 10 per cent, it seemed that Spanish labour had not had it so good for a long time.

Equally remarkable, by 2007 Spain had been transformed from a country of economic emigrants into the host of great amounts of job-seeking immigrants. Between 2000 and 2007 Spain absorbed more than 3 million immigrants, bringing the total to 4.5 million. Over 11 per cent of the population was foreign-born, a level approaching that of traditional destinations of emigrants such as the United States.[5] Immigration provided a welcomed dynamism to the Spanish economy by spurring the creation of new SMEs and enhancing labour flexibility due to immigrants being more willing to relocate than Spanish nationals. The agricultural, construction, health and homecare sectors, in particular, greatly benefited from this influx of immigrants.[6]

This marked improvement in the job market had vanished by 2010. In the first quarter unemployment was reported to be 19.1 per cent, five points above the country with the second highest rate in the OECD, Slovakia (OECD, 2010). The situation for Spanish youth was particularly dire, with almost four out of ten under-25s looking for a job, more than double the rate of 2007.[7] The economically active population had declined by almost six points, to the level of 2003. At 59.9 per cent, it was the fifth lowest among EU members (Eurostat, 2010). Government projections indicated that these figures would keep deteriorating and by late 2010 or early 2011 the situation of the Spanish job market would be worse than during the 1992–3 crisis. This occurred in spite of anecdotal evidence suggesting that tens of thousands of immigrants had left the country, unable to find work or to qualify for unemployment benefits after having lost their jobs. Hence, the gains of 14 years of uninterrupted economic growth were wiped out after three years of crisis. More worryingly, the sharp deterioration of the job market in Spain contrasted with that of most other Western countries, in which the employment picture did not weaken to the extent that would have been expected from the worst crisis since the Great Depression. This reflected the over-reliance of the Spanish economy on construction and tourism. The vast majority of jobs lost between 2008 and 2010 were in these two sectors,[8] an indicator of the dependence of the Spanish economy on sectors of limited productivity.

The budgetary deficit followed a pattern of deterioration similar to that of the job market. When the crisis began in 2007 public finances were in their best shape for over a decade. To ensure continuing compliance with the EU's Stability and Growth Pact, the conservative government had passed the General Budget Stability Law in 2001. The socialist government continued to observe it, with minor reforms passed in 2006 to make it less pro-cyclical. This law obliged all levels of government (central, regional and local) to keep their accounts permanently in balance (Ballart and Zapico, 2010: 244–5). Given the decentralized nature of the Spanish state, with the central government only accounting for 20 per cent of public spending excluding social security costs (Bajo Rubio, 2007: 58), the approval from sub-state governments with which the law was met provided a huge boost to public finances. By 2007, public debt had been reduced to below 40 per cent of GDP, in line with many other advanced economies and far below the 63 per cent of 1995. Between 2005 and 2007 Spain ran budget surpluses.

However, the crisis exposed the deficiencies of the conservative and socialist governments' debt reduction strategy. Rather than cutting spending as much as it would have been advisable, debt had been reduced thanks to greater revenue due to increasing affiliation to the social security system and budging consumption and subsequent growth in tax receipts.[9] In fact, public spending had increased in the two years prior to the crisis. Hence, when affiliations to the social security decreased as the employment rate fell and consumption was also reduced due to job insecurity, the budget deficit grew rapidly. Public debt was predicted to soar to 66 per cent of GDP in 2010 (Banco de España, 2010: 43) with the budget deficit reaching 9.49 per cent of GDP when only two years earlier it had had a surplus.[10] While other countries such as France or the United Kingdom had larger levels of public debt, the inability of the central government properly to control the expenses of sub-state authorities and the decrease in tax receipts as a result of declining consumption and the collapse of the housing market made international investors and organizations nervous at the prospect of Spain being unable to control its debt in the short to mid-term.

The socialist government and the crisis, step two: stern action

Throughout 2008 and 2009 the socialist government introduced an expansionary fiscal policy to contain the effects of the crisis. An 11 billion euro, two-year stimulus package to boost the construction and car industries and employment was unveiled in November 2008.[11] This was followed by tax cuts and measures to stimulate consumer spending valued at 50 billion euro announced in May 2009.[12] Five months later, in October, the government launched a second stimulus package worth 5 billion euro.[13] Public funds were also set aside to support banks with capitalization problems.

Nonetheless, it soon became clear that these measures were insufficient to boost the economy. As we have seen, the problems afflicting the Spanish economy ran deeper than those of other European countries hit hard by the crisis but with better long-term economic prospects. Two events sparked greater fears on the state of the Spanish economy beyond the crisis: sovereign debt problems in Greece and the downgrading of Spain's credit ratings.

Following national elections in October 2009, the newly elected socialist government in Greece announced that its conservative predecessor had tried to cover up the real extent of the country's economic deficit.

Lack of credibility on official economic figures, coupled with a public debt equivalent to 113 per cent of GDP and a budget deficit of 13.6 per cent of GDP led to fears that the Greek government might be tempted to default on its debt, or at least to restructure it. In May 2010 Greece had to activate an EU–IMF joint rescue package to be able to attend its debt payment obligations.[14]

Even though the size of Spain's economy was four times that of Greece's and both its public debt and budget deficit were significantly lower, markets pinpointed Spain, along with Portugal, as the next weakest link in the Eurozone. Spanish and European authorities repeatedly indicated that Spain was in a better position than Greece, with no discernable risk of default and no need to activate international rescue packages. However, this did not satisfy markets aware of the similarities between the Spanish and Greek economies: low productivity and economic competitiveness, debt problems and over-regulation. Avoidance of the problems afflicting Greece was one of the main reasons that led the socialist government in Spain to announce a stern reform package.

A second important reason was the downgrading of Spain's credit rating. Already, in January 2009, Standard & Poor's had downgraded Spain's rating from AAA to AA+. However, problems with ratings grew bigger in 2010. In April Standard & Poor's downgraded Spain's rating to AA with a negative outlook. One month later Fitch stripped the country of the AAA rating that it had held since 2003, cutting the grade to AA+, albeit with a stable outlook. Shortly afterwards, Moody's announced that it would place Spain on a three-month review of its AAA rating, which it could reduce by as much as two notches. The three agencies also reduced the credit rating of a host of regional governments, banks and companies. Standard & Poor's, Moody's and Fitch argued that fiscal problems, poor growth prospects and structural weaknesses were the main reasons behind the downgrading of the Spanish credit rating.[15]

To counter the effects of the crisis and restore market confidence on the long-term prospects of the Spanish economy, on 27 May 2010, the socialist-controlled Spanish parliament approved a 15 billion euro austerity package, aimed at reducing the deficit from 11.2 per cent of GDP to 6 per cent by 2011. Measures included a 5 per cent cut to public sector salaries, a 6 billion euro cut in public sector investment, a 1.2 billion euro reduction in funding to regional and local governments, and a suspension to automatic inflation-linked adjustments for pensions.[16] Absent the option of devaluing the currency and accused of being soft for fear of angering trade unions, the socialist government decided to introduce a package showing the serious measures it was taking to deal with the crisis.

Perhaps more importantly, on 22 June 2010, the parliament approved the most comprehensive labour market reform since the 1980s.[17] The reforms included the creation of 'job-boosting' contracts with lower severance pay, making it easier for companies with financial difficulties to lay off workers more cheaply; creating a government fund to help these companies; allowing companies to forgo collective wage agreements in times of financial instability; and capping the length of temporary contracts.[18] These measures aimed at reducing labour costs and tackling a two-tier labour market in which workers in temporary contracts, which account for 30 per cent of the workforce in Spain against an EU average of 10 per cent, were discriminated against.

In addition, the Bank of Spain and the government put pressure on uncompetitive regional and local banks to merge and create stronger institutions. Spain has a two-tier banking system, with strong private banks sitting in contrast to dozens of less competitive and highly politicized *cajas*. The former were only mildly affected by the financial crisis, and some of them, such as Santander Central Hispano and Bilbao Vizcaya Argentaria, actually strengthened relative to their European counterparts during the crisis. However, a host of *cajas*, or saving banks, often controlled by or with very close links to regional and local politicians, ran into trouble. They were more affected by the burst of the housing and construction bubbles, since during the boom years they had been offering loans to customers and companies that otherwise would have found it difficult to access credit. Pressures for these saving banks to merge began in 2009 and intensified in 2010, leading to several mergers starting from May 2010. Shortly afterwards, in July, the socialist government passed legislation aimed at reducing the politicization of *cajas*.[19]

The labour reform and pressure on politicized *cajas* to merge were seen as steps towards overcoming the long-standing weaknesses of the Spanish economy. Hence, the crisis served as a spark for the socialist government to work on these weaknesses. International institutions and foreign governments welcomed this development, hoping that changes to uncompetitive fiscal and industrial policies, reform of a weak education system and less political meddling on the economy at the regional and local levels would follow.

Conclusion

Spain's long-standing economic weaknesses were exacerbated by the financial crisis. Unemployment and the budget deficit soon soared. After a brief period of deflation, inflation again surged above the EU average. When the 1992–3 crisis struck, three currency devaluations and economic inflows associated to EEC structural funds and the prospect of joining the EMU had helped Spain become more competitive and attract foreign investment. These two options were not available in 2007–10, making it harder for the country to return to stable growth. Moreover, the inability to replace construction and tourism as the most important engines of economic growth since the 1980s aggravated the effects of the crisis, since these sectors were two of the most affected by a reduction in the access to credit. Hence, it is not surprising that Spain suffered from the crisis more than the rest of big economies in the EU.

Nevertheless, by mid-2010 it seemed that the socialist government was taking measures not only to deal with the immediate needs of the Spanish economy, but with its structural deficiencies as well. Following the dictum that a severe crisis might be used to make much-needed changes, the government introduced a substantial reform to the labour market and measures to cut the budget deficit speedily. Further changes to ensure that competitiveness is enhanced by directing public and private investment towards higher value added sectors, thus reducing the trade deficit and inflation, would be necessary. Despite the staggering impact of the financial crisis on Spain, it could end up serving to strengthen the Spanish economy by helping it to move from an obsolete model which served the country well in the past but which does not meet its present and future needs.

Notes

1. Council Directive 88/361/EEC of 24 June 1988 for the implementation of Article 67 of the Treaty.
2. 'Europa – Glossary – Convergence Criteria', available at http://europa.eu/scadplus/glossary/ convergence_criteria_en.htm (accessed 8 July 2010).
3. David Page Polo, 'La aportación del turismo al PIB cae a su mínimo histórico', *Expansión*, 18 February 2010.
4. 'Eurostat – Economically Active Population', available at http://epp.eurostat.ec.europa.eu/portal/page/ portal/eurostat/home/ (accessed 9 July 2010).
5. 'Spain: Immigrants Welcome', *Businessweek*, 21 May 2007.
6. International Monetary Fund, 'Spain – 2007 article 4 consultation, preliminary conclusions of the IMF mission', available at www.imf.org (accessed 9 July 2010).
7. Nelson D. Schwartz, 'In Spain, A Soaring Jobless Rate for Young Workers', *The New York Times*, 21 December 2009.
8. Alasdair Fotheringham, 'Any Green Shoots Wither in Spain as Jobless Figures Rise', *The Independent*, 7 February 2010.
9. International Monetary Fund, 'Spain – 2007 article 4 consultation'.

10. Nigel Davies, 'Spain's Gov't March Budget Deficit 8.9 Bln Euros', *Reuters*, 2 April 2010.
11. Victoria Burnett, 'Spain Unveils €11 Billion Economic Stimulus Package', *The New York Times*, 27 October 2008.
12. Associated Press, 'Spain Unveils Stimulus Package', *Associated Press*, 13 May 2009.
13. L. R. Aizpeolea, 'El Gobierno prevé crear 200.000 empleos con el Fondo Local para 2010', *El Pais*, 23 October 2009.
14. Gabi Thesing and Flavia Krause-Jackson, 'Greece gets $146 Billion Rescue in EU, IMF Package', *Bloomberg*, 3 May 2010.
15. Soeren Kern, 'Spain: A Political Risk Analysis', *The Brussels Journal*, 11 June 2010.
16. BBC, 'Spanish Politicians Approve 14bn-euro Austerity Plan', *BBC*, 27 May 2010.
17. For an overview of previous reforms, see Gil Marín (2002).
18. Tracy Rucinski, 'Factbox: Spain Headed for Job Market Reform', *Reuters*, 16 June 2010.
19. Europa Press, 'Salgado dice que la salida de los políticos de las cajas tendrá un período de transición', *Europa Press*, 9 July 2010.

References

Ayuso, J., Blanco, R. and Restoy, F. (2006) *House Prices and Real Interest Rates in Spain*, Madrid: Banco de España.
Bajo Rubio, Ó. (2007) 'El marco de la política fiscal en España: Sostenibilidad del déficit público e implicaciones de la UEM', *Política Económica en España*, vol. 837, pp. 57–70.
Balfour, S. (2000) 'The Desarrollo Years, 1955–1975', in J. Álvarez Junco and A. Shubert (eds), *Spanish History since 1808*, London: Hodder Arnold.
Ballart, X. and Zapico, E. (2010) 'Budget Reforms in Spain: Anything Else Beyond Budget Discipline?', in J. Wanna, L. Jensen and J. de Vries, *The Reality of Budgetary Reform in OECD Nations: Trajectories and Consequences*, Cheltenham: Edward Elgar, pp. 240–59.
Banco de España (2010 *Informe de proyecciones de la economía española*, vol. 31.
Blanchard, O. (2007) 'Current Account Deficits in Rich Countries', MIT Department of Economics Working Paper 6.
Comín, F. (2008) 'Public Enterprises in Spain: Historical Cycles and Privatizations', *Análise Social*, vol. 43, no. 4, pp. 693–720.
Crespo MacLennan, J. (2000) *Spain and the Process of European Integration, 1957–85*, Basingstoke: Palgrave Macmillan.
Eurostat (2010) 'Economically Active Population', available at http://epp.eurostat. ec.europa.eu/portal/page/ portal/eurostat/home/ (accessed 9 July 2010).
Gil Marín, S. (2002) 'An Overview of Spanish Labour Market Reforms, 1985–2002', Unidad de Políticas Comparadas (CSIC), Working paper 17.
González, P. and Moral, P. (1996) 'Analysis of Tourism Trends in Spain', *Annals of Tourism Research*, vol. 23, no. 4, pp. 739–54.
Harrison, J. and Corkill, D. (2004) *Spain: A Modern European Economy*, Aldershot: Ashgate.

INE (2010) 'Instituto Nacional de Estadística – Contabilidad nacional de España', available at www.ine.es (accessed 8 July 2010).

Lieberman, S. (1995) *Growth and Crisis in the Spanish Economy: 1940–93*, Abingdon: Routledge.

López-Claros, A. (1988) *The Search for Efficiency in the Adjustment Process: Spain in the 1980s*, Washington, DC: International Monetary Fund.

Murphy, B. (1999) 'European Integration and Liberalization: Political Change and Economic Policy Continuity in Spain', I, vol. 4, no. 1, pp. 53–78.

OECD Statistics (2010) available at www.oecd.org/statsportal (accessed 8 July 2010).

Recio, A. and Roca, J. (1998) 'The Spanish Socialists in Power: Thirteen Years of Economic Policy', *Oxford Review of Economic Policy*, vol. 14, no. 1, pp. 139–58.

Royo, S. (2009) 'Reforms Betrayed? Zapatero and Continuities in Economic Policy', *South European Society and Politics*, vol. 14, no. 4, pp. 435–51.

Salmon, K. (2001) 'Spanish Foreign Direct Investment, Transnationals and the Redefinition of the Spanish Business Realm', *International Journal of Iberian Studies*, vol. 14, no. 2, pp. 95–109.

Sosvilla-Rivero, S. and Herce, J. A. (2004) 'La política de cohesión europea y la economía española: Evaluación y prospectiva', *Documento de trabajo. Real Instituto Elcano*, vol. 142.

Viñals, J. (ed.) (1992) *La Economía Española ante el Mercado Único Europeo: Las Claves del Proceso de Integración*, Madrid: Alianza Economía.

10
France: Steering Out of Crisis?

Susan Milner

Introduction

> This crisis isn't really a crisis, for the following reason: France has been living in a state of permanent crisis since 1993.
>
> (Cohen, 2009: 9, author's translation)

In many ways, the banking crisis and economic recession provided less of a shock to the French economy than in many other countries.[1] To start with, France has been managing the tensions of internationalization and the constraints of coexistence within the Eurozone for some time now, and the crisis merely amplified these. Moreover, the continued steering and regulatory role of the French state ensured that the worst excesses of financial deregulation were largely avoided and later provided reassurance of prudential management, allowing confidence to be restored. Finally, France's elaborate system of social protection acted as a shock absorber, mitigating the impact of crisis.

However, this is not to say that the country was not badly hit or that it has necessarily found its way out of crisis. France suffers a persistent balance of payments problem but above all continues to live beyond its means. The labour market is particularly vulnerable to economic downturn and high unemployment in turn creates social tension as well as a waste of human potential. It suffers from governance problems which make reform uneven and sometimes even counterproductive. Moreover, debates have begun in France about the longer-term shifts in the productive system which require not only preparations for the upturn but also thinking about new, post-crisis ways of organizing the economy.

In this chapter, the current state of the French economy and short-term forecasts for growth will be reviewed. Debates around policy choices will then be presented, focusing in particular on the need to tackle unemployment while also reducing public debt.

French banking system

Banks occupy a significant space in the French economy, accounting for 2.4 per cent of GDP in 2008 (slightly down from 2.5 per cent in 2006 and 2007), with insurance contributing a further 1.7 per cent (Banque de France, 2008: 102). French banks account for 10 per cent of the global banking system and 5 per cent of global capital markets (Xiao, 2009).

Overall, French banks appear to have withstood the financial crisis relatively well, partly because within the concentrated sector the large universal banks were able to spread risk, partly because of a tradition of more stringent regulation, and partly because of a more stable domestic environment with high levels of saving (*ibid.*). The relatively large size of mutual funds also acts to stabilize the system.

The French state has traditionally played a significant role in ensuring the stability of the banking and insurance industry, culminating in the 1980s wholesale nationalization of the industry. Even after privatization in the following decade, the French economy was characterized by interlocking relationships between finance and industry which created a system of checks and balances. The government deliberately created two large cross-shareholding groups around Paribas and Société Générale on one hand, and Suez and BNP on the other.

However, this cosy relationship between banks and the state was broken up from the late 1990s as foreign (mainly British and American) institutional investors moved in to take an increasing share of French companies, which in turn found it easier to raise money through equity markets (see Culpepper, 2006). Restructuring through a series of takeovers and mergers led to a concentration of the sector (see Banque de France, 2008: 106–8, 123–8) as well as to an opening-up to international capital, particularly from other big EU Member States. The attempt by BNP's Michel Pébereaus to mount a hostile takeover of both the BNP and Société Générale, blocked by the government and leading to the creation of BNP Paribas (against the initial desire of Paribas to merge with Société Générale), was famously heralded by the leading protagonist as marking the end of *le capitalisme à papa* (daddy's old style of capitalism) and the definitive adoption of a more aggressive role for French banks and a greater importance of investment banking.

As a result, a small number of big banks had grown very powerful, leading both to fears about institutions that were 'too big to fail' (i.e., whose collapse would undermine the entire economy) and to concerns about inadequate supervision. Both fears appeared founded in the wake of the 2008 scandal involving 'rogue trader' Jérôme Kerviel at Société Générale (whose defence lawyers in his June 2010 trial argued that his actions reflected normal practice within the bank rather than rogue activities, a claim which former bank chief Daniel Bouton's sentencing around the same time for insider trading did nothing to dispel). In the summer of 2008, Société Générale announced gloomy results for the second year running, although overall French banks remained in profit in 2008. French banks were also through their international holdings exposed to risks taken by more reckless investment banks and property investors elsewhere, most notably Lehman Brothers but also German company Hypo Real Estate and other European businesses (Hoang-Ngoc, 2009: 429). They lost over $30 billion as a direct result of the crisis (see Hoang-Ngoc, 2009).

Some experts also feared that France's financial system carried inadequate protection against risk, with risk management characterized by the OECD as 'inadequate' (OECD, 2010a: 17). The OECD argued that deposit banks need to be protected from the risk of investment banking activities. The risk (relatively high compared with the US or Japan, but nevertheless significantly lower than in the UK or Germany) of contagion from the banking crisis in France was averted by state action. The French government, working within a coordinated EU action plan, stepped in quickly to set up an interbank loan guarantee fund of 320 billion euros and recapitalize the leading banks through loans totalling 10.5 billion euros; the most vulnerable of the banking groups, the Belgian-French bank Dexia, received 3 billion euros of capital, making the French, alongside the Belgian government, the biggest shareholders in the group. This operation was followed up with a second injection of 10 billion euros in January 2009, despite the concerns raised by the European Commission about the size of the bailout. Domestic sceptics also queried the need for such large-scale expenditure given the overall profitability of French banks and the relatively limited number of banks with serious problems.

The French president also attempted to take a leading role at European level in a large-scale rescue and re-regulation of the banking sector, although his proposal for a 'Paulson' plan met with German resistance. France continued to take a firm stance on regulation of financial markets at home and to attempt to play a leadership role in the EU. French rescue and re-regulation of the banking sector must be seen as a project to inspire a sense of strong leadership and domestic confidence. France, in line with the OECD's advice that regulation would need to be supranational (OECD, 2010a), followed closely the G-20 commitments to financial regulation (Basel II and III) and anticipated the EU's regulatory activities in several respects, in a series of decrees from January 2009 and in the bill adopted at first reading in the lower house of parliament in June 2010 (with full adoption expected in October 2010). With these measures, the government established new rules for transparency and accountability of ratings agencies, new restrictions on the payment of bonuses to traders, a new compensation chamber for derivatives contracts as well as rules for the registration of all contracts (to be set up at European level), new supervisory mechanisms within banks to improve risk management and monitoring, registration of hedge funds and hedge fund managers, a system of colleges to supervise banking and insurance activities, and a new council for financial and systemic risk regulation, to work closely with the strengthened Financial Markets Authority (Lagarde, 2010). With these actions, the French government laid claim to a pioneering role within the EU.

By mid-2010 the big banks looked healthy in terms of profitability, equity capital and lower exposure to investment risks. Job losses in the sector have been relatively small. Christian Noyer, governor of the Banque de France (and member of the ECB's governing council), stated in a radio interview on 29 June 2010 that 'French banks are doing well ... they have a good level of confidence between them and there aren't any big problems here' (Noyer, 2010a), but he also recognized that interbank loans were still at a lower level than before the crisis. Following the ECB's stress tests published on 23 July 2010, which gave a clean bill of health to the four major French banks (Société Générale, BNP Paribas, Crédit Agricole and Banque Populaire-Caisse d'Épargne (BPCE)) which together account for over three-quarters of business in the sector, French banks were 'among the most solid in Europe', Noyer claimed. His remarks echoed those of the finance minister Christine Lagarde who claimed before and after the stress tests that French banks were 'solid' and healthy' (see Ministère de l'Économie, 2010). By 2010, Société Générale, BNP Paribas and Crédit Agricole had repaid their government loans, while BPCE claimed to be on track to repay by 2013.

Economic outlook in 2010: a fragile recovery

Governor of the Banque de France (and Vice-President of the European Central Bank) Christian Noyer, in a radio interview in April 2010, claimed that Europe was emerging from recession and France had 'come out of it quite well' but emphasized the fragility of the upturn, with investment and consumer confidence remaining low (Noyer, 2010b; see also INSEE, 2010a). Growth rates improved in 2010 but in line with the situation in the Eurozone as a whole remain more sluggish than elsewhere in the developed world, reflecting doubts about the solidity of the upturn and the governance of the Eurozone.

Noyer in a later interview confirmed that his forecast of 1.4 per cent growth for the first quarter of 2010 was on target (thus, with lower growth likely in the second quarter his 2009 forecasts for 2010 of just over 1 per cent looked achievable), but it would resume more strongly towards 2011 and could even reach around 2 per cent if there was sufficient confidence in the economy. Noyer forecast between five and ten years of austerity before a return to prosperity. The national statistics office INSEE produced a rather sober assessment of France's economic performance in June 2010, arguing that the economy was still in the middle of crisis, with an initially favourably outlook in the first half of 2010 giving way to difficulties later in the year due to low domestic demand and the high risks associated with international trade due to contract as a result of restrictive macroeconomic policies (INSEE, 2010a).

The fragility of economic growth is underscored by France's longer-term performance which was notably weaker than elsewhere in the Eurozone; thus, the financial crisis 'grafted itself onto [an already] gloomy economic situation' (Hoang-Ngoc, 2009: 422) in the summer of 2008. If anything, the search for the green shoots of recovery masked this longer-term weakness from the beginning of the 2000s.

There were some signs of a return to manufacturing growth in 2010, with manufacturers reporting increased confidence (Société Générale, 2010: 33). Industrial output grew very slowly (less than 1 per cent per month) but steadily in the first half of 2010 after a more irregular pattern of growth and contraction in 2009. However, France's trading position

Table 10.1 Economic growth as % of GDP

	2007	2008	2009	2010 (est.)	2011 (est.)
France	2.3	0.1	–2.5	1.3	1.6
Average for Eurozone	2.8	0.4	–4.1	1.1	1.6
Average for industrialized countries	2.8	0.6	–3.5	2.5	2.3

Source: Société Générale, 2010: 2.

continues to worsen as international markets contract. After improvement in the 1990s, France moved into a trade deficit from 2000 and more markedly after 2005, as the dollar depreciated against the euro and oil prices rose. The trade deficit in May 2010, at a record 5,500 billion euros (Direction Générale des Douanes, 2010), was lower than for the Eurozone average as the bigger Eurozone countries export more outside the zone (60 per cent for Germany and 50 per cent for France) and were therefore helped by the euro's fall against the dollar (Société Générale, 2010: 14). Nevertheless on the basis of current trends France is unlikely to be able to close the trade gap in the near future.

The worsening of France's position in the international economy, particularly in manufacturing, has been a source of concern for some time, with a series of high-level reports drawing attention to the threats posed by international competition. Its exports are still heavily reliant on older industries, which face tough international competition and market saturation, and it has lost 'industrial substance' (see, e.g., Fontagné and Lorenzi, 2005). The current difficulties of the automotive industry (which, together with its subsidiary activities, represents as much as 10 per cent of total employment) are a particular cause for concern given their importance for France's export trade (Cohen, 2009). In this context the need to ensure long-term investment, develop knowledge-intensive industries and support technological development and human capital formation appears paramount. Survey data suggest R&D investment is likely to decrease in a significant proportion of firms (*ibid.*: 46) and that overall it is stagnant. Given that R&D investment as a proportion of GDP (at 1.3 per cent) falls well below that of Japan and the US, concerns about France's capacity to innovate its way out of crisis are substantial.

Rather than businesses, the French public expects the state to provide solutions to the crisis and prepare for post-crisis (Chauvet and Schanze, 2009). Early in the crisis, trade unions staged a series of mass demonstrations aimed at securing a more interventionist economic, industrial and social policy. Following the 'social summit' of February 2009, a countercyclical plan amounting to some 26 billion euros was announced, with sectoral initiatives (particularly in the automobile industry) to support businesses, 1,000 public works projects and increased support for short-term unemployed. In a second phase, a 'grand emprunt' (large-scale loan) was taken out in December 2009 in order to fund infrastructure and research spending, with around two-thirds of the total 35 billion euros going to fund centres of excellence in priority areas (health and biotechnologies, aeronautics, space, nuclear and low-carbon energies). The loan goes some way to responding to accusations, particularly from the left, that the president had not been proactive in investing in the post-crisis economy, but reactions were mixed. A particular criticism, highlighted in economist Daniel Cohen's report to the Centre d'Analyse Stratégique in 2009 and expected to form a major plank of Jacques Attali's report on 'Liberating economic growth' presented in September 2010, is that France has not invested sufficiently in the digital economy, either in the public or private sector. In addition, although there is high political awareness of the 'green recovery' agenda and an emphasis on renewable energy sources in the most recent research and education policies and spending, the crisis has not so far thrown up a clear strategy for building a new model of economic development.

Public debt is high (OECD, 2010a; b) and rising. The public deficit reached 8 per cent of GDP in 2010. In its plan for reducing the deficit presented to the European Commission in January 2009, the French government argued that it could bring the deficit down to 3 per cent by 2013, based on plans to reduce spending by some 100 billion euros year on year, and renewed growth of 2.5 per cent in 2011, 2012 and 2013. Given that even the most optimistic forecasts see growth as reaching around 2 per cent at most over this period, sceptics expressed doubt about the government's ability to reach its targets. However, experts closer to government pointed out that France's structural debt was significantly lower than in many other European countries and saw signs of optimism in the country's relatively high fertility rates, moves to reduce social expenditure (see below) and relatively low levels of private debt (Brand and Passet, 2010).

The austerity measures announced by the government therefore looked relatively cautious when compared, say, to the British government's first round of cuts announced at the same time in June 2010, especially given the size of the savings they are intended to produce. Prime minister François Fillon presented cuts of 100 billion euros over three years, starting with government own expenditure ('train de vie du gouvernement'). No direct public sector cuts were announced, but a freeze in transfers to local government was confirmed (OECD, 2010b). The Attali report made further recommendations on efficiency savings in the public sector. France's public sector at between 21 per cent and 24 per cent of total employment looks large by OECD standards and is a regular target of recommendations by international organizations for cuts in spending (see, e.g., OECD, 2010b: 37).

Overall, then, the crisis as it unfolded has seen the French president and government combining its early, reactive version of 'pocket Keynesianism'[2] or, according to a more critical view 'sectoral and partial

Keynesianism' (Hoang-Ngoc, 2009: 433) with a later return to austerity in broad macroeconomic policy. At the same time, however, the early unconditional intervention to support banking companies was balanced by a relatively tough stance on regulation of the financial sector at European level, while expenditure became more strategically focused with the December 2009 loan to finance investment in higher education and research. The French government sought to promote a deliberate policy of *ri-lance* (a mixture of austerity, that is reduction of state spending, and Keynesian boosterism to finance innovation and R&D, financed by borrowing), which it sought to coordinate at European level.

In social and employment policy, on the other hand, a more classically liberal approach is evident, but constrained by popular unease about the unequal impact of spending cuts. Here, debates have focused on the role of the state in social protection rather than, as in previous economic downturns, on regulation of businesses.

Social and employment policy

Unemployment remained stable at 9.9 per cent in mid-2010 (9.5 per cent in mainland France excluding the overseas territories and departments), suggesting that the peak had passed and leading to forecasts of a reduction by the end of 2011. The main reason the crisis did not result in greater job losses is that firms were able to adapt by cutting hours rather than shedding jobs, and also that, as in the US already in the early 1990s recession (see Peck and Theodore, 2007), temporary agency working absorbed well over half of the total job losses in the current recession (Cohen, 2009: 109–12; see also Eichhorst *et al.*, 2010). Part-time work has risen steadily in France, from 6 per cent of total employment in 1972 to 9 per cent in 1983 and 17 per cent in 2006 (Berrebi-Hoffmann *et al.*, 2009: 195).

Nevertheless, nearly 100,000 jobs have been lost each year during the recession, with a particularly sharp rise of 1.8 per cent in the unemployment rate in 2009 to reach 9.2 per cent or 2.7 million unemployed (ILO definition). Young men between the ages of 15 and 24 were particularly badly hit as youth unemployment rose to 23 per cent (INSEE, 2010b). The youth employment rate has dropped as young people, faced with the unfavourable jobs market, remain in education or training. This is likely to cause further 'crowding out' of the labour market in future years, further widen the gap between those with and those without educational qualifications and fuel societal fears about job insecurity (Maurin, 2009).

By mid-2010, a palpable sense of frustration about employment policies pervaded academic and policy debates in France. The government for its part seemed to congratulate itself on its 'voluntarist' approach which had, it was claimed, caused unemployment to rise less markedly than elsewhere in Europe (Waquiez, 2010), but for most commentators policy since 2007 had not had a significant impact on unemployment. The relatively high unemployment rate and low employment rate in France have been subjects of comment and policy recommendations for some time, with international organizations recommending labour market reform and development of active labour market policies (see, e.g., European Commission, 2009; OECD, 2010a; b). The main measures taken in response to the crisis (in the February 2008 plan for employment) corresponded to the more coercive side of the activation agenda: from January 2009, conditionality of unemployment benefit was strengthened by making it subject to acceptance of job offers, and the Revenu Minimum d'Insertion (a minimum income benefit which previously included a rather weak employment integration element) was replaced from 2009 with the Revenu de Solidarité Active, which is conceived rather as a top-up income for those already in very low-paid work. Criticized by some on the left as 'American-style workfare' (Hoang-Ngoc, 2009), the RSA has nevertheless been hailed by others as a real improvement for the poorest households and, as it is financed by a tax on top incomes, has a strong redistributive logic (see Clerc, 2008).

Between 1973 and 2005, public expenditure on employment rose from less than 1 per cent of GDP to almost 4.8 per cent (significantly above the EU average), and 48 per cent of this total is made up of spending on active labour market policy (Berrebi-Hoffmann *et al.*, 2009: 190). However, a significant proportion of this figure (amounting to 1.03 per cent of GDP) consists of employer subsidies by means of exemptions from social security contributions – for example, under subsidized youth employment contracts or new staff taken on in exchange for reduced working time (*ibid.*: 191), rather than active training measures which might, for example, enhance transferable skills. The share of subsidized jobs in total youth employment rose from 7.8 per cent in 1982 to 27 per cent in 2007 (INSEE, 2010b). Subsidized jobs may have negative effects such as displacement of other employment and 'churning', whereby young people move between subsidized jobs and/or spells of unemployment rather than from subsidized to stable employment. They do not necessarily address longer-term labour market disadvantage.

Concerns have also been voiced in France about the long-term unemployed whose share of total unemployment remains stable even as the overall rate increases. Anti-poverty groups are particularly worried about the increasing number (around a million in 2010) of unemployed people who reach the end of their entitlement to unemployment benefit, most of whom do not qualify for any other benefits. In response to such concerns and lobbying from the main trade union confederations, the government set up a working group to look at the 'social management of the employment consequences of economic crisis' but the group has so far struggled to find consensus, although a likely outcome may be a new unemployment benefit for unemployed older workers who have not yet reached retirement age (Rodier and Tricornot, 2010). Meanwhile the deficit of the bipartite unemployment benefit fund continues to grow each year.

More broadly, the crisis has drawn public attention to social inequalities. France does better in this regard than other developed nations, and certainly much better than the US; in 2008, France held the distinction of being the OECD country which had seen inequality grow least (OECD, 2008), thanks to its redistributive policies as well as to the socialist-led expansion of higher education in the 1990s which helped to shorten the differential between social groups (Maurin, 2009). However, there has been a tendency for the highest-earning groups to see their share of revenue increase disproportionately in recent years (Cotis, 2009; Landais, 2007). The banking crisis highlighted extremely high payments in the financial sector and in the broader economy, in a country where such payouts have long proved controversial. A majority of French people see high wages for company bosses as excessive and unjustified and such views have hardened during the crisis (Chauvet and Schanze, 2009: 169).

A particular feature of the French economy is that working conditions for the relatively small group of very low-paid workers have worsened (Caroli and Gautié, 2009), while the lower and middle classes have seen their purchasing power stagnate especially in relation to those in upper income brackets. The dualism of the French labour market, with heavy reliance on temporary agency work and outsourcing to peripheral labour markets, has been accentuated by the economic recession (Liégey, 2009), leading to calls for employment policy to focus particularly on helping those on the fringes of the labour market, particularly young labour market entrants and the long-term unemployed, to find their way into more stable employment.

In a context of recession, subjective employment insecurity slows down consumer confidence (Maurin, 2009) and a widespread feeling exists in France that the lower and middle classes have borne the brunt of the crisis. A survey carried out by TNS-Sofres in autumn 2009 (Chauvet and Schanze, 2009) found that 85 per cent of wage-earners at all levels feared they would be adversely affected by the crisis, with around one third worried about their jobs and 64 per cent concerned about loss of earning power. The government's fiscal policy has not helped to alleviate public disquiet, particularly the *bouclier fiscal* (fiscal shield) measure of June 2007 which overturned the taxation regime for France's most wealthy individuals and allowed for significant rebates on their contributions (see Hoang-Ngoc, 2009). Stories of 'tax gifts' to the rich appeared regularly the media and satirical websites in the years that followed, and, in July 2010, the move came back to haunt the president and his government with accusations of tax favours to the richest woman in France in return for financial support for the ruling party.

Cuts in social expenditure will only aggravate public perceptions of inequality, particularly as there is evidence that social benefits have cushioned France from the impact of recession (Moatti, 2010; OECD, 2010a). Eurobarometer surveys show the importance of the state's role in social protection for French society, with French respondents both particularly worried about growing poverty in their region and in the EU as a whole, and at the same time feeling that public social care (e.g., family and child support services) has improved during economic downturn (European Commission, 2010). Yet international organizations such as the OECD repeatedly call on France to cut its social expenditure, which at 25.9 per cent of GDP in 2009 is the highest in the EU, and the government is relying on decreased social spending to help balance the books by 2013. Healthcare alone accounts for 9.8 per cent of GDP (2009) and pensions a further 9.9 per cent. No one doubts the need to reduce the healthcare and pensions deficit in France, but proposals for reform constitute a political minefield as cuts tend to fall disproportionately on the neediest groups in society.

Pension reform formed a key part of President Sarkozy's reform agenda. In 2003 the rightwing government moved to align public with private sector pensions already reformed in 1993, on the basis of lengthened periods of contribution. The complexity of the system makes reform difficult (Milner, 2010; OECD, 2010b: 27) and the impact of the 2003 reforms was deferred over several years and differential according to the status of the workers concerned. Projections continued to show rising deficits at constant levels of contributions. More recently, it was estimated that the economic crisis had increased the pension fund deficit by −1.2 per cent due to lower income from contributions (Société Générale, 2010: 16).

The July 2010 reform proposal on pensions aimed to move reform forward but it was presented in a clumsy and seemingly inflexible way, with the government proposing raising the official retirement age from 60 (the flagship reform of the early Mitterrand era) to 62. Although such a change would be in line with reforms elsewhere in Europe and, indeed, the recommendations of the EU and OECD, such a move marked a break with the prevailing thrust of reform to date which was to base retirement age on length of contribution, recognizing that those in lower-income groups tend to enter the labour market earlier than professional groups. A large part of the justification for pension reform since 1993 has been the need to share burdens equitably, which created a broad consensus for reform and defused opposition. The principle of pension reform has wide support in France if it is framed in terms of reducing inequalities between occupational groups, and if it is balanced by fiscal measures which also appear to equalize the burden of austerity.

Beset by accusations of personal and political dishonesty aimed at both his employment minister and himself, President Sarkozy struggled to convince the French public in his television presentation of the reform on 13 July 2010.[3] Moreover, trade unions have the capacity not just to mobilize public demonstrations of opposition, but to hollow out the content of the reform in national-level negotiations on exemptions for workers in heavy or hazardous manual jobs.

Conclusion

To conclude, France has resisted the current economic crisis relatively well and has some advantages that will help it to emerge from crisis. The particular characteristics of its labour market and its complex and costly social protection system have acted as 'shock absorbers' to help it through recession. The relative security of the financial system has helped to sustain business and consumer confidence. The role of the state has also been crucial in helping to restore confidence through injections of capital and interventions to strengthen human capital and boost demand.

However, policy has also been marked by strong tensions and conflicts, particularly around public perceptions of social justice and egalitarian redistribution. Criticisms about the poor overall visibility of political strategy and 'navigating without instruments' rather than setting a clear course have dogged previous French governments (for example, at the end of the 1980s and even more so in the recession of the early

1990s). On the other hand, France has weathered criticism from international organizations over several decades and continued to follow an uneven, often idiosyncratic course, which has given it a certain amount of adaptability to crisis.

Longer term, France will need to find its own solutions to the broader issues about its productive power in the international marketplace (a forward-looking rather than adaptive and piecemeal policy on the production of goods and services) and how to fund the social solidarity its citizens prize. The current economic crisis has merely amplified these issues, and possibly provided a temporary distraction.

Notes

1. French economists within the national statistics agency INSEE's macroeconomic division estimated the impact of the crisis as costing France 4.1 percentage points of GDP in 2009, compared with −5.9 per cent for the Eurozone, 5 per cent for the US, 7 per cent for the UK and 8.3 per cent for Japan. See Lapègue and Mauroux (2010).
2. The phrase was used by journalist Jean-Claude Casanova in his radio interview with Christian Noyer: see Noyer (2010a).
3. See, e.g., 'Sarkozy n'a pas convaincu les Français', Les Échos, 14 July 2010.

References

Banque de France (2008) *Rapport annuel*, Paris.
Berrebi-Hoffmann, I., Jany-Catrice, F., Lucidi, F. and Naticchioni, P. (2009) 'Capitalizing on Variety: Risks and Opportunities in a New French Social Model', in G. Bosch, S. Lehndorff and J. Rubery (eds), *European Employment Models in Flux: A Comparison of Institutional Change in Nine European Countries*, Basingstoke, Palgrave Macmillan, pp. 178–200.
Brand, T. and Passet, O. (2010) 'La France et l'Europe face à la crise économique', *Note de Veille du Centre d'Analyse Économique*, no. 183, June.
Caroli, E. and Gautié, J. (eds) (2009) *Bas salaires et qualité de l'emploi: l'exception française?* Paris: Editions de la Rue d'Ulm.
Chauvet. E. and Schanze, C. (2009) *Nouveaux modèles de croissance: grand public et salariés*, Paris: TNS Sofres.
Clerc, D. (2008) *La France des travailleurs pauvres*, Paris: Grasset.
Cohen, D. (2009) *Sortie de crise: Vers l'émergence de nouveaux modèles de croissance?*, Rapport du groupe de travail, Paris: Centre d'Analyse Stratégique.
Concialdi, P. et al. (2009) *La France du travail: Données, analyses, débats*, Paris: Les Éditions de l'Atelier.
Cotis, J.-P. (2009) *Partage de la valeur ajoutée, partage des profits et écarts de rémunération, Rapport au Président de la République*, Paris: La Documentation Française.
Culpepper, P. D. (2006) 'Capitalism, Coordination and Economic Change: The French Political Economy since 1985', in P. D. Culpepper, P. A. Hall and

B. Palier (eds), *Changing France: The Politics that Markets Make*, Basingstoke: Palgrave Macmillan, pp. 29–49.

Direction Générale des Douanes (2010) *Les chiffres du commerce extérieur de la France*, Paris: Dossier de Presse.

Eichhorst, W., Fell, M. and Marx, P. (2010) 'Crisis, What Crisis? Patterns of Adaptation in European Labor Markets', Discussion Paper no. 5045, Bonn, Institute for the Study of Labor.

European Commission (2009) *Recommendation for a Council Recommendation on the 2009 up-to-date broad guidelines for the economic policies of the Member States and the Community, and on the implementation of Member States' employment policies*, 28.1.09 COM (2009) 34 final, vol. I, Brussels.

European Commission (2010) 'Monitoring the social impact of the crisis: public perceptions in the European Union (Wave 4)', *Eurobarometer Flash*, 289, Brussels.

Fontagné, L. and Lorenzi, J.-O. (2005) *Délocalisations, désindustrialisation*, Paris: La Documentation Française.

Hoang-Ngoc, L. (2009) 'La Sarkonomics entre promesses électorales et crise économique. Bilan d'étape fin 2008', *Modern & Contemporary France*, vol. 17, no. 4, pp. 423–34.

INSEE (Institut National de Statistiques et d'Études Économiques) (2010a) *Au milieu du gué. Note de conjoncture*, June, Paris, INSEE.

INSEE (2010b) *Les jeunes de moins de 26 ans dans les dispositifs de politique de l'emploi*, Tableaux de l'Économie Française, Paris, INSEE.

Lagarde, C. (2010) *G20 finance et avancées de la réforme de la régulation financière*, Dossier de Presse, Paris: Ministry of Finance, 2 June.

Landais, C. (2007) *Les hauts revenus en France (1998–2006): Une explosion des inégalités?*, Paris: Paris School of Economics.

Lapègue, V. and Mauroux, A. (2010) *Crise et dépendances. Note de conjoncture*, Paris: INSEE.

Liégey, M. (2009) L'ajustement de l'emploi dans la crise: la flexibilité sans la mobilité? *Note de veille*, no. 156, Paris: Centre d'Analyse Stratégique.

Maurin, E. (2009) *La peur du déclassement: Sociologie des récessions*, Paris: Seuil.

Milner, S. (2010) 'France's Exceptional Social Model', in T. Chafer and E. Godin (eds), *The French Exception*, Basingstoke: Palgrave Macmillan, pp.55–71.

Ministère de l'Économie, de l'Industrie et des Finances (2010) 'Les banques et les tests de résistance européens', Communiqué de presse, 23 July.

Moatti, S. (2010) 'La France en crise', *Alternatives Économiques: Pratique*, no. 043, April.

Noyer, C. (2010a) Entre cinq et dix ans de rigueur, Interview, Europe 1, 29 June.

Noyer, C. (2010b) Où en-est la crise?, Interview, France Culture, Paris, 17 April.

OECD (2008) *Growing Unequal? Income Distribution and Poverty in the OECD Countries*, Paris: OECD.

OECD (2010a) *Pour une croissance forte et soutenable. Contribution de l'OCDE à la Commission de la Croissance Économique*, Paris, 21 May.

OECD (2010b) *Economic Outlook*, no. 87, May.

Peck, J. and Theodore, N. (2007) 'Flexible Recession: The Temporary Staffing Industry and Mediated Work in the United States', *Cambridge Journal of Economics*, vol. 31, no. 2, pp. 171–92.

Rodier, A. and Tricornot, A. de (2010) 'Un million de chômeurs en fin de droits en 2010', *Le Monde*, 18 January.
Société Générale (edited by O. Garnier) (2010) *Analyse mensuelle. Juin 2010, perspectives 2011 de la situation économique*, Paris.
Wauquiez, L. (2010) 'Pour une politique volontariste de l'emploi', *Les Échos*, 10 May.
Xiao, Y. (2009) 'French Banks Amid the Global Banking Crisis', IMF Working Paper, 09/201, International Monetary Fund.

11
The Effects of the Financial Crisis on the Italian and US Labour Markets

Tindara Addabbo, Fahima Aziz and Jack Reardon

Introduction

The current financial crisis is the most severe since the Great Depression. Although it began in the United States, it has significantly disrupted labour markets across the globe. Given the severity of the crisis it is important to analyze both the short-term cyclical effects on families and individuals and the long-term effects on investment and economic growth. In particular, in this chapter we will analyze the short-term socio-economic effects of high unemployment, while at the same time delineating potential factors affecting long-term growth. We compare the labour markets of the United States and Italy. These two countries had very different labour market experiences before the crisis, and if we are to provide appropriate solutions to the crisis we need a global perspective and global comparison. The first section of the chapter will discuss and compare the two labour markets; the second section will discuss the effects of the crisis on them; the third section contains an estimation of the costs of unemployment in terms of poverty (both subjective and in terms of money income) and in terms of access (with regards to Italy) to health services; the last section will offer concluding observations and policy suggestions.

Similarities and differences between the US and Italian labour markets

The Italian labour market is deeply divided by region – the South and the Centre-North.[1] The former has historically had much higher unemployment rates and inactivity rates than the latter; the South has been characterized also by a much higher long-term and youth unemployment.

In Italy, in 2007, 20.3 per cent of youths aged less than 25 were unemployed versus 15.5 per cent in EU-27. For individuals included in the age range 25–9, higher education does not reduce the risk of unemployment: the unemployment rate is 11.5 per cent in Italy for those with a low level of educational attainment; 8.6 per cent for those with a medium level of educational attainment and 14 per cent for those with tertiary education (Eurostat, 2009). Italy is also characterized by a higher diffusion of the underground economy: on average 11.7 per cent of the total employment (against 5 per cent on average in other EU-15 countries) with a larger incidence of irregular labour in the South of Italy. In 2004 with respect to total employment, irregular labour ranged from 7.5 per cent in Emilia Romagna to 26.2 per cent in Calabria (Cappariello and Zizza, 2009; European Commission, 2004).

Compared to the US, the Italian labour market is characterized by a higher degree of trade union density and union coverage. In Italy, the degree of trade union density decreased from 50 per cent in 1980 to 33.3 per cent in 2007; whereas in the US it decreased from 22 per cent in 1980 to 11.6 per cent in 2007 (www.oecd.org).

Since 1996, the non-standard share of Italian employment (including short-term contracts) has significantly increased. According to ISTAT data (2009a), 13.3 per cent of employees in 2008 are in short-term contracts with a higher diffusion of temporary work among women (15.6 per cent of women employees are in temporary jobs) and young workers (23.7 per cent of employees aged less than 34 are in temporary jobs) (ISTAT, 2009a: 242).

Compared to the US, Italy is characterized by lower activity rates (Table 11.1). Though increasing since 1994, in 2007 women's activity rate in Italy was on average 50.7 per cent, compared to 69.1 per cent in the US.

Table 11.1 Labour force participation rates (1994–2007, women and men, aged 15–64)

	1994		2007	
	M	F	M	F
USA	84.3	69.4	81.7	69.1
Italy	74.2	41.9	74.4	50.7
E-15	78.4	56.5	79.5	64.5
OECD	81.4	57.8	80.5	61.1

Source: Table B, OECD (2008): 337–8.

Table 11.2 Employment rates (1994–2007, women and men, aged 15–64)

	1994 M	1994 F	gender gap	2007 M	2007 F	gender gap
USA	79	65.2	14	77.8	65.9	12
Italy	67.8	35.4	32	70.7	46.6	24
E-27				72.5	58.3	14
OECD	75.4	52.9	23	76	57.5	19

Source: www.oecd.org statistical database.

Turning to employment rates (Table 11.2), in Italy the employment rate of women aged 15–64 in 2007 was 46.6 per cent against 70.7 per cent for men. The gender gap in employment rates is on average 14 percentage points in EU-27, 19 percentage point in OECD countries, 12 percentage points in the US and 24 percentage points in Italy.

The effect of the crisis on the Italian and US labour markets

In December 2009 the US unemployment rate was 10.0 per cent, about 15.4 million people, slightly above the European one, which was 9.7 per cent. This percentage was twice as much that at the beginning of the crisis, in 2007. The unemployment rate in some sections of the US surpassed 25 per cent (Antonopoulous et al., 2010). In December 2009, unemployment rates were 10.2 per cent for adult men, 8.2 per cent for adult women, 27.1 per cent for teenagers, 9.0 per cent for whites, 16.2 per cent for blacks, 12.9 per cent for Hispanics and 8.4 per cent for Asians. For single mothers the unemployment rate stood at 13 per cent and youth unemployment rate at 27 per cent, more than twice the overall unemployment rate (US BLS, 2010a). The number of long-term unemployed (those jobless for 27 weeks and over) continued to increase, reaching 6.1 million in 2009. In December 2009, four out of ten unemployed workers were jobless for 27 weeks or longer.

The civilian labour force participation rate fell to 64.6 per cent in December 2009 from 66 per cent in 2008. The employment–population ratio declined to 58.2 per cent. Of significant interest, especially for the long-term effects of the crisis, is that after the 2001 recession ended the labour force participation rate (LFPR) continued to decline, never reversing itself, unlike any other post-World War II recession. Previously, the LFPR would decrease during a recession, then rebound and better its pre-recession peak within one or two years. During the 1973–5 recession, for example, the LFPR decreased slightly in 1974 and by 1975 it resumed its upward trend and in 1976 surpassed its pre-recession peak in 1973. Likewise, during the July 1990–March 1991 recession the LFPR dipped in 1991 but by 1994 it had surpassed its pre-recession peak; and during the double-dip recessions of 1980 and 1981 the LFPR did not decrease.

While data remain preliminary, one hypothesis is that the financial assets of older workers deteriorated during the collapse of the stock market bubble in 1999–2001 and their assets suffered a further deterioration in housing assets during the current crisis, inducing them to re-enter the labour market. But this still fails to explain why the LFPR for prime-age men and women did not increase after 2001 as it has in every other post-World War II recession. Something is fundamentally changing in the US labour market which predates the financial crisis.

In the US, the gender unemployment gap is the most disproportionate since 1948, when record-keeping began. According to the Bureau of Labour Statistics (BLS), male unemployment rates reached 10.2 per cent in December 2009, falling slightly from 10.4 per cent in November 2009. And for women, the unemployment rate hit 8.2 per cent in December 2009, increasing slightly from 8.0 per cent in November 2009. As of October 2009, males accounted for 5.3 million of the 7.3 million total jobs lost since the recession began; probably because approximately half of all job losses have been in manufacturing and construction, which are overwhelmingly male-dominated sectors.

The US labour market is characterized by sexual and racial discrimination. Women on average earn less than men within and across all occupations. In addition, there is pronounced occupational sex segregation, with male-dominated occupations jobs having higher earnings than female-dominated occupations. Women working full time in wage and salary jobs had median weekly earnings of $638, which was 80 per cent of men's median earnings weekly earnings of $798 in 2008 (US BLS, 2010b).

The current recession will exacerbate both wage discrimination and occupational segregation. Data from the US Census Bureau indicates that, in 2008, real median earnings for full-time, male workers declined by 1 per cent from $46,846 in 2007 to 46,347 in 2008. Real median earnings of full-time female workers declined from $36,451 in 2007 to $35,745 in 2008, a decline of 1.9 per cent. In 2008, 25 per cent of employed women worked part time (fewer than 35 hours per week), compared to 11 per cent of employed men (US BLS, 2010c).

Table 11.3 indicates the OECD harmonized unemployment rates from 2006 until the first quarter of 2009. The change in the unemployment rate since December 2007 was 1 per cent in Italy compared to 4.6 per cent for the US. According to OECD projections the unemployment rate in 2010 (quarter IV) will be 10.5 per cent in Italy and 10.1 per cent in the USA (OECD, 2009: 27). In July 2010 the unemployment rate in Italy was 8.4 per cent (ISTAT, 2010)[2] lower than 10 per cent in the euro area (Eurostat, 2010) with a higher level for women, 9.7 per cent, and a lower level for men, 7.5 per cent.

The increase in the Italian unemployment rates has been particularly high among youth. The unemployment rate for individuals aged 15 to 24 in Italy was 26.8 per cent in July 2010 (Eurostat, 2010); a rate which is higher than the European area average of 19.6 per cent, though lower than Spain (at 41.5 per cent) (Eurostat, 2010). The increase in the 15–24 years unemployment rate by 5 percentage points in the first quarter of 2009 was the highest since 1992. This increase is connected to the reduced number of hiring and the lack of renewal of temporary contracts (Bank of Italy, 2009a). In the US, the unemployment rate for teenagers (16–19 years) in December 2009 was 24.8 per cent, more than twice the overall unemployment rate. The unemployment rate for individuals aged less than 25 was 17.5 per cent (US BLS, 2010d).

Increased youth unemployment is problematic for both developed and developing nations and represents a significant long-term global problem. High rates not only decrease entry-level wages, which tend to persist over the individual's life cycle, but also demoralize potential labour market participants. The loss of current and potential output can significantly impact long-term economic growth.

In the US, according to the BLS, the number of discouraged workers (not currently looking for work because they believe no job is available) increased from 642,000 in December 2008 to 929,000 in December 2009, compared to 349,000 in November 2007, 13 months before the recession officially started. In December 2009, approximately 2.5 million workers were marginally attached to the labour force compared to 1.9 million in December 2009. The marginally attached are not officially in the labour force, but want and are available for work; they are officially not counted as unemployed since they have not looked for work in the four weeks preceding the survey, although they have looked for a job sometime in the prior 12 months. The number of discouraged workers, generally increasing with recessions, shows the greatest increase for young people, blacks, Hispanics and men. These demographic groups were over-represented relative to their numbers in the labour force. Once again this presents a significant obstacle to long-term economic growth.

When one includes part-time workers who were unable to find a full-time job along with discouraged workers, the job deficit exceeds 20 million in the US (US BLS 2010e).

In Italy, the already low activity rate has decreased particularly in the South (Bank of Italy, 2009b). In July 2010 provisional labour force survey data indicated an increase of inactivity rates by 0.4 percentage points since July 2009 for men aged 15–64 (26.5 per cent in July 2010), while the inactivity rates for similarly aged women increased by 0.1 percentage points to reach 49 per cent in July 2010 (ISTAT, 2010).

Another peculiarity of the Italian labour market is the access to the wage supplementation fund. The number of workers who accessed it sharply increased with the crisis: in the second quarter 2009 the number of hours paid by the redundancy fund increased by 60 per cent compared to the first quarter – the highest increase since 1985 (Bank of Italy, 2009b). On the one hand this system alleviates the income loss connected with the crisis; on the other hand, this underestimates the cost of the crisis since those who benefit from the fund are not statistically computed among the unemployed. By including employees receiving redundancy funds among the unemployed, the unemployment rate would increase by 1.4 per cent in Northern-Central Italy and by 0.7 per cent in the South (Bank of Italy, 2010). Another peculiarity of the Italian labour market is

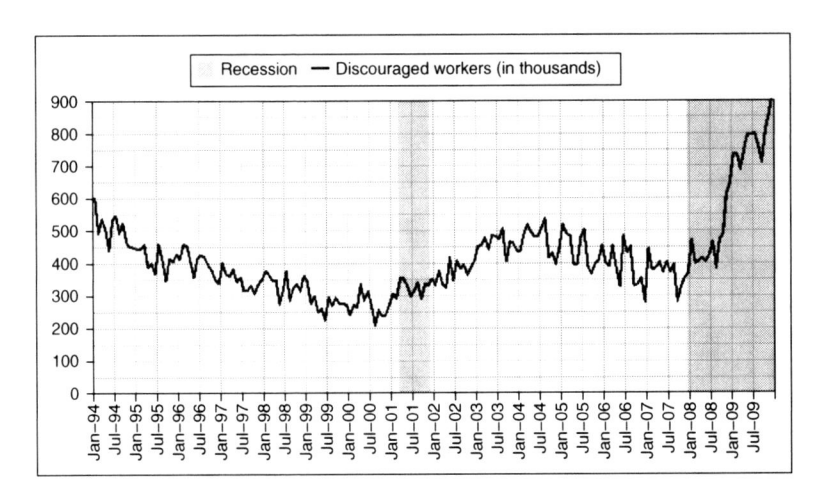

Figure 11.1 Discouraged workers in the US (1994–2009)
Source: http://business.theatlantic.com/2009/09/discouraged_workers_and_seasonality.php.

the high share of discouraged workers. If one included the unemployed who had not been actively seeking a job in the four weeks before the interview but had searched a job before the last month, together with redundancy fund beneficiaries, the Italian unemployment rate in the second 2009 quarter would have increased to 10.2 per cent instead of 7.4 per cent (with redundancy fund beneficiaries accounting for 1.2 per cent while those who did not look for a job within four weeks before the interview accounted for 1.6 per cent of the increase) (Bank of Italy, 2010).

The incidence of long term unemployment (12 months plus) though decreasing, is higher in Italy than in the US. Table 11.4 indicates that in 2008 almost 45 per cent of men and almost 50 per cent of women unemployed in Italy were long-term unemployed compared to 11 per cent of men and 10 per cent of women in the US. The percentage of long-term unemployed in Italy in 2008 is higher than the average of EU-15; whereas the incidence of long-term unemployed in 2008 in the USA was lower than the OECD average.

According to the BLS, data on the net change in employment (difference between jobs gained and jobs lost) indicates that in December 2009 the economy lost approximately 88,0000 jobs (manufacturing 27,000; construction 30,000; government 21,000; and retail 10,000) (NYT, 2010). In order to absorb new entrants, the US economy requires approximately

Table 11.3 OECD harmonized unemployment rates (2006–9, Q1)

	2006	December 2007	2007	2008	2009 Q1	% increase since December 07
USA	4.6	4.6	4.6	5.8	8.1	4.6
Italy	6.8	6.4	6.1	6.8	7.4	1
Euro area	8.3	7.3	7.5	7.6	8.8	2.1
OECD	6.2	5.6	5.7	6	7.5	2.7

Source: Table 1.1, OECD (2009): 25.

Table 11.4 Long-term unemployment rates, 12 months and over (as % of male and female unemployed)

	1994		2005		2006		2007		2008	
	M	F	M	F	M	F	M	F	M	F
Italy	59.6	63.3	50.5	53.8	50.8	54.8	47.3	52.3	44.9	49.9
USA	13.9	10.2	12.6	10.8	10.7	9.2	10.7	9	10.9	10.3
EU-15	46.9	50	43.6	44.6	45.2	44.1	42.3	41.6	38.3	39
OECD	34.9	36.2	32.7	32.8	32.3	32	29.1	29.1	25.4	26.5

Source: Selection from Table G, OECD (2009): 272.

100,000 new jobs monthly. Ben S. Bernanke, the Federal Reserve Bank Chairman, remarked that it would take 'a significant amount of time' to restore the 8.5 million jobs lost in the United States in 2008 and 2009 and cautioned that 'the economic outlook remains unusually uncertain.' (*The New York Times*, 2010).

Differences in the eligibility conditions and in the duration and degree of coverage generate sharp inequalities in the unemployment insurance system in Italy (Anastasia *et al.*, 2009). If one looks at the share of contributory unemployment benefit with respect to previous earnings it ranges from 80 per cent (for ordinary and special wage supplementation funds) to 40 per cent (for ordinary unemployment benefits after the eighth month of the unemployment spell).

Moreover, since eligibility requires previous employment, there is on average a relatively low degree of coverage as evidenced by net replacement rate data. The net replacement rate during the first year of an unemployment spell in 2007 was 37 per cent in Italy and 28 per cent in the US with a five-year average of 7 per cent for Italy and 6 per cent for the US, against a median of 28 per cent (from 72 per cent in Norway to the lowest rate experienced by the US and Korea) (OECD, 2009: Table 1.6, p. 76). In Italy the degree of coverage is also affected by the type of contract: if one considers permanent employees, approximately 96 per cent are subsidized; on the other hand, for fixed-term contract workers the degree of coverage is 70 per cent and about 17 per cent for collaborators (Bank of Italy, 2009a).

The redundancy system has been recently extended in Italy. To compute eligibility to ordinary unemployment benefit according to past months of employment, work experience as collaborators can now also be included. Apprentices who have been fired and had a minimum of three months tenure can now be eligible for ordinary unemployment benefits. However, despite the recent extension of the redundancy system (Italian National Laws 2/2009; 33/2009 and 191/2009), there is still a significant number of workers at risk of being left without any unemployment benefit in case of job loss. According to simulation analyses based on administrative or survey microdata (Bank of Italy 2009a; Berton *et al.*, 2009), they amount to 1.5–2 million workers.

In the US the unemployed are typically eligible for unemployment insurance provided by the government, which provides temporary income support. Unlike Italy, the heterogeneity of the US compensation system is due to differences in eligibility between the states.

A key characteristic of the US labour market is the continued erosion of the economic, and social safety net that has characterized American workers since the end of World War II: 'the tightrope of work is higher, the winds of change that buffet us on it are stronger, but the safety net below is tattered and incomplete' (Hacker, 2006).

The American Reinvestment and Recovery Act of 2009 (ARRA) focuses on short-term cushioning of the unemployed with increased unemployment benefits on investment as the key to long-term economic growth to foster most of the growth in the economy overall.

The following are key benefits from the ARRA, (http://www.progressivestates.org/node/23230):

- Half of the states passed measures to extend unemployment insurance to low-wage workers, women, part-time workers and the long-term unemployed, with an additional 150,000 workers annually eligible for unemployment benefits.
- 21 states changed their laws to extend unemployment insurance benefits by 13–20 weeks if their state's unemployment rate reaches 6.5 per cent. According to the BLS, 33 states have unemployment rates of at least 6.5 per cent.
- UI reform has been a bipartisan effort with nine Republican governors signing legislation, despite initial unwillingness by some high-profile Republican governors. The states enacting changes will receive $3.2 billion of funding.

While extension of unemployment benefits is necessary in the short term, the remaining effects of the ARRA on the long term will be investigated as part of our ongoing research.

A recent study (Antonopoulos et al., 2010) examines job impact of government investment of equal-sized expenditure packages on social care (such as teaching, childcare, and home healthcare) versus manufacturing and transportation. The simulation model's results indicate job creation potential which is approximately 2.1 times larger than the one produced by the same expenditure package on infrastructure (1.2 million jobs in social care as opposed to 556,000 in infrastructure). It was also noted that the three-quarters of new jobs in high- and low-end care services are female dominated and thus would create more jobs for women than men. The study also found that social care expansion would outperform infrastructure in creating jobs for the lower-income households, particularly for home health aides, which is the largest component of social care, and comprised mainly female workers from low-income groups. The study finds that social care expansion would also create more jobs for groups with middle and high income and for groups with low and high educational attainment in comparison to infrastructure spending.

The experience of unemployment in Italy and in the US

This section deals with the costs of unemployment in terms of decreased household income, the perception of not being able to pay for one's basic expenses and having access to health services. The Italian system of unemployment benefits is fragmented and does not cover equally all workers, which led us to disaggregate the unemployed according to their previous working condition.

The costs of being unemployed in Italy in terms of income poverty and access to health services

A first cost of unemployment is connected to the increase in income poverty. In order to disentangle to what extent being unemployed increases the probability of being income poor we have estimated a probit model by using IT SILC 2006 microdata. The results in column 1 of Table 11.5 indicate that unemployment increases the probability of being defined as income poor (when the equivalized disposable income is less than the poverty threshold: 60 per cent of median equivalized disposable income).[3] The probability of being income poor significantly increases among those unemployed who have never had a job. The probability of being income poor increases also for those who are unemployed but formerly self-employed, although this effect is lower than for those who were never employed before. Those who were formerly employed, though experiencing an increase in the probability of being defined income poor, are characterized by a lower effect than those who are currently unemployed but previously in a different working condition.

Turning to the perception of difficulties in making ends meet, we have estimated an ordered probit model to highlight the effect of unemployment, incorporating family, personal and regional variables. Table 11.5 (column 2) indicates that greater difficulties are perceived by the unemployed in making ends meet, with the effect being higher for the unemployed who were formerly self-employed with employees. These results are consistent with the limited coverage of the Italian system of unemployment benefits discussed in the previous section.

Investigating other dimensions of the cost of unemployment, we estimate the probability of having unmet medical or dental needs (Table 11.5, column 3). The unemployed who were formerly self-employed without employees have higher probability of not having access, since they consider the costs too expensive. One should note that this group of self-employed also includes workers under collaboration contract who have a lower access to unemployment benefits and higher income uncertainty.

Table 11.5 Multivariate analyses on poverty probability and costs of being unemployed

	Column 1 Probit model on income poverty	Column 2 Ordered probit on the ability to make ends meet[†]	Column 3 Probit model on unmet medical and dental services
Age	0.046**	–0.025**	0.050**
	(6.54)	(7.24)	(5.99)
Age squared	–0.001**	0.000**	–0.001**
	(7.57)	(9.50)	(5.36)
Female	–0.063*	0.000	0.074*
	(2.37)	(0.03)	(2.42)
Married or cohabiting	–0.118**	0.098**	–0.042
	(2.90)	(5.54)	(0.91)
Separated/divorced	0.349**	–0.213**	0.285**
	(6.58)	(8.07)	(4.42)
Widow	0.074	–0.112**	0.174*
	(0.87)	(2.65)	(2.05)
Secondary	–0.233**	0.182**	–0.148**
	(5.99)	(9.37)	(3.19)
High school	–0.530**	0.530**	–0.359**
	(13.03)	(26.85)	(7.43)
Tertiary	–0.974**	1.021**	–0.655**
	(16.85)	(42.27)	(9.30)
Part time	–0.387**	0.150**	–0.174**
	(7.55)	(6.30)	(2.98)
Unemployed, previously self-employed with employees	0.669*	–0.934**	0.374
	(2.38)	(3.85)	(1.00)
Unemployed, previously self-employed without employees	0.560**	–0.422**	0.366*
	(3.71)	(5.63)	(2.13)
Unemployed, previously employee	0.237**	–0.406**	0.155
	(3.40)	(11.05)	(1.90)
Unemployed, never employed before	0.790**	–0.493**	0.147
	(9.84)	(10.38)	(1.43)

(*continued*)

Table 11.5 Continued

	Column 1 Probit model on income poverty	Column 2 Ordered probit on the ability to make ends meet[1]	Column 3 Probit model on unmet medical and dental services
Inactive	0.159**	0.019	−0.157**
	(3.08)	(0.76)	(2.61)
Chronic ill	0.056	−0.187**	0.408**
	(1.60)	(11.22)	(11.57)
With children from 0 to 5 years old	0.237**	−0.065**	0.066
	(5.80)	(3.43)	(1.45)
With children from 6 to 14 years old	0.249**	−0.146**	0.186**
	(8.32)	(9.87)	(5.19)
With children from 15 to 17 years old	0.250**	−0.083**	0.092*
	(7.52)	(4.53)	(2.16)
South	0.784**	−0.448**	0.252**
	(31.72)	(36.39)	(8.55)
Constant	−1.606**		−2.438**
	(11.20)		(14.09)
Observations	35,219	35,219	35,219

Notes: Robust z statistics in parentheses
* significant at 5 per cent; ** significant at 1 per cent
† The variable on the perceived ability to make ends meet takes the following values: 1 with great difficulty; 2 with difficulty; 3 with some difficulty; 4 fairly easily; 5 easily; 6 very easily.

The costs of being unemployed in the US in terms of income poverty

The most recent data released from the US Census Bureau (2010d), show a significant deterioration in the US labour market. The poverty rate for 2008 was 13.2 per cent, the highest level since 1997 and 0.2 percentage points higher than 2007. The 2008 rate was the first statistically significant increase since 2004. In 2008, 39.8 million people were officially in poverty, up from 37.3 million in 2007. Mean real US household income decreased by 3.6 per cent from 2007 to 2008, from $52,163 to $50,303. We believe these trends will continue at least through 2010.

The poor population can be categorized into two distinct groups: the 'temporarily poor' (those who experience poverty on an intermittent basis; from one to as many as seven times over a ten-year period) and the 'persistently poor' (those who seldom, if ever, have incomes above the poverty line; that is, they are poor in eight or more years over a ten-year period). The group of 'temporarily poor' comprises 90 per cent of the poverty population, which becomes poor due to events such as recessions, illness, disability and divorce. This suggests an important implication for public policy: social insurance programmes should be structured to meet the separate needs of the two distinct groups. The 'temporarily poor' need a brief cushion of substantive financial support to make up for lost income due to unemployment during recessionary periods. The 'persistently poor', however, have very little income from work and have very little work experience to qualify for unemployment compensation benefits. Reducing poverty among the 'persistently poor' requires a combination of income maintenance programmes; food stamps, which provide direct and in-kind benefits based on needs; and job training programmes that give individuals marketable skills (Kaufman, 1993).

In the US, the overall poverty rate fell sharply from the 1960s to the early 1970s but has remained relatively constant during the past 30 years, while very recently trending upward. The poverty rate was 11.3 per cent in 2000 and gradually increased to 13.2 per cent in 2008 (www.uscensus.gov). The aggregate rate obscures that poverty rates have increased for individuals younger than 18 while decreasing for individuals older than 65. One reason is increased government spending in public aid programmes, such as social security and Medicare over time. Also, in the US, poverty rates vary by race and ethnicity groups. A political debate then arises whether government should engage in income redistribution. Measures of income inequality for families, as measured by Gini ratios, increased from 0.432 in 2007 to 0.438 in 2008. Shares of aggregate income received by households indicate that in 2008 the top 20 per cent received 21.5 per cent; while at the bottom 20 per cent received 3.4 per cent of aggregate income in the US. Measures of individual earnings inequality for full-time, year-round workers depict an increase in the Gini index of 0.394 in 2007 to 0.403 in 2008 (www.census.gov), suggesting that income distribution in the US has become less equitable in recent years and may worsen more with higher levels of unemployment during recessionary periods.

In order to investigate the costs of being unemployed we have estimated probit models on the probability of being income poor, using US Census Bureau microdata. Our results underscore the severity of the recession, officially beginning in the United States in December 2007, and now the longest and most severe since the Great Depression of the

1930s. We also believe that this recession and its preponderant causes in the financial market will fundamentally change the direction of capitalist development.

The results of our investigation are reported in Table 11.6. The year 2008 was selected since it was the first full year of the recession and the latest year for which data was available. The year 2004 was selected since it was equidistant from the trough of the 2001 recession and the peak of the expansion (December 2007); moreover, it was the only year of the expansionary period in which the full data set was available.

The UNEMPLOYMENT variable is binary, coded 1 if the individual is out of work and either on lay-off or searching for work; and coded 0

Table 11.6 Multivariate analyses on poverty probability, US

Explanatory variables	2004	2008
Intercept	−3.427	−3.262
	(−475.755)***	(−598.891)***
Unemployed	0.005	0.011
	(2.131)**	(4.103)***
Female	0.010	0.005
	(6.885)***	(3.805)***
Married	0.001	−0.009
	(0.669)	(−7.024)***
Age	0.013	0.012
	(35.741)***	(39.822)***
College	0.002	−0.005
	(1.053)	(−3.160)***
Insurance	0.006	0.005
	(2.417)**	(2.422)**
Black	−0.001	−0.006
	(−0.790)	(−3.530)***
Age squared	0.000	0.000
	(−18.964)***	(−8.748)***
Illness chronic	0.006	−0.001
	(0.648)	(−0.108)
Unemployment benefits	−0.009	−0.007
	(−2.028)**	(−1.849)*
N	19,732	18,593
Chi square	220352.924	337589.668
	(p = 0.000)	(p = 0.000)
df	19721	18582

Source: United States Census Bureau.
Note: *** significant at 1 per cent; ** significant at 5 per cent; * significant at 10 per cent.

if the individual is employed. We hypothesized that the coefficient of UNEMPLOYMENT would be significant and positive – that is, becoming unemployed increases the probability of poverty. This conclusion is far from surprising since, all else equal, losing a job is certainly a preponderant reason for an individual to become poor. Our results indicate that the coefficient is positive and significant for 2008 and for 2004. This confirms our belief that an unemployed person obviously suffers a reduction in income and since poverty is measured by income (along with household size), *ceteris paribus* this increases the probability of becoming poor. This is especially so, given the sustained weakness in the US employment market since 2001, severely exacerbated by the current financial and mortgage crisis.

Having healthcare insurance (INSURANCE – a binary variable coded 1 if the individual has healthcare insurance and 0 otherwise) is positive and significant for 2008 and 2004. What is puzzling, however, is the positive sign. One possible explanation is that having insurance is less important than how it is used; for many Americans a sizeable deductible must be paid, and it is never clear what services are covered. Conversely, the INSURANCE variable hypothesizes that a person without healthcare insurance increases the chances of poverty, but anecdotal evidence suggest that this is often not true in the US, since those without healthcare insurance will obtain healthcare at no cost (to them) at emergency rooms, while those with healthcare insurance can be driven into poverty based on high medical costs and denial of procedures. Unfortunately, our data does not allow testing of these questions. The healthcare legislation recently signed by President Obama is a small step towards rectifying these inequities.

The coefficient of MARRIED (coded 1 if married and 0 otherwise) is positive for 2008 but not significant and negative for 2004. The negative coefficient confirms some well-established findings for the US, that being married significantly reduces poverty. The coefficient BLACK (coded 1 if black and 0 otherwise) is negative and not significant for 2008 and significant for 2004. This is contrary to our hypothesis that being black increases the chance of being in poverty.

The coefficient FEMALE is positive as hypothesized and significant for both 2008 and 2004. The results confirm the statistical profile for the poor in the US, which indicates that more unemployed females are in poverty, especially among black female-headed households.

The ILLNESS CHRONIC variable is coded 1 if the person has a chronic illness and 0 otherwise. It is not significant for 2008 and 2004. Our results do not suggest the vulnerability of the chronically ill during a severe crisis as we hypothesized in the model.

We find a negative and significant (at 1 per cent) coefficient for UNEMPLOYMENT BENEFITS (a binary variable coded 1 if the individual receives benefits and 0 otherwise) for both 2008 and 2004. We hypothesized that this effect would be negative. Our results support the view that the level of unemployment benefits, *ceteris paribus*, is a key factor in reducing the probability of poverty. Unemployment benefits are often referred to as the 'first line of defence' during recessions. Unemployment benefits or insurance are payments (benefits) intended to provide temporary financial assistance to unemployed workers who fulfil the state law requirements, within the guidelines provided by the Federal law. State survey data show that nearly all families spend their entire unemployment insurance (UI) faster than other forms of stimulus that might be saved rather than spent (State of Washington Employment Security Department, 2008). A national survey of a random sample of unemployment insurance recipients found that 77 per cent spent the majority of the UI cheques on food and housing (Hart Research Associates, 2008).

The coefficient of COLLEGE (coded 1 if the individual graduated from college and 0 otherwise) has the expected sign for 2004 but not for 2008 (though for 2008 it is statistically not significant). In 2004, according to the US Census Bureau, 2 per cent of all college graduates were officially poor. Perhaps our sample was muddied by a disproportionate share. Though not significant in 2008, the observed sign suggests that being a college graduate in this severe recession does not insulate one from the probability of becoming poor.

In conclusion, our results underscore the severity of this recession, as well as the need to reconceptualize how we measure poverty and hardship in the labour market. Our results also suggest a more careful gathering of data to understand specific causal relationships. As one example, a record number of Americans in 2008 currently live in a multigenerational household. Currently 49 million Americans (16.1 per cent of the total population) live with relatives in the same household, a significant increase from a post-World War II low of 12.1 per cent in 1980 (Pew Center for Social Research, 2010). Younger people unable to find work have moved in with relatives, usually parents. This is a direct result of the crisis: according to the Pew Center, 2.6 million more Americans were living in a multigenerational household in 2008 than in 2007 (*ibid.*). Such an arrangement by definition reduces poverty, all else equal, even if the person is unemployed or out of the labour force, since poverty in the US is defined by household size and household income. This does not mitigate individual suffering, nor the loss of human capital, but suggests a redefinition of poverty while perhaps using other measures of hardship.

Another reason to fundamentally analyze the conceptualization of poverty is that of the 39.8 million people of the American population that is officially poor, 8.9 million (22 per cent of the poverty population) were among the working poor (US BLS, 2010d). This number increased from 7.5 million adults in 2007. The working poor as a percentage of the US civilian labour force was 6.0 per cent in 2008, compared to 5.1 per cent in 2007 (US BLS, 2010e). Thus, being employed during a severe crisis does not guarantee that the person is not officially poor.

Concluding remarks

Both the Italian and the US economy have witnessed an increase in unemployment rates. The Italian unemployment data must be complemented with data on the beneficiaries of redundancy hours (who are not computed among the unemployed) and with data on discouraged workers to assess more completely the effect of the crisis on the labour market.

In the US, labour force participation, though higher than Italy, has been decreasing continuously before the crisis; in Italy there is a wide share of the population (particularly in the South and among women) that is inactive and discouraged from undertaking job search. There is a need for statistical and econometric techniques able to account for their presence (Brandolini et al., 2006; Jones and Riddel, 2006) and their status should not be neglected in the design of employment and social policies to avoid their permanent exclusion from the labour force.

Though redundancy hours have increased in 2009 and access to wage supplementation funds has been extended by the Italian government as a reaction to the crisis, the Italian system of unemployment benefits indicates a high heterogeneity and, on the whole, low coverage. This can generate high socio-economic costs of unemployment. Using microdata prior to the crisis in Italy, we can detect higher difficulties by the unemployed in the ability to make ends meet; a higher degree of income poverty and a high probability of not accessing medical or dental treatment. In addition, the costs change according to the employment status prior to unemployment. These results call for a reform of unemployment benefits in Italy to achieve a higher equality and coverage of unemployed. US data confirms a sharp deterioration in the labour market. Of crucial concern, especially for the implications of long-term growth, is the high incidence of youth unemployment.

In both countries, unemployment compensation is the most significant short-term programme to alleviate the private and social costs of unemployment. A more progressive compensation insurance system can decrease the private cost of unemployment and thereby the social cost of unemployment.

Given the higher probability of experiencing limits in accessing health services (see above) and the estimated costs in terms of health deterioration (Sen, 1997b) experienced by the unemployed, we believe that actions undertaken by regional governments in Italy (like, for example, the Italian Region Emilia Romagna) to introduce exemptions for temporary prescription charges for medical specialist visits and exams for the unemployed or redundancy fund recipients and their families could have a positive effect in reducing the socio-economic costs of the crisis.

Notes

1. On the persistence of these regional disparities see SVIMEZ (2010).
2. According to provisional monthly Labour Force Survey data.
3. Equivalized total disposable household income has been obtained by using the modified OECD equivalence scale.

References

Anastasia, B., Mancini, M. and Trivellato, U. (2009) 'Il sostegno al reddito dei disoccupati: note sullo stato dell'arte. Tra riformismo strisciante, inerzie dell'impianto categoriale e incerti orizzonti di flexicurity', Isae, Working paper no. 112, April.

Antonopoulos, R., Kim, K., Masterson, T. and Zacharias, A. (2010) 'Why President Obama Should Care About 'Care': An Effective and Equitable Investment Strategy for Job Creation', Public Policy Brief No 108, Levy Institute of Bard College.

Bank of Italy (2009a) *Relazione annuale 2008*, Rome: Banca d'Italia.

Bank of Italy (2009b) *Bollettino Economico*, no. 57, July.

Bank of Italy (2010) *Bollettino Economico*, no. 59, January.

Berton, F., Richiardi, M. and Sacchi, S. (2009) 'Quanti sono i lavoratori senza tutele', www.lavoce.info.

Brandolini, A., P. Cipollone, P. and Viviano, E. (2006) 'Does The ILO Definition Capture All Unemployment?', *Journal of the European Economic Association*, vol. 4, no. 1.

Cappariello, R. and Zizza, R. (2009) 'Dropping the Books and Working Off the Books', Bank of Italy, Temi di Discussione (Working Paper), 702, January.

Cohaney, S. (2009) (United States, Department of Labour, Bureau of Labour Statisticsavailable at http://www.bls.gov/opub/ils/pdf/opbils74.pdf, April (accessed 24 January 2010).

David, K. P. (2009) 'The Jobless Gender Gap'. available at http://online.wsj.com/article/SB10001424052748704576204574531453974382142.html, 27 November (accessed 24 January 2010).
European Commission (2004) *Undeclared Work in an Enlarged Union*, Director General for Employment and Social Affairs, Brussels.
Eurostat (2009) *Youth in Europe: A Statistical Portrait*, Luxembourg: Publications Office of the European Union.
Eurostat (2010) 'Eurostat: news release. Euroindicators' 125/2010 – 31 August, http://epp.eurostat.ec.europa.eu/.
Fan, C. (2009) 'Unemployment Reforms Sweep Nation due to Federal Recovery Incentives', available at http://www.progressivestates.org/node/23230, 25 June (accessed 24 January 2010).
Hacker, J. (2006) *The Great Risk Shift*, New York: Oxford University Press.
Hart Research Associates (2008) 'Unemployed in America: Job Market, Prospects for Employment, and Impact of Unemployment on Families and the unemployed,' commissioned by the National Employment Law Project, December, available at http://www.nelp.org/page/-/UI/show8860.pdf.
Indiviglio, D. (2009) 'Discouraged Workers and Seasonality', available at http://business.theatlantic.com/2009/09/discouraged_workers_and_seasonality.php, September 2004 (accessed 24 January 2010).
ISTAT (2009a) *Annuario Statistico Italiano 2009*, Rome: ISTAT.
ISTAT (2009b) *Rapporto annuale, La situazione del Paese nel 2008*, Rome: ISTAT.
ISTAT (2009c) 'Condizioni di vita e distribuzione del reddito in Italia. Anno 2008', *Famiglia e Società, Statistiche in breve*, 29 December.
ISTAT (2010) 'Occupati e disoccupati, Luglio 2010: Stime provvisorie', Comunicato Stampa, ISTAT, 31 August, www.istat.it.
Jones, S. R. G. and Riddel, W. C. (2006) 'Unemployment and Non-employment: Heterogeneities in Labour Market States', *The Review of Economics and Statistics*, vol. 88, no. 2 (May), pp. 314–23.
Kaufman, Bruce, E. (1993) 'The Economics of Labor Markets', The Dryden Press Series in Economics.
McClelland, A. and Macdonald, F. (1998) 'The Social Consequences of Unemployment', available at http://www.bsl.org.au/pdfs/social.pdf, July.
The New York Times (2010) 21 July, available at www.nytimes.com/2010/business 2010.
'Number of Discouraged Workers: December 2009' (2010) available at http://www.businessinsider.com/number-of-discouraged-workers-december-2009-2010-1, 11 January (accessed 24 January 2010).
OECD (2008) *Employment Outlook*, Paris: OECD.
OECD (2009) *Employment Outlook*, Paris: OECD.
Pew Center for Social Research (2010) 'The Return of the Multi-Generational Family Household', available at http://pewsocialtrends.org/pubs/752/the-return-of-the-mult-generational-family-household, March.Rampell, C. (2009) 'Job Market Pie', available at http://economix.blogs.nytimes.com/2009/04/30/job-pie/#more-10539, 30 April (accessed 24 January 2010).
Schmidt, J., Roe, H. and Fremstad, S. (2009) 'US Unemployment Now as High as Europe', available at http://www.cepr.net/documents/publications/US-EU-UR-2009-05.pdf, May (accessed 24 January 2010).

Sen, A. (1997a) 'Inequality, Unemployment and Contemporary Europe', *International Labour Review*, vol.136, no. 2, pp. 155–71.

Sen, A. (1997b) *The Penalties of Unemployment*, Rome: Banca d'Italia, Temi di discussione, 307.

State of Washington Employment Security Department (2008) 'Claimant Expenditure Survey, Fiscal Year 2007', January, http://esd.wa.gov/newsandinformation/media/uidata/uipublishedreports/claimant-expenditure-survey-2007.pdf.

SVIMEZ (2010) *Rapporto Svimez 2010 sull'economia del Mezzogiorno*, Bologna: Il Mulino.

'Unemployment Benefits' (2009) available at http://www.opencongress.org/wiki/Unemployment_benefits, 1 October (accessed 24 January 2010).

US Department of Labour, US Bureau of Labour Statistics (BLS) (2010a) 'The Employment Situation: December 2009', January.

US BLS (2010b, January 2008) available at http://www.bls.gov/cps/tables. htm#empstat_m (accessed 24 January 2010).

US BLS (2010c, January 2008) available at http://www.bls.gov/news.release/ empsit.t12.htm (accessed 24 January 2010).

US BLS (2010d, January 08). available at http://www.bls.gov/news.release/empsit. nr0.htm (accessed 24 January 2010).

US BLS (2010e) 'A Profile of the Working Poor, 2008', Report 1022, March.

US Census Bureau, (2010), "The 2010 Statistical Abstract: The National Data Book", Web-site: http://www.census.gov/compendia/statab/ as accessed on December 4, 2010.

12
Reaching Out in a Time of Crisis: How External Anchors Assist Southeastern Europe

Jens Bastian

Introduction

With the economic crisis starting to assert itself in the second half of 2008 in Southeast Europe, the manner in which governments and central banks initially reacted highlighted a mixture of political unpreparedness, at times outright denial and exposed manifest institutional limitations to act quickly and decisively. If the economic crisis in the region could be reduced to one single phenomenon, and it is arguably delicate to do so, it would be this: the fact that nobody in power saw it coming and hardly anybody knew what to do next. Put otherwise, crisis management and crisis resistance capacity were both in short supply when a twin external shock started to manifest itself in mid-2008 in the region.

From October 2008 onwards the immediate intervention of multilateral financial institutions became the means of last – and only – resort for governments and central bank authorities in Serbia, Bosnia and Herzegovina, Hungary, Romania, Ukraine, Belarus, etc. At that stage of external intervention the fast-emerging solvency crises lacked domestic policy solutions in Belgrade, Sarajevo, Budapest, Bucharest and Kiev.

Instead of risking going broke, many countries had to 'go cap in hand' to international financial institutions (IFIs); first to Washington (IMF and World Bank) and, subsequently, to London (EBRD, European Bank for Reconstruction and Development) and Brussels (EU, i.e., EIB, European Investment Bank). Only through the availability of such a multiplicity of external (financial) anchors did these countries avoid the modern-day equivalent of financial meltdown, namely having to throw in the 'default towel'.

External anchors such as the IMF, World Bank, EBRD, EU and EIB thus have a critical role to play. The year 2009 has been one of the busiest for such institutions. Through their lending programmes they are redefining a responsibility that consists of sheltering countries in dire need and assisting them in the objective to consolidate their gains after 20 years of complex economic, financial sector and political transition.

These anchor institutions can provide significant financial resources and administrative skills. They equally draw on a wealth of experience and lessons learned when providing emergency assistance in the past to the region. As shall be illustrated, such external anchors have proved to be rather flexible in the adoption and implementation of coordinated rescue programmes based on division of labour, resources and mandate. In a word, a new sense of purpose for such external anchors is emerging.

The consequences of the economic crises across Southeast Europe will nevertheless be felt for many years to come. Painful cuts and delicate trade-offs are in prospect as a result of the economic recession affecting the region. After a decade of GDP growth, countries must now prepare for a new era of austerity. Ultimately, this process will also spark debate about the timing and reasoning for scaling back crisis assistance programmes from such external financial anchors.

The macroeconomic situation

After the onset of the financial crisis in the autumn of 2008, the global economic environment continued to worsen into the first half of 2009 while slightly easing towards the end of 2009 (EBRD, 2010a). Southeastern Europe is among the regions most adversely affected, reflecting dramatic GDP contraction (see Figure 12.1 below), sizeable fiscal deficits and numerous external challenges – for example, current account shortfalls, liquidity problems in foreign currency inflows and declining export capacity (IMF, 2009a).

The economic and financial crises caught up with the economies of Southeast Europe in the fourth quarter of 2008. All countries in the region registered a sharp output decline in 2009, with the Romanian, Serbian and Bulgarian economies particularly adversely affected (IMF, 2009a). Such a combined free-fall in the economies of the Balkans is only comparable to the initial transition period in the early 1990s. The depth of the economic meltdown in the region is reminiscent of the onset of economic transformation two decades ago. The economic and financial sector crises constitute the most significant external shock since the beginning of transition two decades ago (Bastian, 1998).

More specifically, the crises affecting the region since mid-2008 risk setting many of them back to levels of GDP decline witnessed individually

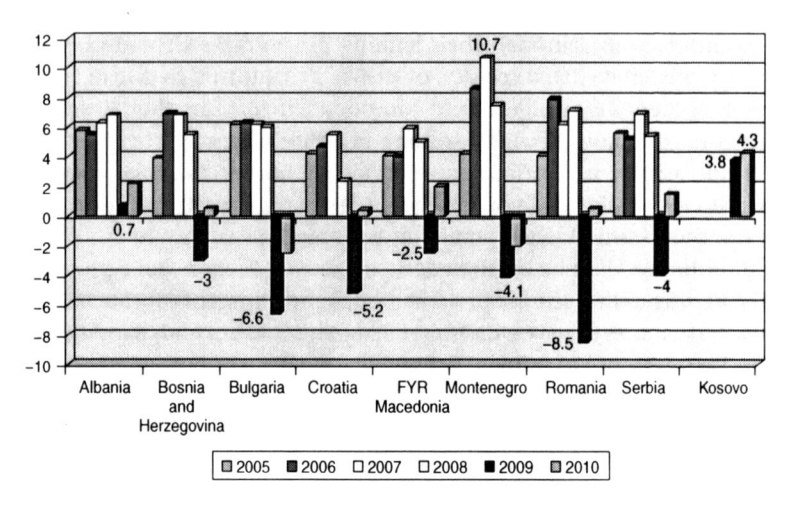

[Figure: bar chart]

Figure 12.1 Real GDP (%) performance in Southeast Europe (2005–10)
Source: IMF (2009b).

one decade ago and as a group of countries in the western and eastern Balkans two decades past. In other words, what is at risk are economic gains and social advancements, privatization benefits and fiscal improvements that these countries' economies and societies sought to consolidate during the past decade (Mitra *et al.*, 2010).

External anchors to the rescue

Against this economic background governments and central banks in the region have had to decide how to modify their policies and adjust their toolbox. The IMF dryly observed in April 2009: 'it is important to realize that the global conditions conducive for the previous high growth rates belong to the past' (IMF, 2009a: 7).

International funding institutions such as the IMF, World Bank, EBRD and EU came to the rescue of eight countries in Central, Eastern and Southeast Europe. Between October 2008 and May 2009 they provided approximately US$110 billion of emergency lending to Romania, Serbia, Ukraine, Belarus, Hungary, Poland, Bosnia and Herzegovina and Latvia to weather the consequences of the economic and financial crises (see Table 12.1 below). Other countries such as Albania, Bulgaria, Croatia, Montenegro and the FYR Macedonia are currently considering their options (WIIW, 2010).

Table 12.1 Crisis lending to countries in Central, Eastern, Southeast Europe

Country	Timing	Volume (US$)	IFIs
Hungary	October 2008	25.4 billion	IMF, WB, EU
Ukraine	November 2008	16.4 billion	IMF
Latvia	December 2008	10.5 billion	IMF + EU
Belarus	January 2009	2.46 billion	IMF
Serbia	January 2009	530 million	IMF
	March 2009	4.0 billion	IMF
	October 2009	1.4 billion	Russian Finance Ministry
Poland	April 2009	20.5 billion	IMF (Flexible credit line)
Bosnia and Herzegovina	May 2009	1.3 billion	IMF (Standby loan)
Romania	March 2009	27 billion	IMF, WB, EU, EBRD
Total external funding		**110.4 billion**	

Source: IMF (2009c).

It is important to understand that the financial assistance programmes provided by different IFIs and the EU include noteworthy distinctions as regards mode of intervention, volume of assistance and level of conditionalities attached. More specifically, the IMF mainly provides *liquidity* assistance to individual countries, while the World Bank, the EBRD and EU institutions can forward *capital* financing and budgetary support (Bastian, 2010a).

Notwithstanding these differences in approach and substance, the combination and coordination of these interventions sent a highly symbolic message to international capital markets during 2010; namely that East, Central and Southeast Europe ultimately have a financial safety net that will be extended across these regions!

In three of the eight cases, namely Hungary, Latvia and Romania, the rescue packages have been worked out in close cooperation between multiple international institutions. The IMF, the EU, the World Bank, the EBRD and other multilaterals are providing to these EU members a variety of financial assistance arrangements with different levels of conditionalities attached to the programmes (*ibid.*).

The Romanian case

The single largest rescue programme concerns Romania. The Finance Ministry and the Central Bank in Bucharest completed talks with the

European Commission, the IMF and other IFIs to seek 'medium-term foreign financial assistance' in March 2009. The rescue package totals US$27 billion under a two-year standby arrangement. The financial details include a loan of US$17.5 billion from the IMF. Another US$9.7 billion of emergency funding is provided by the EU, the World Bank and the EBRD (IMF Agreement with Romania, 2009).

Bucharest's need for external funding stems from its short-term foreign debt repayment obligations in the course of 2009 and the effects of the sharp drop in private capital inflows, in particular in foreign direct investment. The IMF-led rescue programme aims to maintain adequate capitalization of commercial banks and provides liquidity facilities for domestic financial markets. The package also contains specific provisions to increase allocations for social programmes, particularly regarding spending initiatives for vulnerable pensioners and public sector employees (*ibid.*).

The IMF forecast during the negotiations with the government that the Romanian economy was expected to shrink by as much as 4.1 per cent in 2009, while the current account deficit would reach 7.5 per cent of GDP (*ibid.*). Six months later in August 2009, while undertaking the first review of Romania's performance under the US$27 billion agreement, the IMF doubled its forecast for economic contraction in 2009 to as much as 8.5 per cent (IMF Interim Review, 2009). Romania's economy shrank by 7.1 per cent in 2009.

In fact, Romania successfully renegotiated the terms of reference of its lending programme. More specifically, it received permission from the IMF and the EU to run higher budget deficits in 2009 and 2010 (*ibid.*). The revised objectives include an agreed fiscal deficit of 6.8 per cent of GDP for 2010 (*Financial Times*, 21 June 2010).

But even these revised forecasts and adjustments were not enough. In November 2009 the IMF delayed the release of the third financial tranche (1.5 billion euros) to Romania while the country continued to struggle to establish a new government, which would comply with agreed policy targets. The disbursement was only released in July 2010 after the government of Prime Minister Emil Boc agreed to sweeping spending cuts in public sector wages (minus 25 per cent) and a staggering increase of VAT from 19–24 per cent, the second highest in the EU (FAZ, 2010c).

The Serbian case

In the case of Serbia, the authorities in Belgrade had to go cap in hand to Washington twice within three months. After a first emergency loan was approved by the IMF in January 2009, Serbia reached a second agreement for a 27-month, 3 billion euro loan to help its economy address the effects of the global financial crisis in late March 2009. The IMF loans were used to replenish the central bank's foreign currency reserves, a move meant to stabilize the domestic currency, the dinar (Eddy, 2010).

Finally, and for the third time, the Serbian authorities required external financial assistance in October 2009 when they secured a US$1.4 billion loan from the Russian Ministry of Finance. Serbia is the only country that repeatedly required external financial resources during 2009. It is also the country whose funding inflow has the greatest variety of sources from international institutions (Ricard, 2009).

Labour unions and citizens' organizations resented taking on the burden of the IMF's two-year standby credit arrangement with Belgrade while large private sector businesses sought additional government subsidies. The revised 2009 budget cut public spending by US$1.3 billion. Public sector employees' wages were reduced between 10 and15 per cent.

Employment levels in state administration were downsized by 10 per cent until mid-2010. In practice this included redundancies and involuntary early retirement for 8,500 public employees (New Europe, 2009a). In order for the IMF to release the third credit tranche the Serbian government also had to comply with the submission of pension reform legislation in June 2010 (FAZ, 2010b).

Can Albania and Bulgaria be considered outliers?

As one country after another sought multilateral funding from a combination of IFIs; the growing list also exposed those countries that have yet to come forward, and are holding their cards close to their chest.

One such country is Albania. The central bank governor Ardian Fullani urged the government to turn to the IMF for loan assistance in April 2009. Fullani cited a lack of liquidity in foreign currency inflows as the main reason for recommending approaching the IMF (IHT, 2010a). The decision not to seek assistance from the IMF was ultimately taken after the establishment of a new coalition government following the general elections of 28 June 2009.

However, to date the Albanian government has yet to restore full relations with the IMF. Albania is also an outlier in two other respects. For one, it was the last country in the region to receive a credit rating from any of the three leading international credit rating agencies. In June 2007 Moody's Investors Service ranked the country on a par with Ukraine, Indonesia and Jamaica. The B1 rating was four steps below the investment-grade level of Baa3 assigned to Balkan neighbours Croatia and Bulgaria at the time.

Second, Albania only made a successful Eurobond debut on international capital markets in November 2010. Albania debuted its first five-year,

300m Eurobond with a five-year maturity at a maximum interest 7.5 per cent rate. For a decade Albania has been trying unsuccessfully to finance its budget deficit with the issuance of Eurobonds. In 2009 the finance ministry had to cancel Eurobond plans because prices and interest rates in the bond markets were deemed too high. Instead the government took out a 193 million syndicated loan from 20 commercial banks that was managed by Deutsche Bank and Greece's Alpha Bank (*ibid.*)

A second example is the EU member Bulgaria. In the case of Sofia, political and electoral considerations also played a role in *not* approaching the IMF before the outcome of the 5 July 2009 general elections. The political sensitivity of the issue during the election campaign prevented the authorities from seeking a financial agreement with the IMF.

How much an agreement with the IMF became a political football during the campaign was exemplified by the then leading opposition politician, the Sofia mayor Mr Boiko Borissov's party, GERB, which argued in favour of a precautionary agreement with the IMF as part of its economic policy priorities. Mr Borissov subsequently won the elections and went on to become prime minister of Bulgaria. But his government has not sought the financial assistance of either the IMF or the EU.

The amount Bulgaria would need was estimated to range between one half and two-thirds of US$25 billion, the volumes secured from the IMF and the EU by Hungary and Romania in 2009 (Bastian, 2009). While the Bulgarian economy grew by 6 per cent in 2008, a year later GDP contraction reached 5.1 per cent. Such a level of macroeconomic adjustment is remarkable within one year.

Bulgaria's fiscal position is a key reason why the country's authorities have to date successfully navigated around IMF loan assistance. Bulgaria registered a budget surplus between 2006 and 2008 and had the lowest budget deficit in the EU in 2009. However, its economic and financial vulnerability is defined by risks from the private sector, which has high levels of external debt. In 2009 Bulgaria had gross external debt of 37.6 billion euro, equivalent to 111 per cent of annual GDP (Kathimerini, 2010).

Moreover, Bulgaria's foreign direct investment (FDI), which constituted a key driver of GDP performance in recent years, has declined since the end of 2008. FDI plunged to minus 21.9 million euros during the first quarter of 2010, from a positive 926 million euros in January–March 2009 (IHT, 2010c). Declining foreign investment on such a scale signals diminishing prospects for economic recovery among the EU's poorest emerging economy and may yet trigger the need for international financial assistance the country's authorities have so far sought to avoid.

Equally, neither have Croatia, FYR Macedonia and Montenegro negotiated financial assistance from the IMF, the World Bank or the EU. This does not imply that they did not consider it or that governing and central bank authorities always see eye-to-eye on the subject matter. Nor does it suggest that any of these countries are on safer economic and financial grounds today and therefore not in need of such options. However, the apparent difference between those that sought international financial assistance and the cluster of countries in the region that have – so far – successfully held out is all the more striking.

Is the crisis assistance discretionary, tilted towards EU members?

When considering funding assistance from the international [financial] community towards recipient countries a major difference has to be borne in mind. Hungary, Poland and Romania are EU members, with other levels of institutional integration than those of Serbia, FYR Macedonia, Bosnia and Herzegovina, Montenegro or Albania.

This difference highlights a major drawback for non-EU members in the western Balkans. Their only route available for possible bailout operations are presently IFIs, while the EU's hand for immediate financial intervention through its lending institution – the EIB – is limited for non-members. Put otherwise, emergency lending arrangements to Balkan countries may raise the very concerns they are intended to calm: that the crisis threatens to split the region into rival camps.

The EU cannot assist non-EU member countries in the Balkans in the same manner as it did in the case of neighbouring Hungary, Romania and possibly Bulgaria. The EU balance of payment support facility is only available for EU members. Equally, the Commission's budgetary resources are selective and discretionary; favouring the new EU members from Central and Eastern Europe.

In order to counterbalance this structural discrepancy, and divert the criticism that the EU may appear biased, the Commission has sought alternative financial instruments. In the course of 2009 the EU has started to frontload specific funds for countries in the western Balkans. The EU is using one of its core financing instruments – namely IPA – to deliver funding assistance to non-EU members in the region.

IPA stands for Instrument for Pre-Accession assistance. It offers financial assistance to countries aspiring to join the European Union for the period 2007–13 (see Table 12.2 below). The beneficiary countries are

Table 12.2 EU support for non-EU members in the western Balkans and Turkey (2009–10)

	Volume (euros)	Focus	Timing
Bosnia and Herzegovina	39 million	Grant funding	August 2009
Serbia	100 million	Budgetary support	July 2009
	100 million	credit lines	2010
Western Balkans and Turkey	85 million	Grant finance	July 2009
EIB Lending Facilities (Western Balkans)	3.2 billion	Loan finance	2009/10
Western Balkans Investment Framework	130 million	Pooling grants + loans from EU/EIB/EBRD/CEB	2009/10

Source: European Commission (2009c).

the former Yugoslav Republic of Macedonia, Croatia, Turkey, Albania, Bosnia and Herzegovina, Montenegro, Serbia and Kosovo.

IPA resources earmarked for capacity building projects are being redirected as direct budgetary support means. Of this, 85 million euros will be given to western Balkan countries and Turkey to help secure investment in their economies, reform their banking sectors and improve competitiveness. Serbia received 100 million euros from IPA funds of the European Commission for 'general budget support' in July 2009 (IPA, 2009). The Commission noted that such support seeks to 'help with the stabilization of the country and ease the economic and social consequences of the crisis' (*ibid.*: 13).

This form of EU financial assistance to non-members applies for the first time Article 15 of the IPA regulations. This clause foresees that in extraordinary circumstances earmarked resources from IPA can be redirected towards direct budgetary support of an EU candidate or accession country or SAA country (Stabilization and Association Agreement).

In terms of volume and macroeconomic impact, these different measures by the EU and/or in cooperation with other IFIs seek to reiterate the Commission's commitment to the region. They underline that the EU recognizes the institutional discrepancy between EU members and non-members (accession countries, candidate countries and potential candidate countries) as regards funding availability during the global crisis. The Commission is thus prepared to support countries in the western Balkans by existing means and new instruments from its vast (financial) toolbox (Bank of Greece and University of Oxford, 2009).

To further underline this approach, the EU also provided a credit line to Serbia in 2010 in two tranches of 100 million euros each. Equally, the EU approved a 39 million euro financial crisis response package for Bosnia and Herzegovina in August 2009. The 39 million euro grant finance will support the development of small and medium-sized enterprises and provide significant investment in infrastructure in the transport, environment and energy sectors (Szewczyk, 2010).

Funding will also be granted to the Deposit Insurance Agency in order to enable it to prevent deposit outflows due to the financial crisis. The 39 million euros were allocated under the IPA envelope for Bosnia and Herzegovina. A second programme for the country to ensure continuation of institution-building efforts was adopted by the European Commission in autumn 2009 (Castle, 2009).

The Western Balkans Investment Framework (WBIF), which was established in December 2009, is a case in point. The Framework is a joint initiative by the Commission, EIB, EBRD and CEB which seeks to pool grants, loans and technical expertise together to prepare financing for a common pipeline of priority investment projects in the Western Balkans. The WBIF will pool grants from the Commission's budget, IFIs and bilateral donors in two programmes: 1. joint lending facilities and 2. joint grant facilities. As of December 2009, the WBIF included grants totalling 130 million euros, with follow-up lending facilities expected to match this level from the outset of establishing the investment framework (European Commission, 2009c).

Is all this enough? Surely not, and it pales in significance when compared to the funding muscle applied by the IMF, World Bank and EBRD. But the comparison of volumes may in fact be misleading. Rather, we can observe that a division of labour is currently taking place. IFIs are providing large amounts of emergency lending to the western Balkans, with flexible conditionality attached to the rescue programmes. By contrast, the EU Commission is supplementing these interventions with limited, but targeted resources allocations, while being much more proactive as regards the adoption of and adherence to conditionalities for recipient countries.

But this line of argument about EU initiatives or the lack thereof also has a flip side. In many less direct and visible ways the EU, individual EU countries and the European Central Bank (ECB) have assisted non-EU members in the western Balkans and Turkey on a far larger scale.[1]

For one, the ECB extended its liquidity facility to Hungary's and Poland's central banks directly. More specifically, the ECB established temporary reciprocal currency arrangements to support dollar and/or euro liquidity. In autumn 2008 the ECB agreed with the central banks of Hungary and Poland to support liquidity operations in these countries. However, their gain was the neighbouring countries' pain. More specifically, those who are not (yet) members of the EU 'only' have a stabilization and association agreement (SAA) with Brussels and thus have a more limited set of financial support available to them.

Furthermore, at the G-20 Summit in London in April 2009 EU member countries pledged an additional 100 billion euros to the IMF, knowing full well that many of these resources would also end up in Central, East and Southeast European countries' standby arrangements with IFIs (G-20, 2009).

The ECB has also pumped phenomenal amounts of liquidity into the Eurozone financial systems, and those Eurozone-based commercial banks with local subsidiaries and branches in Southeast Europe have taken advantage of this window of opportunity and thereby provided liquidity support to their regional holdings. The sums involved were not inconsequential for the continuation of banking operations at a time when money and credit markets had essentially dried up in late 2008, early 2009.

It could thus also be argued that the Commission, the ECB and individual EU countries have indirectly been bailing out Central, Eastern and Southeast European financial sectors in a fashion similar to the more direct measures they are taking within the EU and the single currency zone.

Eurozone-based commercial banks are huge beneficiaries of funding arrangements such as the ECB's liquidity access programmes. Look no further than Greece, where the commercial banks with significant holdings and investments in the Balkans and beyond have obviously (and fortunately) been able to refinance their operations by taking advantage of accessing various ECB liquidity facilities.

Initiatives to support financial sector stability in Southeastern Europe

Economies in the region are being adversely affected by a financial sector that has relied far too long on foreign currency lending being provided by western parent banks to their local subsidiaries. Any forecast for the timing and scope of economic recovery in Southeastern Europe structurally depends on the region's financial sectors resuming lending to private individuals and the corporate sector.

Since the beginning of the global financial crisis in mid-2008, small and midsize companies have faced a serious credit crunch in all countries of the region (IMF, 2009b). This credit crunch is being implemented by commercial banks majority-owned by foreign parent banks. Table 12.2 above highlights to what degree foreign financial institutions have penetrated banking sectors in the region. With the exception of the EU member Slovenia, every other country in the region posts at least a foreign ownership ration of 60 per cent or more.

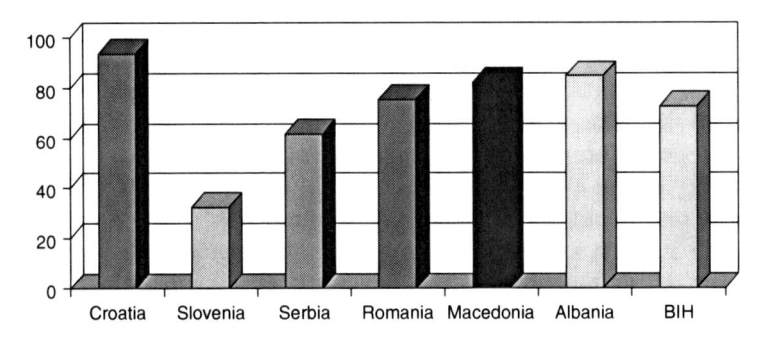

Figure 12.2 Banking assets in foreign ownership in Southeast Europe (2009) (%)
Sources: Central banks' data, Bank for International Settlements (2009).

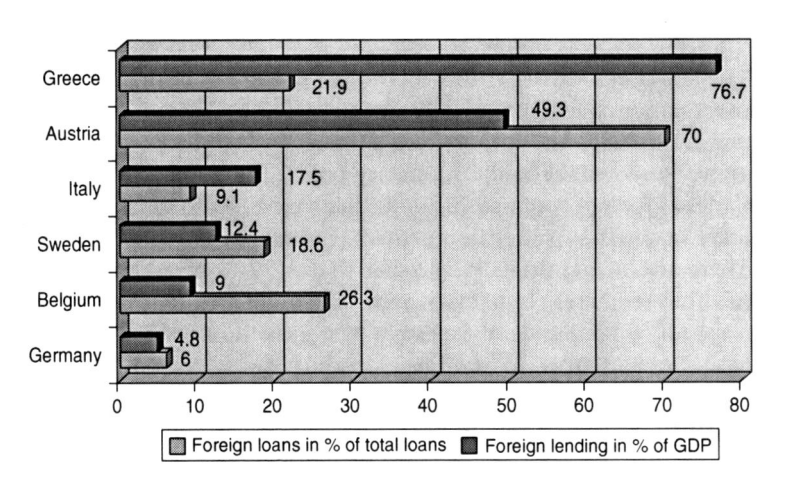

Figure 12.3 Foreign bank lending in Central and Eastern Europe (2008)
Sources: Bank for International Settlements (2009).

As Figure 12.3 illustrates, Greek and Austrian commercial banks are most heavily exposed to countries in Central, Eastern and Southeastern Europe. They had the highest share of lending as a percentage of annual GDP of all EU countries in 2008, namely a staggering 76.7 per cent and 49.3 per cent, respectively (Kerdos, 2010).

These numbers would even be higher if the data also included Serbia, Albania and FYR Macedonia, three additional countries where Greek commercial banks implemented a proactive lending strategy during the past decade. The countries include Poland, Russia, Czech Republic, Turkey, Hungary, Romania, Croatia, Slovakia, Ukraine, Bulgaria, Estonia, Latvia and Lithuania.

Put otherwise, while many competitors initially hesitated, Greek and Austrian commercial banks had the risk appetite to invest early and proactively in the region. Geographical proximity mattered for Greece in Southeast Europe and for Austria in Central Europe. Both countries' banking sector investments subsequently expanded their theatre of operation beyond the initial regional confines.

Such high loan exposure, combined with exorbitant loan growth among private households and an over-leveraged corporate sector, suggests that various parent banks from Western Europe created their own subprime markets in Serbia, Montenegro, Hungary, Albania, Ukraine, Romania and Bulgaria between 2000 and mid-2008. Money from western parent banks fuelled a debt-laden binge in Southeast Europe that blinded investors to the risks of cross-border, foreign currency lending (Bastian, 2010b).

The key characteristic of this subprime market and central driver was foreign currency lending, mostly denominated by Swiss francs and/or euros. Households and corporations alike bet against their own domestic currency and central banks' monetary policy. They found willing subsidiaries of foreign commercial banks that were eager to quickly increase market share *vis-à-vis* their competitors (Ewing, 2010a).

There are further underlying issues that need to be addressed short term. The credit crunch that is currently affecting countries in Southeast Europe follows a decade of excessive loan growth of about 50 per cent a year, in particular in mortgage lending denominated in foreign currencies. Between 2004 and mid-2008 the emerging housing bubble in parts of Southeast Europe was impossible to overlook. Real estate prices doubled within this four-year period in cities such as Podgorica, Belgrade, Tirana and Pristina (Ewing, 2010b).

This gold rush mentality came to an abrupt halt in mid-2008. As evidenced by the so-called Real Vienna in May 2009, the most important annual trade fair for corporate property investment in Central, Eastern and Southeast Europe, investment flows into corporate property development only reached 220 million euros in the three regions during the first quarter of 2009. This level constitutes a decline by two-thirds compared to the fourth quarter in 2008 (FAZ, 2009a).

Cooperation between multilateral lenders and commercial banks

Extending loan guarantees to the real economy and pledging continued support from western parent banks to their local subsidiaries in Southeastern Europe in times of sustained economic meltdown are gradually seeing the light of day. A number of recent policy initiatives highlight the need to identify commercial alternatives to scarce external funding. The focus of these initiatives is to reassure the banks' customer basis and establish coordinated rescue operations with multilateral financial institutions.

One such initiative concerns the provision of capital support to commercial banks operating in the region through multilateral lenders. As Table 12.3 illustrates, in 2009 the EBRD extended lending totaling US$578 million into the Central, Eastern and Southeastern European subsidiaries of the Italian bank UniCredit (UC). The May 2009 agreement

Table 12.3 EBRD capital support to UniCredit in Central, Eastern and Southeastern Europe (2009)

UniCredit (UC) subsidiary	Lending facility	Total volume
UC Bank (Hungary)	SME lending	50 million euros
Bulbank (Bulgaria)	SME lending	50 million euros
Zagrebacka Banka (Croatia)	SME lending	50 million euros
UC Bank (Serbia)	SME lending	30 million euros
UC Leasing (Serbia)	Leasing	15 million euros
UC Bank (Bosnia, Mostar)	SME lending	30 million euros
UC Leasing (Bosnia, Sarajevo)	Leasing	15 million euros
UC Leasing (Ukraine)	Leasing	$25 million
Ukrsotsbank (Ukraine)	Tier 2 capital	$100 million
ATF (Kazakhstan)	SME lending	$70 million
ATF (Kazakhstan)	Energy efficiency	$30 million
ATFBank (Kyrgyzstan)	SME lending	$20 million
		433 – 517 million euros*

Note: * According to US$/euro currency fluctuation.
Source: EBRD/UniCredit (2009).

to provide capital support to UniCredit is the largest in volume to date.

UC is the single largest financial investor and the biggest banking group (by assets) in the three regions (Unicredito, 2010). UniCredit has a network of over 4,000 branches in 19 countries of Central, Eastern and Southeastern Europe. Since the mid-1990s UniCredit has invested about 10 billion euros of equity in the three regions and has approximately 85 billion euros of total customer loans in the regions.

More specifically, the EBRD is providing loan finance to UniCredit's subsidiaries. These loans are not intended to clean up banks' balance sheets in the eight recipient countries. Rather, they are earmarked to support local branches in extending loans to small and medium-sized companies, enable leasing finance and assist energy efficiency projects. The lion's share of the US$578 million will go to UniCredit's subsidiaries in Ukraine and Kazakhstan (EBRD/UniCredit, 2009).

This joint venture illustrates how the EBRD has found a renewed sense of purpose in stabilizing the financial sectors in transition economies. The EBRD also extended similar loan arrangements to Banca Comerciala Romana (BCR), a Romanian subsidiary of the Austrian bank Erste Bank in 2009. The London-based bank is quickly becoming the second most important lending institution next to the IMF in Southeast Europe. Since the beginning of 2009 it increased its investments in the financial sector among 30 member countries by 50 per cent, to 3 billion euros (EBRD, 2010a).

The EBRD's investment is part of a wider crisis response strategy that seeks to implement joint initiatives with the World Bank Group and the EIB. The latter announced in May 2009 that it had launched a two-year loan programme worth 1.4 billion euros to assist Serbia with external funding for small and medium-sized enterprises and priority infrastructure projects (EIB, 2010). Together, the three IFIs have pledged over 24 billion euros in support of the banking sectors in Central, Eastern and Southeast Europe, thereby providing lending alternatives to businesses hit by the global financial crisis (EBRD, 2010a).

The picture that is gradually emerging in Central, Eastern and Southeastern Europe is thus one of delivering comprehensive – and increasingly coordinated – responses to the financing requirements of individual banking groups. These IFI-led responses seek to either stimulate and/or complement joint funding options of western commercial banks operating in the three regions. These interventions by external anchor institutions underscore a division of labour between IFIs and illustrate in practice a high degree of operational flexibility and programme adaptability towards recipient countries.

Exit strategies and shaping the reform agenda? The role of external anchors

The current challenges of the region defy easy categorizations and comparisons. Are the economies in Southeast Europe now discovering their limits – that is, the limits of autonomous economic development, constraints of financial sector integration and the restrictions of crisis management when confronted with the magnitude of such an economic downturn?

These are questions searching for new answers. Governments and civil society face a major task ahead to identify what lessons can be learned, and must be applied, from the economic calamity 20 years after the events of 1989/90.

This task will have to include retooling existing policy responses. As the developments since mid-2008 have shown in the region, crisis management and policy solutions lagged behind the unfolding dynamics of economic events. Equally, the nature of the responses that have since been formulated with the coordinated assistance of the international community may lead various actors involved to reappreciate – and revisit – the notion of *political economy*.

The EU Commission, in cooperation with numerous IFIs, has mobilized unprecedented levels of emergency lending programmes and grant facilities in order to confront the short-term needs of the region. But the Commission, IMF, EBRD, World Bank, EIB, CEB and other bilateral donors are just starting to recognize what will need to be done medium to long term over and above the provision of financial resources. Issues deserving attention in Belgrade, Bucharest, Tirana, Sarajevo and Skopje concern the following.

On what growth model should future economic development be based? GDP performance resulting from credit booms, excessive household and corporate debt as well as over-reliance on foreign capital inflows and unsustainable current account deficits has fundamentally been called into question.

The downside of fast-track financial integration has become increasingly visible. What lessons have to be drawn for financial sector reform and oversight, improving risk management procedures, reducing bias towards foreign currency lending?

The transition agenda must revisit the role of the state, its institutional quality and crisis reaction capacity, redefining instead of minimizing the role of the state, its regulatory scope and fiscal policy-making competence. This endeavour includes rethinking how governments in the region can generate fiscal space *without* having to rely so heavily on IFIs in the coming years?

External anchors coming to the rescue of countries severely hit by the economic downturn in the region cannot extend these levels of lending much longer. At some stage they will have to start moving towards dismantling some supportive policies (IMF, 2010). This implies engaging in winding-down exercises and identifying gradual exit strategies from these programmes, not least in order to avoid creating a culture of dependency. This strategy will considerably test the capacity of domestic anchors to complement and over time replace the activities of external (financial) anchors.

Handling issues such as figuring out exit strategies and/or capital increases is delicate. Discussing such strategies now may spook markets and policy-makers that measures could be withdrawn too quickly and thus undermine the recovery. But the same holds *vice versa*. Being silent about winding-down exercises runs the risk of encouraging markets and authorities in the region to become complacent, thinking IFIs will stick with lending programmes and grant facilities too long. How quickly IFIs unwind the extraordinary support measures put in place since 2008 will critically depend on developments in a still-fragile economic environment in the region.

The process of unwinding has no time limitation. But the funding basis of some IFIs has capital limits. The EIB is already operating at the limits of its funding and lending capacities. It has extended in excess of 6 billion euros to countries in the Black Sea region (including Bulgaria, Romania, Ukraine and Turkey) and approximately 2.2 billion euros for the western Balkans, mostly as credit lines for infrastructure projects and SME lending in 2008–10 (New Europe, 2009b).

The EBRD appealed to members for an extra 10 billion euros to lift its capital by 50 per cent. The additional capital consists of 1 billion euros paid in by the 61 government shareholders, including EU countries, the USA and Japan, and 9 billion euros in callable capital. The request, which was approved at the EBRD's annual shareholders' meeting in Zagreb, Croatia, in May 2010, enables the EBRD to expand its lending and compensate for the sharp decline in private capital flows into emerging European markets (EBRD, 2010b). The need for a capital increase also underscores concerns that the region's economic and financial sector difficulties are far from being overcome.

If the EBRD had continued to operate with its current €20 billion capital, the Bank would have had to limit its annual lending to a record 8 billion euros in 2009–10 and reduce it to 6 billion euros thereafter. The 10 billion euro capital increase allows the EBRD to commit 10 billion euros annually, or 20 billion euros in total extra funding in 2010–15. By mobilizing extra capital from private investors, the total additional funds raised could reach 60 billion euros (Parkinson, 2009).

Such an unprecedented capital increase by the EBRD underlines how precariously any economic recovery in the region is viewed by lending authorities in London and beyond. In February 2010 the World Bank sought support for a capital increase from the bank's shareholders, despite their own fiscal constraints. The World Bank argued that without the capital increase it would need to restrict lending by the middle of 2010 after the worst recession in six decades pushed countries' loan requests to a record high (IHT, 2010b).

Moreover, the depth of the global recession and the additional funding needs expressed by IFIs such as the EBRD and the World Bank illustrate to what degree the downturn is transforming such institutions. Before the crisis struck the EBRD's countries of operation, the US, the biggest shareholder, was keen to reduce the bank's activities on the grounds that its funding role in supporting post-communist transition was nearing the end as market economies were taking root.

But the economic crisis has reduced the amount of private capital available across the region. The EBRD, along with other IFIs, reacted by increasing its own resources thereby extending the development bank's lifespan and *raison d'être*. In a word, the EBRD's job is far from 'mission accomplished' from the Baltic Sea to the Black Sea.

It may not only be a matter of identifying new funding resources or detailing windingdown options, but rather to re-allocate existing resources from lending to capacity building. More specifically, such a shift includes the concentration of resources on the provision of technical expertise in key policy areas whose vulnerabilities have been exposed by the deep recession. The non-financial input that IFIs can provide here primarily concerns the macroeconomic and structural diagnostic capacity of policy-makers – for example, in finance ministries and central banks of the region.

The focus of the EIB is a case in point. Over and above considerably extending its lending resources to countries in the region, it is focusing on making additional financial engineering advice available. This includes technical advice on absorption capacity of available funds for EU members Bulgaria and Romania.

This expertise is all the more pertinent because it includes programmes on how to use these resources before risking losing them for lack of transparency or administrative absorption capacity. The heart of the matter here is the faculty of external actors to help anchor fiscal and structural policy-making capacity that can contribute to greater buffers and deeper crisis adjustment aptitude.

The role of external anchors is also important in one other key arena of policy-making. Through its arsenal of lending programmes and provision of technical expertise they engage the countries of the region in a sustained effort of institutional cooperation and policy coordination. This engagement can contribute to avoid potential alternative avenues of crisis management and risk mitigation in the region. Two such avenues concern individual countries seeking immunity from economic and financial sector vulnerability, adopting Asian-style self-insurance strategies.

The available toolbox for the execution of such strategies includes trade protectionism, competitive currency devaluation, accumulation of foreign currency reserves, considerably increasing capital requirements (in foreign currency) for western parent banks operating in the region and seeking to monopolize the allocation of financial resources. Countries in the region are considering risk mitigation strategies, and it is in the capacity and interest of IFIs and the EU to support them in refraining from adopting counterproductive measures.

This engagement is going to be energized by and shaped through the vehicle of deepening the countries' EU accession dialogue. The magnet of EU integration most convincingly adds to this strategy of engagement and provides the additional political momentum to carry on with the reform efforts in the region.

Two recent developments underscore the importance of revitalizing the EU magnet for the western Balkans. For one, the EU visa liberalization regime, which came into force for citizens from Serbia, Montenegro and FYR Macedonia in December 2009 provided tangible and lasting benefits for citizens across these three countries (European Commission, 2009b). It is hoped that other countries in the region, namely Albania, Bosnia and Herzegovina, as well as Kosovo, can also be included in this visa-free travel programme, provided they have met the conditions set by the Commission.

The other key development concerns the EU Commission's decision to unblock the so-called Interim Agreement with Serbia. This unblocking opened the door for the implementation of the Interim Agreement by all EU members and paved the way for Belgrade to submit its formal membership application in December 2009, before the Swedish EU presidency came to a close (Ricard, 2009).

The EU's continued power of attraction is also mirrored by Albania's and Montenegro's membership applications in April 2009 and December 2008, respectively. Even Iceland's EU application in September 2009 adds a new dimension to the enlargement agenda for the coming years (Reljic, 2010).

Conclusion

The region of Southeast Europe now finds itself in the early and volatile stages of what could be an economic recovery, or an intermission before a renewed downturn. Before rushing to any optimistic outlook or worst-case scenarios, a word of caution is in order. Since many macro-forecasters got it wrong in the past, prudence about any economic outlook for the region is appropriate and rather a sign of considered reflection.

The rate of economic contraction in the region is slowing down. Technically, most countries may be moving out of recession in 2010. According to the EBRD's GDP forecast in 2010, Bosnia and Herzegovina, Romania and Montenegro are expected to continue registering economic contraction (EBRD, 2010a). First-quarter 2010 economic growth in Serbia reached 0.5 per cent (FAZ, 2010b).

At this stage it is pure speculation as to whether the nature of any recovery will be L-, W-, U- or V-shaped in the region's economies. The coming months are still going to feel very much like a recession to many constituencies across Southeastern Europe. In the next years the trend growth rate of most countries in the region will be much closer to 2–4 per cent than in the vicinity of 5–8 per cent, as during the past five years.

Key components of Southeast Europe's economies, such as the unemployment rate, household consumption, residential investment, non-residential construction, capital spending and export capacity remain volatile and trail macroeconomic indicators like GDP development by several months. The value of non-performing loans will continue to increase into 2010. In a word, the economic and financial sector crises could still turn out to be self-reinforcing.

In addition, concerns about the medium-term solvency of governments will soon appear on the radar. In light of their heavy borrowing from IFIs in 2008/9 and possibly beyond, countries such as Romania, Serbia and Bosnia and Herzegovina will face repayment obligations that severely restrict their fiscal policy-making options in the coming years.

The broader concerns across the region are political. How will different constituencies react to economically difficult times and a perception that their hard-earned gains risk being erased? Voters, forced by recession to live more leanly, are irate. Ample opportunities to use elections as a tool for political punishment have already been taken advantage of and will continue to present themselves on the political calendar (Judah, 2010).

Two decades after the collapse of the Eastern bloc, the countries of Eastern and Southeast Europe are facing an uncertain future and the legacies of the recent past. The societies in this region are well schooled and practically experienced in the meaning of imploding states and failed economic systems. They have successfully sought answers to what went wrong before the historical events of 1989–90 (Bechev and Nicolaidis, 2010).

What growth model will they decide to apply while adjusting to the necessary winding-down, scaling-back exercise of relying on IFI emergency funding? Starting in 2010 the proactive lending by external anchor institutions is giving way to a slow unwinding of obligations. Identifying the exit options and repayment requirements will be politically contentious and limit spending alternatives in other budgetary sectors.

In light of what has happened, the trajectory ahead for the countries in Southeast Europe lacks a clearly marked road map. But what is becoming more obvious by the day is the following: the current import-led, financial sector-driven and debt-fuelled transition trajectory of economic development in the region is subject to root and branch re-evaluation.

A broader re-examination by public authorities of the government's role in the economy will have to take place across Southeast Europe. This may include exploring new ways to expand governments' responsibilities. This necessary introspection should not be inward looking and has to avoid protectionist policy solutions. The issues that deserve special placement on the agenda concern:

- the identification and creation of additional fiscal space;
- their crisis management/reaction capacity and regulatory expertise;
- financial sector regulation, in particular regarding foreign currency lending.

More broadly speaking, one of the key lessons learned during the crisis concerns where – and how – the boundary between government and the market should be (re)drawn. The tenets of free-market reform are now under scrutiny. The necessary debate about the demarcation lines has just begun.

This is a time for new ideas, bold thinking and original perspectives. Economic reformers are going to have to make some hard choices about the degree of disappointment they're willing to live with in societies of Southeast Europe. Thought-provoking choices about the nature of their political economies lie ahead.

Note

1. I am thankful to Mr Panayotis Gavras from the Black Sea Trade and Development Bank in Thessaloniki, Greece, for useful arguments on this subject matter.

References

Bank for International Settlements (2009) 'Foreign Ownership of Commercial Banking Sector in South East Europe', September.

Bank of Greece and University of Oxford (SEESOX) (2009) 'Challenges and Prospects of South East European Economies in the Wake of the Financial Crisis', Athens, 16 October.

Bastian, J. (ed.) (1998) *The Political Economy of Transition in Central and Eastern Europe*, Aldershot: Ashgate.

Bastian, J. (2009) Guest Column: 'No Time to Dither Over Policy Options', *Financial Times*, 18 June.

Bastian, J. (2010a) 'External Anchors to the Rescue: Reaching Out in a Time of Economic and Financial Sector Crises in Southeastern Europe', Occasional Paper No. 10/10, February, St Antony's College, University of Oxford.

Bastian, J. (2010b) 'Why the Greek Crisis Matters to South Eastern Europe', *Athens Plus*, 26 March.

Bechev, D. and Nicolaidis, K. (eds) (2010) *Mediterranean Frontiers: Borders, Conflict and Memory in a Transnational World*, London: I.B. Tauris.

Castle, S. (2009) 'In Balkans, a Daunting Money Pit for the EU', *International Herald Tribune*, 1 October, pp. 1, 4.

EBRD (2010a) *Annual Report 2010*, London.

EBRD (2010b) 'EBRD Annual Meeting 2010, Capital Increase Approved', Press Release, Zagreb, Croatia.

EBRD/UniCredit (2009) 'EBRD and UniCredit Join Forces to Support Businesses Across Eastern Europe', Press Release, 7 May.

Eddy, K. (2010) 'Closer Integration with the EU Boosts Growth', *Financial Times*, Special Report Serbia, 11 May.

EIB (European Investment Bank) (2010) *Annual Report of Lending Activities in South Eastern Europe in 2009*, Luxembourg.

European Commission (2009a) http://europa.eu/press_room/press_packs/crisis/index_en.htm, IP/09/1230, Brussels (accessed 11 August 2009).

European Commission (2009b) 'The EU Enlargement Progress: A Year of Progress in the Western Balkans and Turkey', IP/09/1519, Brussels, 14 October.

European Commission (2009c) 'DG Enlargement', Press Releases on the Establishment of the Western Balkans Investment Framework, December.

Ewing, J. (2010a) 'Eastern Europe Bets Again on Euro-Based Loans', *International Herald Tribune*, 7 May, pp. 14–15.

Ewing, J. (2010b) 'Austrian Banks Big Bets on Eastern Europe Turn Sour', *International Herald Tribune*, 26 June, p. 15.

FAZ (*Frankfurter Allgemeine Zeitung*) (2009a) 'Real Vienna zeigt Dimensionen der Hypothekenkrise auf', FAZ, 28 May. FAZ (2010b) 'Serbien muss Stellen Streichen', FAZ, 29 May.

FAZ (2010c) 'IWF-Auszahlung an Rumänien', FAZ, 5 July.

Financial Times (2010) 'IMF Aid Delay Likely After Romanian Court Rejects Austerity Pension Cuts', *Financial Times*, 26 June.

G-20 (2009) *Final Communiqué*, London.

IHT (*International Herald Tribune*) (2010a) 'Albania Plans to Make Eurobond Market Debut', IHT, 16 January.

IHT (2010b) 'World Bank Seeks Backing', IHT, 2 February.

IHT (2010c) 'Foreign Investment Declines in Romania and Bulgaria', IHT, 18 May.

IMF (2009a) *World Economic Outlook, April 2009, Crisis and Recovery*, Washington, DC: IMF.

IMF (2009b) *World Economic Outlook, October 2009, Sustaining the Recovery*, Washington, DC: IMF.

IMF (2009c) http://www.imf.org/external/np/exr/facts/crislend.htm.

IMF (2010) 'IMF Discusses Exiting From Crisis Intervention Policies', Public Information Notice (PIN) No. 10/27, 23 February.

IMF Agreement with Romania (2009) *Three-Year Standby Agreement Between Romania and the IMF*, Washington, DC, http://imf.org/external/np/exr/romania/crislend.htm.

IMF Interim Review of Romania's Standby Facility (2009) September, http://www.imf.org/external/np/exr/romania/interim.htm.

IPA (2009) *2009 Annual Action Programme for Serbia Under the Pre-Accession Instrument, European Commission, DG Enlargement*, Brussels: IPA.

Judah, T. (2010) 'At Last, Good News From the Balkans', *The New York Review of Books*, vol. 57, no. 4, 11 March.

Kathimerini (2010) 'Fitch Says Bulgaria May See Credit Rating Fall to Junk', Kathimerini, 13 May.

Kerdos (2010) 'South Eastern Europe Saved Greek Banks', 6 June, p. 4.

Mitra, P., Selowsky, M. and Zalduendo, J. (2010) *Turmoil at Twenty: Recession, Recovery, and Reform in Central and Eastern Europe and the Former Soviet Union*, Washington, DC: World Bank.

New Europe (2009a) 'Serbia to Draw USD200 Million from IBRD for Public Finances', 6 December, p. 34.

New Europe (2009b) 'EIB Provides 110 mln to Boost SMEs and Microfinance', 6 December, p. 34.

Parkinson, Joe (2009) 'EBRD Seeks More Funds', *The Wall Street Journal*, 30 September, p. 3.

Reljic, Dusan (2010) 'Die Zuckerbrotkrise der EU auf dem Westbalkan', *SWP-Aktuell*, vol. 20, February.
Ricard, Philippe (2009) 'La Serbie s'ouvre la voie d'une candidature d'adhésion à l'Union européenne', *Le Monde*, 9 December.
Szewczyk, B. M. J. (2010) 'The EU in Bosnia and Herzegovina: Powers, Decisions and Legitimacy', Occasional Paper no. 83, March.
Unicredito (2010) *Annual Report to Shareholders 2009*, Milan, www.unicredito.it.
WIIW (Vienna Institute for International Economics) (2010) 'The Crisis Delays the Catching-up Process in Eastern Europe', FAZ, 20 April, p. 12.

13
Russia in Crisis: Implications for Europe

Serena Giusti

> We need to make maximum use of the benefits and opportunities of cooperation in the period of post crisis development.
>
> (Putin, 2009a: 1)[1]

Introduction

The aim of this chapter is to point out the consequences of the global financial and economic crisis for the Russian Federation and its implications for the Russia–EU relationship, the pan-European space and the global balance. Russia has been dramatically hit by the crisis, proving its high integration in the global market. There is not a Russian 'exceptionalism'. The crisis was expected to have serious political implications in Russia where the legitimacy of the ruling elite broadly depends on the country's economic performance. Furthermore, since the first of Vladimir Putin's terms of presidency, the return of Russia among the world powers has been mostly due to its economic rebirth. However, at least in the short term, Russia has reacted well to the external shock and it is already experiencing a recovery, albeit bumpy. The country's 'actorness' has not been seriously hampered. On the international front, the crisis has been rather exploited, strengthening its influence and establishing profitable strategic alliances. The EU has only played a marginal role in its big neighbour's post-crisis plans; relations between Moscow and Brussels are not becoming more involved.

Russia and the crisis

The 2008 financial and economic crisis hit Russia after a long period of rapid expansion during which annual GDP growth rates averaged

7 per cent. Russia has experienced all the difficulties at once: sharply declining export earnings from energy and metals, over-leveraged corporate balance sheets, credit crunch and banking failures, a bursting real-estate bubble and mortgage defaults, accelerating capital flight (capital outflows totalled a net $50 billion in October 2008 alone) and unavoidable pressures for devaluation. Because of the recession, global demand in commodities reduced while the oil price collapsed and Russian total export revenues decreased by almost the 50 per cent (IMF, 2010).[2] As a consequence, GDP contracted by 8 per cent; industrial production tumbled by nearly 11 per cent; exports collapsed by 36 per cent; and state revenues fell by almost 5 per cent of GDP from 2007–9 (World Bank, 2010). Russian banks had a good deal of bad debt and suffered from the same lack of confidence in one another that has been seen in the West. Many of its companies were highly leveraged. Much of their debt was with foreign lenders and against collateral whose value had slumped. The Russian stock market shrunk, suffering a 75 per cent fall in value, and the government had burned through more than 20 per cent of its foreign-exchange reserves (official reserves and accumulated wealth founded were estimated about $750 billion) by August 2009. Confident predictions of 7 per cent GDP growth for 2009 gave way to revised estimates of 3–4 per cent until the first quarter of 2009, when the economy was in recession (*ibid.*). Since the 2009 contraction, the Russian economy has been on its way towards recovery (Russia is likely to grow by 4.5 per cent in 2010, followed by 4.8 per cent in 2011) thanks to increased oil prices, a rising domestic demand and a more flexible exchange rate that helps Russia against the backdrop of oil price volatility (*ibid.*).

Nevertheless, unemployment remains high and credit and investment are limited. Crumbling infrastructure is likely to hamper the economy's competiveness and longer-term growth prospects. Russia needs structural reforms in order to sustain stable growth. The business climate needs to be improved in respect, among other things, of high corruption, influence of the government on the economy and demographic decline. President Medvedev himself has on various occasions denounced his country's over-dependence on the export of natural resources, the rampant corruption, the pervasive and inefficient bureaucracy, dysfunctional governance and legal nihilism. He has called for an ambitious reforming agenda including transparency, competition, accountability and protection of property rights. However, it is still unclear how the Russian presidency will promote the modernization of the state. This seems possible either through experimentation or imitation (by adopting products, technologies, processes and structures that are already in use in more advanced economies with higher productivity and income levels), but no clear position exists so far (Sutela, 2009: 3–4).

In contrast to other big economies, it was feared that the crisis could have endangered Russia's stability. Despite the fact that the first liberalizing reforms in the country were initiated as early as the middle of the 1980s, with a package of radical economic reforms adopted under Boris Yeltsin's presidency in the 1990s, Russia is still in a transformation phase and not yet a full democracy. The political system that emerged in Russia under President Vladimir Putin (2000–8) has been best characterized by the political model of 'partial democracy', 'illiberal democracy' or 'overmanaged democracy'. All these labels refer to a hybrid of democracy and authoritarianism (Zakaria, 1997). The country's political stability has been built and maintained on leadership popularity and its actual capacity to provide economic benefits to people. Political legitimacy of the leadership derives from the economic performance of the country rather than from an electoral democratic legitimacy. As Lo notes:

> The legitimacy of Putinism is not based on relatively abstract concepts such as the rule of law, probity and transparency, but on two things: the regime's capacity to deliver political stability and economic growth; and the ability to hold its nerve in the event of growing socioeconomic tensions. (Lo, 2009: 4)

The two presidencies of Putin, after the crash of the rouble in 1998, marked Russia's best period of economic growth since before World War II. Annual GDP growth averaged 6.7 per cent between 1998 and 2007 (Russia's GDP equalled $1.29 trillion in 2007, putting Russia back into the ranks of the ten largest economies in the world), with persistent budget surpluses between 2000 and 2008, huge current account surpluses and accumulation of $598 billion of reserves by August 2008 – third biggest in the world (Aslund and Kuchins, 2009: 45). This formidable economic expansion positively impacted on society: wages more than tripled in real terms, poverty plummeted by half and unemployment fell by half. Indicators like housing, mobile phone penetration, car ownership and even levels of self-assessed life satisfaction all went up, along with the rise in incomes (Guriev, 2010). Putin embodied the catharsis after the turbulence and frustration of the Yeltsin period.

This explains why the crisis was so feared by the Russian government. Putin passed a stimulus package that increased the government's expenditures from 33.7 per cent of GDP to 40.6 per cent of GDP (Carnegie Endowment for International Peace, 2010). The Russian fiscal stimulus was aimed at the broader middle class (currently around 20–5 per cent of the population), rather than only the poor and 'mono-towns', where residents are almost entirely dependent on a single firm or industry for employment; pensions and minimum wages were also increased. As Kremlin First Deputy Chief of Staff, Vladislav Surkov (2008), warned, 'The main task of the state during the slump must become the preservation of the middle class, the defence of the middle class from the waves of poverty and confusion that are coming from the West.' The defence of the middle class responds to the object of keeping it away from politics and, in particular, from the western notion of democracy. So far, Russia has averted a large-scale social unrest: protests have been selective and localized (Kaliningrad, Vladivostok, Irkutsk) without any major consequence for the political system.[3]

The effects on Russia's external dimension

The crisis in Russia was expected to downsize the country's international ambitions. It is worth remembering that the rebirth of Russia as an international actor was primarily a function of its economic recovery (Giusti and Penkova, 2008). In fact, the two presidencies of Putin sought 'to legitimize Russia's new role and to project its power through economic, as opposed to traditional political-military means' (Stent, 2008: 1089). This sequence – strengthening politically and economically the Russian state → restoring Russia international status → acting assertively – still moulds the Russian concept of foreign policy. Russia aims at establishing itself as a leading economic power and at integrating into global markets. Putin's Russia has developed a mercantilist rather than imperialist posture towards international politics.

As the economic crisis approached Russia, the country had an unexpected and unwanted occasion to show the world its power and reactivity. The war against Georgia (August 2008) to retake control of South Ossetia and Abkhazia, which were then proclaimed independent, had two important effects: on the one hand it cemented the public opinion around the diarchy ('rally around the flag' effect), distracted attention from domestic troubles like unemployment and plummeting incomes; on the other hand, it proved that neither the US nor the EU were willing to support provocations against Russia and to engage in war with a nuclear superpower. At the end the Kremlin took advantage of all opportunities (including the EU division on how to react to the Georgian crisis) to increase its influence in the post-Soviet space.

The crisis also inescapably demonstrated that Russia was well integrated in the global economy, dismissing a country's presumption of 'exceptionalism'. Most Russian policy-makers considered Russia as a relatively safe haven in the world economic crisis until summer of 2008, when the crisis dramatically erupted in the country, ending a ten-year growth spurt (Hanson, 2009: 60). From then, the diarchy (Putin as Prime Minister and Dmitry Medvedev as President) openly admitted that Russia was not immune to financial crisis. At the Davos World Economic Forum in 2009, Putin remarked that, 'The crisis has affected everyone at this time of globalization. Regardless of their political or economic system, all nations have found themselves in the same boat' (Putin, 2009b: 1). The fact that the crisis hit similarly the various world economic giants irrespectively of their domestic regimes proved that capitalism and democratic regimes are not faultless. The crisis equalized the winners of the Cold War and the losers (and this is still a very sensitive issue for the Russians). The western economic and political model that triumphed 20 years ago, to the extent that Francis Fukuyama spoke of the end of history as a result of the ultimate triumph of western liberal democracy and an unabashed victory of economic and political liberalism (Fukuyama, 1989), was dramatically called into question. The relation between democracy and economic wealth also became questionable – making other patterns such as the Chinese one alluring. Although Russia recognizes the value of democracy, a part of its political elite is looking with interest to the Chinese model, a mix of capitalism and Communist rule that has accomplished modernization from the top down within an authoritarian regime.

Russia has neither attacked economic liberalism nor has promoted a 'third way' as an alternative to capitalism and globalization. On the contrary, it has responded to the financial emergency by emphasizing the importance of further reform and the need for more cooperation with other countries. 'In our anti-crisis domestic policy we attach great importance to enhancing international collaboration', President Medvedev (2008: 1) affirmed. Prime Minister Putin warned world leaders against reacting to the crisis by sliding into isolationism and unrestrained economic selfishness. He called on the US President Barack Obama to 'cooperate constructively' (Putin, 2009b: 1) in international affairs. Putin also warned that militarization will not solve the world's problems but only push them back, taking from the economy vast financial and material resources that could be used much better elsewhere.

Putin's Russia, already well experienced in pragmatic relationships based on a limited set of mutual interests, has further broadened its intense network of strategic partnerships. Russian foreign policy is highly de-ideologized. This approach moves from a particular vision of the international system. As Foreign Minister Sergey Lavrov explained,

'The world is becoming a polyarchy – an international system run by numerous and diverse actors with a shifting kaleidoscope of associations and dependencies' (Lavrov, 2007). The fact that Russia is not involved in campaigns like worldwide democracy promotion but leaves the form of governance to the choice of the single country, makes it less constrained in selecting its allies. The concept of 'sovereign democracy' proclaimed by Russia to hold down western influence in the Soviet space helps Moscow to conduct affairs also with non-democratic countries (such as Iran, Syria and Venezuela). Russia's friends are not required to comply with any particular political regime's conditions in order to benefit from its cooperation.

The financial crisis has made the reconfiguration of strategic partnerships and pragmatic friendships both more feasible and more urgent not only for Russia but also for the other major players in the international landscape. Russia has been willing to engage with them on wide-ranging issues. The turbulence of the economic global system opened new windows of opportunity for Russia to extend its traditional influence over the so-called post-Soviet space and to intensify cooperation with the former rival of the Cold War, the US. The paucity of financial resources pushed both of them closer to China, which has proved to be better equipped to face up the 2008 financial shock.

The crisis had also some important irenic implications helping the 'resetting' of the relations between Washington and Moscow. The need for curtailing the budget devoted to defence gave a formidable impulse to Moscow and Washington for the renegotiations and signing (8 April 2010) of a new Strategic Arms Reduction Treaty (START II) replacing START I, which expired in early December 2009.[4] President Obama and President Medvedev put aside the tensions of recent years and declared that they would seek even deeper cuts in nuclear weapons. The policy of the 'reset the button' (Penkova, 2010)[5] of bilateral relations inaugurated by Russian Foreign Minister Lavrov and US Secretary of State Hillary Clinton in March 2009 was certainly the result of pragmatism on both sides, further boosted by the need to contain the crisis effects on the state budget. This happened just a year after US President George W. Bush shelved a civilian nuclear cooperation agreement in protest at Russia military intervention against Georgia in support of Abkhazia and South Ossetia. President Obama did not mention Georgia or the broader issue of Russia's assertiveness with its neighbours. The two presidents also played down their quarrel over American plans to build missile defence in Europe, despite recent comments by Russian officials threatening to withdraw from the treaty if the United States pressed too far.[6] The US

President did not express any public concern about Russian 'hybrid or illiberal democracy', a topic that routinely flavoured discussions during the previous presidency. Even though the reset has not implied a new start in the Russia–US relations, it has nevertheless produced consistent results which the crisis has helped accelerate.

The eruption of the financial crisis in Europe was synchronic to the first version of President Medvedev's proposal for a 'new European security architecture from Vancouver to Vladivostok' (Berlin, June 2008) that was better elaborated in the autumn at Evian (October 2008) and, finally, published on the website of the Kremlin as a Draft Treaty in November 2009.[7] The Russian plan for a new pan-European security was not initiated because of the crisis, but the crisis made the 'clients' of that offer at least more attentive. As Medvedev explained, the draft has to be understood as a purely constructive idea that is not directed against anyone but it is intended to contribute to a full-fledged united and safe European space. In contrast to Gorbachev's idea of a 'Europe from the Atlantic to the Urals', entailing the survival of a Soviet Union that would have simply cooperated with both the US and the EU, Medvedev's proposal presents a post-bipolar view in which Russia is one of the key players and shapers. As the Russian Foreign Minister stressed (April 2010), 'the approach towards the Draft Treaty on European Security is a test-case of sincerity of Russia's partners, including NATO' (Penkova, 2010: 7). The viewpoint of Washington regarding the proposed Draft is of a crucial importance for Russia – if positive it will acknowledge Moscow's fundamental role in shaping the European security architecture; if not – it will fuel once again the position that European stability and security is a matter of US-exclusive responsibility. Russia wants to count more in the international system and in the pan-European space. It seeks to review the institutional setting, inherited from the Cold War (NATO, OSCE) and it wants to strengthen the pro-Russian organizations (Collective Security Treaty Organization and the Eurasian Economic Community). European security will remain incomplete and subject to rupture until a genuine 'common security space' incorporating Russia and its neighbours emerges, while the US–Russian relationship cannot be put on a durably positive and productive basis until there is a common view of the post-Soviet space. Arriving at a mutually acceptable European security arrangement will largely determine the kind of relationship Russia can have with the West, and this in turn impinges decisively on Russia's range of choice in managing relations with other major powers, including China and, more broadly, BRIC (Brazil, Russia, India, China). The EU, absorbed by the crisis and yet divided on how to deal with Russia, has not taken the proposal seriously.

The crisis and the post-Soviet space

As a consequence of the crisis Russia has become closer to China. Russia is looking for fresh financial resources, while China is hungry of energy for its expanding economy. In the course of 2009 the two countries concluded an oil contract worth US$100 billion and Russia's Rosneft and Transneft secured a 20-year credit of $25 billion from the China Development Bank. Rosneft will refinance debts and support an investments programme, while Transneft will direct resources for the construction of the Eastern Siberia–Pacific Ocean pipeline spur to China. Moscow and Beiijng are now negotiating an agreement that would make China the biggest consumer of Russian natural gas. Russia has finally proved to the EU countries that there are alternative consumers to European clients. Europe seems in a weaker bargaining position when discussing energy issues with Moscow. The Sino-Russian bilateral engagement is very pragmatic and it does not have the characteristics of a long-term and comprehensive strategic alliance. Their new entente does not threaten western interests. Moscow and Beijing are more interested in engaging with the West than with each other and China is in a stronger position than Russia to challenge the West's global pre-eminence (Lo, 2008). China is assisting financially and investing into countries that have traditionally been in Russia's area of interest. Beijing, for instance, extended a US$1 billion credit to Moldova, twice as much as Moscow had promised (and so far failed) to deliver.[8] Chinese investments have been flowing into Central Asia at an impressive rate, particularly in the energy, mining and construction sectors. China's involvement in Central Asia is driven heavily by commercial considerations, while Russia's has a much more obvious political undertone. China's 'soft power' is softer than that of Russia, being more mercantilist orientated and less politicized. It is difficult to predict if and when Beijing's economic leverage could result also in a political influence over the region that would clash with Russia's ascendance in the area.

Russia has exploited the crisis as well to reinforce dependency links with the countries of the post-Soviet space. This responds to the Russian aim of limiting the role of both the EU and the US in the region. In January 2009 the Minister of Economic Development, Elvira Nabibulina, called for the creation of a special body that would coordinate public and private efforts to acquire low-priced assets in the Commonwealth of Independent States (CIS); the acquisition strategy was paralleled by an important flow of credits or financial aid to number of countries.[9] As usual, Russia has used its energy power to make many of the former Soviet Republics more acquiescent to its requests. And with the crisis hitting these fragile economies it is difficult to say no to Russian rewards.

The most blatant example of this policy was the agreement reached by Russian President Medvedev and Ukrainian President Yanukovych in April 2010. According to it, Russia granted 30 per cent discount on the Russian gas price of $330 per 1,000 cubic metres over the next ten years (expected to cost Russia $40 billion over that time). The discount of gas prices should help Ukraine to save some $3 billion in 2010 and continue social programmes, adding relevant changes that have already been introduced to the country's 2010 draft budget. The new gas deal has also eliminated provisions on penalties, which constantly posed a threat to the Ukrainian gas national energy company and monopolist Naftogaz. Moreover, on the basis of the discount, Ukraine's gas transportation system will give the country some $6 billion in annual revenues if Kiev manages to persuade Russia and the EU to invest in the modernization of Ukraine's pipelines. At the same time, Ukraine agreed to extend the term of the Russian Black Sea Fleet presence in the country's Crimea for 25 more years after the current lease expires in 2017. The deal, extending Russia's use of a naval base in Crimea, is economically beneficial for both Moscow and Kiev. As far as Russia is concerned, it is not only a question of the redeployment of the Black Sea Fleet or the construction of new coastal infrastructure, but it is also crucial for eliminating the remaining 'uncertainty' in bilateral relations. The ratification of the deal on the naval base provoked chaos in Ukraine. Putin has also proposed that Ukraine could merge Gazprom and Naftogaz by means of assets swaps. The various gas crises, including the one in June 2010 between Russia and Belarus, are of the same tone. Gazprom aims at increasing its stake in Beltransgaz on the basis of the country's full dependency on Russian energy. The dispute centred on Belarus's refusal to accept a hike in the price it pays for Russian gas and the delay in paying off Gazprom. Russia's decision to cut supplies to Belarus was also a 'soft' way to persuade the country to ratify the Customs Union with Russia and Kazakhstan and to show to the European countries receiving gas through Belarus (notably Germany, Lithuania and Poland) its capacity for economic blackmailing.

Russia has proven very dynamic in creating or reinvigorating clubs/ associations/groups with a heterogeneous geographical composition. Russia has used, for instance, the Asia-Pacific Economic Cooperation (APEC), and in particular the BRIC group, to rebrand itself as an emergent and successful economy, despite the crisis. Being identified with these groups is a way to distinguish itself from the stagnant western economies. During the APEC's forum in the autumn of 2008, President Medvedev affirmed that the emerging economies, especially in Asia, will have to

> assume the task to unravel the world economic crisis ... and its role is growing as never before. The APEC member States' market investment capacities, and the high human and technological potential of these countries, allow us to consider that this region will become the locomotive of sustainable world economic development in the future. We believe that many APEC countries will become leaders in the post-crisis period and will gain new positions in key markets.[10]

Russia sought to strengthen its international profile by playing a more active regional role. In particular regional cooperation/integration has been seen as an opportunity to lead the political and economic orientation of its former Republics, especially after the decision to interrupt bilateral negotiations for accession to the WTO. The crisis has offered Russia an opportunity to counterbalance with its lucrative offers the mounting influence of the EU and the US in the region. First of all, Russia wanted to regain a certain control over the CIS, a very loose association involving most of the former Soviet states. In 2009 a common package of anti-crisis measures was implemented and the idea of creating a single economic space like the EU was floated. Meanwhile the EurAsEC (Belarus, Russia and Kazakhstan agreed, on 29 March 1996, to establish a custom union) appeared the most appropriate project for the first stage of economic integration. At a CIS–EurAsEc summit in late 2007, Putin announced plans to establish a Customs Union and a supranational commission in charge of customs regulations on the EurAsEC platform. The Customs Union project that was announced before the onset of the global economic and financial crisis has become especially important now. The desire to protect internal markets from cheap imports stems from the low competitiveness of the goods produced by the participating countries and from the fact that these products are in demand only in the post-Soviet markets. Also, Moscow simply could not ignore the emergence of a contending European project – the plans to create a free trade zone affiliated with the EU and conceived in the format of the EU's Eastern Partnership initiative (EaP), which Azerbaijan, Armenia, Belarus, Georgia, Moldova and Ukraine were invited to join as participants.[11]

The crisis had no major positive impact on Moscow–Brussels relations. The EU remains in the doldrums, greatly divided once more on the anti-crisis measures and on how to bail out its most uncomfortable Member

States, such as Greece. EU–Russia relations have been stagnant for a while. Moscow does not consider the EU as an intriguing partner even at a time of crisis, while it continues to conclude profitable agreements with some of its Member States, notably France, Germany and Italy. Russia is reluctant to deal with the EU, this being an organization whose postmodern nature is not clearly understood in the Kremlin. Furthermore, the EU has irritated its Russian neighbour with the launch of the EaP that has been perceived in Moscow precisely as an attempt to create a European zone of influence in its traditional sphere. Although the European Commission stated that the EaP would be developed in parallel with the strategic partnership with Moscow, the Member States (Poland and Sweden) promoting the EaP led Russia to suspect that it is a less-than-neutral stabilization policy. Moscow feels the EaP may conceal a strategy to co-opt the former Soviet republics into the European integrated area and 'roll back' Russia from her traditional sphere of influence. The EaP thus points to the existence of ongoing competition for control of the post-Soviet area where two rival security systems confront each other: the Euro-Atlantic and the Russian. Paradoxically, epistemological confusion over this cycle of international politics – ever since the Cold War ended the international system has been fluid and unstable – is both keeping the paradigms of bipolarity alive and revealing how inadequate and insubstantial they are. In this 'two-way periphery' area both are employing strategies that reflect their own interests and are based on an acceptable degree of rationality. The EU aim is to repeat the positive experience of 'Europeanizing' and stabilizing Central–East Europe, though if there are no prospects of membership for states in the area its influence is distinctly hamstrung.

By contrast, Russia sees the ex-Soviet area as embodying a sizeable part of her Euro-Asian identity. Target countries vary in their judgements of the EaP according to how much they aspire Europe-wards (there is a weaker sense of European identity here than in Central Europe; the enthusiasm of 1989 has played itself out now) or, conversely, how much Russian ascendance is felt (in various forms). Participation in the EaP does not entail eligible countries having to make a clear choice between one side or the other: many of them are still receptive to overtures from Russia, which has more cultural affinity than the EU and a residual influence in the area. There are sizeable minorities of Russians in EaP countries and their identities have been bolstered by Moscow's passport policy and control over the national media. Equally important is the money sent home by immigrants to Russia and the presence of Russian troops. Despite some increases, the price of Russian hydrocarbons has remained below market cost. Again, with the crisis the flow of Russian capital has stepped up in strategic sectors like energy and infrastructure (Popescu and Wilson, 2009). With the two zones of influence intersecting as they do, a competitive atmosphere has set in. Both seek greater institutionalization, though they differ in their basic values and in what they are able to offer. This has encouraged national leaders (most markedly in Ukraine) to draw tactically on support now from Brussels, now from Moscow, for domestic and often personal reasons. Such oscillation by national elites is hardly conducive to consolidating democracy. The 'two-way periphery' is torn between what still seems too abstract an attraction to the EU and the more concrete promises being made by Russia.

The EU–Russia Partnership for Modernization launched at their Summit in Rostov-on-Don (May–June 2010) does not seem a workable framework for improving relations between the two actors either.[12] The content and the aims of the modernization partnership are too vague. First, the financial and economic crisis has discredited the western model of capitalism in Moscow's view; second, the EU itself has failed to become the most competitive and dynamic knowledge-based economy in the world by 2010, as foreseen in the Lisbon Strategy; third, a debate on what kind of modernization is suitable for Russia should be a precondition for any strategy of this kind.

Conclusion

The Russian economic and political system looks stable on the surface, but it is actually fairly fragile. The failure to modernize and innovate in the country might, sooner or later, call into question the ability of the current political leadership to govern and be seen as a breach of the understanding that the people tolerate an illiberal democracy in exchange of better conditions of life. The crisis has neither weakened the international position of Russia nor reappraised the country's foreign policy ambitions. On the contrary, Russia has taken advantage of it to reset relations, strengthening partnerships and deepening regional cooperation under its leadership. Before the crisis hit, Russia's leaders believed rapid economic growth was shifting the global power balance in their favour; after the crisis they believe the same. The Russian government's desire to delay large increases in military spending contributed to a new round of arms-control agreements with the US administration. Russia was also able to conclude profitable agreements with China. The crisis has therefore consolidated the place of Russia among the 'Great Nations'. Furthermore, Russia has rebranded its image as a strong and growing BRIC economy. The crisis has not improved relations with the

EU. Moscow prefers bilateralism to group negotiations with Brussels. It seems that the EU is still confused on how to engage Russia. The competition over the influence on the grey space between the enlarged Union and the resurgent Russia does not help the transformation of countries like Belarus, Moldova or Ukraine. Actually Russia has exploited their weak economic situation to expand its economic penetration in strategic sectors, increasing its political leverage. The EU has also been unresponsive to the Russia plan for pan-European security. Russia, during the crisis, has been much more proactive than the EU, which might once more have lost the chance to build a constructive partnership with Russia and make safer the environment around its new borders.

Notes

1. Vladimir Putin Speech at the Shanghai Cooperation Organization's Heads of Government Council meeting, 14 October 2009, http://www.premier.gov.ru/eng/visits/world/7889/events/7902/ (accessed on 6 August 2010).
2. In 2008, 65 per cent of exports were made up by hydrocarbons contributing to the 50 per cent of state revenues but only 20 per cent of GDP. Energy accounts for two-thirds of export revenues, almost half of all public sector revenue and around a quarter of total GDP. If metals are added, the basic commodity sector produces some four-fifths of Russia export revenue. While energy is crucial for export and tax revenue, it does not provide many jobs. Only 2 per cent of all Russian workers are employed directly in the energy sector.
3. According to Levada-center only 27 per cent of respondents asked in February 2010 about the possibility for mass actions in their town/district against drop in their standard of living answered that they were quite probable and even fewer (20 per cent) answered that in case of protest actions, they would join (http://www.levada.ru/press/2010031805.html, accessed on 6 August 2010).
4. Under the treaty, if ratified, each side would be barred from deploying more than 1,550 strategic warheads or 700 launchers within seven years. Because of counting rules and past reductions, neither side would have to eliminate large numbers of weapons to meet the new limits. But the treaty re-establishes an inspection regime that lapsed in December and could serve as a foundation for deeper reductions later.
5. To reset the button consists of a new approach to dealing with Russia – addressing top political targets Iran, Afghanistan, international terrorism, energy and non-proliferation – while courting Russia's sensibilities with compensations for previous neglect of its interests, rather than pursuing an explicit and long-term strategy.
6. The Bush administration's plan for building a missile defence system in Poland and the Czech Republic has been a major source of tension with Russia, which fears the weakening of its nuclear deterrent capacity and opposes the establishment of an American military footprint close to the

frontiers of the former Soviet Union. The day after Obama's November 2008 election victory, Russian President Dmitry Medvedev declared in his annual state of the nation address that Russia would station short-range Iskander missiles in Kaliningrad, a Russian territorial enclave bounded by Lithuania to the north and Poland to the south.
7. The main features of the draft are: 1. respect for the territorial integrity of all countries; 2. prohibition of the use of force as well as the threat to use force; 3. insurance of equal security for all (this point alludes to restrictions on military alliances such as NATO that threaten, according to Medvedev, the security of some non-members); and 4. the rejection of an exclusive right of one state or organization to maintain security in Europe (yet further reference to NATO).
8. 'China is gaining a foothold in Russia's backyard', *Financial Times*, 29 July 2009.
9. Armenia ($500 million), Belarus ($2 billion), Kyrgyzstan (a $2 billion loan and aid worth $150 million), Moldova ($500 million promised), the separatist enclaves Abkhazia ($68 million) and South Ossetia ($81 million dollars in addition to the $246 million assigned for post-war reconstruction of infrastructure) and the EurAsEc special fund (out of $10 billion, Russia contributes $7.5 billion). These data and other detailed cases of Russia economic penetration in the neighbour countries can be found in S. Secrieru, 'Russian Foreign Policy in Times of Crisis: Greater Compliance or Resilient Self-confidence?', *CEPS Policy Brief*, No.192/30 June 2009.
10. 'Strengthening Dynamic and Equal Partnership in the Asia-Pacific Region', 21 November 2008, http://www.thejakartaglobe.com/opinion/toward-a-dynamic-and-equal-partnership/300656 (accessed on 12 August 2010).
11. The European Eastern Partnership is an initiative launched by the EU in May 2009 on the basis of a Swedish–Polish proposal on response to the French efforts to promote and strengthen the Mediterranean Union. The aim of the EaP is to enhance the EU's relationship with: Armenia, Azerbaijan, Belarus, Georgia, Moldova and Ukraine. This would imply new association agreements including deep and comprehensive free trade agreements with those countries willing and able to enter into a deeper engagement and gradual integration in the EU economy. The EaP contemplates also the possibility of easier travel to the EU through gradual visa liberalization, accompanied by measures to tackle illegal immigration. Through the EaP, the EU wishes to promote democracy and good governance, strengthen energy security, promote sector reform and environment protection, encourage people to people contacts, support economic and social development and offer additional funding for projects to reduce socio-economic imbalances and increase stability. For more information see the EU website devoted to the initiative: http://www.eeas.europa.eu/eastern/index_en.htm.
12. The Partnership for Modernization implications have not been explicated in detail and the way it will be carried out is not yet clear. The Partnership has been simply defined as a shared modernization agenda to advance the EU and Russian economies and bring respective citizens closer together. The partnership should serve as a flexible framework for promoting reform, enhancing growth and raising competitiveness. Among the priority areas of the partnership are: expanding investment in strategic sectors, improving

trade and economic relations, promoting small and medium enterprises, enhancing cooperation in innovation, research, space, energy and improving the business climate trough the promotion of good governance (see Council of the EU, Joint Statement on the Partnership for Modernisation EU–Russia Summit, 31 May–1 June 2010, Rostov-on-Don, 1 June 2010, 10546/10 Presse 154).

References

Aslund, A. and Kuchins, A. (2009) 'The Russia Balance Sheet', The Peterson Institute for International Economics and the Center for Strategic and International Studies.

Carnegie Endowment for International Peace (2010) 'Russia's Response to the Financial Crisis', event organised on 4 Mayin Washington, DC, available at http://www.carnegieendowment.org/events/?fa=eventDetail&id=2895 (accessed 10 August2010).

Fukuyama, F. (1989) 'The End of History', *The National Interest*, Summer 1989.

Giusti, S. and Penkova, T. (2008) 'Russia Just a Normal Great Power?', ISPI Working Paper no. 30, with the support of the Italian MAE, available at http://www.ispionline.it/it/documents/WP_30_2008.pdf.

Guriev, S. (2010) 'Russia's Economy: Are We Returning to the Soviet Model?', Chatham House, 16 February.

Hanson, P. (2009) 'Russia: Economic Performance and Prospects', *Quaderni di Relazioni Internazionali*, 9 March, p. 60.

IMF (2010) Country Report No. 10/246: Russian Federation: 2010 Article IV Consultation – Staff Report; and Public Information Notice on the Executive Board Discussion, available at http://www.imf.org/external/pubs/cat/longres.cfm?sk=24104.0.

Lavrov, S. (2007) 'Munich: World Politics at the Crossroads', *Moskovskiye Novosti*, 23 March.

Lo, B. (2008) 'Ten Things Everyone Should Know about the Sino-Russian Relationship', *CER Policy Brief*, December.

Lo, B. (2009) 'Russia's Crisis: What it Means for Regime Stability and Moscow's Relations with the World', *CER Policy Brief*, February, p. 4.

Medvedev, D., (2008),"Strengthening Dynamic and Equal Partnership in the Asia-Pacific Region", web-site http://www.indonesia.mid.ru/ros_asia_e_7.html as accessed on December 4, 2010.

Penkova, T. (2010) 'Russia and the US Reset after the New START', *ISPI Analysis*, 7 April.

Popescu, N. and Wilson, A. (2009) 'The Limits of Enlargement-lite: European and Russian Power in the Troubled Neighbourhood', ECFR, London, June.

Putin, V. (2009a) Speech at the Shanghai Cooperation Organisation's Heads of Government Council meeting, 14 October, available at http://www.premier.gov.ru/eng/visits/world/7889/events/7902/ (accessed 2 August 2010).

Putin, V. (2009b) Speech at the opening ceremony of the World Economic Forum in Davos, 28 January, available at http://www.weforum.org/pdf/AM_2009/OpeningAddress_VladimirPutin.pdf.

Secrieru, S. (2009) 'Russian Foreign Policy in Times of Crisis: Greater Compliance or Resilient Self-confidence?', *CEPS Policy Brief*, no. 192/30, June.

Stent, A. E. (2008) 'Restoration and Revolution in Putin's Foreign Policy', *Europe-Asia Studies*, vol. 60, no. 6 (August), p. 1089.

Surkov, V. (2008) Speech on 28 November, as reported at http://www.ng.ru/politics/2008-11-29/100_surkov.html?mthree=1 (accessed 11 August 2010).

Sutela, P. (2009) 'How Strong is Russia's Economic Foundation?', *CER Policy Brief*, October, pp.3–4.

World Bank (2010) *Russian Economic Report*, no. 22, June.

Zakaria, F. (1997) 'The Rise of Illiberal Democracy', *Foreign Affairs*, November/December, pp. 22–43.

Conclusion
Leila Simona Talani

Europe in crisis: always? This might be a legitimate question if we look at the economic and institutional developments in Europe in the last few years. Yes, of course, one needs to specify which crisis we are talking about, as it is undeniable that the financial crisis, the economic crisis, the fiscal crisis and the institutional crisis are distinct phenomena. Also, one needs to make clear whether these crises interest the European integration process as a whole, the economic and monetary union, or only some countries within it (the 'PIIGS'). Yet this book presents a view of 'the crises' affecting Europe and European countries which, somehow, seems to identify many linkages between them.

The first set of linkages is obviously represented by what went on in terms of financial integration in recent years. This produced systemic linkages between Member States and increased the likelihood of risk transmission across the single market as a whole, making the financial crisis a matter of common concern for all Member States.

Moreover, the crisis revealed the limitations of the institutional framework of market and monetary integration, especially the lack of political integration and the related absence of any mechanism allowing for the communitarization of economic and financial risks. It may be argued that the financial crisis gave rise to a constitutional crisis in the EU whose consequences have exacerbated the difficulties already experienced in the aftermath of the recent enlargements. Indeed, the last enlargement raised numerous questions, of both an economic and a political nature.

In addition, and this can be hardly denied, the financial crisis acted as a catalyst to all already-existing structural economic problems in the EU and its Member States. In this context, the ECB's monetary stances in response to the financial crisis of 2007–8 were represented by combination of a very lax monetary policy and a restrictive fiscal policy. This is likely to produce a depression of wages and aggregate demand, with a sharp rise in unemployment (as it is already the case) and, most likely, an increase in the gains arising from arbitrage and speculation.

Besides, from its establishment, the macroeconomic governance framework of the Eurozone did not seem to foster cooperative practices as to favour real convergence, but increased differences.

One solution could be to tackle the problem of financial governance in the broader global context. Indeed, there is an economic literature which recognizes the world leadership of the US dollar as one of the main culprits of the recent global financial crisis.

However, there is no escaping the feeling that something is wrong also in the EU architecture and in the way in which market and monetary integration has been devised. In particular, it seems to the authors of this book that the key problem of the EU, and, especially, of EMU, is represented by the insufficient degree of political integration between its members, as the Greek fiscal crisis clearly demonstrates. Indeed, the Greek crisis has overcome the boundaries of the local turmoil of a peripheral country. It has shown the deficiencies of the EMU policy framework, most notably, the limits of the European fiscal rule and the independence of the ECB. And, most importantly, it has put a question mark on the very long-term sustainability of EMU as it made evident the lack of solidarity between Member States, bordering real hostility on the side of some in terms of intervening financially in support of Greece or any other country risking contagion. As a result of the Greek fiscal crisis, the EMU's limits have been revealed and, in the lack of a political union, one wonders whether it is doomed to disintegrate or to move to a two-speed union.

But if Greece suffered the direst consequences of the financial crisis and risked being submersed, bringing with it the whole EMU project, other EU Member States did not emerge unaffected from the latest events. Spain's long-standing economic weaknesses were exacerbated by the financial crisis. Unemployment and the budget deficit soon soared. After a brief period of deflation, inflation again surged above the EU average.

At the other end of the spectrum, France was able to endure the current economic crisis relatively well thanks to the specificities of its labour market and its social protection net, which acted as 'shock absorbers' to contain recession. Particularly important has been the role of the state in restoring confidence through injections of capital and interventions to strengthen human capital and boost demand. In the longer term, France might need to address its productivity issues and find alternative sources of finance for its social policies.

In the UK the crisis was supposed to undermine the power of the City of London, arguably one of the main culprits for the financial turmoil. But, apart from the rise of unemployment in the financial sector (which, however, does not seem to be more severe than that experienced by other industrialized economies and already shows signs of reversal), and some discussion about entering EMU, there are no clear signs of decline of the hegemonic position of the City. In fact, one could argue that the wave of restructuring and mergers following the crisis has improved the bargaining position of its strongest institutions in both the internal and external context.

Broadening the analysis to 'Europe at large' it seems that European neighbours have been able to emerge from the crisis with fewer wounds. In the case of Russia, the fear that the crisis would weaken its international position or reappraise the country's foreign policy ambitions has proved wrong. On the contrary, Russia has taken advantage of this difficult moment to reset relations, strengthen partnerships and deepen regional cooperation under its undisputable leadership.

Even the region of Southeast Europe, initially shocked by the unexpected crisis, now seems to be in the early and volatile stages of what could be an economic recovery.

Concluding, the various 'crises' hitting the European economy and polity in recent years have clearly demonstrated structural problems that will have to be tackled and somehow solved to avoid permanent crisis.

Index

bold = *extended discussion or concept highlighted in text; f = figure, n = endnote, t = table.*

Abkhazia 245, 247, 255(n9)
absorption capacity 236
'abundant money' 29
accounting rules 23(n5)
Addabbo, T. **5**
Afghanistan 114, 254(n5)
Africa 113t
age 208t, 209t, 211t
aggregate demand 40, 41, 44, 46, 62, 66, 68, 99, 259
  'true drivers' of economic growth 99, 101
Aglietta, M. 25(n26), 26
agriculture 169, 174, 176
AIG (insurance company) 31
Aiyar, A. 88(n23), 89
Albania 220f, 220, **223–4**, 225, 226, 229f, 230, 236, 237, 240
Alesina, A. 96, 105, 162(n16), 163
Alpha Bank (Greece) 224
Ameco dataset 50n, 54n, 58n
American Reinvestment and Recovery Act (ARRA, 2009) **206**
Andalusia 169, 174
Angelini, E. C. xiii, **4**
Antonopoulos, R. 206, 215
arbitrage 39, 44, 49, 259
Argentina 113t, 146
Armenia 251, 255(n11), 255(n9)
arms control agreements 253
  see also Strategic Arms Reduction Treaty
Artis, M. 127, 140(n1), 141
Asia 113t, 113
  monetary integration 162(n14), 163
Asian financial crisis (1997–8) 28
  'South-East Asian crisis' 78
Asian Tigers 107
Asia-Pacific Economic Cooperation (APEC) 250–1, 255(n10)
asset diversification 138
asset prices 31, 37, 38f, 39
asset-backed securities (ABS) 35f, 35
assets
  foreign 70(n1)
  toxic 34–5
Attali, J. 189
austerity 102, 104, 178–9, 181(n16), 187, 189–90, 194, 219
Australia 114f
Austria 58f, 70(n3), 109t, 160, 229f, 230, 232
  output slump (2007–9) 71(n15)
  REER based on ULC (1979–2009) 50f

authoritarianism 244, 246
automatic absorbing mechanisms 76
automatic stabilizers 67
Azerbaijan 251, 255(n11)
Aziz, F. **5**

bailouts 98, 159
balance of payments EU support facility 225
balance of payments crises 87(n4)
balance of payments deficits 183
  see also current account
balanced budgets 66, 95, **154**, 162(n8), 176
  see also budget deficits
Balassa–Samuelson effect 51
Banca Comerciala Romana (BCR) 232
Banco Bilbao Vizcaya Argentaria (BBVA) 179
Bangemann report (1990) 107
Bank of England 130, 139, 141(n18), 141
Bank for International Settlements (Basel) 23(n3), 229n
Bank of Japan 44
Bank of Spain 179
bank-runs 9
banking 12t, 13t, 165, 168
banking crisis 192
banking regulation 12, **130–1**, 184
banking sector 129, 229
  debt transferred to public sector 47, 70(n4)
  weight 87(n10)
banking system
  France **184–6**
  Spain **174–5**, 179
bankruptcy 118
banks 23(n5), 28–9, 47, 53, 134, 138, 155, 156t, 171, 177, 190, 222, 228, 230, 243
  capital requirements 236
  cooperation with multilateral lenders (southeastern Europe) **231–3**
  government recapitalization 34
  interconnections (EU–USA) **41–2**, 43
  Irish and Spanish 29
  'main beneficiaries' of QE 39
  mergers and acquisitions 63
  mutual creditworthiness 46
  refinancing 30, 44
  'universal banks' 184
Banque de France 184, 186, 195
Banque Populaire-Caisse d'Épargne (BPCE) 186

261

Barcelona: Olympic Games (1992) 169–70, 172
Barroso, J. M. 121
Basel II/Basel III 186
Basset, R. 130, 141
Bastian, J. 5–6, 221, 224, 229n, 230, 239
Batool, T. xiii
Bauman, Z. 100, 105
Bear Stearns 31
Begg, I. 24(n17), 26, 128, 140(n2), 141
beggar-thy-neighbour policies **49**, 62–3, 68, 70
Belarus 218, 220, 250, 251, 254, 255(n11), 255(n9)
crisis lending 221t
Belgium 58f, 70(n3), 109t, 156t, 185, 229f
high-debt country 80
REER based on ULC (1979–2009) 50f
Belgrade 230
Beltransgaz 250
Benelux 110
Benetton, M. 87(n9), 88(n21), 89
Benigno, P. 103, 105
Bernanke, B. 31, 32, 33, 44, 205
'monetarist faith' 43
Bianchi, P. **4**, 111, 117, 123
bilateralism 252, 254
bipolarity 248, 252
Bishop, G. 129, 140(n4), 141
Black, J. 25(n34), 26
Black Sea Fleet (RF) 250
Black Sea Trade and Development Bank 239(n1)
BNP Paribas 184, 186
Bobba, M. 77, 89
Boc, E. 222
bond markets
global share 79t, 87(n10)
public and private 156
bonds
'government bonds' 136, 146, 147, 156, 162(n10)
Italian 103
rated AAA 79t, 87(n10)
re-financing on maturity 36
Spanish 103
see also covered bonds
bonus payments 186
thirteenth and fourteenth month pay 150
see also low income
Borissov, B. 224
Borri, N. 103, 105
borrowing
short-term (versus long-term lending) 83
Bosnia-Herzegovina 218, 220f, 220, 225, 229f, 231t, 236, 237, 241
crisis lending 221t
institution-building 227
IPA 226t, 226, 227

bouclier fiscal (fiscal shield, 2007) 193
boundaries
economic versus political 63
Bouton, D. 185
Brazil 113t, 114f
Bretton Woods regime
Bretton Woods I (1944–72) 2, 88(n14)
Bretton Woods II (1989–2007/8) 2, 76, 81, 87(n7)
Bretton Woods III (prospective) 2
'exorbitant privilege' of USA (de Gaulle) 76, 87(n6), 89
see also international monetary system
BRIC 85–6, 107, 111, 248, 250, 253
broad money aggregates 37
Brown, J. G. 128, 130, 133
budget deficits 83, 95, 165, 166, **167**, 168, 173, 174, 176, 179, 180, 222, 259
'fiscal deficits' 219
Greece **150–1**
ratio to GDP 152, 154, 171, 172, 177, 178, 181(n10)
see also public deficits
budgetary support 221, 226t, 226
budgets
short-term/long-term aspects 152
surveillance 25(n37)
Buiter, W. 128, 140(n3), 141
Bulgaria 109t, 219, 220f, 220, **224**, 225, 230, 231t, 234, 236, 240
fiscal position 224
Bundesbank 49
bureaucracy 243
Bush, G. W. 247, 254(n6)
business cycles 53, 62, 65, 76
'economic cycles' 149, 159, 162(n15)
synchronization 53, 76, 149, 159, 162(n15)
business environment 120
business services 110, 111t

cajas (saving banks) 179, 181(n19)
Calabria 199
Calvo pricing 51
Canada 113t, 114f, 114t
capital 24(n10), 252–3
capital controls 22f
capital financing **221**
capital flight 243
capital gains 41
capital markets 117, 120, 131, 135, 140(n4), 171
'broad, deep, liquid' 82
global 184
international 40, 221, 223
liberalization 48
post-Big Bang 139
capital mobility 10, 20, 49, 84, 79, 170
capital outflows 147
capitalism 105(n7), 246
western model 'discredited' (RF) 253

Index 263

capitalisme à papa 184
car industry 98, 174, 177
 'automotive industry' 188
car ownership 244
Carbaugh, R. 76, 88(n23), 89
carry trade 44
cartels 120
Casanova, J.-C. 195(n2)
Catalonia 159
'CEB' 226t, 227, 233
Central Asia 249
Central Bank of China 71(n17), 78, 84
central banks 3, 5, 28, 49, 64, 78t, 79, 88(n21), 131, 218, 220–3, 225, 227–30, 235
 governors 18
 loss of control of money market (Minsky) 32
 macro-prudential supervision 17, 25(n27)
Central and Eastern Europe 110, 120, 121, 221, 228, 231t, 232, 252
 crisis lending 221t
 'Eastern Europe' 40, 132
 foreign-bank lending (2008) 229f, 230
 see also Southeast Europe
'central government' 103
CESifo 88(n18), 89
Chicago Board of Trade 137t
Chicago Mercantile Exchange 137t
children 193, 206, 209t
Chimerica 89
China 2, 83, 87(n8), 89, 121, 147, 246, 247, 253
 expenditure on research and development (2008) 113, 114f
 financing of US trade deficit 78
 foreign exchange reserves 78, 85
 foreign reserves (dollar-denominated) 79, 88(n14)
 foreign reserves (shift from dollar into euro) 84
 GDP 86, 111–12, **112f**
 lack of democracy 84
 merchandise exports (1983–2008) 113t
 relations with RF 249, 253, 255(n8)
 soft power 249
 trade imbalance (with USA) 63
 'under-valued exchange rate' 63
China Development Bank 249
Chiodini, F. 24(n16), 26
Chiti, E. 25(n22), 26
City of London 5, **127–42**, 260
 international money market 134
 'pragmatic adaptation' 139
classical economics 117, 118
Clerc, D. 191, 195
Clinton, H. 247
Cohen, D. 183, 189, 190, 195
cohesion funds (EEC) 169
Cold War 87(n1), 247
 see also post-Cold War era

'collaboration contract' 207
collateralized debt obligations (CDOs) 35f, 147
Collective Security Treaty Organization 248
colleges of supervisors 15
Collignon, S. 129, 140(n7), 142
commercial law 23(n9)
commercial paper 30, 32, 34
Committee of European Banking Supervisors (CEBS) 12t, 13t 131
Committee of European Insurance and Occupational Pension Supervisors (CEIOPS) 12t, 13t
Committee of European Securities Regulators (CESR) 12t, 13t
commodity bubble 88(n13)
'common pool' problem 49
'common security space' 248
Commonwealth of Independent States (CIS) 249, 251
Communication on European Financial Supervision (European Commission, 2009) 24(n15), n18)
communism 246
 fall 74–5, 116, 238, 252
 fall: twentieth anniversary 123
competition 92, 243
 avoidance of abuse 120
 competitive advantage 72(n22), 172
 competitiveness 4, 46, 47, 49, 51, 53, 57, 61–2, 64, 72, 76, 78, 89, 96–7, 100, 147, 148, 155, 158, 161–2(n4), 165–6, 169–70, 174, 180, 251, 255(n12)
 eroded (Spain) 167
 'competitiveness policy' (terminology) 107
complementarity strategy 68
confidence 10, 29, 80, 97, 183, 194, 259
Conseil d'Analyse Stratégique 189, 195
construction 110, 111t, 165, 173–4, 176, 177, 179, 180, 201, 204, 249
consumers 15, 25(n24), 37
consumption 40–1, 95
contagion 144, 150, 161, 185, 259
contract continuity 135, 136
contract law 118
core–periphery analysis
 Euro Area 4, 46–9, 53–4, 56, 57, 61–5, 67, 70, 70(n2–3), 72(n22), 79–80, 143, 259
 global 81
corporate banking 138
corporate debt markets 135–6
corporate governance 53
corporate sector 230
corporatism 96
corruption 243
counter-cyclical policies 67, 68, 71–2(n18), 93, 103, 176, 188, 194
covered bonds 29, 43
 definition 35

covered bonds – *continued*
  see also eurobonds
creative accounting 144, 154
credibility 82–3, 85, 154, 155, 156, 170, 178, 194
credibility theory 76
Crédit Agricole 186
credit default swaps (CDS) 31, 33, 148f, **152**, **165(n7)**
credit lines 226t, 227, 234
credit ratings 32, 146, 177, 178, 181(n15), 186, 223
credit supply 37
Crimea 250
crisis management 5–6, 25(n37), 26, 154–5, 218, 233, 238
crisis reaction capacity 234, 238
crisis resistance 5–6, 218
Croatia 220f, 220, 225, 226, 229f, 230, 231t
Culpeper, P. D. 184, 196
culture 101, 102, 117, 158
currencies 87(n5)
  international status (economic and political relevance of country) **82–3**
  international status (four criteria) **82–3**, 84
  international status (preconditions) 82
  see also exchange rates
currency convertibility 84
current account 54, 56, 57, 62, 65, 71(n14), 153t
  divergences (Euro Area) 72
  'major determinant' 57[–]61
  surpluses reversed (2007–9) 71(n15)
  see also trade balance
current account deficits 46, 47, 48, 56, 57, 71(n12), 76, 147–8, 174, 219
current account surpluses 46, 57, 148, 161–2(n4)
customs unions 250, 251
Cyprus 109t
Czech Republic 109t, 113, 114f, 230, 254(n6)

data deficiencies 211, 212
data manipulation 154, 155
Datastream 145n
Davos World Economic Forum (2009) 246
de Gaulle, C. 87(n6)
de Larosière, J. 12
de Larosière Report (2009) 13, 15, 17, 24(n17), 25(n23)
debt 47, 102, 151
  transnational 97
  see also Greek debt crisis
debt-financing 103
debt-repayment 40, 41, 43
debt crisis
  appropriate cure **148**
debt deflation 69
default 146, 150, 165(n7)

deflation 33, 37, 43, 63, 68, 72(n22), 93, 179, 259
'delinquent mortgages' 30
Della Posta, P. xiii, **4**, **74–90**
Delors Report (1989) 23–4(n10)
demand 94–5, 194, 259
  domestic/internal 62, 63, 85, 100, 148, 161–2(n4)
  domestic versus foreign (appropriate balance) 62
  domestic impulse 61, 62, 71(n16)
  excess 57
  low 96
  world boom (2004–7) 57, 62, 65
  see also aggregate demand
demand shocks 56, 97–8
democracy 129, 169, 245, 253, 255(n11)
  obstacle to implementation of correct policies 96, 104(n4)
  'partial, illiberal, over-managed, hybrid' (RF) 244, 248, 253
democracy-promotion 247
demography 96
Denmark 109t, 110, 132
dependency culture (avoidance) 234
Deposit Insurance Agency 227
deregulation 171, 183
derivatives 33, 34, 37, 41, 43, 46, 137, 186
  'credit derivatives' 1, 32
Deutsche Bank 224
Deutsche Mark (DM) 49, 64, 75, 88(n22), 134, 135t, 141(n18)
Deutsche Terminbörse 137t
devaluation 148, 153t, 168, 170, 174, 180, 236, 243
  competitive 49
  nominal 51, 53
developing countries 83, 120
Dexia (bank) 185
diarchy (RF) 245–6
dirigisme 91, 98–9, 102
Discount Houses 139
discouraged workers 202, 203f, 204, 214
distress dependence (global) 42, 42f
division of labour/specialization 117, 118
Dodd–Franck Financial Stability Act 41–2, 43
Donnelly, B. 129–30, 140(n8), 142
Drèze, J. H. 162–3(n16), 163

early retirement 223
Eastern Partnership Initiative (EaP/EU) 251, **252**, 255(n11)
Eastern Siberia–Pacific Ocean pipeline spur to China 249
ECOFIN 12t, 154, 156
  (2009) 17, 24(n15)
  (2010) 25(n36)
  see also European Council of Ministers
econometrics within-EMU macroeconomic imbalances **54–62**, 71(n12–16)

economic blackmailing 250
'economic constitution' (Eurozone) 93–6, 98–102, 104
Economic and Financial Committee 24(n15)
economic governance 21, 25(n37), 154–5, 163
economic growth 4, 5, 57, 92, 103, 117, 128, 144, 145t, 165, 167, 171, 172, 198, 244, 255(n12)
  aggregate demand factors 'true drivers' 99, 101
  conditions 96–7
  drivers/engines 120, 180, 224
  Europe versus USA 91
  export-led 99–100
  'GDP growth' 71(n12)
  long-term (obstacles) 202
  preconditions 93, 94–5, 99, 102
  products 102
  slow rates 104
  Spain versus EU 173
economic homogeneity **159**
Economic and Monetary Union (EMU) 22, 23, 74, 88(n19), 116, 171, 180
  absence of political union 69
  case for UK to join **127–33, 140–1**
  core–periphery analysis 46, 47, 70(n2–3)
  costs and benefits of membership 149, 158, 160, 160f
  disintegration 160
  economic characteristics 149
  'EMU period' (2000–9) 56, 67
  evolution of real divergence (1979–2009) **48–54**, 70–1(n4–11)
  'limits revealed' 259
  long-term prospects **157**, 161
  macroeconomic governance **46–73**
  macroeconomic governance (alternative views) **64–9, 71–2(n18–21)**
  macroeconomic imbalances **54–62**, 71(n12–16)
  membership risks 150
  'not an OCA' 149
  policy coordination (argument against) 64–5
  policy framework (deficiencies) 259
  second phase (January 1994–) 170
  'second-best world of markets' **68**
  similarities (economic, political, social, cultural) **160–1**
  solidarity weakened **157**
  stability versus dollar and yen 71(n8)
  structural vulnerability 150
  twin deficit hypothesis 'does not seem to apply' 56
  'two speed' **144, 157–61, 162–3(n12–17)**, 259
economic recessions 93, 200–1, 210–11, 213
  'normally seen as temporary' 95

post-11 September (2001) 62
  see also global financial crisis (2007–)
economies of scale 71(n13), 77, 86–7
Economist, The **91–2**, 94, 96–9, 102, 104(n3–4), 105
economy size 82, 84
ECU (accounting currency) 77, 135t, 137
education 101, 102, 119, 120
educational attainment 206, 208t, 211t, 213
  risk of unemployment 199
Eichengreen, B. 92, 105, 162(n14), 163
Eichhorst, W. 190, 196
electrical machinery 110, 111t
electricity 172
Eleventh of September (2001) 56, 62, 65
elites 166, 253
emergency lending 233
emerging countries 72(n21)
emigration 166
Emilia Romagna 199, 215
empiricism 49, 53, 62, 67
employment 72(n19), 109t, 109, 119, 128, 148, 153t, 188, 189, 223, 254(n2)
  non-standard share (Italy) 199
  part-time 190
  subsidized 191
  see also labour markets
employment creation 206, 215
employment status 208t
'end of history' thesis (Fukuyama) 246, 256
energy 97, 171, 189, 227, 231t, 249–50, 253, 254(n2, n5), 255(n11)
enterprise policy 119
enterprises 109t, 109–10
environment 115, 119, 120, 122, 227, 255(n11)
environmental efficiency 119
epistemology 252
equity markets 184
Erste Bank (Austria) 232
Estonia 109t, 230
ethnicity 210
Eurasian Economic Community (EurAsEC) 248, 251, 255(n9)
Euro 2, 25(n39), 188, 228, 230, 231t
  'accounting device' (1999–2001) 77
  exchange rate 66
  initial expectations 74, 75
  in international monetary system **4, 74–90**
  international status ('does not qualify to replace US dollar') 83
  introduction of banknotes and coins (2002) 77
  loss of credibility 47
  'next leading international currency' **83–4**, 88(n18–21)
  overvalued 100
  performance (first decade) **77–9, 87(n9–14)**, 89

Euro – *continued*
  reasons for creation 74–6, **87(n1–8)**
  reserve currency 74, 78, 100–1
  reserve currency status (synthetic index) 79t
Euro Area *see* Eurozone
'Euro taxes' plan 163(n17)
'Euro-euro' bond market 136
Eurobarometer surveys 193
eurobonds 98, 103, 136, 223–4
  see also German Bunds
eurointelligence.com 141(n16)
Europe 86
  financial crisis (consequences) **79–81**, 88(n15)
  financial crisis (general issues) **3–4, 7–124**
  industry (structure) **108–11**
  real divergence (limits of macroeconomic governance) **46–73**
  structural problems 260
'Europe in Crisis' conference (Florence, 2010) xiii
Europe of regions 162–3(n16), 163
European Bank for Reconstruction and Development (EBRD) 218, 220–2, 226t, 227, 233, **234–5**, 237, 239
  capital support to UC (2009) **231–2**
  crisis lending 221t
  shareholders' meeting (Zagreb, 2010) 234
European Banking Authority 13t, 24(n21)
European Banking Committee 12t
European Central Bank (ECB) 3, 5, 15, 18, 21–2, 23(n1), 25(n29), 27, 42, 46, 49, 64, 65, 66, 72(n22), 80, 101, 128, 131, 133, 134, 143, 146, 170, 174, 227–8, 258–9
  creation (June 1998) 172
  Greek crisis **155–7**
  independence 161
  interventions (secondary public bonds market) 69
  liquidity injection 43
  monetary policy 40
  monitors international status of euro 88(n17), 89
  original interest-rate-rise mistake 28, 34, 43
  response to financial crisis 28–9, **34–7**
  'rigid statute' 47
  ECB General Council 17
  ECB Executive Council 153t
  ECB governing council 186
  ECB securities markets 151
European Commission 12, 13, 14, 16t, 18, 19f, 19, 21, 22, 23(n5), 24(n15, n21), 25(n37), 64, 66, 68–70, 122, 124, 152, 154, 185, 222, 225–7, 233, 236, 252
  author/data source 57–61, 71(n16), 72, 149, 163, 191, 196, 226n

Lisbon Strategy 121
macro-prudential oversight 17, 25(n29)
European Commissioners 141(n15)
European Community 116
European Constitution
  ratification failure (2005) 114
European Council 21, 23(n5), 24(n20), 25(n29, n38–9), 143, 150, 156
  'Council, the' 13, 16, 19f, 19, 20t
  'Council of EU' 256(n12)
European Council of Ministers 12t
  see also ECOFIN
European Economic Area (EEA) 10
European Economic Community (EEC) 75, 84, 87(n1), 107, 120
  boon of membership (for Spain, 1986–) **168–9**, 170
'European economic government' 98
European Financial Stability Facility (EFSF) 21, 143, **151**, 155, 162(n5)
European Financial Stabilization Mechanism 21, 25(n35)
European Insurance and Occupational Pensions Authority (EIOPA) 13t, 24(n20)
European Insurance and Occupational Pensions Committee 12t
European integration 26, 108, 122
  centripetal versus centrifugal forces 2–3
  economic 115–18, 120–1, 123
  legal strategy 20, 25(n31)
  monetary 5
  political 118, 120, 121, 123, 129–30, 158, 160, 161, 163(n17)
  see also EU enlargement
European Investment Bank (EIB) 218, 225, 226t, 227, 232–4, 239
  focus (Southeast Europe) 235–6
'European Monetary Fund' (advocated) 153t
European Monetary System (EMS, 1979–) 70(n5), 71(n7), 75, 133
  'asymmetric' functioning 72(n22)
  EMS economies 57
  'EMS period' (1979–90) 54, 55t
  'hard EMS' 48, 49, 53, 64
  'single currency' 53
  'soft EMS' 48
  see also exchange rate mechanism
European Parliament 12t, 13, 16t, 24(n20), 25(n29), 140(n4, n8)
European Securities Committee 12t
European Securities and Markets Authority (ESMA) 13t, 24(n20)
European single financial market 9–10, 23(n2), 27
  incompatibility of objectives 10
  integration ('onion layers', 1973–) 21, 22f
  law and regulation 12t, 20
  'regulatory public good' notion 22

Index 267

European Single Market 3, 10, 51, 53, 97, 118, 119, 131, 140(n4)
European social model 98–9, 102
European Stabilization Fund 151
European Supervisory Authorities (ESAs) 3, 12–13, **13–17**, 21–2, **24–5(n16–23)**
  characterization 25(n22)
  cooperation with ESRB 17, 18, 19f, 19, 20t
  non-compliance 14, 16t
  regulatory instruments **16t**
  responsibilities and powers **14–15**
European System of Central Banks 21–2
European System of Financial Supervision (ESFS) 12–13
European Systemic Risk Board (ESRB, 2009–) 3, 13, 15, **17–20**, 21, 22, 25(n24–9)
  'act or explain' mechanism 18, 19
  governance structure 18
  previously 'ESRC' 17
  regulatory instruments 20t
  requests for information from ESAs 18, 20t
  risk warnings 18, 19f, 19–20, 20t
  tasks 17
  tools and mechanisms **19–20**
European Systemic Risk Council (ESRC) 17
European Union (EU) 220–2, 225, 245, 248
  agencies 25(n22), 26
  'always in crisis' 258
  constitutional crisis 258
  crises (linkages) 258
  crisis lending 221t
  directives 24(n20)
  'economic giant but political miniature' 108
  'economic and institutional developments' 258
  expenditure on research and development (2008) 113, 114f
  GDP 111–12, 112f
  industrial policy **4, 107–24**
  merchandise exports (1983–2008) 113t, 113
  political integration 258, 259
  political weakness 83
  public budget 70
  relations with RF **251–2, 253–4**
  relations with RF (energy issues) 249
  RF in crisis (implications) 242–57
  trade 112, 113t
  visa liberalization regime 236
  wealth disparities 160
  'world economic power' **111–15**
European Union (EU-15) 199t, 204t
European Union (EU-27)
  business indicators (2006) 109t

employment rates 200t, 200
  structural trends 111
  value-added (non-financial business activity) 111t
European Union 2020 Strategy 3, 4, 108, 119, 121, 124
  adoption (June 2010) 122
  'failure to identify structural changes required' 119
  objectives 119
  see also Lisbon Strategy
European Union enlargement 108, 121, 123, 258
  impact on Lisbon Strategy (2000–) 116
  see also Eurozone political integration
European Union law 12, 12t, 14, 16t, 22, 24(n12)
European Union legislation 18, 23(n7)
European Union securities markets 23(n2), 26
European Union transfers 174
European Union–Russia Partnership for Modernization (2010) 253, 255–6(n12)
European University Institute (EUI) Alumni Association xiii
Eurostat data 108, 109n, 111n, 123(n1)
Eurosystem 15
Eurozone/Euro Area 3, 10, 102, 156t, 195(n1)
  convergence (nominal versus real) 69, 72(n22)
  core 98
  debt problem 151
  dependence on USA 83, 88(n18)
  existence at risk 91
  external imbalances 147–8
  federalization of monetary policy 11, 23–4(n10)
  financial markets (current situation) **39–41**
  institutional architecture 97
  lack of fiscal policy coordination 80
  macroeconomic governance 259
  macroeconomic situation 4
  monetary response to financial crisis (US comparison) **28–45**
  'muddling through' 92–5, 98–9, 104, 104(n1)
  'needs to function like American states' (Krugman) 104(n2)
  no-bailout clause 'flawed' **69**
  north versus south 159
  political fragmentation 4
  public debt crisis 77
  relative decline 100
  'second violin' (to USA) 100
  structural issues 96, 122–3
  weaknesses 102
  'would benefit from mutual risk insurance' 70

268 Index

Eurozone political integration
  'calls for alternative theoretical
    perspective' **99–103**, 104–5(n6–7)
  obstacle (standard macroeconomic
    theory) **94–9**, 104(n4–5)
  'solution to financial crisis' **4**, **91–106**
  see also European integration
Excessive Deficit Procedure (EDP) **154**
exchange controls 82
exchange rate crises (1970s) 1
exchange rate mechanism (ERM) of
  EMS 24(n10), 133, 138, 171
  bilateral bands 48
  see also European Monetary System
exchange rate policy 139
exchange rates 82, 129
  adjustable 149–50
  euro–US dollar 77
  fixed 49, 71(n12), 73, 75, 78, 149–50
  fixed system (fall, 1972) 2
  flexible 49, 71(n12), 73, 76
  free-floating 132
  nominal realignments 51
  pegged 78t, 79t, 84–5, 138
  real versus nominal 49
  see also foreign currency reserves
executive decentralization 22
export capacity 219, 237
export earnings 243
export elasticity 51
exports 41, 57, 62, 65, 71(n12–14), 82, 85, 113t, 170, 254(n2)
  France 188
  German strength 63–4
external imbalances **147–8**, 161–2(n4)
external-anchor' institutions **218–41**
Extremadura 169, 174

factor productivity 148
family 193, 198, 215
family ownership 117, 166
Fannie Mae/Freddie Mac 31
Farina, F. xiii, **4**, 49, 56, 65, 67, 70, 72(n22), 73
Federal Reserve 3, 28–9, 37
  author/data source 35n, 36n, 38n, 44
  balance sheet 42–3
  failures of understanding 30, 32, **33**, 43
  monetary policy 40
  policy response to crisis (2007–) **30–3**
  'quasi-fiscal agent of the state' 40
  special facilities 31, 32, 42
Feldstein, M. **153t**
Ferguson, N. 84, 89
Ferguson, T. 31–2, 44
Ferran, E. 23(n2), 26
Ferrarini, G. 24(n16), 26
Fillon, F. 189
finance (sector) 165
financial assets 70(n4)
  dollar-denominated 72(n21)

high-risk 72(n21)
  price-recovery 40–1
financial bubbles 62, 65
financial capital 117
Financial Conglomerates Committee 12t
financial crisis situations
  definition 14
financial deregulation 183
financial futures and options 137t
financial institutions 10, 14, 16t, 18, 20t, 37, **39**, 43, 155
  balance sheets (level of foreign assets) 70(n1)
  cross-border 23(n9)
  failing (ECB non-intervention) 34
  liquidity granted by ECB 46
  liquidity problems 30
  market for fund exchanges 32
  rescue expenses 40
  stability 17
  see also international financial institutions
financial integration 23(n6), 88(n18), 149, 258
financial markets 35, 80, 83, 147, 185
  current state (USA) **37–9**
  Euro Area (current situation) **39–41**
  globalized (inter-connectedness) 69
  integration (Europe) 63
  interconnectedness 47
  international 132, 146
  international currency status 82
  sophistication (USA) 83, 88(n13)
  speculative attacks 83
financial regulation 33, 42, 131, 238
  weaknesses (EU level) 13, 24(n16)
financial sector 132
  stability (Southeast Europe) **228–31**
financial services 26, 27, 110, 129
  cross-border 24(n10)
Financial Services Action Plan 131
Financial Services Authority (FSA) 131, 142
financial services law 13, 14
financial stability 16t, 21, 25(n27), 102
  'trilemma' **10**, 20, 23(n6), 27
Financial Stability Board (FSB, 2009) 17, 25(n28)
financial structure (international currency status) 82
Financial Times 140(n11), 152, 153t, 163(n17)
  FT–Harris poll 162(n11)
Financial Times Deutschland 141(n16)
Finland 58f, 70(n3), 109t, 110
  output slump (2007–9) 71(n15)
  R&D expenditure (2008) 113, 114f
  REER based on ULC (1979–2009) 50f
firms
  'corporations' 71(n13)
  efficient versus non-efficient 117

Index 269

'multinational corporations' 83, 171
non-financial 110
fiscal activism 56
fiscal authority (centralized) 103
fiscal consolidation/retrenchment 57, 65, 70
fiscal discipline 21, 94, 95, 98
 'budgetary discipline' 146
fiscal federalism 149
fiscal independence 87(n4)
fiscal indiscipline (Eurozone) 91–2
fiscal policy 48, 49, 66, 72(n20), 93, 147, 172, 193
 active 103
 common (absent) 47
 contractionary 40
 counter-cyclical efficacy 67, 68, 71–2(n18)
 deficit-financed expansion 71(n12)
 discretionary 104, 105(n7)
 expansionary 33, 46, 177, 180(n11–13)
 pro-cyclical 56–7
 rescue of financial institutions 29
 restrictive 44
 stability 70, 96, 99
 sustainability 47, 64, 69
 see also public finances
fiscal responsibilities 15–16
fiscal rules/procedures 5, 152, 154, 157, 161
 enforcement mechanism 155
 'strict budget rules' 93, 104(n3)
fiscal sovereignty 21, 22f, 26(n40)
Fisher, I. 69
Fitch (ratings agency) 178, 240
Fitoussi, J. P. 100, 105
'five economic tests' (UK) 128, 133
Fontagné, L. 188, 196
Fonteyn, W. 25(n32), 26
foreign currency lending 230, 233 238
foreign currency reserves 78t, 79t, 88(n13), 223, 236, 243
 China 78
 denominated in euro 78, 88(n12)
 held in US dollars 78
 see also international currency
foreign direct investment (FDI) 71(n10), 83, 147, 222, 224
 'foreign investment' 180
foreign exchange intervention 78t
foreign exchange swap market 34
foreign exchange transactions 79t, 87(n10)
France 5, 59f, 63, 70(n3), 75, 91, 100, 104, 109t, 109, 110, 114f/t, 114, 154, 156t, 171, 175, 177, **183–97**; 252, 255(n11), 259–60
 banking system **184–6**
 current account deficit (shrinkage, 2007–9) 71(n15)
 economic outlook (fragile recovery, 2010) **186–90**
 economic performance 'notably weaker than Eurozone' 187, 187t

GDP 195(n1)
inter-bank loan guarantee fund 185
loss of 'industrial substance' 188, 196
merchandise exports (1983–2008) 113t
'permanent crisis' (Cohen) 183
protectionism 98
REER based on ULC (1979–2009) 50f
signs of optimism 189
social and employment policy **190–4**
structural problems 195
France: *Ministère de l'Économie* 186, 196
Francoism 166–7, 168, 175
Frankel, J. 149, 158, 163
Frankfurt 12t
fraud 80
free markets 1, 80, 238–9
 see also market forces
free trade 162(n16), 251, 255(n11)
 see also trade
Frijdal, A. xiii
fuel processing and chemicals 110, 111t
Fukuyama, F. 246, 256
full employment 62, 95, 102, 104(n6), 167
Fullani, A. 223
fund management 138
Fundamental Principles of Financial Regulation (2009) 25(n25)

Galì, J. 71–2(n18), 73
Galicia 174
Gavras, P. 239(n1)
Gazprom 250
GDP (gross domestic product) 71(n10), n12), 111, 112f, 114f
 world 82, 86
 see also economic growth
gender
 pay gap (USA) 201
 unemployment gap 201
General Budget Stability Law (Spain, 2001) 176
general elections 223, 224
geographical proximity 230
Georgia 251, 255(n11)
Georgian War (2008) 245, 247
GERB [*Grazhdani za Evropeysko Razvitie Balgariya*] 224
German Bunds 146, 147
 see also Greek bonds
German Constitutional Court 26(n40)
German syndrome (economic giant, political miniature) 108, 122
Germany 44, 54, 57, 59f, 67, 70(n3), 72(n22), 91–2, 94–5, 99, 100, 104, 109t, 109, 110, 114f, 151, 154, 156t, 160, 161–2(n4), 165, 171, 175, 185, 188, 229f, 250, 252
 balanced budget rule 162(n8)
 beggar-thy-neighbour policies **62–4**, 147–8
 current account surplus 147–8

270 Index

Germany – *continued*
 domestic demand (government reluctance to foster) 63–4
 foreign reserves 88(n14)
 macroeconomic imbalances 62–4
 measures on short-selling and CDS 152
 merchandise exports (1983–2008) 113t
 output slump (2007–9) 71(n15)
 patents 113–14, 114t
 propensity to save 41
 public opinion 157, 162(n12–13)
 REER based on ULC (1979–2009) 50f
 resistance to joining EMU 155
 re-unification (1991) 75
 'third-largest exporter' 76
 trade balance 62
 trade direction 62
 trade imbalances 63
Gil Marín, S. 181(n17), 181
gilt contracts 137
Gini ratios 210
Giusti, S. 6, 245, 256
global financial crisis (2007–) 1–6, 65, 69, 72(n21), 74, 78, 108, 258–60
 'became global *economic* crisis' 80
 chronology 23(n3)
 consequences in Europe 79–81, 88(n15)
 differential impact 165
 effect on European institutional setup, governance, and architecture 3–4, 7–124
 effect on Greece 146–7
 effect on labour markets (Italy versus USA) 200–6
 future avoidance 87
 impact on GDP (China, EU, USA) 112, 112f
 impact on single European countries 3, 4–6, 125–257
 impact on Spain 165–82
 macroeconomic problems 33
 monetary policy response: Euro Area versus USA 3–4, 28–45
 narrative reconstruction 31, 44
 post-Soviet space 249–53, 255–6(n8–12)
 public debt crisis 1–2, 80–1, 82, 87(n4); *see also* Greek debt crisis
 Southeast Europe 218–41
 Spain 173–4, 180(n3)
globalization 28, 98, 100, 121, 246
 balanced 120
 financial 34–5, 41, 46, 70(n1), 128
 impact on Lisbon Strategy 116–17
 phase I 88(n16)
 phase II 88(n16)
 phase III (neo-liberal) 1, 81, 86, 88(n16)
 'phase IV' (prospective) 1, 81, 87
Goldman Sachs 31
González, F. 168
good governance 255(n11), 256(n12)
Gorbachev, M. S. 248

Gorton, G. B. 32, 33, 44
government borrowing 98
government guarantees 36, 39
government intervention (in economy) 80
government sector (employment) 204
governments 5, 44, 48, 93–4, 94–5, 99, 104, 118, 151, 157, 159, 163(n16), 165, 218, 220
pragmatism 97–8
rescue of financial institutions 40
spending cuts 41
grand emprunt (2009) 188
grant finance 226t, 233
Great Depression (1930s) 40, 198, 210–11
Greece 2, 3, 47, 59f, 70(n2), 83, 91, 105, 109t, 165, 166, 228, 229f, 230
 anti-corruption legislation 150
 budgetary figures (alleged falsification) 146
 current account–GDP ratio 145t
 deficit–GDP ratio 144, 145t
 'devastating speculative attack' 80
 'fiscal sustainability problems' 69
 public debt–GDP ratio 144, 145t
 public finance situation 63, 144–6
 public finances 'in disarray' (not the whole story) 147
 public finances and trade balance (deterioration) 57
 REER based on ULC (1979–2009) 50f
 see also PIIGS
Greek bonds/securities 103, 143, 146, 147, 156t
see also public bonds
Greek debt crisis 5, 10, 103, 108, 115, 143–64, 239, 252, 258, 259
 catalysts 146, 147
 causes 144–8, 161–2(n1–4)
 consequences for EMU 152–61, 162–3(n8–17)
 ECB independence and no-bailout clause 155–7, 162(n9–11)
 EU–IMF rescue plan (2010) 21, 80, 146, 151–2, 162(n5)
 external imbalances 147–8, 161–2(n4)
 'faltering behaviour' of Germany 146
 impact on Spain 175, 177–8
 'important lesson' 150
 limits of SGP 152, 154–5, 162(n8)
 Papandreou government's cuts to deficit 150–1
 policy responses 150–2, 161(n5–6)
 prospective solutions 152, 153t
 restricted solidarity hypothesis 157–61, 162–3(n12–17)
 structural causes 149–50
 'two speed EMU' 157–61, 162–3(n12–17)
 world financial crisis (2007) 146–7
 see also public debt
Green, D. 131

Index 271

'green recovery' agenda 189
Gros, D. 153t, 163
Group of Seven (G-7) 86
Group of Twenty (G-20) 17, 25(n28), 186
    London Summit (2009) 228, 240
Guardian, The 140(n6)
'hard EMS' 48, 49, 53, 64
Hardy, D. 23(n8), 26
harmonization 14, 21, 22, 97, 98, 99, 159, 160f, 161
Hazell, D. 131, 140(n12), 142
health and healthcare 5, 97, 102, 176, 198, 206, 209t, 211t, 212–13
    expenditure (France) 193
    unmet needs (Italy) **207–9**
hedge funds 80, 186
Hedrick, R. 76, 88(n23), 89
Herring, R. J. 23(n9), 26
Hertig, G. 23(n7), 26
High-Level Group on Financial Supervision in EU (2008–9) 12, 24(n14)
High-Level Working Group (2008) 24(n15)
higher education 192, 199
history 74–5, 94, 118, 121, 123
Hoang-Ngoc, L. 185, 193, 196
home-country control 10, 11, 21, 22
home healthcare 176, 206
home price index 37, 38f, 38–9
home purchasers
    fiscal discounts 37
Honohan, P. R. 71(n9), 73
host countries 11, 22f
household consumption 237
household income 207, 209, 214, 215(n3)
household size 212, 214
households
    female-headed 212
    multi-generational 213–14, 216
Houses of Parliament (UK) 140(n4)
housing 177, 201, 213, 244
    excessive lending 35
housing bubbles 62, 65, 173–4, 179
    generally absent (Euro Area) 40
    Southeast Europe 230–1
human capital 194, 214, 259
Hungary 109t, 218, 220–1, 224–5, 227–8, 230, 231t
    crisis lending 221t
Hutton, W. 131–2, 140–1(n13)
hydrocarbons 254(n2)
Hypo Real Estate 185

Iceland 9–10, 128, 130, 132, 237
identity 100
Île de France 110
immigration 96, 255(n11)
imperialism 245
import elasticity 51
imports 57, 62, 71(n12), 75, 117

'inclusive growth' 119
income redistribution 102, 210
incomes 245
    see also household income
independent fiscal agency (prospective) 155
India 2, 113t, 114f, 121
    see also BRIC
individuals 118, 198
industrial policy 4
    'constructivist' approach 107
    definitions 107, 117
    'integrated' approach 122
    'long-term vision of development' **117–21**
    need for long-term vision **107–24**
    'wide sense' 108
industrial production
    impact of financial crisis (2008–9) 110–11
inequality 41, 192
inflation 4, 37, 49, 70, 71(n7), 95, 145t, 147, **167**, 170–4, 179–80, 259
    excessive 165, 166
inflation avoidance 43
inflation differentials 64
inflation rates 51, 65, 73
inflation targeting 68, 69, 72(n19), 96, 99, 101
inflationary expectations 76
    central bank creation (in order to avoid deflation) 33, 43
infrastructure 101, 102, 166–7, 172, 188, 206, 227, 232, 234, 243, 253
innovation 113–14, 114t, 119, 122, 123
    factor for economic change 120
INSEE 187, 195(n1), 196
insider trading (France) 185
insolvency law 23(n9)
institutional barriers 117
Institutional Fund Managers' Association 138
institutional investors 41, 137, 184
institutional mediation 101
institutional stabilization 118
institutions 120
Instrument for Pre-Accession Assistance (IPA) 225–6, 227
IPA regulations (Article 15) 226
insurance 12t, 13t, 138, 141(n17), 156t, 168, 184, 186
interbank market 31–2, 34
    France 186
    global dimension **41**
    'task of central bank' 35
interest rate 3–4, 28, 30, 34, 36–7, **39**, 71(n12), 101, 130, 132, 133, 137, 145t, 146, 170, 171, 174, 224
    ECB control 66
    nominal 65, 71(n7)
    'only ECB policy instrument' 65
    real 48, 62, 65, 68

272 *Index*

interest rate – *continued*
  short-term versus long-term 33, 37, 43, 44
intergovernmentalism 122
international currency
  Chinese strategy and tactics 85
  functions 77, 78t
  private and official functions 78t, 83
  privileges and drawbacks 76
  'reserve currency' 76, 89
  see also NEER
international finance 84–5
international financial institutions (IFIs) 218, 221–3, 225–8, 232–4, 236–7
  see also non-bank financial institutions
international financial transmission 46
International Monetary Fund (IMF) 17, 21, 115, 143, 153t, 218, 222–5, 227–8, 232–3
  author-data source 38, 42, 42n, 45, 220n, 220, 221n, **240**
  conditionality programmes (LDCs) 79
  crisis lending 221t
  Greek rescue plan (2010) **151–2**, 162(n5)
  Spain 180(n6)
  stability objective 'myopic' 79–80
  voting weight 80
international monetary system: future **81–6, 88(n16–23)**
  euro ('next leading international currency') **83–4**, 88(n18–21)
  'multipolar' **85–6**, 88(n22–3)
  'unipolar' **81–3**, 88(n16–17)
  yuan ('next leading international currency') **84–5**
  see also Bretton Woods
international reserves 63
international socialism 168
investment 37, 56, 57, 65, 72(n21), 95, 101, 102, 128, 198
  'search for quality' 63
investment banks 63, 72(n21)
Iran 247, 254(n5)
Iraq War (2003–) 114
Ireland 2, 21, 40, 47, 57, 60f, 65, 70(n2), 80, 109t, 110, 147, 159, 165
  current account deficit (shrinkage, 2007–9) 71(n15)
  REER based on ULC (1979–2009) 50f
  sovereign debt crisis 143
  see also PIIGS
Irkutsk 245
Iskander missiles 255(n6)
isolationism 246
Issing, O. **153t**
ISTAT 199, 216
IT SILC 2006 microdata 207
Italian labour market versus US counterpart
  effects of global financial crisis **5, 198–217**
  similarities and differences **198–200**

Italy 60f, 70(n2, n6), 75, 97, 99, 100, 105, 109t, 109, 114t, 143, 147, 156t, 159, 229f, 252
  Centre-North versus South 198–9, 203, 209t, 214, 215(n1), 217
  crisis (1929) 40
  current account deficit (shrinkage, 2007–9) 71(n15)
  high-debt country 80
  merchandise exports (1983–2008) 113t
  poverty probability (multivariate analyses) 208–9t
  REER based on ULC (1979–2009) 50f
  R&D expenditure (2008) 113, 114f
  regional governments 215
  unemployment: experience 207–9, 215(n3)
  unemployment: harmonized rates 202, 204t
  unemployment: poverty and unmet health needs **207–9**, 215(n3)
  see also PIIGS

J. P. Morgan Chase 31
Japan 33, 63, 107, 185, 188, 195(n1), 234
  crisis (1990s) 44
  foreign reserves 88(n14)
  merchandise exports (1983–2008) 113t
  patents 113–14, 114t
  R&D expenditure (2008) 113, 114f
Johnson, R. 31–2, 44
Joint Committee of European Supervisory Authorities 13t
joint grant facilities 227
joint lending facilities 227
joint ventures 232
Juncker, J. C. 104(n4)

Kaliningrad 245, 255(n6)
Kazakhstan 231t, 232, 250, 251
Kenen, P. 82, 89
Kerviel, J. 185
Keynes, J. M. 69, 87(n2), 127
Keynesian expansionary effect 66
Keynesianism 2, 80, 88(n16), 94, 96, 100, 101, 194
  current versions 104–5(n6)
knowledge-based economy 108, 115, 119, 122, 188, 189, 253
  see also Lisbon Strategy
Korea 114f, 205
Kosovo 220f, 226, 236
Krugman, P. 33, 77, 78n, 88(n22), 89, 92, 96, 102, 104(n2), 105
Kyrgyzstan 231t, 255(n9)

La Malfa, G. 162(n16), 163
Labory, S. **4**, 111, 117, 123
labour-intensive sectors 174
labour costs 98, 110

Index 273

labour force
 workers 'marginally attached' 202
labour force participation 199t, 214
labour force participation rate (LFPR) 200-1
Labour Force Survey (Italy) [202], 215(n2)
Labour Governments (UK, 1997–2010) 127
labour market
 dualism (France) 192
 flexibility 68, 168, 175–6
 institutions 67–8
 peculiarities (Italy) 203–4
 policies 96–7, 119
 reform 179, 180, 181(n17–18), 181, 191
 rigidities 173
labour markets 54, 67, 70, 92, 96, 171, 172, 183, 194, 196
 inefficient 101
 Italy versus USA (effects of financial crisis) 5, 198–217
 see also workers
labour migration 98
labour mobility 149
labour productivity 54f, 57, 65, 173
labour standards 91
Lagarde, C. 186, 196
Lamfalussy framework (2001) 12, 24(n12)
Laming, R. 132, 141(n14), 142
Lane, P. 71(n9)
Lapègue, V. 195(n1)
Latin America 113t, 169
Latvia 109t, 220, 221t, 221, 230
Lavrov, S. 246–7, 256
law 31, 102, 117
Lea, D. (Lord Lea of Crondall) 129, 140(n5), 142
Lee, E. 88(n21), 89
legitimacy 244
Lehman Brothers 30–1, 185
less-developed countries (LDCs) 78, 83
 IMF conditionality programmes 79
'Levada-center' 254(n3)
Level 3 supervisory committees 13
Levy Economics Institute 33, 45
liberal democracy 246
liberalization 48, 64, 79, 171, 172, 244
life satisfaction (self-assessed) 244
liquidity 3, 23(n5), 37, 41, 46, 151, 162(n10), 223, 228
liquidity assistance 221, 222
liquidity injections 33, 34, 42, 43
liquidity risk premia 129
liquidity trap 29, 33, 43
lira 48
Lisbon Strategy (2000–10) 3, 120, 253
 evolution 121
 failure 4, 84, 97, 102, 108, 114
 failure (reasons) 115–16
 industrial policy 'in classical sense' 119
 'industrial policy for coherence of EU' 115–17

'national progress' monitored by European Commission 115
 see also 'EU 2020 Strategy'
Lisbon Treaty (2007; in effect, December 2009–) 3, 15, 24(n21), 86, 114, 122
 Article 290 14
 ratification 26(n40)
Litan, R. E. 23(n9), 26
Lithuania 109t, 230, 250
living standards 119, 121, 253, 254(n3)
Lo, B. 244, 256
loans 36f, 37, 226t
London 12t, 131, 232
 see also City of London
London: G-20 Summit (2009) 228, 240
London Foreign Exchange market 134–6, 135t
London International Financial Futures and Options Exchange (LIFFE) 137t, 137–8
London Stock Exchange 136–7
Lorenzi, J.O. 188, 196
Louis, J.V. 25(n35), 26
low income 40, 191, 192, 206
 see also public sector pay
lower (and) middle classes (France) 192–3
LP price index 38f
Luxembourg 24(n15), 104(n4), 109t, 156t

M1 monetary base (USA) 37
Maastricht period (1991–9) 54, 55t, 64
Maastricht Treaty (Treaty on European Union) 48, 53, 56, 67, 71(n7), 93, 94, 131, 138, 149, 171
 convergence criteria 171–2, 180(n2)
 entry into force (1993) 170
 industrial policy 107
 origins of EMU 87(n3)
Macedonia (FYR) 220f, 220, 225, 226, 229f, 230, 236
McKinsey
 currencies (index of international rank) 77–8, 79t, 89
macro-prudential oversight 17, 25(n24), n29)
macroeconomic adjustment 158, 224
macroeconomic equilibrium 57, 58–61f
 'relies on level of economic activity' (peripheral countries) 62
macroeconomic governance 46–73
 alternative views (EMU) 64–9, 71–2(n18–21)
 cooperative 69
 'interdependences not recognized' 69
 policy mix 68, 70
macroeconomic imbalances 21, 25(n37), 63, 68–9, 70, 79, 147, 154–5, 160
 country-specific structural deficiencies 65
 within and between currency areas 62–4, 71(n17)

macroeconomic imbalances – *continued*
  within EMU (econometric
    assessment) **54–62**, 71(n12–16)
macroeconomic policy 51, 120, 130
  France 190
  Germany 'only country gaining'
    (Eurozone) 148
  restrictive 187
macroeconomic theory 93
  orthodox versus alternative 104
  standard 104
  standard (obstacle to Eurozone political
    integration) **94–9**, 104(n4–5)
macroeconomics 101, 105
Madoff case 80
Majone, G. 25(n33), 26
Malta 109n
manufacturing 51, 110, 111t, 132, 188,
  201, 204, 206
Marché à Terme International de France 137t
marital status 208t, 211t, 212
'market-maker of last resort' 28–9
market-makers 30
market adjustment 51, 53, 54, 66–7, 97
  'complementary' strategy 65
market forces 98–9
  see also free markets
market imperfections 64, 97
market integration 6, 11, 20–1
market liberalization 64
market share 62
markets 53, 54, 93, 104(n5)
  'disintegrating' **9–13**, **23–4(n3–15)**
  efficient working 96, 118
  global 100
  imperfect 49
Mauroux, A. 195(n1), 196
Mayer, T. **153t**, 163
McCallum, T. 88(n23), 89
'means of exchange' function 76
'means of payment' function 78t, 83, 84
media 130, 193, 252
Medicare 210
Mediterranean Union 255(n11)
Medvedev, D. 243, 246, 247, 250, 251,
  255(n6)
  'new European security architecture'
    (2008–9) 248, 255(n7)
member states 9, 10
Mény, Y. xiii
mercantilism 245, 249
Merkel, A. 143, **146**, 151, 156–7
metals 110, 111t, 254(n2)
Metrik, A. 32, 33, 44
middle class 244–5
Middle East 113t
Milner, S. xiii, **5**, 193, 196
minimum wage 67, 99, 245
Minsky, H. 32, 45, 69
Mirror Group 130
Mitterrand, F. 75, 194

modernization
  EU–RF 253, 255–6(n12)
  Spain 167
Moldova 249, 251, 254, 255(n8–9, n11)
Monacelli, T. 71–2(n18), 73
monetarism 138
monetary authorities 156t
monetary policy 22f, 48, 49, 95, 98, 103,
  139, 174
  heterogeneous impact 67–8
  lax 44
  'one size fits all' 67
  response to crisis (Euro Area/USA) **3–4**,
    28–45
monetary stability 64, 99, 102
monetary union
  optimal and long-term sustainable **158**
  restricted (optimal dimensions) **158–9**
money market mutual funds 32, 33, 34
money markets 133, 139
  central bank loss of control (Minsky) 32
  wholesale 139
'mono-towns' 245
monopolies 172
Montenegro 220f, 220, 225–6, 230, 236–7
Moody's 178
moral hazard 39, 46, 69, 146, 155, 157
mortgage debt 39
mortgage defaults 243
mortgage securities 31
mortgage-backed securities (MBS) 35f, 43
mortgages 35, 37
  denominated in foreign currencies 230
  foreclosures and/or strategic defaults 38
  subprime crisis 9, 24(n3), 46, 147,
    174–5, 212
  variable-rate 37–8
'muddling through' scenario 92–95, 98–9,
  104, 104(n1)
multilateral lenders
  cooperation with banks (Southeast
    Europe) **231–3**
multilateral surveillance **152**
multipolarity 74, 86–7, 121, 123
  monetary **85–6**, 88(n22–3)
  stability **86–7**
Münchau, W. 132, 141(n16), 142
Mundell, R. 73
Mundell–Fleming model 56, 71(n12)
Mundellian theory 149, 164
Mundschenk, S. 141(n16)
Munster 122
Murdoch, R. 130
mutual funds 156t, 184
mutual recognition 10, 11, 21, 22, 23(n4),
  26–7
mutual risk insurance 47
mutualization of risks 10

Nabibulina, E. 249
Naftogaz 250

Index 275

national boundaries, re-drawing 159, 162(n16)
national champions 120
national interest 22, 92, 93, 99, 104, 122
national savings 148
national supervisors 14–15, 16t, 16–17, 19, 22
'national system of innovation' 101
nationalization 184
NATO 248, 255(n7)
natura non facit saltum argument 94
natural gas 172, 249, 250
'navigating without instruments' (France) 195
negative equity 37
neo-classical theory 104–5(n6–7)
neo-Keynesianism 1, 81, 87
neo-liberalism 80, 86, 87
  comeback 1–2
neo-protectionism 1
Netherlands 50f, 60f, 70(n3), 71(n14), 109t, 110, 156t
network externalities 86–7
New Classical Economics 64, 66, 68
New Keynesian Economics 66
New Labour 4
New Neoclassical Synthesis 93
New York 134
New York Fed 31
New York Times 33
no-bailout clause **143**, **155–7**
nominal effective exchange rate (NEER) 52t, 53, 71(n9)
  see also REER
nominal rigidities 67, 68, 72(n19)
non-bank financial institutions 32, 39–40
  weight 36
  weight (EU versus US) 43
non-discrimination
  basic principles 10
non-financial institutions
  refinancing by central bank (USA) 30
non-performing loans 39, 237
non-tariff barriers **117–18**
North Rhine–Westphalia 161(n3)
Norway 205
Noyer, C. 186–7, 195(n2), 196
nuclear energy (civil) 247
nuclear non-proliferation 254(n5)
nuclear superpower 245
Nyberg, L. 24(n15)

Obama, B. 123, 131, 215, 246, 247, 255(n6)
  healthcare legislation 212
Obama administration 81, 146
  counter-cyclical plan 93, 103
Observer, The 140(n13)
occupational segregation 201
OECD 114n, 123(n2), 176, 182, 185–6, 189, 191–4, 196–7, 199n, 200n, 204n, 205, 215(n3)

harmonized unemployment rates 201–2, 204t
off-shore markets 134, 136
oil 168, 172, 249
oil price 75, 88(n13), 167, 188, 243
open coordination method 115, 121, 123(n3)
Optimal Currency Area (OCA) 76, 96, 160f, 160–1
  'benefits would exceed costs' 159
  criteria 129
  endogenous criteria **149**, 163
  fulfilment of criteria (*ex post* versus *ex ante*) 149
  Mundellian theory 149, 164
  traditional theory 158, 162(n14–15)
Ortino, M. 23(n4), 26
OSCE 248
outliers **223–5**
output 41, 148, 153t
output gap 46, 51–7, 67, 70, 72(n18)
  'central role played by REER' 62
output–inflation trade-offs **65**
outsourcing 110
over-the-counter (OTC) markets 138

P variable 71(n9)
Pacheco Pardo, R. xiii, **5**
Padania 159, 162(n16)
Padoa-Schioppa, T. 23(n10), 25(n27), 26, 153t
Palmer, J. 129, 140(n6), 142
pan-European security (RF plan) 254
Papandreou, A. 146
Papandreou government, cuts to deficit **150–1**
Paribas 184
Paris 12t
Paris summit (12 October 2008) 10, 23(n5)
Partido Popular (PP) 170, **171–3**
Partido Socialista Obrero Español (PSOE) **168–9**, 171
  and global crisis, 1: denial **174–7**, 180–1(n4–10)
  and global crisis, 2: stern action **177–9**, 180, 181(n11–19)
  regained power (March 2004) 173
patents 97, 113–14, 114t
patriarchal social model 166
Paulson, H. M. 31, 42
Pébereau, M. 184
Peck, J. 190, 197
peer review 16t
Penkova, T. 245, 256
pension funds 41, 156t
pension reform **193–4**, 195(n3), 223
pensions 12t, 13t, 98, 150, 178, 222, 245
perception **157**
peseta 168
Pew Center for Social Research 213, 216

Phelps, E. 96, 105
PIIGS 144, 145t, 148f, 258
pipelines 249, 250
Pisani–Ferry–Sapir **153t**
Pistor, K. 23(n4), 27
Pittsburgh Summit (G-20, 2009) 25(n28)
'pocket Keynesianism' (Casanova) 189, 195(n2)
Podgorica 230
Poland 109t, 110, 151, 220, 225, 227–8, 230, 250, 252, 254(n6), 255(n11)
crisis lending 221t
political credibility 2, 83, 84
political economy **233**, 239
political integration
  solution to Europe in crisis **4, 91–106**
political stability 83, 244
political will 4, 98, 103, 108, 122, 158
polyarchy 247
Portugal 2, 40, 61f, 70(n2), 72(n20), 80, 109t, 143, 159, 178
  REER based on ULC (1979–2009) 50f
  see also PIIGS
Posen, A. 84, 89
post-Cold War era 246, 248
  security systems **252–3**
  see also world wars
post-Keynesianism 1
'post-Soviet space' 247, **249–53, 255–6(n8–12)**
pound sterling 48, 128, 129, 132, 134, 135t, 135, 137
poverty 119, 191–3, 195, 198, 244–5
  ability to make ends meet 207, 208–9t, 214, 215(n4)
  Italy **207–9**, 215(n3)
  probability of unmet medical needs 207, 208–9t
  unmet health needs 214, 215
  USA **209–14**
  USA (categories) 209–10
pragmatism 97–8, 104, 246, 247, 249
prescription charges 5, 215
preventive arm **152**
price competition 100
price flexibility 49, 53, 70
price rigidities 97
price stability 96, 155
prices 51, 62, 65
  commodities and raw materials 37
primary balance 57, 62, 71(n12)
Pristina 230
private credit 155
private debt (ratio to GDP) 40
private investment 95
private markets 31, 42
private sector 57, 82, 147, 224
  financial markets 80
  stability 95
privatization 150, 171, 172, 184
Prodi, R. 115, 122, 123, 155

producer price index (PPI) 37, 38f
product markets 92, 96
product quality 71(n13)
production 119–20
production function 101
productive structure 76
productivity 65, 97, 147, 173, 174, 244
productivity growth 57, 64, 101
profit motive 165(n6–7)
propensity to invest or consume 101
property rights 243
protectionism 98, 102, 108, 236, 251
protest demonstrations 151, 188, 194, 254(n3)
prudential management 183
Przyrowski, J. xiii
psychology 101
public bonds 35, 151
  interest differentials (Euro Area) 36–7
  secondary market 69
  see also sovereign bonds
public debt 5, 48, 63, 64, 147, 189
  default 47
  dollar-denominated 78
  'foreign debt' 77, 78
  'government debts' 28–9
  Greece 80
  'national debt' 37, 103, 171
  ratio to GDP 46–7, 71(n7), 171, 176, 177, 178
public debt crisis (current) 1–2, **80–1**, 82, 87(n4)
  see also sovereign debt
public deficit 47, 56, 64, 148, 155, 171
  adjustment 68
  ratio to GDP 46–7, 56, 62, 71(n7), 162(n8), 189
  see also balanced budgets
public expenditure 68, 101, 172, 176, 177, 223
  cuts 222
  France 191
public finances 57, 63, **144–6**, 147
  mismanagement 64
  worsening 40
  see also fiscal policy
public goods 119
public opinion 130, 132, 141, 158–9, 162(n11–13), 188, 195, 238, 245
  France 192–3
  Germany 146, 157, 162(n11)
public policy 210
'public primary balance' 55t, 56
public sector 57, 167
  efficiency savings 189
  imbalances 79–80
public sector employees 222
public sector pay 150, 222
  see also salaries
public transfers **153t**
public works 172

Index 277

Putin, V. 242, 244–6, 250–1, 254(n1), 256
qualified majority voting 16
quality 63, 71(n13)
'made in Germany' 100
quantitative easing/asset purchases 29, 33, 39, 43, 44, 162(n10)
race 200, 201, 202, 210, 211t, 212
'race to bottom' 70
radical economists 1
ratings agencies 186
see also credit ratings
real divergence
evolution across EMU economies (1979–2009) **48–54**, 70–1(n4–11)
limits of EMU macroeconomic governance **4, 46–73**
real effective exchange rate (REER) 48–51, 52t, 54–7, 61–2, 65, 67, 71(n9)
based on ULC (EU-15, 1979–2009) 50f
see also currencies
real estate 29, 35, 41, 43, 147, 230–1, 243
see also housing
Real Vienna (trade fair, May 2009) 230–1, 240
Reardon, J. 5
'rebalancing behaviour' 88(n21)
Recine, F. 24(n15, n19), 27
redistribution 98, 191, 192, 195
redundancy 203–5, 214–15, 223
regional independence 162–3(n16), 163
regions 171
regressions **51–62**
regulation 130–1, 184, 185–6
common European mandate 23(n8), 26
European financial market (post-crisis) **3, 9–27**
failures 13
home versus host country (lessons of crisis) 10, 23(n4), 27
'micro-prudential supervision' 12–13, 17
national 10–11, 12, 20, 23, 23(n6, n8–9)
technical standards 14
Regulations of EP and the Council 13
'regulatory public good' notion 22
Reichlin, P. 103, 105
religion 117
renmimbi *see* yuan renmimbi
rentiers 39
repressive mechanism **152**
Republican Party (USA) 206
repurchase agreements/'repo' market 32, 34, 44
reputation 82–3
research and development 101, 115, 188, 190
expenditure (global, 2008) 113, 114f
'reserve of value' function 75, 78t, 82, 83
reserve requirements 133–4, 138

'reset the button' (RF–US relations) 247, 254(n5)
restricted solidarity hypothesis **157–61**, 162–3(n12–17)
long-run perspective **159**
retail sector 110, 111t, 204
retirement 97, 150, 157
see also pension reform
Revenu Minimum d'Insertion (France) 191
Revenu de Solidarité Active (RSA) (France) 191
ri-lance policy (France) 190
Ricardian equivalence 66
Ricciuti, R. 56, 67, 73
right to exchange (on markets) 118
risk 10, 11, 67, 86, 118, 224, 230
'risk dashboard' 15
risk management 17, 185, 186
risk premia 36, 47, 161(n2)
risk transmission 258
risk warnings 22
Rodríguez Zapatero, J. L. 174, 175
Romania 109t, 110, 218–20, **221–2**, 224–5, 229f, 230, 234, 236–7, 240
crisis lending 221t
Romania: Central Bank 221–2
Romania: Finance Ministry 221–2
Romanian government 222
Rose, A. K. 149, 158, 163
Rosneft 249
rouble 244
rule of law 244
rules 118, 119
rules of game 84–5
Russian diaspora 252
Russian 'exceptionalism' 245–6
Russian Federation (RF) 85, 114f, 230, 260
'actorness' 242
in crisis: implications for EU **6, 242–57**
economic indicators 244
economic and political power 245
foreign aid programme 249, 255(n9)
foreign policy 253
foreign policy (effects of global crisis) **245–8**, 254–5(n4–7)
'fragility' 253
GDP 242–3, 244, 254(n2)
global crisis **242–5**, 254(n2–3)
pan-European security plan (2008–) 248, 255(n7)
passport policy 252
post-Soviet space **249–53, 255–6(n8–12)**
'rebirth as international actor' 242, 245, 253
regional cooperation/integration 251, 253
relations with China 249, 253, 255(n8)
relations with EU **251–2**, 253–4
relations with Ukraine 250
relations with USA **247–8**, 254–5(n4–6)
stimulus package 244–5
structural reforms required 243

Russian Federation: Ministry of Finance   221t, 223

salaries   40, 41
  see also wages
sanctions   154
Santander Central Hispano (bank)   179
Sarkozy, N.   193–4, 195(n3)
saving rate   39
savings   37, 56, 57, 62, 63, 72(n21), 184
  global glut   78, 81
savings paradox   69
savings propensity   40–1
Say's Law   95
Schinasi, G. J.   24(n13), 27
Schoenmaker, D.   23(n6), 27
Schularik, M.   84, 89
Scialom, L.   25(n26)
SEAQ (Stock Exchange Automated Quotation)   137
secondary market activity   136
Secrieru, S.   255(n9), 257
'sectoral and partial Keynesianism' (Hoang-Ngoc)   189–90
securities   12t, 13t, 155
  foreign exchange denominations   34
  'government securities'   171
  Greek government   156t
  legal and regulatory system (2003–10)   12
Securities Investment Board (SIB)   139
Securities Markets Programme (ECB)   36
securitization   30, 32, 41, 43, 46
  'Europe' versus USA   34, 35f
seigniorage   75–6
self-employment   207
self-insurance strategies   236
Selmayr, M.   26(n41), 27
Sen, A.   105(n6), 105, 215, 217
  capabilities approach   102
Serbia   218–20, **222–3**, 225, 229f, 230, 231t, 232, 240–1
  crisis lending   221t
  IPA   226t, 226, 227
Serbia: Interim Agreement (with EU)   236–7
service sector   51, 97, 101
services   110
  non-financial   110
severance pay   179
Seville: Universal Exposition (1992)   169–70, 172
Seymour, D.   130, 142
'shadow bailout' (2007–8)   31, 34, 42
shadow banking system   33
shareholders   41
shocks   51, 53, 54, 56, 67, 68, 70, 71–2(n18), 219, 220f
  asymmetric   76, 149, 150, 159
  'different propagation effects'   65
  symmetric   149
  see also global financial crisis

short-selling   **152**, **165(n6)**
Slovakia   109t, 176, 230
Slovenia   109t, 229, 229f
'smart growth'   119, 124
SMEs   175, 227, 229, 231t, 232, 234
  cost of financing   32
Smith, A.   117, 119–20
social care   206
social cohesion   119, 122
social expenditure   68, 193
social insurance programmes (USA)   210
social market economy   122
social policy   214
social protection   67, 183
social solidarity   195
'social summit' (France, 2009)   188
social welfare   4, 102, 104(n6), 174, 177, 222
  costs   172, 176
Société Générale   184, 185, 186
socio-economic imbalances   255(n11)
'soft coordination' method   97
soft power   249
solidarity   162(n14)
  definition   157
  restricted definition   **157–8**
  see also restricted solidarity hypothesis
Soros, G.   92, 103, 105
South Africa   114f
South Ossetia   245, 247, 255(n9)
Southeast Europe
  banking assets (foreign ownership, 2009)   229f
  cooperation between banks and multilateral lenders   **231–3**
  credit crunch (2008–)   229, 230–1
  crisis assistance 'tilted towards EU members'   **225–8**
  crisis lending   221t
  external anchors   **5–6**, **218–41**, 260
  external anchors: exit strategies   **233–7**, 238
  external anchors: to the rescue   **220–1**
  external anchors: role   **233–7**
  future economic development model   233
  GDP   219–20, 220f, 237
  growth model   238
  initiatives to support financial sector stability   **228–31**
  institutional cooperation and policy coordination   236
  issues deserving special placement on agenda   238
  'key lesson'   238–9
  lessons for financial sector reform   233
  macroeconomic indicators   237
  macroeconomic situation   **219–20**
  political concerns   238
  'questions requiring answers'   233
  'shaping reform agenda'   **233–7**

Index 279

subprime markets 230
trend growth rate 237
sovereign bonds 150, 152
  see also bonds
sovereign debt 21, 129, 153t, 177
  speculative attack 91
  see also debt
'sovereign democracy' 247
sovereignty 129, 139
Spain 2, 40, 47, 57, 61f, 65, 70(n2), 80, 91, 95, 97, 109t, 109, 143, 147, 159, 259
  boon of EEC membership (1986–) **168–9**, 170
  credit-rating downgraded 177, 178, 181(n15)
  crisis (1992–3) 169–70, 173, 180
  economic growth and modernization (1970s, 1980s) **166–7**
  'economic miracles' 165, 166, 171, 173, 174
  economic recession and boom (1990s–) **169–71**
  economically active population 175, 176, 180(n4)
  emigration–immigration transformation 175–6, 180(n5)
  GDP 169, 173
  guarded optimism 180
  'high-inflation country' 62
  impact of global financial crisis 5, **165–82**
  industrialization 166–7
  'lack of competitiveness' 165–6
  'miracle' to 'crash' **165–82**
  public debt as percentage of GDP 169
  quadrennial development plans (1964–) 166
  recession (1992–3) 169
  REER based on ULC (1979–2009) 50f
  structural deficiencies 165–6, 173
  sub-state governments 176, 177, 178
  see also PIIGS
Spanish government 166
Special Drawing Rights (SDRs) 85, 86, 88(n23), 89, 90
special facilities 29
Special Purpose Vehicle 151
speculation 39, 44, 259
speculative attacks 74, 80, 83, 91, 155, 162(n9), 164
speculators 98, 150
spillovers 47, 48–9, 65–70
Spolaore, E. 162(n16), 163
SROs ['self-regulatory organizations'] 139
Stability and Growth Pact (SGP) 5, 21, 25(n37), 47, 56–7, 62, 64, 68, 69, 70(n4), 93, 94, 103, 114, 116, 143, 161
  crisis (2003) 154
  deficit–GDP ratio 67
  'deflationary bias' 67

  lessons of Greek crisis (2010) **152**, **154–5**, 162(n8)
  reform (2005) 154
  theoretical underpinnings 66–7
Stabilization and Association Agreement (SAA) 226, 228
Stabilization Fund *see* EFSF
Standard & Poor's 178
state aid 120
state companies 166
state role 118, 194, 234, 238, 259
state-ownership 117, 120
Steltzer, I. 96, 105
Stevenson, N. 130, 140(n9), 142
Stiglitz, J. 92, 96, 103, 105
stock market capitalization 82, 87(n10)
stock market indexes 39, 40
stock markets 243
stock prices 37, **39**
store of value 84
Strategic Arms Reduction Treaty (START II, 2010) 247, 254(n4), 256
Strauss Kahn, D. **153t**
stress-testing 15, 16t
strikes 151
structural dynamics, view of Adam Smith 119–20
structural funds (EEC/EU) 168, 174, 180
structural reforms 92, 93, 96, 98–9, 101–2, 104(n3), 154
  difficulty of implementation 97
subprime mortgage crisis (2007–) 9, 24(n3), 46, 147, 174–5, 212
Suez 184
supply and demand 95
supply factors 101
supply-side 96–7, 99, 104(n5)
Surkov, V. 245, 257
'surprise inflation' 49
sustainable development 122
'sustainable growth' 119
Sutherland, P. 132, 141(n15), 142
SVIMEZ [*Associazione per lo sviluppo dell'industria nel Mezzogiorno*] 215(n1), 217
Swaminathan, S. 88(n23), 89
Sweden 109t, 110, 113, 114f, 151, 229f, 252, 255(n11)
Swiss franc 135t, 230
Sylos Labini, P. 117, 124
synergies, European-level 115, 116–17, 121
Syria 247
systemic instability 33, 42
systemic risk 15, 16t
  see also European Systemic Risk Board

Tabellini, G. 95, 97, 104(n5), 105
Talani, L. S. xiii, **5**, **127–42**, **258–60**
Tamborini, R. 49, 65, 66, 70, 73
tariff barriers 117

tariff union 120
tariffs 166, 169
taxation 41, 95, 101, 102, 103, 115, 150, 151, 153t, 163(n17), 171, 172, 177, 191, 193, 254(n2)
  corporate 98
  harmonization 91
  teaching 206
technical standards 16t
technocracy 91
technological development 84
technological gap 101
Teixeira, P. G. **3**, 23(n1–2), 24(n12–13, n15, n19), 27
telecommunications 97, 104(n5), 168, 171, 172
temporary contracts 150, 179, 202
temporary staffing 190, 192, 197, 199
term auction liquidity facility (TALF) 32
territorial integrity 255(n7)
territory 120, 123
terrorism 254(n5)
Thatcher Government 138
Theodore, N. 190, 197
Thessaloniki 239(n1)
Thygesen, N. 130, 140(n10), 142
Tier 2 capital 231t
tight demand policies 94–5, 96
time 117, 118
Tirana 230
Tison, M. 23(n4), 27
TNS-Sofres 193
Togati, T. D. **4**
Tokyo 134
'too big to fail' 185
total factor productivity (TFP) 54
tourism 165, 166–7, 170, 173–4, 176, 180, 180(n3)
trade 22f, 41, 46, 66, 82, 84–5, 87(n10), 88(n18), 112, 113t, 159, 165
  see also WTO
trade balance 47, 51, 56, 57, 63, 64
  see also balance of payments
trade deficits 57, 169, 173, 180, 188
trade union density 199
trade unions 151, 168, 178, 188, 192, 194, 223
training 119, 120
transaction costs 74
transactions
  cross-border 34–5
  international 82
transition economies 235
Transneft 249
transparency 40, 236, 243, 244
transport sector 206, 227
Treaties of Rome (1957) 87(n1), 120
Trichet, J.-C. 156, 162(n10)
Triffin's dilemma 76, 86
Tropeano, D. **3–4**, 32, 45, 88(n15)
trust 44, 101t, 102

Turkey 226t, 226, 227, 230, 234, 240
'twin deficit' hypothesis 56
'two speed EMU' **144**, **157–61**, **162–3(n12–17)**, 259
'two-way periphery' area **252–3**

Ukraine 218, 220, 230, 231t, 232, 234, 251, 253, 254, 255(n11)
  crisis lending 221t
  relations with RF **250**
under-employment 190, 203
unemployment 5, 29, 37, 40, 41, 44, 49, 81, 153t, 165–6, **167**, 169–77, 180(n8), 179, 183, 211t, 211–12, 213, 217, 237, 243–5, 259
  France 190–1
  Italy 198–9, 214
  long-term 191–2, 198, 204, 204t, 206
  socio-economic costs **214–15**
  USA 200, 214
unemployment benefits 98, 192, 211t, **213**, 214, 215
  conditionalities (France) 191
  Italy 205, 207
  USA **205–6**
UniCredit (UC) Bank **231–2**
  subsidiaries 231t
Union of Soviet Socialist Republics 248
  see also 'post-Soviet space'
unipolarity
  efficiency **86–7**
  financial **86**
  monetary **81–3**, 88(n16–17)
'unit of account' function 75, 78t, 82, 83, 84
unit labour costs (ULC) 49, 50f, 51, 57, 61, 64, 147
  growth rates in EMU economies (1999–2009) 54f
  nominal 54f
unitary decision-making 22
United Kingdom 25(n34), 70(n6), 75, 85, 109t, 109, 110, 114f, 114t, 114, 147, 156t, 165, 177, 185, 195(n1), 260
  budget cuts (2010) 189
  capital and financial markets 88(n19)
  case to join EMU **127–33**, **140–1**
  and euro in aftermath of global crisis **4–5**, **127–42**
  euro membership (referendum promise) 130
  GDP 128
  merchandise exports (1983–2008) 113t
  referendum on Common Market (1975) 130
  refusal to join EMU **133–8**, 141(n17)
United Kingdom government 133
United States 86, 104, 105(n7), 107, 114f, 114t, 114, 118, 147, 185, 188, 195(n1), 234, 235, 245, 248
  capital inflow (reasons) 83

Index 281

costs of being unemployed (income poverty) **209–14**
current account deficit 81
economic hegemony 2
experience of unemployment **209–14**
financial markets (current state) **37–9**
financial reform law 33
'fiscal stimulus' (Obama) 81
fiscal sustainability 63, 71(n17)
GDP 79, 86, 88(n14), 111–12, **112f**
harmonized unemployment rates 202, 204t
merchandise exports (1983–2008) 113t, 113
missile defence in Europe 247, 254(n6)
monetary response to financial crisis (Euro Area comparison) **3–4**, **28–45**
'one-fifth of world economy' 88(n11)
poverty probability (multivariate analyses) 211t
presidential election (2008) 31, 255(n6)
public debt 63
public deficit 72(n21)
relations with RF **247–8**, 253, **254–5(n4–6)**
short-term borrowing versus long-term lending 83
states 205, 206
temporary staffing 190, 197
trade deficits 72(n21), 78
trade imbalance (with China) 63
'twin deficit' 56
US Bureau of Labour Statistics (BLS) 201, 202, 204, 206, 217
US Census Bureau 201, 209, 210, 211n, 213, 217
US Congress 43
US dollar 2, 4, 71(n8, n17), 72(n21), 74, 81, 89–90, 100, 134, 135t, 138, 141(n18), 188, 228, 231n
 appreciated throughout 2008 34
 continuing supremacy **83–4**
 global reserve currency 88(n11)
 international role 75
 international role (performance of euro in its first decade) **77–9**, **87(n9–14)**
 reserve currency 89
 'safe haven' 76
 synthetic index of degree of reserve currency status 79t
 world leadership 259
US labour market
 effects of global financial crisis (Italy comparison) **5**, **198–217**
 versus Italian labour market (similarities and differences) **198–200**
US Senate 44
US Treasury 32
Usher, J. 23(n7), 27

value-added 108–9, 109t, 110, 111t
value-added tax (VAT) 150, 222
value chain 169, 173
Van Gerven, W. 23(n7), 27
Van Rompuy Task Force 21
Vancouver 248
Venezuela 247
Verde, A. xiii, **5**, 157, 160, 162(n9), 164
Versailles Treaty 87(n2)
visa liberalization 236, 255(n11)
vision **117–21**
 industrial development **107–24**
Vladivostok 248, 245
Volcker, P. 33
'voluntarist' approach (France) 191

wage flexibility 70
wage moderation 57, 64
wage rigidity 62
wage supplementation fund (Italy) 203, 205, 214
wages 41, 44, 51, 67, 72(n20), 168, 172, 244, 259
 'compensation per employee' 54f
 cuts 65, 70, 71(n15)
 entry-level 202
 national contracts 68
 nominal increases 68
 public sector 223
 see also bonus payments
Waigel, T. 162(n12)
wealth of nations 119–20
 'key determinant' 117
Weiler, J. H. H. 25(n31), 27
Werner Plan (1970) 75, 87(n5)
Western Balkans Investment Framework (WBIF) 226t, 226, 227
wholesale trade 110, 111t
Williamson, J. 88(n23), 90
women 166, 175, 201–3, 206, 208t, 211t, 212
 employment rates (Italy versus USA, 1994–2007) 200t, 200
 labour force participation 214
 temporary work 199
workers
 fixed-term contract 205
 full-time 210
 part-time 203, 206
 see also employment
working poor 214
World Bank (WB) 218, 221, 222, 225, 227, 232, 233, 235
 crisis lending 221t
World Trade Organization (WTO) 113n, 251
 see also free trade
world wars
 World War I 75, 87(n2), 88(n16)
 inter-war era 244
 World War II 75, 123
 post-war era 1, 88(n16), 116, 200–1, 205–6, 213

world wars – *continued*
  see also Cold War
Wouters, J. 23(n7), 27

Yanukovych, V. F. 250
Yeltsin, B. 244
yen 63, 71(n8), 79t, 88(n22), 134, 135t, 141(n18)
youth 176, 180(n7)
youth poverty (USA) 210

youth unemployment 190–2, 198–200, 202, 215
yuan renmimbi 2, 63, 74, **84–5**, 86, 100
  international status ('does not qualify to replace US dollar') 83
  'systematic undervaluation' 84–5

Zilioli, C. 26(n41), 27
Zingales, L. 159, 164

Lightning Source UK Ltd.
Milton Keynes UK
UKOW02f0116031214

242570UK00008B/125/P